Fashioning Acadians

McGill-Queen's Studies in Early Canada / Avant le Canada

SERIES EDITORS / DIRECTEURS DE LA COLLECTION : ALLAN GREER AND CAROLYN PODRUCHNY

This series features studies of the history of the northern half of North America – a vast expanse that would eventually be known as Canada – in the era before extensive European settlement and extending into the nineteenth century. Long neglected, Canada-before-Canada is a fascinating area of study experiencing an intellectual renaissance as researchers in a range of disciplines, including history, geography, archeology, anthropology, literary studies, and law, contribute to a new and enriched understanding of the distant past. The editors welcome manuscripts in English or French on all aspects of the period, including work on Indigenous history, the Atlantic fisheries, the fur trade, exploration, French or British imperial expansion, colonial life, culture, language, law, science, religion, and the environment.

Cette série de monographies est consacrée à l'histoire de la partie septentrionale du continent de l'Amérique du nord, autrement dit le grand espace qui deviendra le Canada, dans les siècles qui s'étendent jusqu'au début du 19ᵉ. Longtemps négligé par les chercheurs, ce Canada-avant-le-Canada suscite beaucoup d'intérêt de la part de spécialistes dans plusieurs disciplines, entre autres, l'histoire, la géographie, l'archéologie, l'anthropologie, les études littéraires et le droit. Nous assistons à une renaissance intellectuelle dans ce champ d'étude axé sur l'interaction de premières nations, d'empires européens et de colonies. Les directeurs de cette série sollicitent des manuscrits, en français ou en anglais, qui portent sur tout aspect de cette période, y compris l'histoire des autochtones, celle des pêcheries de l'atlantique, de la traite des fourrures, de l'exploration, de l'expansion de l'empire français ou britannique, de la vie coloniale (Nouvelle-France, l'Acadie, Terre-Neuve, les provinces maritimes, etc.), de la culture, la langue, le droit, les sciences, la religion ou l'environnement.

Fashioning Acadians

Clothing in the Atlantic World, 1650–1750

— — — — — —

HILARY DODA

MCGILL-QUEEN'S UNIVERSITY PRESS

Montreal & Kingston • London • Chicago

ISBN 978-0-2280-1892-6 (cloth)
ISBN 978-0-2280-1949-7 (ePDF)

Legal deposit fourth quarter 2023
Bibliothèque nationale du Québec

Printed in Canada on acid-free paper

This book has been published with the help of a grant from the Canadian Federation
for the Humanities and Social Sciences, through the Awards to Scholarly Publications
Program, using funds provided by the Social Sciences and Humanities Research Council
of Canada. Funding was also received from the Donald J. Savoie Institute.

  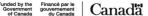 

We acknowledge the support of the Canada Council for the Arts.
Nous remercions le Conseil des arts du Canada de son soutien.

McGill-Queen's University Press in Montreal is on land which long served as a site of meeting
and exchange amongst Indigenous Peoples, including the Haudenosaunee and Anishinabeg
nations. In Kingston it is situated on the territory of the Haudenosaunee and Anishinaabek.
We acknowledge and thank the diverse Indigenous Peoples whose footsteps have marked
these territories on which peoples of the world now gather.

LIBRARY AND ARCHIVES CANADA CATALOGUING IN PUBLICATION

Title: Fashioning Acadians : clothing in the Atlantic world, 1650–1750 / Hilary Doda.
Names: Doda, Hilary, author.
Series: McGill-Queen's studies in early Canada ; 7.
Description: Series statement: McGill-Queen's studies in early Canada / Avant le Canada ; 7 |
    Includes bibliographical references and index.
Identifiers: Canadiana (print) 20230477119 | Canadiana (ebook) 20230477143 |
    ISBN 9780228018926 (cloth) | ISBN 9780228019497 (ePDF)
Subjects: LCSH: Acadians—Clothing—Nova Scotia—History. | LCSH: Clothing and dress—
    Nova Scotia—History. | LCSH: Acadians—Nova Scotia—History.
Classification: LCC FC2350.5 .D63 2023 | DDC 391.0089/114—dc23

For Richard, who has always believed in me.

Contents

Tables and Figures

Tables

Figures

Acknowledgments

SO MANY PEOPLE have contributed so much to allow this project to take flight. The culmination of six years of research, writing, rewriting, coffee infusions, and more rewriting would not have been possible without their support, critiques, mentorship, gentle redirecting, and examples of grace under pressure. I am deeply grateful to Jerry Bannister and Lynn Sorge, not just on this book project but for the years leading up to it as well. You have taught me so much that I'll carry with me for the rest of my life. Thank you to Katie Cottreau-Robins and Marc Lavoie, for the miles travelled, the advice and boundless energy, the joy and generosity with which you shared your expertise and guided my research, the microbrews, and the seafood lasagne. And thank you particularly to Katie for introducing me to material entanglement theory, which aimed a light on my theoretical fumbling in the darkness. Thank you to Richard Morris, the artist who brought some of these artifacts to life on the page, and Tim Chisolm and Vanessa Smith for their excellent photography of the others. I owe a debt of gratitude to Rachel Smyth, my research assistant, without whom this book would have had many fewer images and be much the worse for it.

Thanks to all those who have helped with research and guidance along the way. To Jack Crowley and Beverley Lemire, for teaching that I hope I've put to good use. To Charles Burke, Sara Beanlands, Janet Stoddard, Kevin Jenkins, and the rest of the Parks Canada crowd for letting me play in the cabinets, and for all your patience with my questions. To the archivists and staff at the Nova Scotia Provincial Archives for research assistance, microfilm reader help, and laughs on quiet afternoons. To Lesley Armstrong at LaHave Weaving Studio for opening up the world of weaving to me. The barn loom is still my favourite.

Thanks as well to Catherine Butler at Archives Canada, Heidi Moses and Elizabeth Tait at Fortress Louisbourg, and Maura McKeough at the Parks Canada Cape Breton Field Unit, for documentation and primary-source genius; Kathy Stay at the Atlantic Theological Seminary for fielding a hundred strange questions; Roger Lewis at the Nova Scotia Museum for taking the time to direct me away from the pitfalls of the past; to Tom Cohen for writing advice that honed my skills; to Krista Kesselring, Cynthia Neville, and Dianne Kristoff for shaping the trajectory of my academic life;

and to Val and Tina at the Dalhousie History office and my colleagues at the Fountain School of Performing Arts for making the campus a home.

Thank you to my family, in-laws and outlaws alike. To my mother, may she schep all the nachas, and my father, who tried to teach me to think like an engineer. To Laurie and Helen, and to Dave and Christine, for their encouragement and support throughout. And most of all for Richard – translator, artist, cartographer, sounding board, life coach, slack-taker-upper, tissue-provider, באַשערטר, the heart and soul of our home. This is your labour of love as much as it is mine. Jenny and Alex, my owlets. Your patience with Mom's weird fixations and the drifts of papers scattered all over the house has gone above and beyond the call of duty. I love you.

And finally thank you to the Social Sciences and Humanities Research Council, Dalhousie University, the Killam Trust, the Pasold Institute, the Fountain School of Performing Arts Endowment, and the Gorsebrook Research Institute for financial and logistical support that allowed me to focus on completing this book in a timely manner. I would also like to extend my gratitude to Professor Donald Savoie and the Donald J. Savoie Institute at the Université de Moncton for its generous financial support for this publication.

This research was supported by the Social Sciences and Humanities Research Council of Canada, the Gorsebrook Research Institute of Atlantic Canada Studies, the Pasold Foundation, the Fountain Endowment Grant Program, and the Killam Trust.

Fashioning Acadians

Introduction

> They had no dye but black and green, but in order to obtain scarlet –
> of which they were remarkably fond – they procured the English scarlet
> duffil which they cut, teized, carded, spun, and wove in stripes to decorate
> the womens' garments.[1]

— — — — — — —

SETTING SAIL in the first half of the seventeenth century, responding to a call from a patron who promised farmland, comfort, and support, a group of French settlers arrived on the eastern shores of Canada. The land was not empty, of course, having already been occupied for close to thirteen thousand years by the People of the Dawn.[2] Carving living space and resources for themselves from Mi'kmaw land, over the next hundred years, the people who would become known as the Acadians expanded through what is now Nova Scotia, New Brunswick, and Prince Edward Island. Land ownership continued to be contested, theoretical title to Acadia passing back and forth between French and English imperial authorities with varying degrees of enforcement until the mid-eighteenth century. And in an act of terror that began in 1755 and continued for the next eight years, the majority of the French-speaking, Catholic, Acadian population were forced into ships and sent into exile. Some of the Acadian survivors returned to Nova Scotia, though not to their original lands, while many others remained in the diaspora.

That is the summation of a well-known history, and the cultural mythology that surrounds the Acadians has grown in waves since then. The pastoral romanticism in some early writings about the colony set the tone for the development of an archetype of Acadians as distinct from other settler groups, an image which culminated in folkloric shorthand that mythologized the people as well as the land: rustic, unambitious peasants treading out their daily routines in Longfellow's forest primeval. This perception began early in Acadian tenure, in the simple poetry of Sieur de Dièreville's

1710 travelogue, and Abbé Raynal's subsequent publication on Acadia and its environs. Descriptions of Acadians as plain dressers with limited resources can be found in documents dating as far back as the seventeenth century. The speakers overwhelmingly describe a people living in relative isolation, working the land in their simple homespun clothes. The national mythologies that have grown out of those images are something of a mixed blessing. The enduring positive imagery of the so-called Acadian Golden Age became a rallying point for a community rebirth, a focal point for pride and connection, but the simplification allows us to overlook some of the complexities of Acadian life in the hundred years leading up to the Expulsion.

Over the years prior to the deportation, governors, officials, and clergy variously described Acadians as self-sufficient, proud, slovenly, devout, argumentative, lazy, indolent, and industrious. Many of those wonderfully contradictory descriptions do not fit with the growing body of archaeological and manuscript evidence of daily life in Acadian settlements.[3] Given the limited documentation available, and almost none of it from the Acadians' own writings, we need other ways to evaluate the truth behind these stereotypes. One of the ways we can catch a glimpse of daily life is through wardrobe and the culture of Acadian dress. Buckles and beads, scissors, and lead seals survived the centuries under the earth, and through these artifacts we can trace the shapes of the garments that once bore them up. These ghosts still exist, figures that we can rebuild through examination of context, tools, decorations, and patterns of trade.

This material culture study takes a new look at the question of Acadian exceptionalism through the lens of clothing and textiles. In other words, what can Acadian clothing choices tell us about the nature of their society, and how can dress and fashion help to explain the mixed and often negative reactions of colonial authorities? We can answer those questions through an exploration of Acadian textile culture and the symbolic significance of the Acadians' embodied practices. Human beings gain understanding of the world by manipulating the material things around them, and clothing can be a powerful tool for idiomatic communication. The early modern period in the West saw more rapid changes in clothing and clothing culture than ever before, and the ways in which people adjusted their wardrobes to their circumstances give us insight into their perceptions of their outer world and their inner selves.

The history of textiles and dress in the region shows us the growth of a novel Acadian material identity as Acadian dress and adornment changed from something French to a distinctly local vernacular. Acadians were not a monolith, and the environments and communities in which groups found themselves played a large role in how their sartorial selves were expressed. A new and distinctive style of dress was developing in Acadia prior to the deportation, a style much more nuanced and influenced by contemporary New England and French fashions than previously believed. This was partially tied to trade patterns, geography, and potentially due to some deliberate code-switching for outside observers, as seen in other colonial communities. Changing priorities and engagement with styles and practices of other groups, including the Mi'kmaq, and European authorities at the nearby forts, led to changes in Acadian self-presentation and group identity – shifts that indicate the growth of unique and localized dress cultures influenced by their physical and social environments. These changes confused outside observers and may have contributed in part to this mixed descriptive bag, a misunderstanding of symbols and visual cues that carried different resonance internally and externally. Those misunderstandings, in turn, contributed to growing imperial unease around Acadian allegiances and political intentions.

Interest in dress study as part of material culture has grown over the past fifty years and the developing field has engaged with a number of theoretical takes, including symbolic interactionism; semiotics, or the reading of symbols embedded in objects; and class- or gender-based analyses of consumption.[4] Each of these frameworks draws new information out of clothing choice, which can then be incorporated into object-based analysis. The notion of embodied information and physical communication draws upon semiology, but also engages with historical projections of clothing as an extra layer or boundary to the body. Textiles are now understood to contain as much symbolic meaning and transformative power as any other ritual or utilitarian object, and dress becomes an individual communication within a broader culturally imposed "grammar," a signifier of the training and socialization required for the creation of socially acceptable personal appearance.[5] Choice of clothing both affects and is affected by the engagement that individuals and groups have with their political and domestic environments. Dick Hebdige's theories discuss this relationship, framing dress choice as part of a continuing conversation about power and status, self-fashioning, and moral pressure.[6] Extant articles of dress can bring us as close to the once-corporeal body as diary entries to the original mind of the author, and we can read them as a surviving shed skin that maintains the shape, habits, and priorities of the person who lived within.

In this book, I demonstrate the ways in which Acadian dress was changing and evolving over the course of their first settlement period in Nova Scotia. Engaging with current streams of thought in material culture and dress studies, this book also presents a methodology for determining the nature of clothing worn in a given area when the articles themselves no longer exist for study. This methodology relies on artifacts discovered in both archaeological and historical contexts – found in the ground and passed down through the generations, respectively – as well as exploration of the various local environments and a complete review of available documentation. When wardrobes cannot be found, this data can be used systematically to determine the original shapes and styles of the clothing that was worn.

A useful scaffolding with which to support a study of this type is the framework of *material entanglement*, championed by historical archaeologist Ian Hodder.[7] The metaphor of material entanglement as it is currently used in historical archaeology is an attempt to bridge the gap between object analysis and social theory. In brief, material entanglement theory holds that it is the connections between *things* – the humans, physical items, social structures, habits, beliefs, and relationships between all of the above – that define a culture and cultural moment.[8] It suggests that by knowing the nature of the *things* present in a particular system, space, and time, we can divine the ways in which those *things* influenced, constrained, and compelled one another. That is to say that every *thing* has dependences: preconditions that must be in place for the object or condition both to exist and to be necessary. The existence of a car presupposes the existence of wheels, for instance, as well as sheet metal, factories, and paved roads. This holds true for non-physical concepts as well: illegitimacy of birth first requires the concept of legally defined marriages, the social desire to restrict sexual couplings to within those constrained relationships, and some notion of personal property that can be privately passed down to subsequent generations.

Along with dependences, Hodder argues, *things* also come with affordances, the consequences of their existence. Once an object has been culturally integrated, the behavioural patterns of the humans who interact with it change so that suddenly being without it would cause visible disruption. These entanglements themselves change over time, as new technologies, modes of interaction, and societal rhythms evolve.[9] Prior to the rise of modern fast fashion, for example, the expense of clothing and textiles compelled the wearer to either learn and practise washing and mending, or to organize domestic arrangements with someone who had those skills. Marriage or labour exchange were two solutions to that need, each coming with its own extensive series of connections and prerequisites. On the physical side, mending a torn garment required scissors, thread, and a needle, access to which depended on either the presence of a local manufacturer or someone importing sewing tools, which in turn relied on the existence of trade networks and the availability of either money or goods for barter and export. Those entanglements also change over time. Since the 1990s, a torn T-shirt has instead connected the owner to networks that include clothing sweatshops in Indonesia, big-box stores with low-price policies, and the continuing economic erosion of the middle class. In this way, one seemingly simple aspect of life – wearing clothing – embedded people in a series of networked processes that existed in various states of interdependent tension.[10]

Hodder and other scholars who have worked with the metaphor of entanglement suggest that the webs of engagements present in any given set of relationships can be determined by close examination, and that the objects and relationships in turn generate semi-predictable types of tensions between them. I posit the reverse to be true as well: once the shape of a network is known, and surviving *things* put into position, we should then be able to hypothesize with some degree of confidence which *things* are still missing. Specifically, by exploring the connections and the processes that archaeologists Lindsay Der and Francesca Fernandini have called "feedback loops," I argue that it is possible to reconstruct some of the factors that time and destruction have removed from the modern record.[11] That is, by building the rest of the puzzle to the best of our ability, we can determine the shapes of missing pieces.

Pre-deportation Acadian dress is the perfect case study for this methodology, situating a nascent Acadian fashion system within its specific context in the seventeenth and early eighteenth centuries. Through a close examination of surviving artifacts connected with textile use and production, as well as an exploration of the specific entanglements that affected Acadian material culture, we can produce a finer-grained, more detailed look at what Acadians were wearing. That in turn tells us new things about how the Acadian domestic and sartorial worlds were shaped, how they reacted to change, and how others reacted to the changes in them. Historian Régis Brun first tackled this question, analyzing coastal traffic and trade records that revealed some Acadian engagement in contemporary fashion.[12] Integrating archaeological data and further contemporary documentation into the analysis reveals even more nuance. What we find during this decoding process is a society active in trade networks and the burgeoning capitalist economy. A combination of factors, including geography and local environment, cross-cultural contact, and the intriguing role Acadia played in local and international trade, came together to mark Acadia as a society distinct from that of New England and New France. At the same time, residents were not isolated from the prevailing whims of fashion. Rather, the development of distinctly Acadian styles in different communities reveals both their awareness of and participation in fashion trends of the metropoles, and the simultaneous development of not one but multiple regional fashion vernaculars.

If this is the case, then why did contemporary descriptions and commentary paint the Acadians as rustic and self-sufficient, at a distant remove from the mercantile marketplace? I suggest this was because the traditional image of Acadian settlement as a land of simple agricultural labourers appealed to the imperial designs of both England and France.[13] Acadia was to be developed as a breadbox for the colonies, a farming-specific space to generate profitable produce and, as John Reid has posited, to act both as an arm of settlement-colonialism and a tool for the British empire.[14] Once agriculture had become well established in places like the Minas basin, grain exports became an income-generating activity for Acadia, as did livestock sales for Beaubassin.[15] In seventeenth-century France, however, particularly those areas from which Acadians had originally emigrated, grain was rarely sold as a cash crop and cultural focus was not on the farm as a profit centre. Rural incomes in places like Brittany often relied instead on the sale of women's labour and of textile goods produced by the female heads of household.[16] The different income stream in the settlements, focusing on grain and cattle, freed Acadian women's labour to be deployed in new directions – no longer directed toward spinning and weaving textiles for sale, but into activities like decorative needlework for personal and community use. This change in focus demonstrates some of the shifting priorities of a newly emerging social identity alongside a newly forming political self.

Much has been made of the ways in which the forces of Atlantic empire found the Acadians to be something of a headache, politically speaking. Various authors have placed the blame on imperial concerns over Acadian political agency, how settling families claimed and managed land use, their blurred social structures with lack of a distinct elite group, and their engagement with Indigenous communities.[17] One factor that has not yet been considered is the way in which the Acadians rejected colonial control over their physical bodies – not solely in the ways their movements were limited, and land claims organized, but in how they moved away from the sartorial control of the metropole. Colonial power was vested in control, over colonists and their environments as well as their bodies. Keeping those populations culturally aligned with European sensibilities and social aesthetics, including concerns about nakedness and civility, meant that the uncertainties and anxieties surrounding new spaces could be kept in check.[18]

Acadians blurred the social boundaries between European and North American, and their new environment inspired the development of a new visual culture. Similar movement towards a more syncretic style of dress occurred in other colonial spaces, as explorations of colonial Louisiana have shown.[19] These changes demonstrate a shift away from early modern French emphasis on the particular styles and manners that helped define the social structure of the ancien régime. This added to the sense that the Acadians were rejecting their inherited aesthetics and Eurocentric understandings of the "civilized body" and becoming unpredictable.

Elite culture of the early modern era in France saw emphasis on appearance and manners as windows to states of being, and tensions built when people did not dress in a manner that befit their social and economic stations.[20] Literature and manners instruction of the time emphasized the role of dress and comportment in defining and demonstrating identity, and the emerging Acadian fashion systems disrupted those closely held systems. In so doing, Acadian dress was partially responsible for the growing perception of Acadians as a group whose values differed from those of the Continent. This shifting entanglement created a new form of tension – anxiety related to that waning sense of imperial hold over a people who were increasingly difficult to define.

THE HISTORY OF THE EIGHTEENTH CENTURY is often traced in goods. In the production revolution, the consumer revolution, the beginnings of capitalist consumption, and search for catalyst commodities, we attempt to define the ways in which objects have shaped the beginnings of the modern era. Production and consumption are not, however, the only means by which material things shape and define us. The combined acts of deconstruction and reconstitution, blending old and new into a third liminal creation, is an intrinsic part of the colonial settler experience. It can be seen as a simultaneous reshaping of both objects and the identities defined by those same objects: the touch of the human alters the landscape, and the nature of the landscape inherently alters the ways in which humans can touch and shape it. Moving into a new environmental and cultural space, the French settlers who would become the Acadians over the course of the next 120 years were shaped by their new context, and they shaped it in return. Like the red duffel wool described by Boston merchant Brook Watson, Acadians unravelled the cultural understandings they had brought with them, laid them on their looms next to new threads from their new home, and rewove them into something both unique and still grounded in their symbolic past.

The artifacts described here came predominantly from sites in Kespukwitk, Sipekne'katik, and Siknikt (around the Minas Basin and the Chignecto Isthmus), and the addition of Fortress Louisbourg in Unama'kik (Cape Breton). Recovered during archaeological excavations between 1960 and 2012, the assemblages from Beaubassin,

Belleisle, the Melanson Site, and the Acadian homes in Fortress Louisbourg give us a cross-section of different modes of Acadian life, domestic conditions, and a sense of urban versus rural priorities. In some places, it has proven useful to compare and contrast the evidence recovered from these sites against assemblages from other colonial sites of the period, particularly the archaeological reports on Fort Michilimackinac, a strategic outpost on the south side of the Straits of Mackinac, in Michigan, and seventeenth- and eighteenth-century domestic sites excavated through the Strawbery Banke Museum in Portsmouth, New Hampshire.[21]

In addition, this book interrogates both competing notions of pre-deportation Acadia: as a series of isolated settlements of French-accultured colonists on the outskirts of empire, or a fully realized ethnicity and community distinct and separate from surrounding peoples. The evidence suggests instead that Acadians in these Nova Scotia settlements were engaging with contemporary fashion and the transatlantic marketplace. They participated more heavily in colonial French and English culture than previously understood from examination of documents alone.

Adding the evidentiary base of the artifact assemblages opens new directions for discussion, and provides evidence that Acadians were consciously using clothing as a means of communication, as well as a tool for cultural and economic connection. We can see from the objects left behind that there was more than one Acadian dress vernacular; the assemblages from Beaubassin, Belleisle, Melanson, and in houses occupied by Acadian families resident in Louisbourg are all that little bit different from each other. Given time, those differences might well have continued to grow and develop into a set of distinct and identifiable Acadian styles, but the process was indelibly altered thanks to the traumatic events of 1755.

Objects worn on the body, whether made locally or imported, have a great deal to say about the world in which the Acadians lived, and how they engaged with it. Studies have been done along these lines on foodways, glass, and architecture, and this book adds clothing and dress-related artifacts into the discussion. The following chapters examine the geographical and historical contexts of four Acadian settlements in Nova Scotia, the tools used to manufacture and decorate the textiles and garments, the varieties of textiles and fibres to which Acadians had access, the notions and accessories that completed their outfits, the garments themselves, and finally overviews of the wardrobes and local fashions from the sites. Far from being isolated, the Acadians were indelibly connected to the wider Atlantic commercial network, the mercantile marketplace, and the global network of things.

The Acadian World

[S]ince the English have been masters of the country, the residents who
were lodged near the fort have for the most part abandoned their houses
and have gone to settle on the upper part of the river. They have made
their clearings below and above this great meadow.[1]

— — — — — —

WHEN IT COMES TO CHOOSING OUR CLOTHES, context matters. Factors such
as the climate and weather, the availability of materials, and social expectations all
directly influence what we wear, and how we wear it. These preconditions can be
ancient and all-pervasive, like wet winter weather on the northeast coast of North
America, or short-lived and individual, as with a fashion fad or a preference for the
colour pink. Geography, climate, environment, religion, social pressures, age, and
expectations surrounding gender all contribute, as do factors including access to
materials, participation in local and international trade, and the economic status of
participants in purchase and production. In order to understand what people wore
and why they wore it, we need to know the world in which they made those choices.
Only then can we begin the task of reconstruction.

The geography, climate, political, and social environments surrounding the French
settlers in Acadia played significant roles in the evolution of their dress culture. Over
the course of the century-plus between settlement and deportation, different groups of
Acadians began to differentiate themselves and their dress from one another, as well
as from the fashion systems of France, New England, and New France. This differentiation was spurred on by a complex intersection of environmental and social factors,
including the physical environment as well as the changing nature of their contact
with the Mi'kmaq, the distances between Acadian settlements and seats of imperial
power, Acadians' commercial position and trade habits vis-à-vis New France and New
England, and the influences of the dominant cultures present in the migrants' points

of origin. Along with these macro forces we also find the micro – the networks of families, trading partners, and individuals living and working in the settlements.[2]

Environmental conditions play a large role in what materials are practical and available, and these conditions can include everything from the geography of a region to the available flora and fauna. The moisture content and pH of the soil determine the types of crops that can be grown, as does the number of healthy bodies available for agricultural labour. The presence or absence of calm harbours and cleared trails alters the possibilities for trade, and the size and abundance of fur-bearing animals determine whether one hide or twenty is needed to cover an adult human body. Those preconditions alone, however, are not enough to explain dress choice. The economic realities of a region also play a powerful role, both in the availability of traded materials, the diversity or homogeneity of access to resources, and the nature of existing networks of exchange.

Acadia is often described as remote, a borderland made inaccessible by multiple-week travel times from Quebec and France, and the relative dangers of sailing on the capricious Bay of Fundy. The geographic isolation, it has been suggested, made Acadian farmers increasingly vulnerable and self-reliant, each homestead working semi-independently and engaging in infrequent trade for items that could not be produced on-site.[3] The region, however, was far from uninhabited or isolated. Siknikt (the Chignecto Isthmus) had been a hub for trade and engagement with the outside world prior to the arrival of European settlers and continued to be so following their arrival. New scholarship instead describes these kinds of cultural and environmental borderlands as bridges, regions of intersecting and overlapping engagement between peoples. Coastal spaces in particular are regions shaped by these perpetual negotiations, the spaces at the water's edge defined by constant movement and change.[4]

Acadian occupation spread upward from La Hève and outward from Port Royal in the mid- through late seventeenth century, settlers establishing a series of homesteads and villages along the rivers, marshes, and coasts. The traditional interpretation of the engagement between existing Mi'kmaw communities and the new arrivals was at first one of peace and mutually beneficial engagement, including intermarriages, mixed settlements, and military assistance against the English.[5] Surviving parish registers do not indicate large numbers of intermarriages between non-elite Acadians and the Mi'kmaw community, however, though some families undoubtedly maintained closer relationships than others. Time played a role, communities drawing closer together when mutual support was needed, drifting apart later as their political goals diverged.[6] More engagement certainly took place at trading hubs than would have been seen at predominantly farming-focused sites, but even then the answer is not so clear-cut.

Pre-Colonial Mi'kma'ki

The Mi'kmaw Nation has inhabited the northeast of North America for at least 13,000 years. Referring to themselves as L'nuk – The People – groups, according to one tradition, originally migrated to their territory from the southwest of Turtle Island, the continent of North America.[7] Mi'kma'ki extended over 130,000 km² at its height, including Nova Scotia, Prince Edward Island, parts of New Brunswick, northern Maine, and into the Gaspé Peninsula in Quebec. Estimates of the population for pre-contact Kiskukewe'k L'nuk give numbers of about 3,500–6,000 people, while others have suggested as many as five times that amount.[8] Their seasonal rounds following the harvests included hook, spear, weir, and basket fishing in the spring and summer, shellfish harvesting, and the collection of seabirds and eggs during the spring, summer, and autumn, while winter hunting revolved around moose, beaver, bear, otter, caribou, and other mammals. Travel was primarily along waterways, using cedar and birchbark canoes.[9] Proximity to the water shaped their material culture, with groups living in the interior adapting to wetland resources, and those on the coast developing technologies more suited to marine resource gathering. Their annual routine moved them from coastal regions in the summer farther inland in winter. Subsistence activities included fishing, hunting, gathering, and small-scale horticulture. A cultural mandate for sharing resources and communal oversight of lands encouraged policies of stewardship and harvesting only enough to account for current needs, rather than viewing land, flora, and fauna as profit-generating commodities.[10]

The Atlantic Maritime Ecozone, of which Mi'kma'ki is a large part, experiences cool summers and mild winters overall, as a result of proximity to the Atlantic Ocean. The relative humidity is high, and the area is prone to storms and hurricanes. The soils are highly acidic, which impedes the preservation of organic materials except in extraordinary circumstances, but which supports mixed coniferous and deciduous forest, and a wide range of flora and fauna. Many areas of the highlands are ill-equipped for farming, and the short growing season makes agriculture difficult. The lowlands, especially the marshlands of the Chignecto Isthmus and the Bay of Fundy, are much better situated for agricultural use.

While not nearly as extensive as the practices of fire ecology and fire hunting among Indigenous groups farther south, the Mi'kmaq did have the small-scale practice of very carefully managed controlled burns to change the landscape – clearing space for berry bushes, and firing meadows to improve fertility.[11] Desirable plants were planted and maintained for small-scale use, and regular campsites enriched with

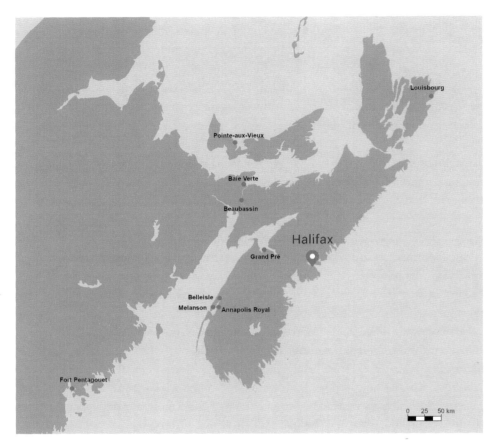

FIGURE 1.1 • Map of selected Acadian settlements and major locations.

compost and burned wood over thousands of years of occupation. Agricultural activities took place throughout the year, including the tapping of maple trees for syrup, and the growing and harvesting of tobacco. Local experts have suggested that the Mi'kmaq also farmed crops like pumpkins and beans, trading them with the Abenaki farther south. Hunting grounds were allocated by district chiefs, and prior to the fur trade protocols were in place for game management.[12]

Descriptions of Mi'kmaw dress at the time of contact come solely from European perspectives, subject to cultural bias and misunderstandings. Seventeenth-century writings from Nicolas Denys, Marc Lescarbot, and Abbé Biard describe wardrobes based on leather, a preference that began to shift once tightly woven wool fabrics called strouds were made available as trade goods.[13] Denys described men's main garments as loose tunics made from white moose-skin, painted with red, violet, and blue dyes in a wide variety of geometric and representational patterns, the colours sealed by pressing with a heated bone in a manner that Denys compares to the gilding process. Tunics were tied together at the sides rather than sewn, and worn open over a loincloth and leather leggings.

Women's clothing was similar in composition, but covered more of the body. Their moose-skin tunics were tied over both shoulders and belted around the waist with a girdle. They wore this dress style with knee-length leggings and sometimes with separate sleeves, tied on at the back.[14] They made moccasins from old moose leather, elaborately decorated with quillwork embroidery in red and violet. Quillwork and other embellishments were common and prized by French onlookers, as were accessories made from local materials. Garments were decorated with shell and seed beads, local copper, stone, bone, teeth and claws, and brightly dyed quills. They used locally gathered ochres, roots, barks, and berries for dyes to paint both clothes and bodies.[15] Smaller furs such as otter, martin, squirrel, and beaver were used for winter wear, and cold-weather cloaks were made of bear, deer, moose, or lynx.[16]

European contact came first in small doses: meetings with Basque and Portuguese fishermen in the early sixteenth century introduced new trade goods into Mi'kmaw circles. Jacques Cartier's arrival in 1534 began an era of wider trade with France, and by 1550 French fishermen were common sights on the coast and in the Gulf of St Lawrence. The fur trade developed alongside the fishery, and those changes began a permanent disruption in established patterns of exchange and land use. The Mi'kmaq became dependent on materials imported by Europeans, particularly once over-trapping and European encroachment on hunting grounds began to deplete the available game. Migration patterns changed along with the establishment of trading posts, the introduction of alcohol, and the behavioural shift from hunting for food to hunting for trade.[17] The arrival of French settlers in Kmitkinag in the 1630s caused more changes, both to land use and to exchange and engagement. The precise level of contact and communication between the Mi'kmaq and the Acadians is unknown, but some knowledge exchange certainly took place over the following century and a half, connected both to proximity of living spaces and the needs of the fur trade. What can be generally assumed from surviving references is that contact between the Mi'kmaq and French settlers began relatively amicably, with land peacefully co-occupied thanks to different requirements from the landscape. Tensions likely began to grow as the cartographic fiction of "Acadia" began to usurp the concept of "Mi'kma'ki," and the Mi'kmaq were drawn further into imperial struggles for domination over the region.[18]

Mi'kmaw settlements were recorded at Port Royal, Cape Sable, La Hève, Minas, Musquodoboit, Cape Breton, and Chignecto in 1708, with a combined population of 836 persons.[19] This is undoubtedly only a fraction of the number of nomadic Mi'kmaq living in the region, as not even the agriculturally sedentary Acadians are fully enumerated on the official censuses. These settlements were summer villages rather than full-year residences, occupied primarily for trade and community exchange. The amount of cultural exchange grew as more settlers arrived, then diminished in later years as conflict increased, land use came under interrogation, and Mi'kmaw and Acadian priorities diverged. Jesuit missionaries invested a great deal of energy into the conversion of Mi'kmaw communities, and many Jesuits served both Acadian and Mi'kmaw groups during their postings to Mi'kma'ki. Intermarriage between Acadian men and Mi'kmaw women took place in earlier years, though how frequently those marriages occurred, or how many went unrecorded, has remained a contentious point of debate. Attempts to use DNA testing to resolve some of these questions have encountered problems with the reliability of commercial services and the data pools required to make confident matches.[20] What we can be sure of is that while colonial officials discouraged mixing, social ties still developed in settlements like Beaubassin where contact was more frequent.[21] Contact levels may be described using Rani Alexander's label of "cultural entanglement" – a "long-term, gradual, and non-directed" process of social and material change as the result of the slow spread of Acadian settlement through Mi'kmaw territory.[22] These situations of mutual influence, based neither on conquest nor assimilation, created a new set of relationships that changed social and cultural relations, patterns of production, and eventually the participants' concepts of self.[23]

Social engagement between many groups of Mi'kmaq and Acadians lessened following the British conquest of 1710. While military alliances against the British saw Acadians and Mi'kmaq working together, British policy and retaliations against Acadian communities increased tensions between the two – particularly in the 1740s and 1750s.[24] The 1720s saw rising conflict between the Mi'kmaq and the British in Mi'kma'ki, and efforts to push the British out of the region led in some cases to the British targeting Acadians for retribution instead, as they were believed to be allies. Ultimately, hostilities between France and Great Britain spread the conflict. The antagonism supposedly formally ended with the signing of a set of peace treaties with the British in 1749, 1752, and 1760–61, but the ways in which the provisions of those treaties were enacted or ignored set the stage for future problems.

French Settlement and Expansion

The first French settlers in Nova Scotia spread out across the salt marshes on the Bay of Fundy, employing dyking technology developed in Europe to desalinate the land at the mouths of the rivers and streams. Agricultural rhythms at the homesteads were ruled by the Fundy tides, the pressures of water and silt settlement requiring careful balance between risk of damage to the dykes and fields, and the necessary re-fertilization of the settling soils inside them. The first seventy years saw slow immigration from various regions of Europe, the majority of new settlers collecting from the west and southwest of France. While some families were connected with European aristocracy, the bulk of the newcomers were members of France's Third Estate – labourers, soldiers, and tradesmen.[25]

The community was originally centred around Port Royal, but political conflicts and population pressures encouraged Acadian migration away from the town. Settlers moved along the coast of central Nova Scotia and the Minas Basin, west to Annapolis, and north and east into Siknikt (Shepody River, New Brunswick, and Amherst). They primarily built smaller villages often centred around single-family clusters, rather than larger urban environments. Close to 2,500 Acadians were living in the region by 1711, about five hundred settling around Port Royal.[26] Mainland Acadia (not including Ile Royale, modern-day Cape Breton) was handed over to notional British control in the Treaty of Utrecht in 1713, subsequent negotiations between the Acadians and the European empires reforming the connective tissue between them. Over the next few decades more families moved away from Port Royal, establishing farms and small kin-focused settlements in surrounding regions. Church records show only a few marriages between British and French residents in Nova Scotia, though Acadians continued to marry French-speaking Catholics from outside their community, and some families made marital connections with Massachusetts. Marriages often took place between the groups, with as many as a third of Acadian marriages involving spouses from different settlements.[27]

Community support was vital for these marriages and the kinship networks they forged. As Brook Watson wrote in 1791, describing marriage customs among Acadians: "Whenever a marriage took place the whole village set about establishing the young couple, they built them a log house, and cleared land sufficient for their immediate support, supplied them with some cattle, hogs, and poultry, and nature, aided by their own industry, soon enabled them to assist others."[28] Marriages created and reinforced existing familial ties, strengthening connections and the system of labour-sharing that was common across Acadia. New immigrants to the region married into established families, assuming roles in this existing network of mutual aid.[29] Average family size was around six to seven children per couple, with approximately 75 per cent of Acadian children surviving to adulthood.[30] Births were approximately two years apart, with some cases of twins and even one of triplets. The timing suggests that wet nurses were not commonly used and that Acadian women weaned infants around their first birthday, with fertility returning quickly thereafter.[31] Children were valuable as hands for domestic and farm work and continued to be an asset into adulthood. It was a common practice for older Acadian parents to divide up their property among their heirs in return for a promise of continual elder care.[32] These multi-generational households gave younger parents access to childcare and made more hands available for light domestic and farm labour. Subdivision of land between adult children and general expansion of settlements meant that by the time of the 1707 census most of the families were cultivating between four and twelve arpents of land, if they had land of their own.[33]

The following sections explore the history and populations of four different Acadian settlements in Nova Scotia. While more sites have been partially surveyed, many of which remain undisturbed, these four are notable for the quantities of documentary and archaeological evidence associated with them, evidence that can give us a window into the lives of Acadians prior to the deportation of 1755. These are known colloquially as the Melanson site, a settlement within the banlieue of Fort Anne; Belleisle Marsh, a series of rural farms along the Annapolis River; Beaubassin, a trading hub on the Chignecto Isthmus; and Acadian households in Fortress Louisbourg, an urban environment under French colonial authority. Each represents a different way of living, with varied demographics, perspectives, and priorities. The environmental and geographical differences between the settlements influenced the development of local cultures, as well as their fashion systems and identities.

Melanson

The Melanson site lies about six kilometres west of Annapolis Royal and ten kilometres from the Digby Gut, where water flows from the Annapolis Basin to the Bay of Fundy. The Annapolis region has significant salt marshes along the coast, with large shellfish populations in the mud flats. Local temperatures are mild thanks to the generally sheltered nature of the area, though snow lasts longer in the winters than farther east in the Valley. The region is generally suited for agriculture, particularly once the marshlands were dyked and the water drained, as Charles Morris, a

Massachusetts-born army officer and surveyor, described in 1748: "the Villages [are] divided from each other with long intervalls of marshes and they at great distance bounded by Hills covered with Trees the Natural growth of the Country [.] here may be seen rivers turning and winding among the Marshes then Cloath'd with all the variety of Grain."[34]

This fertile region was settled by brothers Pierre and Charles Melanson and their families in the late seventeenth century. The brothers were the sons of a French Huguenot and his English wife and spent the early years of their lives in England; that heritage affected the ways in which the brothers and their families played local politics. Charles Melanson *dit* La Ramée, son of Pierre Laverdure, and his wife Marie Dugas, the daughter of Port Royal armourer Abraham Dugas, were wealthy compared with other settlers, owning the second-largest land concession in Acadia and the largest herd of cattle.[35] They had fourteen children, eight of whom settled their homesteads nearby. As cousins by marriage to families living in Boston, Belleisle, and at Fortress Louisbourg, the Melanson family were at the top of the region's social ladder. Their wealth was regularly diminished, however, by attacks from the British colonies aimed at their herds of livestock.[36]

The Melanson children's marriages solidified their family's ties within and beyond the Acadian community. One daughter, Marie Melanson *dite* Laverdure, married David Basset, a Huguenot trader, and moved with him to Boston.[37] Following imprisonment in France for smuggling prisoners of the Governor of Plaisance to Boston, Basset returned to become the master of the British ship *Porcupine*, raiding French sites and privateering up and down the east coast. Basset was one of a large group of traders that brought illicit goods from New England to Acadian settlements in the twenty years prior to the Treaty of Utrecht (1713). Another daughter, Cécile Melanson, married trader Abraham Boudrot, an important merchant with strong ties to Boston. The Boudrot family originally settled near Cécile's parents in the expanding Melanson settlement, but following her husband's death and her subsequent remarriage, the widow Boudrot moved away.[38] Other siblings were involved in the political life of nearby Port Royal, as seen in Claude Melanson's 1733 appointment as an overseer of the "Herds and fflocks," to inspect the community's sheep and regulate use of common grazing lands.[39]

Their brother Charles Melanson brought wife Anne Bourg to live in Melanson around 1701, becoming part of a shifting rotation of daughters and daughters-in-law revolving around the main house. The house next door to Melanson and Bourg was the residence of Melanson's sister Madeleine, who originally lived there with her husband Jean Charles Belliveau *dit* le jeune, and their children. Belliveau died fighting off an English raid on Port Royal in 1707, and his widow and children remained living in the house only fifteen metres from her brother and sister-in-law. These couples were part of the intricate community network that connected the string of Acadian settlements along the Bay of Fundy. Among other ties, Charles's brother Michel was already married to Anne's sister Elizabeth, those Melansons living in the settlement of Beaubassin. The Melanson-Bourg house was first excavated in 1983 and is the source of most of the domestic finds we have from the settlement.[40]

Anne Melanson, sister to Charles, Marie, Claude, and Cécile, returned to the settlement around 1700 following the death of her first husband, Jacques de Saint-Étienne de La Tour. She soon remarried and established a household with second husband Alexandre Robichaud and her four children from her first marriage.[41] De La Tour had been local nobility, inheriting shared seigneurial rights from his parents Charles de Saint-Étienne de La Tour and Jeanne Motin. "Lady Anne" gained the informal title thanks to her marriage, and her children by de La Tour inherited his shares in the land. The connections between the Melansons, Boston money, and the high status of the local seigneurs placed the settlement squarely in the middle of the economic and political tensions that swirled around the area, especially in the first decade of the eighteenth century.

A map made in 1708 by engineer Pierre-Paul Delabat allows us to place the various members of the Melanson extended family in their respective houses (see figure 1.2). The houses are close together, strewn across the landscape in a haphazard way with buildings erected where useful as the need arose, a common pattern for colonial and frontier settlements. Many of the outbuildings would have been large enough to house looms and other large equipment necessary for agricultural and domestic production.

Nine households had set up residence at the Melanson site by 1714, and most of those families included multiple young couples themselves beginning married life. Sons often stayed nearby to work the land, while daughters might remain local to access shared domestic labour.[42] Three generations of Melansons are believed to have been deported on the *Pembroke* in 1755, becoming part of a group that rebelled against their captors and seized the ship.[43] They eventually made their way to Quebec, though many died shortly after arrival thanks to waves of illness that swept through the Acadian refugee community.[44] The closest of these four settlements to the colonial headquarters at Port Royal, at the mouth of the harbour entrance, those living at the Melanson settlement had easy access to the official seat of government in the region. The Melansons' close association with the La Tour family gave them a certain amount of political cachet, and potentially higher interest in following European

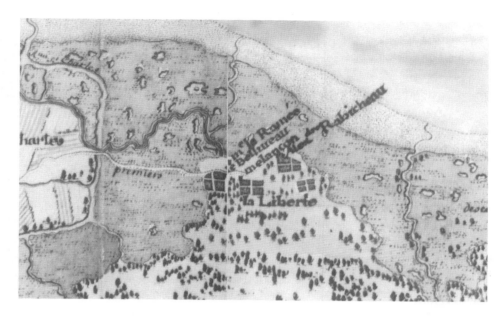

FIGURE 1.2 • Plan de la banlieu du Fort Royal a l'Acadie et environes et de ses environs, 1708.

fashion trends and cultural mores. Their dress items, discussed in later chapters, show that some of the members of this settlement owned and wore fashions common to the middling classes and elite.

Belleisle Marsh

The Belleisle marsh held an Acadian settlement and farming community, with settler presence recorded from before 1679. The original wetland was over 700 hectares in size, which gave ample room to support the farms that dotted the area by 1748.[45] The settlement was built approximately eleven kilometres east of Port Royal on the north side of the Annapolis River, close to and in the same ecological zone as Melanson. On excellent land and near to a large metropolis, Belleisle became one of the most heavily populated settlements in the region.[46] The farmers living in and around Port Royal had brought with them an understanding of freshwater and sea-coast marshes, including techniques of reclaiming the land that had been refined in regions like the Poitou for generations, and the Belleisle tidal marsh made for ideal land to test techniques of reclamation and large-scale dyke-wall construction.[47] The high tides of the Bay of Fundy brought advantages as well as challenges, the high-rising waters keeping the banks free of trees and encouraging the meadows that had so enthralled Lescarbot in 1606.[48]

The marsh was populated by a small number of families, either already linked by blood or marriage or soon to become so. A census taken in 1688 listed ten houses and seventy-four people residing at Belleisle, twenty-four of whom were adults; a map drawn in 1733 shows twenty-four houses in the vicinity.[49] There are some well-known Acadian names among the residents of Belleisle, including Michel Richard *dit* Sansoucy, merchant Michel Richard *dit* Lafond, and militia officer Pierre LeBlanc. Along with marriage, families were connected by mutual obligation, sharing the labour of tilling the fields and maintaining the dykes. Patriarch Guillaume Blanchard owned and worked land in Belleisle until leaving to travel, founding Village des Blanchard (in modern-day New Brunswick) in 1699.[50] After Blanchard's death, his land was managed by a group consisting of his son René, his brother Antoine, and Pierre Gaudet *dit* Will Denis. Pierre Gaudet and Antoine Blanchard had other properties in Belleisle but René Blanchard had no other land under his name, and most likely continued to occupy his father's house. René Blanchard married Marie Savoie, the daughter of his neighbour Germain, and together they raised thirteen children. Blanchard died in 1754, while Marie Savoie survived the deportation and died in Duxbury, Massachusetts, in 1767.[51]

Two of the Blanchard-Savoie children, a son also named René and daughter Marguerite, never married. They likely remained at the homestead and would have provided more pairs of working hands. René Blanchard *le fils* disappears from the records after his baptism, but Marguerite Blanchard and her mother both reappear in the civil registry of Duxbury, Massachusetts, after 1755.[52] Marguerite Blanchard's status as an unmarried woman makes her significant. Approximately 90 per cent of rural labourers in France married, and the rates in Acadia were higher, with "virtually all young men and women" espoused.[53] Marriage would not have excluded her from the pool of joint labour required to maintain the family's holdings, so something else must have informed her attachment to her single life. Living together at the house in Belleisle following René-le-père's death, the widow Blanchard and her daughter were then sent together into exile.

As of the census of 1707, Germain Savoie was farming the land to the east of Pierre Gaudet Sr, and his house was partially excavated by archaeologists in 2005. Savoie took the land over from his father François, who had been cultivating it since the middle of the seventeenth century. Property transfers between fathers and sons often happened on the occasion of the son's wedding, maintaining that association of land ownership with familial and generational ties.[54] Savoie and his wife Marie Breau *dite* Vincelotte had at least eleven children, one born on average every two years. Of the sons who appear in the records, the second born, François-Xavier Savoie, married Marie-Josephe Richard; her first cousin was Marguerite Richard in Louisbourg, solidifying the link between the families. By the time the residents of Belleisle were exiled in 1755, Germain-le-père and Marie Breau had passed away. The two sisters for whom we have records married and moved to Port Royal and Beaubassin respectively, their families later travelling to New Brunswick and Quebec.[55]

Belleisle was a thriving community, the families engaged in shared labour and tied together by two generations of marriage and mutual support. Residents travelled to Port Royal for church on Sundays, and mingled and married with those from other towns and settlements. Unlike the Melanson family, however, the households at Belleisle did not have strong familial and social connections to the British authorities, nor to the local gentry. If the Melansons could be conceived of as very minor aristocracy, Belleisle's residents were the slightly less couth country cousins. Many were financially comfortable, but the stratification that still existed in Acadian society in earlier years led to a different relationship with social display than seen in other areas.[56]

Beaubassin

Thanks to the survival of some parish records, Beaubassin, situated far from Port Royal at the apex of the Bay of Fundy, is one of the better-documented settlements in Acadian history. A series of archaeological explorations have also revealed physical evidence of Acadian homesteads, some of which remained undisturbed by later British and Planter activity. Recent analyses done on the records exposed a rich and vibrant network of families in the region, supporting one another through rituals of godparenting and the bonds of marriage.[57] Geographically more distant from centres of imperial influence than Melanson and Belleisle, Beaubassin was outside of the radius of territorial control of both the French and the English. As such, Acadians living there had more social freedom to establish new practices.[58] By the first half of the eighteenth century, Beaubassin was a thriving community involved in proto-capitalist trade with both New England and Louisbourg.[59]

Geography and Environment

The Acadian village of Beaubassin was located at a strategically important point in the area originally known as Siknikt – the Isthmus of Chignecto – in the overall region also known as Beaubassin. The narrow seventeen-mile span between the Bay of Fundy and the Northumberland Strait made the region the best choice for portages between the two waterways, a pathway used by Indigenous peoples for generations before European contact.[60] Four rivers drained into the Cumberland Basin, running through narrow river valleys and picking up fertile sediment along their twelve- to fifteen-mile-long travels.[61] Forested highlands separated the river valleys, providing a source for lumber both for use and for sale. Prior Mi'kmaw use of the area had been primarily for the collection of shellfish and other marsh resources.

The village of Beaubassin was founded between 1671 and 1674 by Acadian migrant Jacques Bourgeois from Port Royal, and by 1750 the isthmus supported a population of more than 2,500.[62] Predominantly French-speaking Acadians, the population of Beaubassin also included a handful of immigrants from places like Ireland and Portugal.[63] The fertile soils of the Fundy salt marsh allowed for the planting of shallow-rooted crops in the lands reclaimed by dyking.[64] The region was attractive to newcomers seeking to enclose and work agricultural lands. The wetlands and marshes of the southern region of the isthmus were more fertile than the rocky, mixed-forest uplands, and Acadian settlers made their homes on the edges and low elevations of the uplands.[65] Antoine Cadillac's 1692 memoir described the Beaubassin area as having "meadows as far as the eye can reach from all the shores. There are numbers of little rivers with small valleys, and with pasture-lands to support an infinite number of cattle."[66] Settlements were already in existence by this point, approximately five leagues (~28 kilometres) from the portage to Baie Verte.

Beaubassin's extensive meadows made the environment ideal for cattle, and beef production played a major role in Beaubassin's economy. Farmers from Chignecto transported cows into Cape Breton through the late seventeenth and early eighteenth centuries, much to the dismay of British officials.[67] By 1707 the shift in agricultural focus from crops to livestock seemed to be well under way. The number of heads of livestock had more than doubled across all the enumerated categories by that year, and sheep had multiplied by a factor of five.[68] The settlement grew rapidly, with a dramatic increase in population after the region came under British control in 1710. It is after this date that Beaubassin hit critical population mass, becoming – and remaining – the third-largest French settlement in the region, following Minas and Port Royal.[69] Geography played a vital role in the choice of locations and the ways in which resources were used. The lumber mills, the short portage to Baie Verte on the Northumberland Strait, and marine access to both Port Royal and Louisbourg would come to define the settlers' roles.

Ecology and sustainability aside, Beaubassin was an attractive settlement point for logistical reasons. De Meulles describes a trip of approximately six weeks from Quebec to Beaubassin in October and November of 1686, and another two weeks

FIGURE 1.3 • Detail, *Carte de l'Acadie, isle Royale et païs voisins. Pour servir à l'histoire generale des voyages. Par M.B. Ingr. de la Marine. 1757.*

beyond that from Beaubassin to Port Royal by ship, making Baie Verte and the portage to Beaubassin a natural stopping place and route for travellers from New France.[70] The 550 kilometre run from Baie Verte to Louisbourg through the Northumberland Strait was safer than bringing ships through the Cumberland Basin with its unpredictable tides. Acting as a crossroads between Acadia and New France, Beaubassin's central location gave it greater reach and influence with other Acadian settlements than more distant Port Royal.[71] Beaubassin developed a livestock-based economy, exported goods to other Acadian regions, and included members of prominent wealthy Acadian families as well as those still eking out a basic living. Subsistence and luxury goods passed through the area with frequency, and the Acadians of Beaubassin dressed in clothing that followed current fashion alongside garments made according to their own particular vernacular. Bartered materials and cash influxes kept the local economy growing.

Shipyards and mills sprang up thanks to the easy access to good lumber in the region and a flour mill and sawmill were among the earlier buildings erected, constructed from parts brought in by New England merchants.[72] The largest ship ever to be built in Acadia – Jacques Vigneau *dit* Maurice's 100-tonne vessel – was under construction in nearby Baie Verte in 1754.[73] By 1755, Baie Verte had become a small and thriving waypoint and trading centre, as Colonel Winslow described: "This Vilage Contains about Twenty-five Houses a Chaple and Priests house well Furnished, and the Inhabitants of this Vilage Live in better form and more after the English Manner than Any I have Seen in this Province and have an open Communication with the Island of St John and the Inhabitants of Cape Briton whome the Furnish with Lumber Indian Goods and, from whome they recive all the Conveniencys of Life in return."[74]

Beaubassin is perhaps most widely known for the method of its destruction, the village itself burned to the ground by Abbé Le Loutre's followers in 1750. This was hardly an uncommon fate for Acadian settlements in the early eighteenth century, but the main distinction to be made is that unlike other settlements on the isthmus, Beaubassin village was targeted by theoretically "friendly" fire.[75] There were fewer residents still living in Beaubassin at that point than might have otherwise been the case, as many had already moved north of the Missaguash River to a region administered by the French.[76] The British built Fort Lawrence in 1750 on the southern side of the river, on the land originally occupied by the village, and the French constructed Fort Beausejour in 1751 on the opposing bank. The other Acadian settlements on the south side of the Missaguash were abandoned once Beaubassin was destroyed and Beausejour built, while those on the north – Pitkoudiac, Chipoudy, and Memramcook – were folded in under the administrative umbrella of Fort Beausejour. This split has for all intents and purposes become the modern Nova Scotia–New Brunswick border.

The People

The first European settler on the Chignecto isthmus was Jacques Bourgeois, who sold off land in Port Royal in 1672 and moved northeast between 1671 and 1673.[77] Bourgeois and his family made their way northeast in the early 1670s to establish a new settlement on the Tantramar marshes. Bourgeois would have been familiar with the area thanks to his prior involvement in the fur trade, and had contacts with local Mi'kmaw groups.[78] Michel Leneuf de La Vallière, governor of Acadia (1683–84), received the seigneurial grant to the isthmus in 1676 and moved there himself in 1705. Over the years he facilitated the emigration of settlers from Canada, many of whom integrated into existing Acadian communities; a census of Beaubassin in 1686 shows 127 settlers living on 426 arpents of cultivated land.[79] Twenty-two houses had been built on hills near the wooded uplands, and kin compounds generally included three or four main buildings to house family units and livestock.[80]

Diversity and Indigenous Relations

The population of Beaubassin was a mixed group beyond the Acadians from Port Royal and La Vallière's French imports from Canada. Emmanuel Mirande *dit* Tavare, a Portuguese sailor from the Azores, married Jacques Bourgeois's daughter Marguerite sometime between 1675 and 1680. Roger Caissie, an Irishman, married Marie Françoise Poirier of Port Royal, and their family were among the first settlers in Beaubassin.[81] Michel Haché *dit* Gallant, of mixed Indigenous and French descent, married Anne Cormier, the daughter of the Beaubassin militia captain, somewhere around 1688–89, and they settled in Ouescoque. Wealth and holdings varied among the families in the region, the settlement containing poorer families such as that of Robert Cottard, with his wife, one young son, two arpents of land and a handful of livestock, through to the seigneur, de La Vallière, with sixty arpents cultivated, fifty-three large animals (cows, pigs, and sheep), and his own gunsmith hired to care for his seventy different firearms.[82]

The region that archaeologist Sara Beanlands has dubbed the "Oesgag Triangle," the space between the Mi'kmaq settlements of Oesgag, Weehekage, and Oegôgômigeg, played host to the fur trade and was an important contact zone between the Acadians and the Mi'kmaq.[83] According to the 1686 census, about one-fifth of the population of the area was Mi'kmaw and they remained a significant local presence. The so-called "Indian census" of 1708 recorded a hundred Indigenous persons living in Chignecto, though those communities were not in regular close contact with the Acadian population.[84] The fur trade brought the groups into contact more often in the community's early years, though later conflicts grew over land use and ownership of livestock, particularly escaped cattle or wenjooteam – the "French Moose."[85] Acadians from Beaubassin also traded for furs with the Malecite of the Saint John River Valley.

Intermarriage, if it took place in any formal way, does not appear in the written records. No Mi'kmaw names appear on censuses taken of the Acadian settlements at Beaubassin, nor in marriage records in surviving parish registers. Acadian men recorded as bachelors, or those living in the woods and unrecorded on the censuses, may well have had unofficial arrangements with Mi'kmaw women that would not appear in contemporary documentation. However these relationships may have proceeded, they do not seem to have happened often enough or in great enough numbers to have shifted the gender balance in the Acadian settlements through the loss of young bachelors, or to have produced many, if any, children out of wedlock.

The social hierarchy in Beaubassin strengthened and solidified during the last generation before the deportation. Status and power relations rearranged as time went on, as newcomers entered Beaubassin society and other family groupings moved out.[86] Counter to Clark's assertion in the 1960s that sophisticated European fashions were restricted to the areas close to Port Royal, Beaubassin's residents engaged in contemporary style and had direct contact with the Atlantic marketplace.[87] Beaubassin shows us a society that was more isolated than urban regions in France and New England, certainly, but was neither self-sufficient nor interested in becoming so. Rather than turning inward, residents of Beaubassin engaged in a multi-faceted material culture, drew influences from the groups surrounding them, adapted to the local environment, and in turn developed their own vernacular. This marked them not only as Acadians, distinct from other French groups but still able to engage in a form of "conditional French-ness," but also distinct from the other major Acadian settlements in Port Royal and Louisbourg.

Acadians in Louisbourg

Founded in 1713, the French military outpost of Fortress Louisbourg was a later addition to the coastline of Nova Scotia. Initially known as Havre à l'Anglois, Louisbourg became the location for the central French colony on Ile Royale in 1719, as well as the home for French fishermen who had moved from Newfoundland. The fishing port subsequently grew to become a major commercial port and a strongly defended fortress. The walled fort was built in 1720 and survived as a garrison for the French Navy, protection for Quebec City, and a sea link to France. Conquest in 1745 resulted in British control of Louisbourg until it was ceded back to the French three years later, and British re-conquest in 1758 finally saw the fortress demolished. The inhabitants were primarily French soldiers and officials, fishermen originally from Newfoundland, and eventually, a number of Acadians – most of them women – who married into French families or who came to live and work at the fortress alongside the French majority. Fifty-one Acadian women and twenty-six Acadian men appear in the surviving marriage records in Louisbourg, and others had married French officials in places like Port Royal, and moved to Ile Royale together.[88]

Louisbourg was an urban centre at its height, in contrast to the rural farming settlements typified by Belleisle and Melanson. By 1737 there were 1,436 civilians living in Louisbourg, added to a garrison of approximately 550 military men, a number that rose to a total of 2,454 as of the census of 1752. Demographically diverse, it was home to a moderately sized community of Black men – both previously enslaved and not – a few hundred Germans and Basques, a small community of Spanish soldiers at the garrison, and a range of individuals who might not show up in the church or court records, including Catholic Irish and at least one Jewish man.[89] The majority culture was French, and heavily informed by official and trade connections to the metropole. As early as 1707 the French authorities had tried to bring Acadian settlers in to swell their numbers, but few accepted those early invitations.

Reports from the garrison suggest that the isolation made a posting there an unpleasant temporary duty rather than an attractive option for permanent residency,

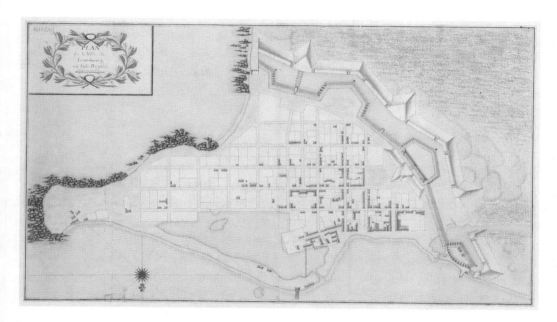

FIGURE 1.4 • *Plan de la ville de Louisbourg en l'Isle Royale.* 1745.

the steady ratio of eight to ten men to every woman not helping matters.[90] The presence of markets, notaries, and other services alongside the garrison, however, did make Louisbourg a useful destination for those already local. A few Acadian women married French government officials and military officers who had been stationed at Port Royal, moving with them to Louisbourg following the British takeover of their hometown. Once there, despite being seen as culturally distinct from French society, Acadians partially integrated into local high society, even socializing with the governor.[91] Other Acadians travelled to the fortress as merchants or for work such as carpentry or domestic service. A handful of houses in Louisbourg were occupied by Acadians or French inhabitants with Acadian spouses, four of which were excavated during Parks Canada's reconstruction of the fortress in the 1960s and 1970s. The Louisbourg families are special because of the availability of written documentation in the forms of probate inventories, something unknown elsewhere in Acadia.

Jeanne Thibodeau, an Acadian woman originally from Annapolis Royal, married Mathieu de Goutin, the French-born *lieutenant général civil et criminal*, and colonial secretary. The match was the subject of critique, as de Goutin was from a minor noble French family. Despite their differences in origin – despite Thibodeau's father's

political connections, the governor lamented that de Goutin had married "a peasant's daughter" – the marriage appears to have been stable, and produced thirteen
children.[92] The family lived in France between 1711 and 1714, returning to Ile Royale
when de Goutin was appointed as king's notary for the colony. He died that year and
Thibodeau remained in Louisbourg with her children. She died a wealthy widow
in April 1741, and her probate inventory displays the kind of material environment
appropriate for a woman of rank. Inventories of this kind provide a valuable resource
for understanding the daily lives of those whose goods were recorded. The property
of three other Acadian women and one young girl was inventoried after their deaths:
Marie Josephe Le Borgne de Belleisle, Anne Levron, and Marguerite Terriau.

Anne Levron of Port Royal married Pierre Benoist, an apothecary's son and en-
sign in the Louisbourg garrison, in 1713. They set up house in Louisbourg in 1722,
in a section of the fortress town that would become a centre for Acadian life.[93] The
Levron/Benoist household was one of the few Acadian households in Louisbourg that
owned enslaved people – in this case a young Black man named Charles, originally
from the West Indies. Charles's primary occupation would have been outdoor tasks
on the property, cutting wood and tending to the family's fires and stove. He appears
as property in Levron's probate inventory, one of more than two hundred enslaved individuals held in Louisbourg.[94] The wardrobe of Anne's young daughter was included
in the inventory of Anne's property following her passing.

Marguerite Terriau was twenty-four when she became the second wife of thirty-
one-year-old Pierre Bouisseau. His first marriage had been childless and Marguerite
bore nine children, three of whom died in infancy. Pierre died in 1755 and his belongings were inventoried together with Margeurite's, as was common practice under
French laws.[95] Together, their inventories open a world of information about their
wardrobes, possessions, creditors and debtors, and their use of domestic spaces.

Marie Josephe Le Borgne de Belleisle, born in 1711 to Alexandre Le Borgne de
Belisle and Anastasie d'Abbadie de Saint-Castin, was Mme Thibodeau's niece. Her
maternal grandmother was the daughter of Abenaki chief Madockawando, placing
her family at an intersection of Acadian, French, and Indigenous cultures. Le Borgne
was raised in Pentagouët, and moved to Louisbourg in her early teenage years to live
with her aunt Anne Le Borgne de Belleisle, there marrying Jacques Philipe Urbin
Rondeau, a notary and agent of the treasury of the Marine.[96] Le Borgne, from a family
that had been involved with trade – particularly of furs – for more than a century, engaged in the family tradition of trade and sales, particularly of textiles and dressmaking supplies. The inventories made after Rondeau's and Le Borgne's deaths separate

out personal belongings from damaged goods from saleable merchandise, giving us a glimpse into the kinds of import/export activities and commodities available to the network of Acadian women and their families in the fortress and beyond.

Commodities trade was a vital point of connection between Acadian communities, though the volume of goods moving between Acadia, New England, and Louisbourg, both legal and contraband, was treated by many contemporaries as primarily a problem of economic control. New England traders brought cod, French wines and brandy, tobacco, and sugar up from the West Indies, in return for food, building materials, and tools. Acadian farmers' role in the exchanges was the supply of provisions, specifically livestock and vegetables, in return for tools and domestic materials including textiles and ceramics.[97] As Louisbourg's population grew, trade that had formerly been focused within Minas moved to the town to take advantage of the bigger markets. Charles Morris described the movement of goods between Louisbourg and the Minas Basin in 1748: "Vessells from Cape Britton Spring and Fall come to Minis ... bring Wine, Brandy and Linnings which they can afford four pence and Six pence in a Yard cheaper then our [British] Traders can Possible doe, And Take from thence nothing but Wheat & Cattle which they Kill there & Salt up and from Chignecto ... They Drive Cattle over to Bay Vert and from thence Transport them ... The French Inhabitants haveing the sole Trade with the Indians & what our Traders get is intirely from the French."[98]

VIBRANT PARTS of a closely interlinked community, Acadian families throughout the Maritimes were connected by blood and by trade. As John Reid originally described, they lived at an intersection of spaces, a crossroads between the French, English, and Indigenous peoples where both goods and ideas circulated with relative freedom.[99] Acadians had access to supplies entering from England, France, and the Continent, as well as New England – both before and after such colonial trade was legal. As spouses, cousins, or co-operating landholders, the Richards, Dugas, Blanchards, Melansons, and the Belleisle Savoies formed a kinship network that transcended the bonds of ancestral villages.[100]

Their living environments played a strong role in the ways the different groups presented themselves to the outside world. Livestock and herds were the major agricultural focus in Beaubassin, supplying wool and leather, while Melanson and Belleisle, in Annapolis, were in a zone that favoured lush orchards and gardens. Embroiled in the politics of the fort and connected through marriage to the seigneurs and to Boston trade, the Melansons engaged with European and colonial power to a greater extent than more-distant Beaubassin. At Beaubassin, a region that had a strong Indigenous presence, Acadians looked to their trade partners and nearest neighbours for style and materials cues, the fur trade and closer contact with Mi'kmaw families shaping their aesthetic along new lines. Belleisle's settlers and the Acadian families at Louisbourg, while linked by kinship ties and similar in terms of wealth, engaged with fashion very differently. Louisbourg was a French urban environment, one in which Acadians moved but did not control. Louisbourg also had easier access to trade goods than Belleisle, and the patterns of that trade and commerce in general shaped the material culture of the settlements in different and complementary ways.

Allies and Smugglers

Historical descriptions of Acadia and modern nostalgia drive an image of Acadian homesteads as self-sufficient and disconnected from the broader world. Abbé Raynal is one of the main sources for this idea, painting a portrait of independent solitude: "The neutral French had nothing else to give their neighbors, and made still fewer exchanges among themselves; because each separate family was able, and had been accustomed to provide for its own wants."[101] The description is deeply misleading, as trade was a vital part of the Acadian economy. Along with importing goods, trading partners also maintained and strengthened contacts with other communities. This section examines the realties of trade in three regions with an Acadian presence – the Chignecto Isthmus, the Minas Basin, and Fortress Louisbourg. Each region played a role in the kinds of goods circulating through Acadia, the network of merchants, their families, connections, and suppliers entangling Acadia in a web that extended from Montreal to Indonesia.

Trade has a variety of functions, from the very practical and surface-level goods-and-services subsistence level, through to the more esoteric and nebulous. A single exchange is always about more than the specific items bought and sold. Each item passes through and is transformed by the process of becoming a commodity, the act of acquisition itself marking the goods as something different, often more valuable, than a homemade equivalent. Fundamentally, the movement of goods through a space impresses the space upon the goods, and the goods upon that space.[102] The arrival of copper kettles with Basque whalers in the sixteenth century, for instance, changed the material landscape of the east coast First Nations. Not only did it alter direct physical behaviour such as burial practices, but the presence of the copper kettles added the visual beat: "here is something new." "Here is something From Away."[103]

Changes in Acadian dress relied partially on their own skills as homesteaders, but also heavily on trade. The paths the goods took, the hands they passed through, and the end users' intents all contributed to the layers of meaning the fabrics accumulated along the way. Travel time between Port Royal and France, or Port Royal and Canada, was lengthy, and the distance encouraged illegal cross-border trade into Boston, which was much closer.[104] At the same time, European markets had little to no interest in goods produced in Acadia, as the excessive cost of transport made them unattractive compared with similar products from England and Ireland.[105] It made more sense to trade local goods locally, into Louisbourg, Acadia, Canada, and New England, rather than run up surcharges that could not be earned back.

Trade goods can also be understood as a means of staking out territory. The presence of certain items in a network lent prestige to the origin points of those goods, even if only in the minds of rivals. English strouds became a signpost for the British empire in this way, taking a space in the textile market denied to French woollens. Borders of contact regions pushed outward along with the goods even when not followed by the people, some of the signifiers of foreignness remaining even as goods and their primary meanings changed hands and shapes.[106] Bringing French-ness into Mi'kma'ki, European traders and the settlers who followed were part of a wave of visual takeover. The new people-shapes moving across the landscape were different in silhouette, colour, and detail than anything that had been seen there before. Those visual cues followed settlers into the forests, where explorers and traders in turn took on the clothing and body modifications of the Indigenous peoples they encountered.[107] Dress placed a European stamp on the land, the sight of farmers in skirts and trousers creating the cultivated pastoral landscape so closely associated with contemporary civilization. The baroque curves and gingham squares of imported textiles brought the aesthetic of India and Indonesia to Acadia, alongside the motifs of England, Italy, Spain, and France. The visual evocation of distant shores existed alongside the continued intrusion of European aesthetics into Indigenous spaces.[108]

Early Acadian settlers arrived with wardrobes consisting of imported fabrics and garments, but quickly began to make their own textiles from local materials. These homespun fabrics did not completely replace imports, especially since luxury textiles like silk and cotton could not be made locally. Settlements farthest removed from the forts made most of their clothing from linen and wool, while Acadian women in more urban areas added imported silks and cottons by the second quarter of the eighteenth century. They also incorporated local materials and goods, weaving the threads of settler and Indigenous fashions into their own vernacular. These alterations from the fashions of the French countryside changed the impact of the Acadian presence. By letting go of some of the markings of imperial clothing culture, incorporating what they learned and found around themselves, they created their own language on this different visual battleground. This can be seen as an act of resistance toward imperial incursion, a modification in the plan as though to say *we are different now. We are from France but no longer of France.*

WE CAN DEMONSTRATE how necessary trade was to the survival of early Acadian settlements by looking at the mathematics of wool. The old assumption has been that the Acadian herds were their main source of wool fibre and woollen textiles. Villebon describes the Acadian fleeces as of very good quality and writes in his memoir that "the clothing worn by the majority of the men and women is made of it."[109] His descriptions from 1699 suggest that most of the wool clothing worn in the Minas Basin was produced from local materials: "As for the women they are always busy, and most of them keep their husbands and children in serviceable linen materials and stockings which they make skillfully from the hemp they have grown and the wool produced by their sheep."[110]

Haliburton concurred thirty years later, with a very similar description from Abbé Reynal: "Their usual clothing was in general the produce of their own flax, or the fleeces of their own sheep ; with these they made common linens and coarse cloths."[111] The Reverend Andrew Brown, writing a retrospective of pre-deportation Acadian culture, claimed that "The whole community was clothed in domestic manufactures, the Exclusive product of female industry."[112] De Meulles reported much along the same lines:

> Most of the women make themselves woolens with which they dress themselves and also their husbands, They make almost all of the socks for their families and they go without buying; They [*ils* – now including men as well] use only moccasins which they make themselves. An English barque comes to this place every year in the month of April which brings them their little necessities that they buy with the furs that they had from the savages [*sic*].[113]

TABLE 1.1 • Wool yardage needs in Acadian settlements

1707 census	Men	Women	Children	Sheep	Minimum annual yardage req'd (clothing only)	Estimated annual production capacity, wool yardage
Cobequid	28	22	32	121	844	305
Mines	159	148	265	718	5,342.5	1,795
Beaubassin	72	71	127	500	2,492	1,250
Port Royal	160	149	238	1,245	5,291	3,115

The overarching narrative in all these cases is self-sufficiency, traders predominantly bringing in luxuries or "small necessities" that could not be manufactured locally rather than fulfilling essential survival needs. However, far more fabric was required to clothe the growing populace – not to mention the textiles needed for blankets, table linens, bedrugs, bags, and wagon covers around working farms – than the sheep population could reasonably supply. Basic articles of clothing for an average-sized adult would take somewhere from three or four yards for a woman's skirt or a pair of men's trousers, to upwards of eight or ten for a full formal gown or men's working outfit with jacket.[114] Adrienne Hood has calculated that it would have taken approximately sixteen and a half yards of fabric per year to create and maintain a basic wardrobe for a working man, consisting of a good suit, five shirts, two pairs of trousers, two pairs of drawers, a waistcoat, and a coat.[115] A woman's basic wardrobe required thirteen yards, and by incorporating hand-me-downs, a child could be clothed for about three yards a year. A family of six, by these numbers, would need on average about forty-two yards of fabric per annum in clothing alone to maintain basic levels of coverage and cleanliness. None of the settlements in the 1707 census come close to that level of production.

Roger Quessy (Caissie) and his wife Marie Poirier owned six sheep as per the 1686 census, but by 1707 their four sons, all of them married and with children of their own, owned forty-six sheep between them.[116] The Quessys' six sheep, sheared once a year, could produce six to fifteen pounds of wool for spinning, yielding potentially between twelve to thirty yards of finished wool cloth.[117] With very careful management and the extensive use of hand-me-downs, as well as accommodations made for the flax and hemp they would have been growing and processing for linen, the high end of that estimation would have been barely enough to clothe the family of seven for the year.

The household economy would have to be extremely carefully managed and rely on gifts, second-hand clothing, or imported textiles to achieve a basic standard of living. The Quessy family would have needed to purchase at least fifteen yards of fabric per year from elsewhere in order to survive, much less thrive.

Their neighbours Pierre Mercier and Andrée Martin – and their ten children – had no sheep in 1686, meaning that all their wool fabric must have been sourced from elsewhere. That situation must not have been ideal, as by the 1693 census they had acquired a flock of fourteen animals as well as married off their eldest child, considerably improving their sheep:shawl ratio.[118] Fourteen sheep could potentially have given them up to seventy yards of unfulled wool for clothing, or six and one-third yards per person, per year. Not quite enough for fancy dress, but enough for each member of the household to have a new skirt or jacket (or knitted mittens and stockings) each winter and spring.

Pierre Hebert's family, on the other hand, had thirty sheep in 1707. Their fleece would have been enough raw material to be made into 100 to 120 yards of finished cloth, far more than necessary to clothe Pierre, his wife, and their two sons. Wool was not a notable export from Acadia, so this extra fleece would have been part of their household economy – shared, sold, or bartered between families, either as fleeces or prepared rovings. Spinning was woman's work, and the lack of daughters in the family meant a serious dearth of female labour to process the fleece into thread, unless Mme Hebert took in daughters from other families as helpers and informal apprentices in a fairly common form of invisible domestic economy.[119]

By 1707, the last year for which we have livestock recorded on the census, none of the settlements were producing enough wool to meet their basic needs. That extra material had to come from somewhere, and that gap was filled by trade. Wool arrived as an import. Red and blue cloth listed on a cargo manifest along with knitted wool stockings, and textile seals found at multiple sites confirm the presence of bolts of fabric from multiple European sources.[120] The New England colonies were forbidden from exporting wool textiles after 1699, so all legal imports to Acadia were coming from Canada or Europe. The illegal movement of textiles through smugglers, however, was prolific.[121]

Along the Sea Coast

From the earliest days of the colony, long before the marshes had been drained and crops established, through to the import of supplemental and luxury goods in the later years of the settlements, ships of all sorts found their way to Acadian trading posts. Official support for trade varied as borders shifted and land changed hands, clandestine exchanges continuing even after various control measures were attempted. English merchants coming up from Boston were threatened with sanctions in the 1670s when fishing permits were revoked to get the English out of French waters, and Acadians complained heavily about losing the New England sources for "small necessities."[122] As empires rotated in and out and legalities changed, Acadian traders reaffirmed their policies of surface-level accommodation and backup sources of materials, through Louisbourg, Boston, and Mi'kma'ki.[123] Merchants like Henri Brunet travelled back and forth between Plaisance, Acadia, and Boston, establishing ties between the locations. Acadian merchants moved in and out of Boston's harbours despite Massachusetts bans on trade to French colonies after 1714. They took goods on consignment, and even petitioned for redress for wrongs suffered across the border. Tools for agriculture, manufacturing, and domestic life were imported from Massachusetts, and Boston merchants like John Nelson made annual trips to "La Baye Françoise."[124]

Many residents of Acadia traded with New England between 1671 and 1707, despite the illegality. Governor Meneval was accused of encouraging English trade with Port Royal, and in a series of letters sent between 1693 and 1701, Villebon describes English ships coming semi-openly to Port Royal: "17 April 1693: two English vessels had arrived at Port Royal, one of 30, the other of 25 tons, with fifty men in both: they were laden with merchandise and asked only to trade." The following year, 18 July 1694, a known privateer, Baptiste, took a ship "loaded partly with cloth from Lancaster in England," though that and two other of his prizes were recaptured by Boston sailors.[125]

Clandestine commerce was not isolated to the governors, of course. Jacques de Meulles's 1685 report on Beaubassin describes supply runs coming in from English traders, with whom the Acadians traded local furs in return for tools and other useful goods.[126] In 1707, a canal was proposed to cut across Siknikt in order to put an end to the illegal trade, "which now is all done by the English, and which is quite considerable, since each summer three or four ships from Boston, sell at whatever price they want to charge, all their merchandise to the inhabitants."[127] On 24 November 1720, Governor Philipps of Acadia wrote to the Commissioners of Customs, reporting on legal trade with Boston – "Trade considerable, by four or five sloops from Boston, bringing English woollens and W. Indies goods for furs and feathers. Value £10,000" – as well as the illegal – "French settlements up the Bay carry on clandestine trade with C. B. Garrison too weak to prevent."[128] This was still continuing in 1734, and L. Armstrong reported on it on 13 September: "There is clandestine and unlawful trade in the province, to the detriment of trade and the prejudice of the fair trader, C. is empowered 'to Examine into these Unlawful practices and to take and bring into this Port all Such Vessells and the Masters thereof Whether they be foreigners, Strangers or subjects that are not qualified to Trade in this province According to Law': to be there further examined.'[129]

Intimately connected to leading Acadian families, traders brought tools, fashions, and new aesthetics back and forth across the Atlantic harbours. Beyond familiarity with trade goods, the local land and resources, and their connections with urban life, settlers would also have remained familiar with the tools and skills brought to Acadia by their great-grandparents. Techniques for patterning and making clothing, woodworking, knitting stockings – all of these would have been part of the original migrants' repertoires, the cultural knowledge of home, and one of the foundations for the skill sets and equipment generated and used by families in Acadia decades later.[130]

Trade in Chignecto

European involvement in the Siknikt region began as an extension of Acadia, focused on mission work and fur trading. The arrival of settlers in the 1680s changed the balance in the area, though the region did not become politically relevant to Great Britain and France until rival forts were built in the area in 1750 and 1751. Like many Acadian settlements, Beaubassin was often dismissed as unimportant in the grand scheme of things. Unlike many, its location, demographics, and geography made it perfectly positioned to become a centre for commerce that flew under the radar of imperial interests.[131] In 1686, Jacques de Meulles described his experiences in Chignecto with the English merchants who persisted in sailing north from Boston to sell commodities to Acadian locals. His concerns focused on the problems this trade created for the future of New France, since the distance required to bring goods from Quebec to Acadia was far greater than the short sail between Boston and Port Royal, or Boston and Beaubassin. A canal, on the other hand, cutting across the top of the isthmus, would create "une belle Rivière" for Quebec's ships and make that route much more attractive.[132] Not coincidentally, this manoeuvre would also diminish the importance of the portage route between Minas and Baie Verte, the primary avenue by which goods were moved by Acadian middlemen from one end of the region to the other. Despite interest from various involved parties, however, those plans never came to fruition.

France's continued perceived lack of interest in maintaining strong economic connections with Acadia prior to 1710 helped to reinforce Acadian connections with local trading partners, from whom they happily received European goods. In the early years trade connections continued to be forged and exploited between Massachusetts and Acadia. A number of known merchants with ties to Port Royal and Boston were based out of Beaubassin or travelled there regularly, including Robert Hale of Boston, Jacques Bourgeois, who founded the original settlement, and Zacharie Richard, son of Michel Richard *dit* Lafond, who also transported Acadian goods for export.[133] Bourgeois, a surgeon and ship owner as well as merchant, was partially funded by John Nelson, the nephew of Boston resident Thomas Temple, himself a former governor of Nova Scotia. Settlers from Beaubassin made trips into Port Royal for trade, and then brought some of those goods across to Baie Verte for the next leg of the journey. They would be sailed down the Northumberland Strait to be traded again in Louisbourg, along with isthmus-raised cattle and grain.[134]

European goods came in from Canada by way of Baie Verte, or through the Minas Basin by Boston and Acadian traders. In 1695, an agent of the Acadian Trading Company reported that trade relations between Port Royal and the St John River settlements were low to non-existent out of fear of the English, but that other trade was ongoing:

> The settlers of Port Royal do almost no trade with the French of the St John river because of their fear that, if the English learned of it, they would be burned out. However, M. de Villebon assured me that M. Dubreuil, who lives there and who returned recently from Boston, will come here for cloth and other merchandise. Three settlers came from Minas and Chignecto, who have taken away some goods, and are to return shortly for more so that they may go trade in Cape Breton Island next winter. All the settlers are, like these, extremely timid about venturing into this river, especially if they come in shallops, because they fear to be caught by English vessels which frequently cruise about these waters.[135]

In 1718, Captain John Doucett, British lieutenant-governor of Annapolis Royal, described the kind of price undercutting taking place: "The French from Cape Britton Bring Wine Brandy and Linnings which they can afford four pence and sixpence in a yard cheaper than our traders can possibly doe."[136] The trade included textiles and had been going on in both directions since long before the British takeover: "They [the Acadians] furnish't [the fort] with Cattle and other Live Stock and took in Exchange; Rum sugar Cotton Molasses Wine and Brandy."[137] The things most in demand were "Little ordinary Stuffs" of British manufacture, like "Woolings, as Strouds, and Duffles."[138] We get more of a description of these British imports from Governor Phillipps in 1731, noting the textiles were "Cheifly Red and Blew strouds, Kerseys and stufs of various kind and Linnens."[139] This circuit had more stops: the settlements at Pentagouët even after the fort's destruction in 1674, Louisbourg, Boston, and Canso. Boston merchants like Peter Faneuil and Joshua Scottow brokered deals with Acadian go-betweens and proxies to get goods in and out of restricted regions.[140]

By the 1740s, some households in Beaubassin were producing clothing articles for export. In June 1743, Michel Richard's son Zacharie took out a cargo including thirty to forty pairs of woollen socks "fabriqué a laccadie," and five women's skirts.[141] Montreal was a welcoming market for items like stockings, with hosiery in demand. The difference from fifty years prior is noteworthy, when Charles de La Tour was bringing "Two dozen halfe stockins" *in* to Acadia for sale in 1696, or 1707 when the number of sheep in the settlement was barely enough to cover the region's own needs.[142] Richard's manifest is the only one to include manufactured clothing, though it is unlikely to have been a single-instance anomaly. Acadian traders preferred to sell to New England merchants rather than locally, as they received better returns on the transactions. British traders were also offering employment, both as middlemen and as interpreters, and an "Arsenau" from Beaubassin was listed as someone employed in that capacity.[143] Other dealings included trade with Gorham's Rangers, a British-allied Ranger unit more normally found on the opposite side of conflicts from the Acadians. The potential conflict of interest didn't seem to bother either the Rangers, or the more than half-dozen Acadian men with transactions in the Rangers' record books.

While Acadians were engaged in the kind of clandestine sea commerce that involved tiny boats zipping among the reeds at night, they also engaged in far more sophisticated and legal trade practices. A multitude of small shipyards and mills sprang up throughout Acadia in the early eighteenth century. As early as 1719, Acadian traders were purpose-building sloops to be loaded with cargo, sailing them to Cape Breton, and selling both cargo and the ships to dealers located there. Letters from de Brouillan, governor of Ile Royale, to Doucette in that same year describe the Acadian-built vessels as "little ships ... [which] they were obliged to sell almost for nothing to English merchants" due to a lack of rigging.[144] Low prices were not always the case, however, as records show that in 1743 Beaubassin resident Pierre Cyr sold his 45-tonne ship *Marguerite* to fellow Acadian J. Vigneau for the remarkable amount of £2,800.[145] Jean Vigneau had been involved in large trade in previous years, selling a single 11-tonne ship (the *Sainte-Jean*) to Ruellen & Chaufaux for £1,738 – more than the net worth of many entire households in Ile Royale.[146] The transactions are reported in terms of total cost, but it is more likely that something other than cash was in play.

Walking back home to Baie Verte with £2,800 in cash in one's purse would have been difficult, if not dangerous to impossible at the time, but partial payments and sophisticated arrangements such as mortgages were certainly known at the time.[147]

Some of that sold cargo was textiles, as in the knitted stockings mentioned above, but the bulk of the export items moving out of Beaubassin and Minas were cattle. They were brought to the fortress alive ("on the hoof"), slaughtered, and salted on-site.[148] Beaubassin could not and did not supply all of the beef consumed at Louisbourg; Cape Breton had some of its own cattle producers, and military officers as well as civilians kept livestock including cattle and pigs for their own uses.[149] Using locally built ships gave them a cost advantage over other traders, the Nova Scotia wood used for masts, yards, and bowsprits being less expensive than buying shipbuilding materials or bringing labour from abroad.[150] While trade with New England was a relatively common thing – the English having been granted fishing permits in the region – the relationship was not always amicable. Settlements in Beaubassin were burned by Benjamin Church and a group from New England in September 1696, despite pleas from Germain Bourgeois. Bourgeois's house was spared, along with a few others nearby, but the rest of the region was sacked. A second English attack followed in 1704, the English burning crops and houses alike.[151]

Trade in Fundy

Acadians in Port Royal traded extensively with Boston, a major supplier for goods. A wide variety of ceramics styles present in the assemblages from both Melanson and Belleisle, as well as pottery from Saintonge, English lead crystal, and other imported French and German items confirm the settlers' active participation in contemporary Atlantic trade networks.[152] The trade was not clandestine, but very much commented on even in New France. In 1671, Intendant Jean Talon wrote to Jean-Baptiste Colbert with a proposal to redirect Acadian trade from New England to New France, by making those desired items more readily available:

> It is necessary to stop without violence the trade which the English carry on with Port Royal, from whom they take every year a quantity of meat in exchange for some druggets and other cloths made in Boston; it would be enough, in my feeling, to send from France, or from here [Quebec] to Port Royal, some stuff [wool cloth] to fill their most pressing needs, and even some looms which the colonists asked me for, in order to use the wool from their sheep and the hemp that the earth gave them thanks to the work of their hands.[153]

One merchant's invoice from 1691 included listings for over 135 yards of assorted fabrics, including gingham, red and blue cloth, 155.5 yards of silk lace, twelve pairs of stockings, 93 yards of plain ribbon, and 46 yards of silk ribbon, all of it shipped from Boston to be sold on consignment in Port Royal.[154] Ribbon in the seventeenth and eighteenth centuries was made from silk, silk-linen blends, and occasionally precious metal threads, including silver and gold, and archaeological finds from seventeenth-century Boston include silk ribbon of middling quality.[155] All of these "little necessities" found their way into Acadian wardrobes in Annapolis and beyond.

Other merchants brought goods for sale to Port Royal and Cape Sable, and surviving invoices confirm that textiles and sewing equipment were often among the cargo.[156] Along with Abraham Boudrot and David Basset, Michel Richard *dit* Lafond brought goods into Acadia in general and the Belleisle settlement specifically, his routes including dealings with Guillaume Delort, a trader who brought merchandise in from La Rochelle and New York. An invoice between Boudrot and Boston supplier André Taneuil from 1691 includes a list of the goods that Taneuil had commissioned Boudrot to sell at Port Royal on his behalf, including fashionable fabric, silk ribbons, silk lace, and pairs of stockings.[157] In September of 1695, Charles de La Tour carried cotton, serge, thread, buttons and lining, vermillion dye, stockings and shoes, and "two doz: sizzers" from Suffolk County, New York, to Cape Sable on Nova Scotia's southernmost tip.

During the English years, trade continued to come both through and around the renamed Annapolis Royal, and connections expanded further. The Melanson settlement within the *banlieue* of Port Royal and Fort Anne is interesting for its strong connection to the English, at least by Acadian standards.[158] The Melansons had Huguenot in-laws in Boston, which gave them more access to textiles from New England. In 1690 Pierre Faneuil, and David Basset, the Melanson in-law, negotiated with Abraham Boudrot and Jean Martel for consignment sales of linens and other fabrics.[159] Six years later, Charles Melanson informed Massachusetts Governor William Stoughton that Boudrot was leaving for Boston, bringing two boats loaded with wheat and coal.[160]

The Savoie family in Belleisle produced at least one Acadian delegate, and the presence of Saintonge pottery in the house affirms their continued connection to France. Geneviève Massignon located the Savoies' origins in southwestern France – Martaizé, in the Loudon.[161] They had social capital, the Savoie family one of the largest and most prosperous in the region.[162] Joseph-Nicolas Gautier *dit* Bellair's holdings on the south side of the Annapolis river were not officially part of Belleisle, but his location between the marsh and the Fort, as well as his social influence and the saw and grist mills that he ran, made him an extremely important player in the Belleisle world of goods. Rejected in 1720 as a potential Acadian delegate because he was still "transient," by the 1730s he had built himself a small trading empire.[163] His sloops sailed to the Caribbean, bringing goods from the colonies there to Ile Royale as well as France, New England, and to his home base only a few kilometres from Annapolis Royal.[164] In the 1740s Gautier's close alliance with Sieur François Duvivier against the British undoubtedly put him in the path of Duvivier's cousin and sister-in-law, Marie Josephe Le Borgne de Belleisle.[165] Her strong presence in Louisbourg trade had likely made them business associates earlier than that, the webs of kin and trade connections expanding with every generation.

Trade in Louisbourg

For the Acadians living in Louisbourg itself, life looked a little different than for those trading materials in from the outside. Illicit trade in and out of Louisbourg was still an issue leading into the expulsion; Mascarene had complained to the Lords of Trade about French trade in Cape Breton in 1741 and 1748.[166] Materials also came in from the West Indies, Europe, Indonesia, and beyond. One Acadian in particular, Marie Josephe Le Borgne de Belleisle, played a remarkable role in the acquisition and production of a great deal of textile, garment, and accessory wealth. Born in Pentagouët in 1712, Le Borgne died in Louisbourg in 1754. Not only Acadian, Le Borgne's mother was of mixed French and Indigenous ancestry, the granddaughter of Abenaki Chief Madokawondo.[167] Le Borgne married in 1733 to Jacques-Philippe-Urbain Rondeau, the treasurer of the Marine in Ile Royale. As treasurer, Jacques Rondeau could not be seen to be engaging in trade, but his wife's participation allowed the family to participate while absolving him of the appearance of conflict of interest. Her second husband, Joseph Dupont Duvivier, was a military officer, and records show that she continued to work as a merchant under her own name, with his permission, even after her second marriage.[168] The various inventories related to Le Borgne, her husbands, and her shop give us insight into the wide variety of goods that textile merchants were bringing in to the colony.

The property evaluation Le Borgne had performed in 1750 prior to her marriage to Dupont Duvivier included Acadians on her list of debtors, and at least one debt that she owed in Acadia in return.[169] The name of Joseph Munier, "accadien," in debt to Marie Le Borgne for 116 livres, appears in the list of deportees from Grand Pré five years later. Munier was Le Borgne's cousin through their shared grandmother, and her parents were also his godparents.[170] A reference in the minutes of the council at

Annapolis Royal in 1734 described Munier as "Munier a half-Indian" and a clandestine trader, in league with "one Bently of Charlestown in New England" and his uncle François Meneux of St Castin, of Penobscot.[171] The different emphasis in the two entries for Munier is intriguing. Le Borgne claims Munier as hers – Acadian – and part of her community, while the British writers of the minutes reject any kinship or responsibility. "Pierre Doucez, accadien," in debt to Le Borgne for 112 livres, is probably Pierre Doucet, though two men by that name feature on the 1752 Acadian census.[172] Both lived in Rivière de Nanpan, a settlement southeast of Beaubassin. Both Doucet and Munier owed Le Borgne large sums of money, enough for forty yards of very good wool, fourteen of silk taffeta – or fifty-six pairs of wool socks. This would have been enough to cover a small collection of goods bought to sell on consignment, or a year's worth of personal expenditure on clothing.

Louisbourg was not at the forefront of fashion; styles from the metropole necessarily took time to cross the Atlantic and take hold in the colonies. Despite that, merchants drew on multiple supply lines – legal and otherwise – to bring in desirable merchandise, including materials that were illegal elsewhere (see chapter 3, under Cotton). Le Borgne's inventory puts her at the centre of a web of trade that linked Acadian and Indigenous buyers with suppliers in Britain, New England, the West Indies, Asia, and France.

Indigenous Connections

Mi'kma'ki was an Indigenous space for tens of thousands of years prior to European arrival, and some of it remained so even after the intrusion of European colonizers. Siknikt remained a hub of activity for Mi'kmaw travel and trade, while settlements more distant from Port Royal and Grand Pré maintained some level of engagement even as political relations between Mi'kmaq and Acadians grew more distant into the 1730s and 1740s. The presence of French trade goods designed and produced for the fur trade confirms that Beaubassin was an important point of contact between Acadia and the Mi'kmaw groups living nearby.

These shared contact spaces were not permanent installations like the forts, but created as moments in time, structured by the effort to make contact and connect.[173] The places of intersection were defined by intangibles like co-operation as much as by lines on a map. Mi'kmaw settlements at Siknikt were some of these intersectional places, the winter census of 1688 showing a village already established near

Beaubassin.[174] While co-operation with Acadian settlers was not always smooth, the evidence shows some level of generally peaceful interaction. Acadians and Mi'kmaq shared mobile geographical spaces, travelling along waterways and engaging with coastal resources. Acadian boat builders used the rivers as highways, permeating the boundaries of Mi'kmaw space. That knowledge of the coasts and water networks moved into the European consciousness when the British called in Acadian pilots to help them navigate the unfamiliar waters.[175]

Many Europeans felt a growing anxiety about the young men who shed their clothes to join the Mi'kmaq, a reaction that had its grounding in early modern understanding of how clothing shaped and built both individual and collective identity. Those anxieties suggested that the action of putting on Indigenous clothing could move young men from one culture to another, shedding their European natures under the influence of leather breechclouts. The reverse was also considered true, and the encouragement of European dress was as much a tool of colonization as religious instruction and conversion.[176] Images from the sixteenth century suggest that Indigenous children along the east coast were given fashion dolls dressed in European clothing during the early contact period, and gifts of shirts and yardage were common.[177]

These attempts at normalization of European dress did not prove effective with everyone. In 1612 Abbé Biard described Mi'kmaw use of French clothing, but in 1691 Father LeClercq explained Mi'kmaw women's disdain for European women's fashion: "They say they cannot make themselves like this dress, and that it would be impossible for them to walk or to work freely with the clothes of our Frenchwomen … they are so enamoured with their own, that they are not willing even to hear ours mentioned."[178]

Rejecting stays and long skirts, the Mi'kmaw women whom LeClercq encountered maintained their own more practical styles of dress. Under this model, spreading European clothing as the ideal into Indigenous spaces became a challenge. Identification with the French by way of French goods, and more so, the changing of the Mi'kmaw inner self into something Frenchified, became a marker of psychological conquest for one side. Those taking the goods and reworking them to fit within their own perspectives and processes saw that transformation in an entirely different light.

The contact space encouraged trade along predetermined lines, goods designated for the fur trade shipped into the colonies from France, England, and the West Indies. Furs brought in by Mi'kmaw hunters were used as trade goods between Acadians and traders in Massachusetts, changing hands outside of the reach of the various fur trade companies.[179] The Sieur de Bonnaventure, commanding the French ship *Envieux*, brought cotton fabric, thread, ribbons, tapes, and pins, among other things, to trade

FIGURE 1.5 • Trade silver buckle, Beaubassin.

for furs at Beaubassin in 1699.[180] Three types of artifact in particular – trade silver, trade beads, and textile seals – speak to the ongoing nature and value of the contact spaces and the exchanges made within them.

Trade Silver

Silver was a common metal for trade ornaments, popular decorative accessories alongside glass beads and wampum. Brooches, buckles, beads, and hair ornaments made of wampum were traded for pelts and quickly incorporated into Indigenous dress. Between the mid-seventeenth and the nineteenth centuries trade silver was ubiquitous, lightweight pieces smithed in Montreal and Quebec City as well as abroad. The trade was more common in the late eighteenth century, however, so the presence of the ring brooch at Beaubassin prior to 1750 was less expected than it would be even thirty years later.[181]

The basic ring brooch style was an extremely common form of trade silver, with almost identical examples appearing in assemblages as far away as Ohio. The silver ring buckle shown in figure 1.5 was one of many produced in New France. It would have travelled to Beaubassin down the Saint Lawrence. Brooches of this type were used as jacket and cloak closures across the northeast, worn by all genders. The use of silver as dress ornament may indicate adoption of forms of European status signalling, silver replacing copper as a preferred material for ornamentation throughout the seventeenth and eighteenth centuries.[182] The aesthetic environment created by the exchange of textiles and adornments was a blending, a visual indication of the social engagement of the two groups.

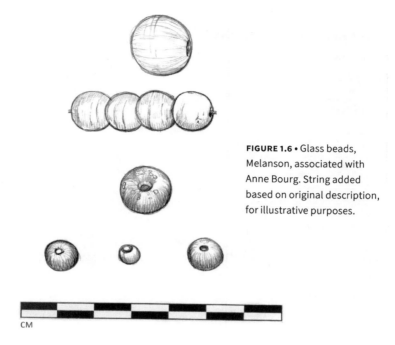

FIGURE 1.6 • Glass beads, Melanson, associated with Anne Bourg. String added based on original description, for illustrative purposes.

CM

Beads

At least as late as 1750 in some areas of colonized Mi'kma'ki, trade beads were an integral part of settler engagement with Indigenous peoples. Indigenous dressers wore large beads in necklaces and bracelets, and strung them for rosaries, while small seed and glass beads were sewn as embellishments or as part of embroidered designs onto garments and accessories.[183] While older sources suggest that trade beads were falling out of favour by the 1730s, the discovery of a barrel of beads at Fort Beausejour – a fort built in 1751 – indicates that they were still in demand in the region.[184] Glass beads manufactured in Venice and Amsterdam were particularly valued, though beads were manufactured across Europe to be funnelled into the colonial trade.[185]

The Mi'kmaq prized beads, embroidering them on to caps, leggings, and moccasins as well as wearing them on strings around their necks, wrists, ankles, and other joints. The beads served a function similar to trade silver when worn, and as Loren argues, the presence of glass beads in quantity at a colonial site suggests Indigenous dressing styles in play alongside European ones.[186] Amber, white, green, and blue beads were popular, as were long beads carved from clay pipestems. Glass beads found at Beaubassin match these types, though in a scattered context it is difficult to be sure whether they were intended for trade or were being used on clothing.

TABLE 1.2 • Beads found at three Acadian sites

	Belleisle	Melanson	Beaubassin
Glass beads	1	11	40
Seed beads		1	11
Clay beads (pipestem)			6 possible
Stone beads			5
Wood and bone		1	3

The negligible number of trade beads found at Belleisle and Melanson suggest these settlements did not engage in on-site trade with Indigenous partners.[187] Beads found at Melanson appear to have been part of Anne Bourg's personal jewellery rather than set aside for trade purposes, and only one glass bead of this type has been found at Belleisle so far. The difference is likely one of geography. Melanson and Belleisle are within a few kilometres of Port Royal, a trade centre focused primarily on exchange with New England. Beaubassin engaged in different networks, its place within a short portage of Baie Verte and the Northumberland Strait giving trade beads more immediate purpose.

Other bead finds at Beaubassin included a broken pipe stem scored in preparation to be cut, and discs that appear to have been carved from the remnants of other pipe stems. A wide-ranging survey conducted by Karlis Karklins in 2015 found that pipe-stem beads have a 100 per cent correlation with Indigenous or fur-trade sites: no pipe-stem beads to date have been discovered at European settlements that were not officially part of the fur trade. Most of the sites where these beads have been found are in the northeast of North America and dated between the seventeenth and early eighteenth centuries. The western sites were occupied during the later eighteenth and nineteenth centuries, indicating a westward movement of the style.[188]

The discs from Beaubassin are distinctly different in size from those found elsewhere. While Karklin's sites have beads ranging in length from 11.5–56 mm, those from Beaubassin are all under 8 mm in length. The possibility exists that those without wear patterns could be discarded remnants of other work on pipe stems, but the consistency in their shape and size, proximity to other beads on site, and the presence of what appears to be a wear pattern on two of the discs suggests this may not be true in every case. The disc shape would allow them to be strung and worn with the stone rosary beads and glass trade beads found nearby. Made on site rather than imported,

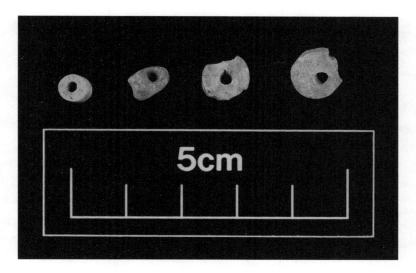

FIGURE 1.7 • Pipe stem fragments, possibly beads. Beaubassin.

clay pipe-stem beads are an example of cultural transformation in action, repurposed out of imported European goods that had been originally designed for the use of an Indigenous consumable. Turgeon's investigation of bead use among the First Nations found that beads were multi-faceted builders and conveyers of individual identity. They were worn on the joints – elbows, knees, wrists – to strengthen and protect, and to convey power beyond the physical. If the hardness of the glass and stone beads influenced the hardness of the body, then the softer fired clay, prone to eroding between the teeth and easy to score and break, was of no use for symbolic protection. Their value lay instead in the ease of change and in the simplicity of scoring to snap and painting to colour, moving between contexts and crossing meanings as they went.[189]

Rosary spacers, the only beads without a prayer in the chaplet, are similarly liminal. They mark beginnings and endings, separating beads and groups of beads into discrete sections for prayer, filling the same essential function as a period at the end of a sentence. For both traditions the clay beads do not, then, represent power, but the counterpoint – the malleable breathing space in contrast to which strength, hardness, and power can be more fully seen. Beaubassin is an outlier as a settler site that was not an official trading post, but the beads, lead seal evidence, and the close presence of allied Mi'kmaw villages in the Oesgag Triangle confirm its role as an active hub within the local fur trade. The distinction between formal sites of exchange and the more informal nature of the trade at Beaubassin is embodied in the smaller, more flexible bead, appropriate for embroidering onto clothing as well as being strung as spacers in a rosary.

Textiles

European trade goods moved through Mi'kma'ki, and textiles played a special role in these exchanges. Bale seals, small lead tokens used as tax and import labels on commodities such as textiles, fill in some further connections. One textile seal found at Beaubassin bears the arms of the Compagnie des Indes (the French East India Company), which held the monopoly on the Canadian beaver-fur trade between 1719 and 1769.[190] Along with the fur trade, the Compagnie owned Louisiana and held monopolies on both the sale of tobacco in France and the local slave trade. The Compagnie had a major advantage in the French fur trade as the only French institution allowed to import English strouds, the woollens most highly prized by Indigenous traders. The strouds, or *écarlatines*, were brought through La Rochelle to Montreal and then spread further, the cloth permitted in the colony only for the sake of the fur trade.[191] Compagnie seals found at Beaubassin and at the British encampment at Grand Pré in non-domestic contexts suggests the presence of strouds as trade goods.[192]

Indigenous traders had limited interest in French woollens, disdaining their poor quality as cheap imitations of English wool.[193] While they could have traded for strouds from the English, the Compagnie was able to provide the fabric at lower prices. Not being subjected to British duties meant their costs were measurably less.[194] Écarlatines circulated from their origin in the town of Stroud in Gloucestershire County to the port of La Rochelle in the possession of the Compagnie des Indes, where they were measured, checked for quality, and importantly, tagged with the Compagnie's lead seal. Loaded on ships, the red, blue, black, and green fabrics were sailed across the ocean to stop first in Louisiana, and then head north to Louisbourg.[195]

Being part of the circuit of the Compagnie des Indes adds a new circle of influence for the Acadian shores, expanding their access out of the Atlantic. The Compagnie traded extensively across the northeast, the Great Lakes area, and down the Mississippi River, collecting an average of 166,000 pelts per year.[196] Receiving agents brought in goods from the ships in Quebec City and distributed them to voyageurs, who took the trade goods to the trading posts. They brought the furs they received in trade back to Quebec City, where they were shipped onward to France. The Compagnie's trading routes extended into the Indian and Pacific oceans, creating intersecting networks of production, trade, and consumption.[197]

French laws forbade exports to British colonies, making trade through Beaubassin prior to 1710 something more exciting than straightforward, and many Acadians were engaged in smuggling and redistribution operations. Albany was a hub for the clandestine fur trade between the English and Haudenosaunee, despite the fact that Albany was blocked from westward trade. That appetite for English goods could be fed through spaces like Beaubassin with less worry about interception or interference.[198] While systems and regulations theoretically changed after British conquest, the rise instead of French privateers and Acadian disinterest in British rule meant that the maritime trade continued, as textiles, trade silver, Jesuit rings, and tools passed from one sphere into another through contact zones like Beaubassin.[199] The furs and trade goods sat in ships' holds next to Indian calicoes and Malaysian ginghams, English wools, and French silks. The Compagnie des Indes' trade circles linked Acadia with textile producers in Chandanagor in Bengal, Nîmes in France, and Lorient in Louisiana, joining the Acadians and Mi'kmaq in an overlapping diagram of trading partners, spheres of influence, and empires.

Conclusion

These four Acadian communities are as similar in some ways as they are distinct in others, their particular geographies, environmental constraints, periods of occupation, and locations in respect to other settlements determining their character. That diversity helps to explain the variety of lifestyles and attitudes among the Acadians of these regions, their cultural geographies and senses of self marked by the locations in which they grew and thrived. Bringing with them aesthetic senses honed by their former homes, the first wave of settlers understood the language of clothing with which they had grown up in France. Successive generations were shaped by other forces, by the different visual and cultural cues that began from but were not entirely like those of their parents' generation.

The climates of the Acadians' original homes in France and their new settlements in Mi'kma'ki were similar in some respects, but Maritime winters were far harsher than those experienced in the Loudon. Comparisons of textile purchases in other French colonies show that New France, subject to winters of similar duration, used far more woollens both for themselves and for the fur trade than the warmer, linen- and cotton-dependent colonies in Louisiana and Saint-Domingue.[200] Flora and fauna in the region varied as well; differences in dyestuffs, in the breeds of sheep that thrived on local forage, and in the kinds and quantities of flax that could be grown in Acadia all contributed to which textiles could be made locally and which had to be imported. And those factors in turn determined how much and what kind of trade they needed in order to maintain the lifestyles they wanted.

If we try to predict Acadian wardrobes based on climate, geography, and available materials, we should expect to see more footwear designed to withstand the wet and cold. We should also expect to find woollen socks and outerwear, more use of furs than seen in Continental French clothing, as well as some evidence of influence drawn from the clothing of local Indigenous groups. If human beings dressed only according to practicality and environment, however, then clothing for similar biomes would be much more alike than it is. While some physical aspects remain the same – looser clothing in hot, arid regions, use of furs and hides in colder ones – the human element has a powerful influence over aspects such as style, fit, and decoration. The Europeans who settled Acadia came primarily from farming settlements in western France, part of a western European Catholic culture steeped in visual and oral tradition. Prone to early marriage and large families, the first wave of settlers in the 1630s spread out rapidly along the Acadian marshlands, using technology developed in Europe to alter the terrain. Despite the distance between the settlements, kinship networks, strong ties between family members, and community-centric labour practices kept interpersonal bonds strong.

Local community standards and expectations undoubtedly played a role in choice of dress, part of the ongoing process of determining and displaying social identity. The day-to-day choices of which clothes to wear become an embodied practice of disclosure, concealing and revealing the nature of self as the wearer deemed appropriate.[201] The number of people in a family and their ability to generate and process linen, hemp, and wool impacted their need to trade for imported goods, and imbalances in production on the local level may have exacerbated visible differences between families, or encouraged domestic labour exchange and barter. Distance from authority and interest in connecting with British or French administrators would have affected exposure to contemporary continental fashion and levels of interest in replicating those styles for oneself.

The lines between "elite families" and farmers blurred quickly thanks to limited choices for marriage partners. In the early years, this may have included marriages of French men with Mi'kmaw women. These marriages created pathways for Indigenous production techniques to be brought into European households, as well as extending important kinship networks into the Indigenous community. We can see those networks in action in Marie Josephe Le Borgne's commercial trade, her personal connections to the Mi'kmaw and Acadian communities kept alive despite her marriage to a French official. She moved goods into Louisbourg, and then out into the communities at Port Royal, Beaubassin, and Grand Pré. She and the other merchants discussed here were part of the greater context describing Acadian access to imported goods and materials.

In the end, spaces, neighbours, networks, and tools all have a major impact on dress choice. Proximity to power, emotional and political connection to people or places, trade relationships, and the role of clothing in diplomacy, trust building, and identity all had an impact on the different modes of dress deployed in different regions of Acadia. With the context of these decisions now in place, we can turn to look at some of the surviving items that we can use to trace out the outlines of these long-gone garments.

The Sewing Box

[I]n that bit of white rag with the invisible stitching, lying among fallen
leaves and rubbish that the wind has blown into the gutter or street corner,
lies all the passion of some woman's soul finding voiceless expression.[1]

— — — — — — —

TOOLS DETERMINE THE KINDS of textiles a population can produce, the complexity of their weaves, the ways fabrics are cut and sewn together, and the styles of decorative embellishments that can be produced. The designs of the tools in turn tell us the story of the materials they were used to make. Heavier tools produce thicker threads and cut heavier fabrics, and decorated embroidery scissors speak to a different set of tasks than large tailor's shears. Beyond that, the tools can teach us about the priorities of the people who used them – were tools intended to be useful, beautiful, or a combination of the two? How were they displayed in public settings, by whom, and for whose benefit?

This chapter explores the surviving production tools associated with Acadian sites and places them in their contexts. Patterns of gender relations, social status, labour division, and community engagement are all made visible through the networks surrounding scissors, sewing kits, and spinning wheels. Archaeologist Mary Beaudry has created a framework for classifying sewing tools by task, separating necessary work like plain sewing, knitting, and repairs, from those used for decorative arts.[2] The types and sizes of spinning tools and sewing equipment are diagnostic evidence for the long-gone textiles produced by and manipulated with them. With that information, we can use the surviving archaeological evidence to extrapolate what textiles Acadians were making and using. The social dimension can be explored through this lens as well. To outside observers, Acadian women's fancy-work was bordering on subversive, claiming a skill that was at the centre of a contemporary shift in perceptions of elite femininity. Embroidery became a tool for inculcating values of femininity, and as Rozsika Parker has argued, femininity and aristocracy became indelibly associated with the art.[3] Fine sewing and sewing tools were a crucial part of the definition of elite European womanhood, and their presence at the settlements sheds new light on Acadian value systems and means of navigating complex colonial social structures.[4]

Nineteenth- and twentieth-century gender roles mean that most of us associate sewing with women's work, though it has never been an exclusively gendered activity. Sewing kits including scissors, pins, and thimbles were part of soldiers', farmers', and sailors' equipment from the medieval period to the modern day, as maintenance and repair of uniforms and gear were vitally important tasks. Changes in mindset in the seventeenth and eighteenth centuries, however, associated embroidery and fancy-work with the performance of femininity. Artifacts connected with women's labour and the body gained a particular kind of importance in this period. Women wore personal items like bodkins and embroidery scissors as accessories, artists used them as focal points in portraits, and through all this, they became objects of social display and status negotiation. Decorative tools associated with women's labour added a layer of prestige to work, silvered scissors and embellished snips transforming a subsistence activity into an elite one.[5]

Scissors

In the early modern period, visual symbols of textile labour carried a great amount of social meaning. Scissors moved fluidly between Igor Kopytoff's categories of meaning – from commodities, to subsistence items, to prestige items, to markers of relationships and social exchange.[6] The types and quality of the tools used for production give clues as to the tasks sewers used them for, the quality and purpose of the work, and the social standing and display practices of the needleworkers.[7] Sewing and fancy-work accessories appear frequently in depictions of elite women. Throughout the seventeenth and eighteenth centuries artists frequently depicted scissors, needles, bobbins, and lacemaking pillows alongside other tools and symbols of domesticity. Jean-Étienne Liotard captured the young embroiderer in his portrait entitled *Jeune fille brodant* in a moment of preparation, her large tapestry needle threaded and poised, her scissors attached to her apron by a blue silk ribbon that matched the colour of the silk thread in her lap. Stephen Daniels described the artistic use of sewing tools like these as "emblems of activity": markers of the sitter's industry and skill.[8] Liotard's subject is engaged in decorative needlework rather than plain sewing, and the ribboned scissors with decorative handles become a symbol of her status. The luxurious silks, her fancy embroidery snips, and the tapestry in her lap show that she spends her time on art and decorative household goods instead of subsistence labour.[9]

Tensions between productive and misused time are apparent in the way in which the term luxury transformed during the eighteenth century in France. Prior to the 1750s, the word "luxury" was a derogatory term and almost always referred to the unearned use of elite goods by those of lower status. Rising access to consumer goods and luxury items confounded pre-existing categories of those who could afford high-end goods and those who could not, and changed the symbolic meaning behind women's use of luxury sewing tools. Scissors became a signifier of a broader social discourse about the nature of appropriate gendered activities and the value of leisure.[10]

Access to fine tools looked different in Acadia than in London or Paris. While blacksmiths had been present in Acadia since the first arrivals, most of the scissors found there were likely imported.[11] King Philip's War (1675–78) and the subsequent unrest all but halted tool production in Maine between 1676 and 1740, and Sheffield was the likely source for the majority of the scissors found at American colonial archaeological sites.[12] Those scissors then found their way north. In 1696, Charles de La Tour brought a cargo including "Two doz: sizzers" from Massachusetts to sell at Cape Sable, and scissors would have been available for purchase at Louisbourg.[13] Larger scissors are associated with English manufacture, and French scissors were known for their delicacy. In the seventeenth century, French-made scissors were often heavily embellished with precious metals, decorated with cast and inlaid embellishments, or paired with exquisitely delicate metal sheaths.[14]

Every household engaged in any kind of domestic textile or garment production – that is, the vast majority of settler households – would have owned at least one pair of scissors. Scissors were standard household items, needed to build and repair clothing as well as carry out a variety of domestic chores. Some of the pairs of scissors found at Beaubassin, Belleisle, Melanson, and Louisbourg are decorated prestige items, and the assemblages from all four sites include many more pairs than necessary for basic daily activities. Most of the scissors found at Acadian domestic sites were embroidery or fancy-work scissors and many were decorated in one manner or another. The differences between the utilitarian domestic workhorse scissor and the fancy-work hobby scissor are in the quality and embellishments, revealing important information about how the women living in each community considered and performed their social identities. A fancy pair of silver-plated scissors hanging from a woman's belt was a strong visual cue about her place in society.

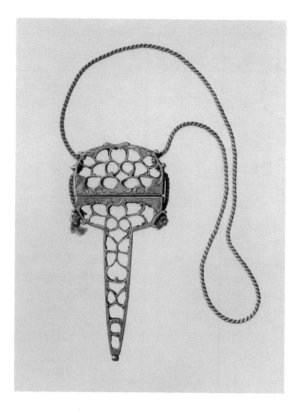

FIGURE 2.1 • Scissors case, French, 17th century. Believed to be a wedding gift. Steel.

The Collection

Scissor styles indicate the activities they were designed and used for. Size and blade-to-handle proportion are the key factors in that identification process. Some specialized forms of scissors have unique blade shapes that make useful diagnostic features, such as the knob at the end of the blade for lace-making scissors, but the corrosive nature of Nova Scotia soils makes identifying some of those details difficult.[15] The differences between standard domestic multi-purpose scissors and tailor's shears are easy to list but more difficult to discern in practice. As anyone with a sewing box is well aware, scissors originally intended for one task are often borrowed for others by incautious members of the household, and general-use scissors can be repurposed for sewing tasks. Nevertheless, some styles can be more closely associated with specific chores.

TABLE 2.1 • Scissors found at four Acadian sites

Type	Size / features	Beaubassin	Belleisle	Louisbourg	Melanson
Snips / embroidery scissors	<12 cm long, narrow, tapered blades, often decorated.	3	6	8	4
Domestic scissors	10–15 cm, thin blades, plain.		5		4
Sewing scissors	12–20 cm, decorated	2		1	
Dressmaking / tailoring scissors	20–30 cm, offset bow, broad blades.		1		1
Fragments	Not enough survived to tell		2		7
Total		5	13–14 possible pairs	9	9–16 possible pairs

Mary Beaudry's examination of colonial-era sites in New England found a ratio of one pair of utility scissors per site.[16] One assemblage with another surprisingly large number of scissors, Fort Michilimackinac, included twenty-seven pairs of scissors or fragments of pairs. Of those, three fragments were brass, two of those brass fragments were decorated with engraving, and none were plated.[17] The numbers are intriguingly different in Acadia (table 2.1). The scissors found in Acadia fall into four different categories: snips, tailor's shears, sewing scissors, and domestic scissors. Embroidery scissors or "snips," with very narrow and tapered blades, are perfectly designed for cutting single threads or making very precise cuts in the warp or weft of a textile.[18] Tailor's scissors or shears are at the opposite end of the scale, their long blades and proportional handles the most efficient design for cutting quantities of heavier material.[19] Sewing scissors in the mid-length range, designed for cutting cloth in straight lines, are the most difficult to differentiate from regular domestic scissors. Scissors of similar style and different size categories are found together more often than not, such as a set of silver-plated scissors and snips at Beaubassin, or the pairs of sewing scissors and snips found together in the Blanchard house in Belleisle. The combination often indicates the presence of a sewing kit, especially when found in conjunction with pins and other sewing tools, an indicator of areas of the property used for textile labour.

Many of the pairs were decorated through either moulded detail or surface treatments. Three of the five pairs of scissors found at Beaubassin were silver or tin-plated.[20] The Belleisle assemblage included a mix of plain and fancy scissors, about half of them small enough to be embroidery snips. Two of the pairs of larger domestic scissors were found in association with snips, suggesting they were part of sewing kits. One larger pair has an extended rivet, of the type seen in contemporary illustrations of tailors' shears. The Melanson site contained many small, corroded pieces of larger scissors and snips, most of those appearing to be plain in design.[21] The home of the widow Dugas at Fortress Louisbourg provided one pair of mid-range scissors and four pairs of snips of varying sizes, one similar in decorative style to the snips recovered at Belleisle. The collections show disparities in style and quantity, though given the circumstances of the sites' abandonment it is difficult to know the original numbers. We cannot know, for instance, how many pairs of scissors family members were able to retrieve as they left for the final time. Nor can the snapshot in time tell us whether Madame Savoie bought and gave away or lost other pairs of scissors over her lifetime. Only one of the sites has multiple use layers to give us a chronology, and so we must assume that the pairs discovered were a minimum number rather than a complete catalogue.

Beaubassin

Beaubassin's collection of scissors are styles predominantly associated with fancy-work and precise dressmaking. One set of sewing scissors and embroidery snips were found together and mostly intact, including the silver or tin plating that originally covered them. Plating one metal with another is a technique that goes back centuries, and gilded spurs were common adornments for male nobles in the Middle Ages. In the eighteenth century silver plating was a common method used to make brass items look like solid silver, and both brass and silver scissors had a distinct advantage over iron ones in that they were protected from rust.[22] Those who could afford the luxury would sometimes indulge in an upgrade from wrought iron to silver, as did one successful French seamstress in 1770, with her purchase of silver scissors and a matching silver thimble.[23] The Beaubassin set is a mid- to late seventeenth-century style, with wrapped loops and a rectangular cross-section to the hafts. The larger sewing scissors have a plain design while the snips have fancier curved handles, a combination that was fairly common.[24] Simpler than some of the later rococo scissors, these plated snips were still a luxury expense. The plating and decoration on both pairs gave this set more significance than basic workhorse domestic scissors.

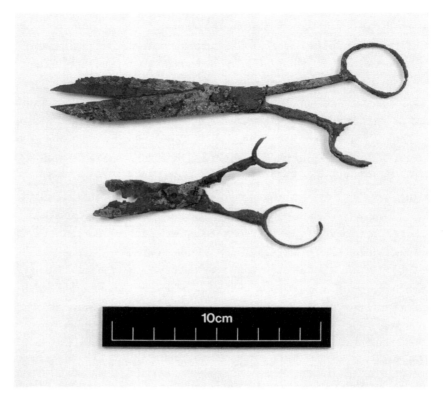

FIGURE 2.2 • Plated scissors and snips found at Beaubassin.

The owner of this set probably used them outside, as the pairs were found together with other household artifacts beneath a burned layer of earth on the south side of a domestic structure.[25] Whose house this was is unclear, but even without knowing the identities of the residents, we can learn much about their use of space from this discovery. The sewing kit was discovered along the south wall of the structure, the side that would receive the greatest amount of sun.[26] While excavations did not find the house door, we do know that the door was not in the fully mapped south wall, which in turn means that in this case the sewing kit was not found outside because it had been stored beneath the front stoop, as has been seen in other locations.[27] More likely, it was found where it had been used, the owner sitting in the afternoon sunshine with her handwork and her mending. This use of public space for domestic work was common, turning an intimate activity into group experience. The prime loci for sewing work prior to the invention of electric light were the hearth and the solar, workspaces

FIGURE 2.3 • Snips, Beaubassin.

FIGURE 2.4 • Iron snips handle found in association with the awl, Beaubassin.

designed to maximize available light and heat. Moving to the outdoors, a practical solution in geographies and seasons where weather permitted, shifted the action from the closed world of the family into communal space.

The other pairs from Beaubassin are less decorative, but no less interesting. These are smaller, and two with surviving tips have a blade shape associated with embroidery scissors. Images from the 1740s show almost identical scissors available for general purchase (figure 2.5). The peddler carries his wares in a box along with reading glasses, shoe buckles, buttons, and other items related to easy domesticity. The context of the finds explains their use: three pairs of scissors were found in artifact

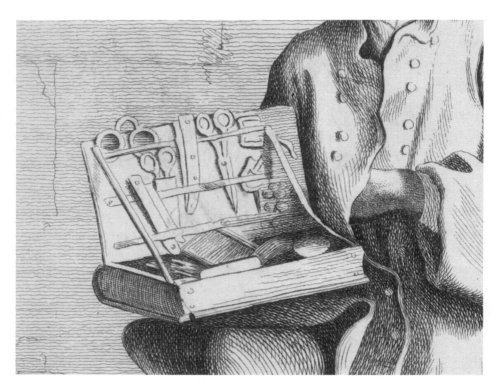

FIGURE 2.5 • Detail, *Peddler of Knives, Scissors and Combs.*

groupings with beads, both finished and half-complete, and a small sewing awl. The collection of sewing and embellishment-related objects suggests remnants of lost or abandoned sewing kits. The small size of the scissors indicates that they were used for fine handwork, possibly involving the beads found nearby.

Another pair of plated embroidery scissors stands out in this assemblage as a second level of luxury consumer good. Embroidery snips indicate the presence of feminized aesthetic work, while the extra expense of plated tools adds a layer of prestige and social display. Badly crushed and bent at some point prior to being interred, these scissors are plated with a silvered coating. Owning fancy scissors like these indicates an emphasis on the visibility of gendered tasks and the social value they accrued as part of the owner's sense of self. Wealth can be displayed overtly through gems and buckles, expensive fabrics, and fancy stockings, but the expense of purchasing silvered sewing tools incorporates embroidery and fancy-work as expressions of feminine identity. In the classic *The Subversive Stitch*, art historian Rozsika Parker separates

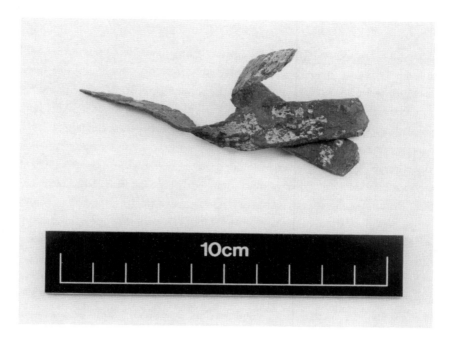

FIGURE 2.6 • Plated scissors, Beaubassin.

the categories of plain sewing and embroidery on both the practical and ideological levels. While plain sewing was a requirement to furnish a household in the eighteenth century, embroidery signified access to an aristocratic lifestyle where access to leisure time for art was proof of gentility and economic privilege. Fine embroidery was intrinsically connected to a household's status and part of the way in which a genteel family maintained its social position.[28]

The silvered scissor sets and fancy snips from Beaubassin reveal the presence of a system where fine sewing was a marker of elite womanhood. This is not the kind of activity commonly associated with the archetypical "outpost" or "border" labels often used to describe Beaubassin.[29] Rather, it speaks to an investment in changing social norms that separated subsistence living from leisure crafts, with the latter as a venue for conspicuous consumption. Beaubassin, the large settlement farthest away from the concentrations of European power at Fort Anne and Fortress Louisbourg, also included the highest number of fancy scissors in the assemblages found to date. Those living there appear to have been in the process of developing their own social elite, a status reflected in both dress and the tools used to produce it.

Louisbourg

The excavated and reconstructed residential area of Fortress Louisbourg includes four houses known to have been occupied by Acadians. The house of the widow Dugas (Marguerite Richard) on lot 2E was the source for most of the scissors found in Acadian contexts at Louisbourg. She lived there with her second husband, Charles de St-Étienne de La Tour, and their daughters, just prior to the British occupation.[30] Most of the scissors recovered from this site are small embroidery snips and all but one pair have been dated prior to 1750, when the original house was destroyed.[31] The other is of unknown date but of a style common to the early 1700s. It must be noted that there is a chance that some items found there could be from the brief period of the British governor's occupation, 1745–49. Any remains from that brief occupation would have been mingled in the rubble from the 1750 destruction of the house, a common problem with multi-use sites.[32]

Of the four pairs of mostly intact snips recovered from the site, three are on the larger end of the category, and one much smaller (see table 2.1). They range from standard sewing scissors to delicate snips potentially small enough to have been used by a young child. Given the lack of other child-sized sewing tools on site, however, it is more likely that they were used by an adult to clip threads and perform other fine detail work. Two of the larger pairs of snips are plain-handled with no decoration, and the third has a haft decorated with geometric cast iron designs (figure 2.8, top), a type of decoration most frequently found on embroidery scissors. An identical scissor handle was found across the street in Lot 2I, residence of the French de la Vallière family

FIGURE 2.7 • Scissors, with extrapolation of broken section.

FIGURE 2.8 • Scissor handles, Louisbourg.

(figure 2.8, bottom). These pieces are so similar that they could easily be two halves of the same pair, except that they are both designed for the same side. An increasing number of decorated scissors were being mass-produced at this time, and these handles probably represent two different pairs cast from the same mould.[33]

The larger iron scissors from the widow Dugas's house measure 13 cm from end to end. Only one side of the scissors survives and that is corroded, the tip missing. Even so, enough remains of the haft to see the light ornamentation, the haft curving into a baluster before connecting to the circular loop, a style common in the early 1700s.[34] The width and length of the blade suggest general-use domestic scissors, though a similar pair with almost identical haft design and blade shape in the collection of the

FIGURE 2.9 • Plain snips / scissors, Louisbourg. Iron with copper alloy rivet.

Winterthur Museum have been identified as sewing scissors. The boundaries between the types are blurry, and scissors designed and purchased for one set of tasks may be easily repurposed for other chores in the home.

An entry in Jeanne Thibodeau's probate inventory describes "scissors with a cover," which make an interesting addition to the list. The description of Mme Thibodeau's scissors does not include information on the material, but seventeenth- and eighteenth-century scissor covers were often metalwork rather than fabric or leather. Wright's *Portrait of a Woman* (1770) shows a similar sheath for the gentlewoman's scissors on the table (figure 2.10). These covered scissors were small tools meant for both use and display as status objects. The contents of Thibodeau's sewing basket listed in the inventory provide more information about her craft, including 151 skeins of linen thread, six skeins of colourful silk thread, ribbons, taffeta, and braid. By all indications she was engaging in handwork appropriate to a genteel woman, not spending her time on practical or subsistence sewing.[35]

Louisbourg was on Atlantic trade routes, and while fashions were delayed getting to Ile Royale from Paris, those living in the fortress were still aware of and interested in following the fashions of the empire. The similarities between the scissors owned by Acadian and French families in Louisbourg show integration into the symbolic life of the community. The connections to those from the other settlements suggest a shared aesthetic, as well as communication and trade. The variety in size means the equivalent variety in the tasks being performed, the presence of sewing scissors

FIGURE 2.10 • Detail, *Portrait of a Woman*, Joseph Wright, ca 1770.

indicating engagement in either dressmaking, tailoring, or both. There seems to be limited local influence in this area, with the emphasis on fancy-work tools and the attendant Eurocentric marking of feminine-coded tasks.

Belleisle

Belleisle was an older community than Beaubassin and survived five years longer, destroyed in 1755. The scissors found there in 1983 and 2004 tell a tale similar to those from the other sites.[36] As many as thirteen or fourteen pairs of scissors are represented in the Belleisle assemblages, at least half directly connected to dressmaking and fancy-work rather than kitchen or general household use. The Blanchards, the family who owned the property where most of the sewing tools were found, were among the wealthier residents of Belleisle. Brothers René and Antoine held four separate plots of land, sharing maintenance with brother-in-law Pierre Gaudet.[37] Pierre Blanchard was listed as a deputy for Belleisle in 1740, empowered in a letter from Mascarene to organize road building around part of the marsh and arbitrate fence disputes between neighbours, indicating his higher status within his community.[38] The Blanchards' wealth and Pierre's role as a deputy make the Blanchards a nominal part of the so-called "elite" Acadian families – mostly defined as the wealthiest and most politically connected families in Acadia, a group often centred around the Melansons and de La Tours.[39]

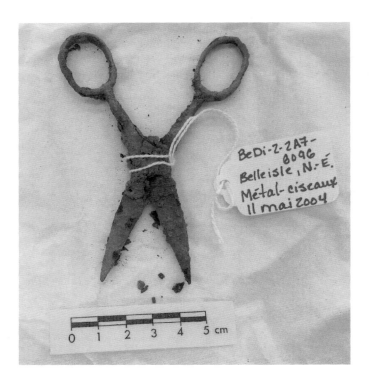

FIGURE 2.11
Scissors, Belleisle.

Belleisle lay outside the banlieue of Fort Anne, the distant region that Clark described as "liv[ing] in the same bucolic fashion as their cousins in Grand Pré and Beaubassin," without marks of European "elegance."[40] This has since been proven simultaneously true and false. Families in Belleisle lived in similar fashion to their cousins at Beaubassin, but both had access to and showed use of similar sorts of luxury goods and status markers as those in urban areas like Louisbourg. The inverse of Clark's statement also appears to be true as far as sewing tools and linens are concerned: the fanciest scissors, and pins for the finest linens, were found at Beaubassin, farthest from the centres of imperial control. The Gaudet, Savoie, and Blanchard houses in Belleisle were furnished more simply. The plainest sewing tools of all were found at Melanson, which was also the closest site to the British presence at Fort Anne. Something other than wealth was on display there – a signalling that did not correlate directly with available income.

The most complete set of scissors to date was uncovered at Belleisle in 2004 in the house of Germain Savoie (Germain-le-père) and his family. The intact scissors are heavily corroded but in otherwise good condition, 10.5 cm in length, with symmetrical

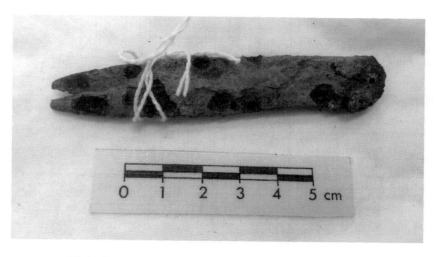

FIGURE 2.12 • Blades from domestic scissors, Belleisle.

loops. They bear a striking resemblance to the snips on display in the peddler's sale case (figure 2.5), though the haft is straight and the blades are wider. From visual examination, the separate symmetrical handles, round hafts, and blade shape confirm a likely manufacturing date in the first or second quarter of the eighteenth century. As with all of the scissors recovered in Acadia so far, there is no visible makers' mark; if there had been one originally, it has since been entirely concealed by corrosion. A second set from the 2004 excavation was found in the same lot as a sewing needle, suggesting a connection, though that lot also contained a great number of bones and domestic waste, including pottery sherds and pipestems.[41] The likelihood, given the size, shape, and archaeological context, is that these were domestic scissors used for kitchen and other household tasks (figure 2.11). Germain's wife Marie Breau *dite* Vincelotte died in 1749, so it is possible that one or both of these pairs began life in her sewing kit, moving to the collection of her daughter-in-law following Vincelotte's death.

About four hundred metres away across the path at the Blanchard residence, the overall collection includes at least four pairs of snips, one possible pair of tailoring shears, and at least one set of small sewing scissors out of a group of, at minimum, nine separate pairs. Most of the recovered hafts are relatively plain, though one pair of snips was found with similar ornate hafts and blades to those found in Louisbourg (figure 2.13). The decorative style suggests an eighteenth-century date of manufacture.[42] The remains of the other pairs of scissors found at the site are in a less complete state. Portions of two larger pairs of domestic scissors of approximately the same

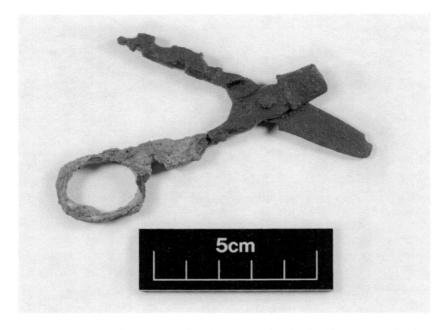

FIGURE 2.13 • Snips, Belleisle. Objects found together in the Blanchard house, unit A, level 1.

size have also been recovered – the handles and parts of the loops of one, and the blade and rivet section of the other (figure 2.12). The size and shape of these scissors suggest general sewing use: too large for snips but with blades narrower than would be expected for tailor's shears.

Another piece of a blade appears to be the middle of a set of scissors of similar size and shape, perhaps a little smaller. An extended rivet in the centre of the blade portion strongly resembles the elongated rivet on the tailors' shears shown in Diderot's 1771 encyclopedia entry for the tailor's shop (figure 2.14), and the surviving portions of the blade are of similar proportion. The final two pieces from Belleisle are loops from different pairs of snips of the same general shape and size (figure 2.15). One loop has been drawn-forged, an older technique in which the iron was pulled into a circle and then wrapped around to connect again with the haft. The other appears to have been forged as a separate piece before being attached, indicating that the loops are from two different pairs of scissors, one likely manufactured at an earlier date than the other.[43] Both loops are simple iron, with no evidence of decoration.

The presence of three different kinds of sewing scissors at the Blanchard house suggests activities beyond basic garment production and repairs, carried out by more

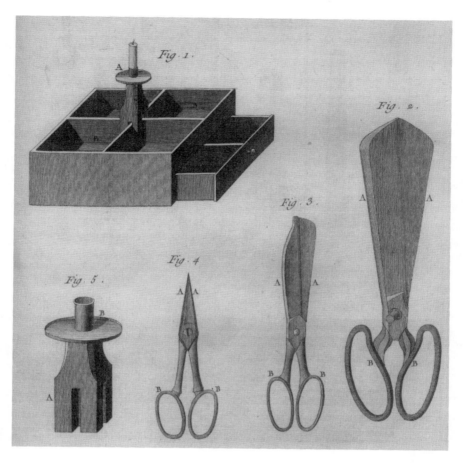

FIGURE 2.14 • Detail, "Tailor of suits and tailor of bodices." *The Encyclopedia of Diderot & d'Alembert.*

than one individual. Each woman would have had her own sewing basket with tools ranging from the basic to the brilliant, including needles, thimbles, scissors, and other assorted tools such as bodkins and awls.[44] Assuming one owner for a set comprising the shears, scissors, and snips, and the fancy snips as a gift or a special pair, we are left with enough variety and quantity for multiple members of the household to be actively engaged in textile labour.

Without chronological markers it is difficult to track changes over time in the Belleisle assemblages. At the time of the deportation, René Blanchard's wife Marie Savoie and their unmarried daughter Marguerite Blanchard were the adult women in residence and the logical owners of the sewing equipment found on site. The

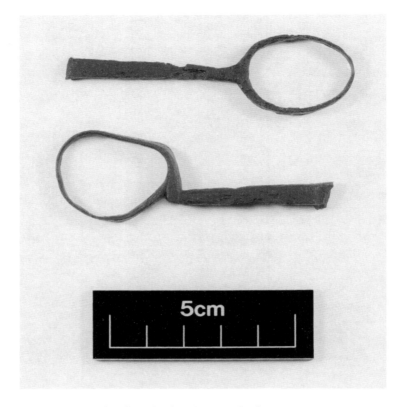

FIGURE 2.15 • Snips handles, Blanchard house, Belleisle.

Blanchard and Savoie houses are about a five- to fifteen-minute walk apart, depending on weather and original terrain, making it less likely for shared household goods here than at other sites.[45]

Removed from both the bustle of Annapolis Royal and the trade routes passing through Beaubassin, Belleisle residents were by no means cut off from luxury goods but may have been less able to access the kinds of varied and profitable trade that flowed through more connected communities. The assemblage is suggestive of a craft culture in Belleisle that valued ornate tools less than Beaubassin. The fancy plated scissors and snips found in Beaubassin have no equals in Belleisle, while the similarity of the snips found in the Blanchard house to the cast iron snips from Louisbourg possibly indicate an origin as a gift, an imported luxury purchased at the Fort. The decorated embroidery snips from Belleisle bear witness to their pastime, and their sewing kits to their engagement in the global world of goods, buying materials from traders like

Michel Richard *dit* Lafond and Marie's grandfather Guillaume Blanchard, whose cargoes of silks, ribbons, lace, and pins were an anticipated supplement to home-grown flax and wool. Acadian women at Belleisle certainly valued fancy-work enough to own tools designed for its execution. The simpler designs and material composition of the scissors, however, indicate they placed a lower priority on the use of sewing tools as a form of feminine-coded status display.

Melanson

One source of information we have at Melanson that is not available for the other sites is a chronology. The earth at Beaubassin was disturbed during the construction of Fort Lawrence, Belleisle's remains are dated primarily by the 1755 destruction, and Louisbourg's artifacts and inventories can only pick out specific points in time for specific individuals, on a timeline interrupted by the British conquest. The Melanson homestead, on the other hand, saw four different structures on site demolished on separate occasions, from a fire in 1707 to the final destruction in 1755, each incident leaving its own evidentiary pattern behind. As a result, the homestead of Charles Melanson (*le fils*) and Anne Bourg gives us a clearer look at their pattern of occupation.

Four different structures have been identified on the site, each one leaving a layer behind. The most dramatic of these events was a house fire in the late 1730s or early 1740s, resulting in a debris field that was not completely cleared away.[46] Instead, as part of the rebuilding process, clay taken from the collapsed chimney flue was spread across the hearth and surrounding area. Clay was also used to reseal the cellar, and this action sealed in the debris left over from the fire in both locations. Fragments of either one or two pairs of scissors discovered in the early midden at Charles Melanson's house are the oldest based on their archaeological context, but not enough remains of them to make any kind of confident identification. Two pairs of scissors survived from prior to 1740 – the pair of sewing scissors caught in the clay used to reseal the basement following the fire, and a fragment of the handle of a plain pair of snips (figure 2.16).

The remaining seven pairs of scissors and snips were found above the burned layer of the third structure, meaning that they were either saved from the fire and later discarded, or were acquired between 1741 and 1755 following the rebuild of the house but before the inhabitants were deported. One distinct pair is what we might call dressmaker's shears or tailor's shears, long-bladed and heavy. These speak to the wide range of dressmaking tasks taking place in the house. The hafts and loops are missing, meaning that we cannot be certain of the proportional length and the cutting power

FIGURE 2.16 • Blade tips of small
sewing or domestic scissors
and partial haft and loop of snips,
Melanson.

of the shears, but others with blades of a comparable size and shape could be domestic
scissors for kitchen or household use, for sheep shearing, or for cutting out garment
patterns and long seams. The blades are a similar width almost all the way along
before narrowing to a point, a curve similar to the shape and proportions of tailors'
scissors portrayed in fifteenth- and sixteenth-century artwork.[47] The other pairs associated with Bourg's household were designed for a different function. Between 10 and
12½ cm long, the three or four pairs represented by four individual pieces are all of a
similar style, with a sharply curved blade that comes to a point, and an angled stop.
Features of these scissors correspond with various types identified as being from the
middle of the seventeenth century, earlier than those from Belleisle and Louisbourg.[48]
The ratio of three pairs of snips to two pairs of scissors and one pair of specialty
shears at the Bourg residence is similar to others seen across the Acadian settlements,
indicating interest in fancy-work, embellishments, and embroidery. The larger
Melanson snips are plain and more typical of the earlier style of scissors. The set
consists of one pair of general work scissors and multiple small snips, used for fancy-
work. These may have been older pairs rescued from the house before or during the

fire, perhaps along with a sewing basket. Overall, the predominance of small scissors indicates smaller-scale production aimed at dressing an individual family rather than a production or putting-out system, where one dressmaker's workshop supported many families.

Labour was distinctly gendered in Acadia, with men doing the bulk of the travel, field labour, and engagement in public life, leaving the women to run the dairies, gardens, and domestic sphere. Bourg had no daughters to teach to sew, or to do her finishing work, but she did have her widowed sister-in-law Madeline Melanson, the widow Belliveau.[49] In 1710, Belliveau had four children ranging in age from four to thirteen, and her only daughter was seven. Following her husband's death in 1707, she would have relied on her brother Charles and her sister-in-law Anne for assistance on the homestead. A married couple created the minimum economic and labour unit required to run a farm settlement, meaning that Belliveau would have been folded into Charles and Anne's labour pool – or perhaps they, into hers.[50] The close proximity of their houses would have given Belliveau and Bourg the ability to task share and divide the labour of running the homes and raising the children. It is easy to picture Belliveau and her young daughter Marie traipsing across the grass to Anne Bourg's house, their sewing tools and mending tucked into the baskets they carried beneath their arms. The women would have sat and sewed on the stoop in the summer sun, taking advantage of the light to complete their fine needlework and mending before having to move inside to sit by the fire. Trestle tables made space to lay out lengths of wool for cutting, the heavy shears slicing through homespun and imported strouds alike. The design of the shears with their rivet extension made for easy balance and the ability to estimate seam allowances by eye, making sewing up of the pieces simple enough for even those daughters still learning the task.

Three pairs of basic scissors served for lighter fabrics or smaller cuts, slicing through curves for armscyes and bodice seams with much greater control than the heavy shears. Each woman had her own, nestled beside pairs of snips to cut the finely spun sewing threads. Beyond construction, the fine-tipped snips would have been useful to unpick tangles and trim the threads and cords used to sew on the kinds of round glass beads found in a few places on the site. Buttons discovered in the yard might have been lost from clothing, but could also be lost from mender's fingers, or when a sewing basket accidentally spilled into the longer grass. The little accidents of life lie waiting to be uncovered, busy hands working their way through the stacks of mending that come from regular wear and farm labour, tacking split seams, patching holes, and replacing buttons lost from a husband, brother, or son's waistcoat or trousers. Conversation would make the work fly faster, a pin or needle lost in the dust and left to lie, unnoticed, the remainders of a constant and vitally important chore.

The fancy scissors and snips found at Beaubassin and to a lesser degree at Belleisle are nowhere to be found at Melanson. The plain nature of the scissors suggests a more utilitarian intent rather than display, an intriguing distinction. It may have been a question of replacement cost, tied to the need to put assets into rebuilding the home that had been destroyed by fire. On the other hand, the Melansons were not poor, and other status-carrying items have been found at the settlement, including sleeve buttons and a spur buckle, to which we will turn in later chapters.

THE DIFFERENT STYLES OF SCISSORS found at the sites may reflect distinctions in how femininity was embodied and displayed within the different Acadian communities. Beaubassin was on a highway of sorts, and as a trade centre it hosted groups of travellers from many directions. Traders from New France came down the Northumberland Strait and through Baie Verte, while New England traders sailed in through the Bay of Fundy to bring their goods to Acadia, and the Mi'kmaq circulated along their millennia-old portages and trails. Being able to appear as European-sophisticated as possible was an asset when trading with partners from New France or Louisbourg, awareness of trends and the ability to access expensive goods for feminine-coded activities both signs of prestige. Some women in Beaubassin saw power and pride in silvered plating and in the skills which the scissors represented. Their use in the construction of a high-status feminine identity would have been immediately understandable and visible to anyone who came through the settlement.

With their proximity to Port Royal, the Melansons were never far from the eyes of power. At the same time, the women living at the Melanson site had little to gain by presenting themselves as high-status members of the privileged elite. Anne Melanson had returned to her birth family and taken a local man as her second husband, bringing her connections, status, and the rights to administer the La Tour estate with her as resources for Alexandre Robichaud, at least until her children came of age themselves. Lady Anne Melanson had no need to display her status to those at Fort Anne, and indeed may have been better off keeping to the simpler lifestyle afforded to Madame Robichaud.

Marie Savoie and Marguerite Blanchard at Belleisle had a minimum of five sets of scissors between them, three of a type dedicated to fancy-work – and not only plain ones, but decorative snips of good quality. This suggests that embroidery was a passion and a pleasure for at least one of the residents. Marguerite Richard, the widow Dugas, had six unmarried daughters in the house in 1745 when the British took Louisbourg for the first time: her eldest two with Joseph Dugas, the two daughters of her second husband de La Tour, and the eight-year-old twins they shared, and we have fragments from this site of six pairs of scissors: one set of larger scissors and five sets of embroidery snips.[51]

What we see in Acadia, contrary to other colonial sites, is one pair of utility scissors per adult woman and at least one pair of snips for every adolescent and adult. Where there are multiple adult women and a traumatic departure, as with Belleisle, we see plain work and fancy-work scissor sets for each adult woman. The fire at Melanson left one pair of large scissors and three or four fancy-work pairs in the rubble, suggesting one main garment worker and a handful of others associated with finishing and embellishment. The departure from Louisbourg may have left Marguerite and her daughters enough time to pack the larger items, but the snips were left behind. However the materials ended up where they were, we are still left with one pair of larger working scissors for the adult woman in the house, and five pairs of snips.

Never just simple tools, the scissors, snips, and shears used by Acadians for clothing construction and decoration speak to the priorities, goals, and self-image of the women who owned them. The rest of their kits, the pins, needles, awls, and thimbles that made sewing work possible, fill out the remaining space in the sewing baskets and huswifs, helping us build a broader picture of their working lives and priorities.

Sewing Kits: Pins, Needles, Awls, and Thimbles

Sewing kits, collections of tools including scissors, pins, needles, and thimbles, were vital possessions for women in the early modern period, and their use plays a large part in engagement with domestic and public spaces. The amount of labour required to clothe a family meant that sewing kits saw daily, if not constant, use. At Belleisle, archaeologist Marc Lavoie discovered sewing kits placed beneath the front stoops of the houses, while sewing tools have been discovered in outdoor spaces at Melanson.[52] We can extrapolate use patterns from the locations of these finds, thanks in particular to the size of the items in question. Small items of low value tend to be left where they fell, much as people today will pick up a dollar coin but are more likely to leave a penny on the ground. The cut-off size for these remnants appears to be approximately

9 cm, which would include items like the needles and pins found at Belleisle and Melanson. Whether the pins and needles were deliberately stored underneath the stoops or accumulated there through periods of industry, both point to sunny spots outside the house as sites where sewing work took place.[53] This paints a pretty picture of domestic labour in the summer warmth, but there are other implications as well. When sewing in the sunlight on the front stoop, the domestic world was brought into the public sphere. The community aspects of sewing work, textile production, and processing were a vital part of Acadian women's regular routine.

Shared labour created intimacy, and the tools used for the task connected the hands with the material being manipulated. Stitchers sat closely together, bending over the fabric by sunlight or firelight, needle and small scissors in hand. Their knees touched, hands brushing, making physical and emotional contact over the textiles later used on a marital bed, on a household's dining table, or to protect a child's delicate skin. Each hour spent working on a quilted petticoat or a smocked shirt this way also meant an hour in the company of one's sisters, daughters, and friends. Sewing was a communal activity which women used to strengthen their independent social bonds while maintaining the required levels of production for a well-run household.[54] Webs of connection were forged by barter and labour exchange, and entangled with concepts of family, community, and caregiving. The physical nature of the work created deep and abiding investment in the well-being of the recipients, the stitchers becoming in a way part of other households along with their art. The tools they used for these tasks – pins, thimbles, awls, and needles, and the bodkin that drew ribbons and lace through hand-worked eyelets – are tantalizing clues as to the garments and household draperies that have long since returned to the earth.

Pins

Ubiquitous finds at any pre-modern site, pins were primarily used in the premodern period for holding clothing together. Sleeves could be pinned on to bodices, kerchiefs to hair, and fichus tucked and pinned in place for modesty. Domestic sewers were more likely to use pins than professional dressmakers or tailors, who relied on quicker forms of basting techniques.[55] Prior to around 1744 pins were sold by weight, wrapped in paper. By the mid-century it was possible to purchase pins both in pin-papers, or in boxes of specific weights.[56] Tin-plated copper pins would have been used most often for holding garments together, while plain copper were less decorative but could have been used in case of a wardrobe malfunction. The lengths and gauges of the wire used for pins differed based on their purpose, and the linen hair coverings, fichus, sleeves,

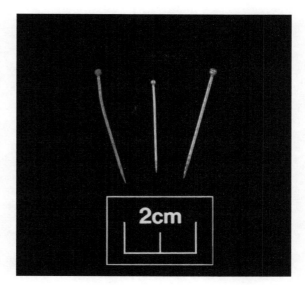

FIGURE 2.17 • Short white pins from Beaubassin, Type C compressed wound-wire head and mostly intact tin plating.

and apron bibs held on by pins also came in different weights and styles.[57] The sizes of the pins found at the sites can give us clues as to the kinds and quality of textiles in use. The contexts in which the pins were found tells as much of the story as their sizes, shapes, and styles.

Beaubassin

Approximately half of the pins found at Beaubassin were between 20 and 30 mm long and 0.5 mm wide. These were a style known as "short whites," common pins used primarily for dressmaking and everyday sewing. Another third were long whites, over 30 mm in length and usually around 1 mm in diameter, which were used for heavier fabrics. Four pins in the assemblage were twice the width and more than twice the length of the long whites, large enough to be used for pinning blankets or utility fabrics, including sail canvas or leather. The overwhelming majority of the pins were made of a copper alloy, the most common material for that purpose in the seventeenth century. The sizes fit the mean distribution for pins associated with seventeenth-century colonial sites, slightly longer than the pins used in the eighteenth and nineteenth centuries.[58] The bulk of the pins at Beaubassin were found in relatively close proximity to other trade goods, including trade silver, textile seals, and beads. It is likely that many of the items found in operation 7B17 were in storage for future exchange, rather than community circulation.[59]

TABLE 2.2 • Pin types found at Beaubassin

Type (adapted from Beaudry, *Findings*)	Sizes	Quantity
Small pins	≤23 mm long, <0.75 mm diameter	23
Short whites	23–30 mm long, 0.75–1 mm diameter	39
Long fines	>23 mm long, but <0.75 mm diameter	17
Long whites	>30 mm long, ≥0.75 mm diameter	20
Data missing	Original length and/or diameter unknown	21
Total		120

TABLE 2.3 • Pin head types found at Beaubassin

Type (adapted from Caple, "Detection and Definition")	Description	Quantity
Type A	2 twists of wire fixed to shaft with adhesive. Dominant style in the 15th cen.	2
Type B	2 twists of wire loosely crimped onto top of the shaft. Dominant style in the 16th cen.	14
Type C	2 twists of wire tightly crimped onto the top of the shaft, forming a spherical head. Dominant post-1600.	74
B or C, inconclusive.		7
Corroded or small and bulbous head	Corrosion or damage makes it difficult to determine with naked eye or microscope.	10
Broken / unknown		13
Total		120

There are three major forms for the heads of wound-wire pins, all of which are represented among the pins at Beaubassin (see table 2.3).[60] The collection indicates reliance on imported pins from England, France, or New England. Metallurgical analysis of some of the pins from Beaubassin indicated that they were once tin-plated, and of a soft alloy commonly used for pins in European manufacture.[61] The prevalence of longer short, white pins at Beaubassin suggests the use of fabric on the heavier side for headdresses and kerchiefs. The use of slightly cheaper, older, longer pins than the height of fashion in the 1740s suggests that they were using older pins, either from earlier occupation or due to delay in receiving goods from France; alternatively, the colonies may have been receiving cheaper, lower-quality goods than was available elsewhere.

Belleisle

The four pins found at Belleisle are too small a sample size to make even educated guesses as to how they were being used. Three of the four were associated with the same small feature in the Blanchard house, possibly a storage closet, and are all copper-alloy with soldered, wire-wound heads indicating professional off-site manufacture.[62] One broken copper alloy pin is fine-weight and delicate, two are standard sewing pins, and the fourth is large and heavy. The single pin fragment found at the Savoie house is heavy and thick, suggesting it was originally of similar size to the largest from the Blanchard house.[63] The long double-white pins were used for blankets and cloaks, but could also be for farm-related chores such as tack repair.

Melanson

A handful of needle fragments and a single copper pin were found at Anne Melanson's house, mostly in the area associated with the house's midden, where broken pins could have been easily tossed there with the garbage. Most of the pieces were iron, more likely to be sewing needles than pins, and the single copper pin recovered was very fine and delicate. Pins this narrow were more commonly used for holding together delicate fabrics like fichus, rather than for sewing. By contrast, thirty pins were found at Anne Bourg's house higher up the hill, many of them in the yard area. These varied in diameter and length, some very fine and small, of the kind used for fine linens and silks, and others larger and more durable designed for domestic sewing. This quantity of scattered pins suggests that Bourg and companions used her outdoor space for sewing on a regular basis.

Twenty-five pins at the house of Jean Belliveau and Madeleine Melanson were also all found in the yard exterior to the house. Using sunlight to sew by in the warmer months created less eye strain than attempting to do the same by firelight or candlelight in winters. While necessary repairs would have happened throughout the year, the rhythm of the seasons may lend itself more to fine sewing the spring and summer months, as the days grew longer, the sunlight clearer, and the chance to sit outdoors and take advantage of the clear natural light kinder to cold fingers. Acadian women and girls sitting and sewing on their stoops would be a consistent presence in the settlements' public sphere.

Needles and Thimbles

Needles and thimbles were integral parts of any sewing kit, and finding them at a site is a more likely indicator of sewing activity than the presence of pins. These packages of sewing tools often vanish from the written record, going unrecorded on inventories or listed in advertisements, but archaeology gives us some of the evidence that they were there. Needles were forged from wire, drilled, grooved, and sharpened. They were both ubiquitous and precious, particularly for those living in regions where replacements for the delicate items were not immediately available. While needles were inexpensive enough by the seventeenth and eighteenth centuries for even rural farmers to own multiples, their importance made their care and use a non-negligible chore. Needles were kept in needle cases, some of which have been preserved at Louisbourg (figure 2.19), or in wool panels in needle books. As with pins, the size and shape can tell us something about the kinds of work they were used for, from delicate lace needles to the heavy-duty iron needles used for net repair.

Two major kinds of thimbles were used by the seventeenth century: tailors' thimbles (not necessarily used only by tailors) with no built-in cap, and full thimbles made with a cap to cover the tip of the finger.[64] Some full thimbles were cast in one piece but others were made in two separate sections, composed of a ring and top.[65] That cap had a tendency to pop off over time and with corrosion, making it more difficult to tell one from the other. Indented around the sides to catch the needle, the size of the thimble's divots revealed the size of the needles with which it was designed to be used.[66]

Thimbles were made in a range of sizes to suit different users. Brass thimbles, the most common form, were cheap and came in three sizes: child, maid, and woman.[67] Thimbles were also used as trade goods with Indigenous communities, either for use with sewing lessons, or to be cut apart and used as tinklers for dress decoration.[68] Britain imported large numbers of thimbles to the colonies, beginning with some destined for trade with Indigenous populations, and continued to do so through the eighteenth century.[69]

TABLE 2.4 · Other sewing tools in Acadia

	Beaubassin	Belleisle	Louisbourg	Melanson
Sewing needles	38	4	–	12
Thimbles	2	–	–	3
Needle cases	–	–	2	–

As with the scissors, fancy thimbles could be status symbols. By the seventeenth century even the middle classes in France were regularly using silver thimbles, partly due to the much wider availability of the precious metal for domestic use following the looting of Central American silver. The thimbles imported to Acadia were mostly brass, however, as were all the thimbles and pieces thereof found at Acadian sites. These pieces from Acadian contexts have minimal decoration. They have plain rims like English thimbles, which tended to be simpler than German- or French-made ones. The full brass thimble found in Louisbourg is an eighteenth-century Lofting style, shorter than later versions.[70] The owner, likely a member of the Dugas family in the 1750s, was tuned in to the current fashion in sewing accessories and probably purchased that thimble as an English import. The even machined spacing of the indentations on the recovered thimbles dates them all to after 1650, indicating that these were purchased locally rather than being family heirlooms of great value.[71]

Made to fit the body, the intimacy of the finger inside the thimble – sweating inside them, the metal leaving traces on the fingertips in return – suggests the sensuality of lovemaking.[72] Knowing someone's hand well enough to size a thimble as a gift was a sign of intimacy, thimbles occasionally becoming a preliminary or replacement wedding band. A decision as closely fit as her bodices and involved in all of her handwork, choice of thimble was an expression not only of a woman's working life but how she wanted that life to be seen by others. Thimbles were integrated into all areas of domestic life, used for measurements in cooking as well as for sealing letters.[73] They also represented a woman's earning potential, particularly in a barter-style system as seen in Acadia where domestic labour was shared. A thimble and full needle case indicated a woman's ability to engage in the community aspects of production and enter into reciprocity with her neighbours.[74]

Needle sizing became standardized in the late eighteenth and early nineteenth century as production became more industrialized, but the associations of size with specific activity came earlier. Certain needle types are naturally suited to certain activities, and while we cannot assume that the appropriate tool was always used for a specific activity, the catalogue gives us a sense of the types of work that were being done at the time. Seventeenth-century professional needle makers had a series of specific types of needle, described in more general terms than they would later acquire. Randle Holme, in his 1688 treatise on society and trades, listed the types with some useful descriptions:

Pearl Needle, is the least size of Needles.

The first, second and third sort of Needles, according to their sizes;

so numbred till you come to ten.

Ordinary Needles.

Bush Lane Needles.

Glovers Needles have square points.

Book Binders Needles are long and round point

Sow-Gelders Needles are flat pointed.

Chyrurgions Needles are the same, flat pointed.

Pack Needles, crooked at the point, and some flat, others three square;

others with a Back and Edge (like a Knife) at point.[75]

All the needles found at the four sites were ordinary needles with rounded points, the type commonly used for domestic sewing and repair work on looser-weave or coarser fabrics. The recovered samples are badly rusted and degraded, but surviving eyes are 2–3 mm in length, with the suggestion of thread grooves above and below. The fact that the only needles found so far have been large does not preclude the possibility of fancy work, as small pearl needles used for embroidery and lace making may well have rusted away in the intervening centuries.

Needles, needle cases, and most especially thimbles have a special place in early modern sewing kits, their practical and symbolic value exceeding their relatively low prices.[76] Carried in a woman's pockets, these tools straddled the line between private and public, mediating personal and communal spaces.[77] The presence of sewing kits under the stoops of Acadian homes exposes sewing as a part of the communal domestic space, while thimbles and needle cases carried inside the pockets, as close to the skin as possible, brought them deep into a woman's personal space.

Beaubassin

All the thimble fragments found at Beaubassin have rims and regular indentations, marking them as post-1675 in manufacture.[78] Those for which we can tell a size are made for adult hands, made of copper alloy (brass), at least one is clearly machine-stamped, and the surviving pieces are unadorned. These utilitarian pieces are unlikely to have played much of a direct role in negotiation of social status.[79]

FIGURE 2.18 • Brass tailor's thimble (left) and copper thimble fragment (right), Beaubassin.

Belleisle

The four sewing needles found at Belleisle – one from the Savoie house and three from the Blanchard house – are incomplete. They are on the heavier end of the scale for standard sewing needles, and some might be darning needles, but we cannot know for sure because the eyes are mostly missing.[80] The very small sample suggests the trend at Belleisle, even more so than at Beaubassin, was towards utilitarian and durable. Heavy pins and needles would have been much more useful for basic sewing, mending, and wool embroidery or tapestry work than for lace making or sewing delicate fabrics like silk. It is tempting to suggest that the sewing work done at Belleisle was predominantly done with utilitarian materials, but the problems of needle survivability and the small percentage of the site that has been excavated make this a dangerous assumption.

No thimbles have yet been uncovered at Belleisle, a gap that certainly does not indicate lack of use. Particularly since the needles found were on the heavy side, meaning that they were being used for heavier materials, the use of a thimble becomes even more vital to protect the hands. Small and easy to tuck into a pocket, both the utilitarian and the fancy thimbles are likely to have been on the bodies of their owners when the deportation began. The lack of broken pieces or discarded thimbles at Belleisle may also indicate the value placed on them – they were kept close, perhaps less easily replaced. And when the sides dented too badly, or the caps began to come loose, they could have been melted down for the brass content, or sent away for repair rather than being tossed in the midden and forgotten.

Melanson

The discovery of thimbles under the hearth at Melanson gives tangible life to theories of use of domestic spaces. Work is intimately tied into architecture, the size and layouts of rooms allowing certain kinds of labour, the placement and directionality of light determining the possibility of others. The hearth was the centre of the Acadian home, the source of light, heat, and cooking during long winter and short summer nights.[81] One thimble was discovered in the stratigraphical layer corresponding to the destruction of the first structure built on the site, one that did not appear to have a hearth. The thimble was discovered near a porcelain sherd and a seed, suggesting nevertheless that sewing work was being done in a space also used for food preparation or consumption. The other two thimbles were found in the remains of the penultimate structure, a house destroyed by fire circa 1740.[82] Found buried near the building's hearth, these thimbles were also in close association with seeds, an expected find so close to the cooking area and bake oven. Work, especially in winters, would continue into the evening hours and the fire in the hearth would be the most useful indoor source of light. Sewing had a place next to food preparation in the centre of Acadian domestic life.

The needles at Melanson, like the pins, were primarily found outdoors: both in the yard area and in the middens. Bourg's midden also included other sewing and dressing equipment, including a bone bodkin (figure 2.23), three brass buttons of varying sizes, two fragments of small scissors, and a small iron ring, perhaps of the sort used to support thread buttons or eyelets. Sewing outside, while useful to catch sunlight, also lent itself to the risk of losing small items in the grass and dirt. A lost needle or pin that fell from a garment could be swept up into the nearby garbage pile without being noticed, as certainly seen with a straight pin and pair of pewter sleeve link buttons found in a pig's grave elsewhere on the site.[83] The other objects found in Bourg's midden are less likely to have been accidentally disposed of, however. The bodkin especially was quite large – approximately 5.1 cm long – intact and easily visible, as well as being an item vital to daily dressing.

Found in the middle layers of the midden, above the layer of tamped-down clay associated with the 1707 rebuilding, the bodkin, buttons, iron ring, and one pair of scissors were in close association with a needle.[84] This collection almost certainly represents a repair or dressing kit, the kind of maintenance and repair items often found contained in fabric rolls called hussifs, or "housewifes," and carried in women's pockets. The hussif demonstrates the portability of sewing work. The spinning wheel and loom kept operators confined to the workshop and hearth, but the small, fabric-wrapped sewing kits, commonly carried in deep pockets close to the body, also travelled with their owners.[85] The brass buttons found with this particular kit were the type worn on men's jackets and waistcoats, while the bodkin was a tool primarily used for relacing women's gowns and bodices. Armed with notions and a needle, wearing her kit in the pocket hanging beneath her clothes, Bourg, in her preparedness, represents the kind of emotional labour that went along with the physical work of maintaining a household and raising a family.

Louisbourg

Acadian women living in Louisbourg had greater access to quality goods, and the fancy tools found in their houses at the fortress show that they took advantage of local merchants' wares. Many of these women were wives of French officers, adding pressure to keep up the appearance of sophistication.[86] Anne Levron and her daughter Marianne Benoist carried their needles in ivory and wood needle cases. Made by joiners and other professional artisans, needle cases with their tightly fitted screw ends were better at rust protection than hussifs and fabric needlebooks. Pin poppets, a slightly shorter derivation of needle cases, held the fine copper pins used to pin garments together. Intricately carved needle cases and pin poppets were another visible status marker and a sign of the social attention paid to needlework, dress, and the demonstration of respectability.[87]

Two intact brass thimbles and one piece of a third were also found at the Dugas and Richard residences. The knurling on the complete crowned thimble, which goes up

FIGURE 2.19 • Needle case, Louisbourg. Likely belonged to Anne Levron, Marianne Benoist, or Anne Jacau.

FIGURE 2.20
Wooden and iron
awl, Beaubassin.

and over the top in a continuation of the impressions on the body, is similar in shape
and style to later Dutch brass thimbles found at St Mary's City in Maryland.[88] The lack
of visible wear suggests that it was a recent purchase and not used much before being
lost. The short band and the larger indentations on the second thimble from the Dugas
house in Louisbourg mark it as a tailor's ring thimble, used by catching the needle on
the side of the finger rather than the tip.[89] These ring thimbles were commonly used for
heavier fabrics (saddle and harness making, sail making, shoemaking), and were often
larger, to fit on men's fingers.[90] The variety of styles present indicates the performance
of multiple types of sewing work, including the construction of heavier garments.

Sewing Awl

The awl discovered at Beaubassin (figure 2.20) is interesting both for itself and for the
artifacts with which it was found. Awls are multi-purpose tools, used for boring holes
in leather, cloth, and other soft materials. They appear on lists of trade goods with
Indigenous groups including the Mi'kmaq, the metal tips popular replacements for
traditional bone awls for piercing and preparing hides.[91] Colonial shoemakers used a
round-headed awl to drive holes into leather for footwear, and a tailor or dressmaker
used an awl or the very similar stiletto to unpick seams and draw threads out of fabric
for cutwork or whitework embroidery.

Because of awls' versatility, it is often difficult to identify a purpose for a specific
example without further contextual detail. Shape can tell us some things. The awls
used for footwear and garment construction had round handles or were mounted on a
curved handle to fit in the palm.[92] The user would twist and apply pressure to slip the
point between fibres and open a hole. In this case, the small awl, with a spike about

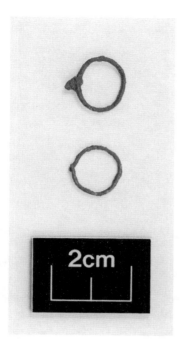

FIGURE 2.21 • Iron rings from Beaubassin.

FIGURE 2.22 • Detail of woman's embroidered jacket with lacing rings, ca 1780.

5 cm long, was found in close proximity to a broken pair of snips.[93] The spike of the awl has a diameter of 4 mm at its widest point, the right size for making holes for small eyelets for lacing. Similar awls have been recovered at sites like Fort Michilimackinac, the distribution at that site showing they were used frequently by both civilian and military personnel, as well as for trade goods.[94]

Lacing was an extremely popular method for closing and connecting garments in the late seventeenth and early eighteenth centuries. When not closed edge to edge with hooks and eyes, bodices and stays were drawn closed with laces. Men's breeches often had a lacing placket in the back waist for size adjustments, and knee bands could have eyelets if they were tied with points rather than closed with buckles.[95] These eyelets would be worked with silk or linen thread, with a metal ring slipped between the fabric layers to provide stability.[96] Iron rings of about the right size have been found at Melanson and at Beaubassin (figure 2.21), which may have been used for this purpose. Another form of lacing used between the fourteenth through the nineteenth centuries was lacing rings, where the metal rings were partially stitched down to the surface

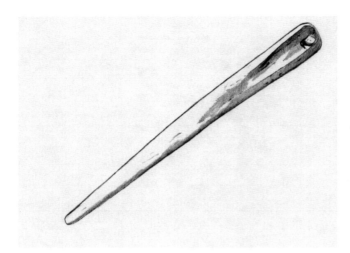

FIGURE 2.23
Bone bodkin, Melanson.

of the garment rather than bound into eyelets. These could be moved more easily than eyelets, allowing for alterations to the garment without the need to poke more holes in a bodice or gown. A later example of a waistcoat from Colonial Williamsburg (figure 2.22) has elaborate lacing rings with extra curlicues to secure the ring to the bodice, adding fashionable flair to a structural necessity.

Bodkin

A bodkin is a tool very much like a large blunt needle or an awl, used to draw ribbons or laces through eyelets or casings in clothing. All forms of clothing could be laced with the help of a bodkin, though they were mostly used to make it easier to lace corsetry and bodices. Some fancy silver or copper-alloy bodkins could be worn tucked into the coif or the apron as a piece of personal jewellery and may even have been monogrammed with the owner's initials. The bodkin had an intimate relationship with the body that it dressed, and while both men and women used bodkins for lacing, the tool held particular social significance for women.[97] A bone bodkin was found in the midden associated with Anne Bourg's house at the Melanson settlement, alongside two buttons and one of the pairs of scissors. While bone bodkins were utilitarian rather than decorative, they still played a role in the construction of female identity in the seventeenth and early eighteenth centuries. Bodkins filled the same signalling space as buckles: necessary tools to wear the fashionable clothing of the seventeenth and eighteenth centuries, but capable of carrying multiple layers of meaning.

The bone bodkin found at Melanson was most likely made locally and does not show the usual sorts of decoration or attachment points for jewels seen in more expensive models.[98] The simplicity of the design and the use of bone suggest that this bodkin was homemade, possibly by Bourg herself from the bone of an animal raised on the farm. Bone buttons were made on site, so the manufacture of accessories from bone was well known locally. Bone also smooths from use, showing the passage of time and thread with every worn section, and the long, natural shape of a simple bodkin would have been easy enough to sand down even for a non-expert. This act of creation was an intimate act by the owner, especially for an item she wore tucked into her bodice or in a pocket, warm from her body and her hands, a regular and required part of her daily life. This bone bodkin is not a decorative piece to signal social status; rather, it roots its owner in both her land and her herd.

Modern maternity wear comes with a wide variety of options for breastfeeding access, but women's clothing in the colonial period was not specialized for pregnancy and nursing. Instead, most women's clothing laced for closure and could be supplemented with stomachers – cloths that pinned across or behind lacings to cover a widened opening – or aprons worn high, allowing for adjustment of size and fit as the pregnant body changed shape.[99] Nursing access demanded front-closing bodices and jackets, and a quick means of unlacing and lacing in order to feed a hungry infant with minimal disruption. A bodkin, designed to speed up the dressing process, would be a vital part of a mother's daily kit and needed to be carried on her person. It spoke to her practical needs as well as provided a place for display and purpose. More poignantly, despite the recorded fecundity of women in Acadia, pregnancy and childbirth in the early modern period were still extremely high-risk. The loose-laced bodices of the last few months of gestation were both a testament to a woman's fertility – and a potential countdown to her death. In this context, the bodkin takes on new meaning. When used to relace a gown for a nursing mother, the simple bodkin becomes an expression of survival.

All these small tools and notions, the insignificant detritus of daily life, clothing use and repair, come together to tell a story about the labour and labour sharing that connected families, and the places and spaces used for sewing-related chores. Sewing kits, thimbles, and bodkins were necessary tools as well as symbols of women's role in maintaining the family's appearance and well-being. Decorative versions of utilitarian objects spoke to status differences, while hand-made versions connected the user to the land. Often overlooked archaeologically, these scattered pieces actually have a fair bit to tell us about the lives of their original owners.

Spinning: The Spindle Whorl and Distaff

Spinning was a cultural constant for European women, a gendered task taught young and practised throughout her life. The tools used and type of thread being spun impacted how a woman or girl moved through both private and public spaces. Without any surviving textiles from the pre-deportation period available for examination it is impossible to know precisely what style of spinning and weaving was being done in Acadia, though we can extrapolate from the evidence that did survive. Documentation and artifacts show us that Acadian women used both spinning wheels and drop spindles to make their thread and yarn. The spinning wheel was a standard part of a French labourer's household in the seventeenth and eighteenth centuries, and the slower drop spindle with its weighted whorl had been a staple in one form or another as far back as the Stone Age.[100]

The drop spindle was a simple device used for spinning fibres, made by placing a whorl – a disk of even weight and diameter – on the bottom of a straight stick to balance it and generate spin. Spindle whorls were made from many different solid, durable substances, including wood, stone, and repurposed pottery. Similar discs or bowls without drilled holes were often used as catches for the point of the spindle for supported stationary spinning. While spinning can be done without a whorl, the use of the whorl creates smaller-diameter threads or cords, of a more consistent size, faster and more efficiently. In order to be useful, the size and weight of the whorl must be calibrated for the type of fibre being spun – the smaller the whorl, the faster the spin, and generally the shorter the staple of the fibre used with it. Large, heavy whorls are best suited for the production of flax and thick wool threads (>1 mm in diameter). Smaller, lightweight whorls have been associated in South and Central America with cotton production; in the case of Acadian home textile production they would have been used for fine woollen threads, between 0.2 and 0.7 mm thick.[101]

A small spindle whorl was discovered outside the Blanchard house in Belleisle. This example (figure 2.24) was quite light (originally 11–18 g), sheared in half at some point before discovery, and was only 36 mm in diameter. The Blanchard whorl was made of what appears to be local clay, perforated – albeit at an angle – to allow for the insertion of the spindle.[102] The size and shape, as well as the angled perforation, suggest that it was locally made by an amateur. Based on the size and projected original weight, this whorl and the spindle it was attached to would have been best suited to the production of very fine wool thread.

FIGURE 2.24 • Spindle whorl, Belleisle. Made of clay, likely local.

The drop spindle was inexpensive and simple to make but was generally ineffi-cient. Many who could afford to replaced their drop spindles with spinning wheels. The spinning wheel was faster and more efficient, but it restricted women's activities in ways the drop spindle didn't. The spinning wheel forced the spinner to stay in one place, while lightweight drop spindles could be spun in the air while walking, allow-ing gravity to do some of the work. The drop spindle's portability meant that the user could engage in other tasks and public social life while working. The spinning wheel, on the other hand, usually lived in the main room of the home, and the stationary chore left the spinner disconnected from public life. Spinning bees could be organized if one had a portable wheel, but even the smallest wheels were unwieldly by compar-ison to the drop spindle. The presence of a drop spindle outdoors on the Blanchard property confirms that some women from families with means were still using the less expensive tools, perhaps in addition to a spinning wheel, suggesting that the motivation was mobility rather than poverty.

The type of spinning wheel the Acadians used was invented around 1600, based on Chinese or Indian designs that entered European use in the thirteenth century. Linen and wool required different wheels, a small "Saxony" or flax wheel for spinning linen fibres, and a larger "great wheel" or "walking wheel" for spinning wool. Some

FIGURE 2.25 • *Standing Woman Holding a Spindle, and Head of a Woman in Profile to Right*. Antoine Watteau, ca 1714–18.

FIGURE 2.26 • Detail, *Peasant Interior*, the Le Nain Brothers, 1642.

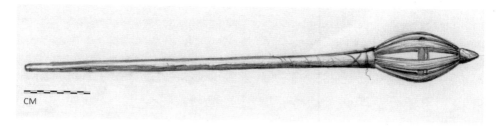

CM

FIGURE 2.27 • Distaff for linen, eighteenth-century Acadian. Fort Beauséjour.

households would have had both.[103] Wheels were ubiquitous but relatively expensive considering their necessary role in the production of household textiles. The cost to purchase one in England in the early seventeenth century was two shillings and four-pence – but rose to about five shillings a hundred years later.[104] While no parts of the main body of a spinning wheel have yet been found at a pre-expulsion Acadian site, an Acadian distaff in the museum at Fort Beausejour is 68.5 cm in length, the right size for use with a spinning wheel (figure 2.27).[105] At that length it is shorter than a distaff designed to be used with a drop spindle, which was usually closer to a metre in length. Using a wheel and distaff, a skilled spinner could spin an average of two skeins of linen thread in a day, or six skeins of wool.[106]

The only evidence we have for looms in Acadia are Dièrville's first-person ac-counts, and inventories that describe looms in the households of Acadian refugees in New England following the deportation.[107] Some households had them, but likely not all. In New England only 65–80 per cent of households owned wheels by 1750. By comparison, only 6–10 per cent had looms. This is relatively unsurprising considering the workload required to produce enough thread to fill a loom, with multiple spinners required per weaver.[108] The looms used at the time were two-harness floor looms, the same style later used in both Louisiana and northern Acadian settlements. This basic loom was capable of producing two different weaves, a plain and a tabby, with basket weave and other variations made possible by changing the threading of the harnesses.[109] The tabby weave was the most common in later Acadian weaving, with pattern banding created through manipulation of weft colours.[110] Fancier patterns like brocades, satins, and damasks were not physically possible.

Weaving had traditionally been a male-coded task, a changeover taking place in the mid-eighteenth and into the nineteenth centuries. Data from southwest England show that women began to train as weavers around 1700, after having been exclud-ed from the profession for approximately two hundred years.[111] Looms became more common in New England household inventories post-1750, around the time when co-lonial production appears to have moved from the professional to the domestic sphere, with female textile workers supplementing purchases of imported cloth. Later, wom-en and children would be among the first users of power looms in the English cotton industry, though as production requirements increased, so did the number of men running the looms.[112] While the image of a weaver often reflects the domestic arche-type of Penelope at her loom, the genders and ages of weavers varied with cultural, economic, and technological changes.

This shift in the locus of production from male specialist to female domestic pro-duction must have begun earlier in Acadian circles than elsewhere, as by the time of the deportation it is Acadian women being given the credit for weaving. Mathieu Martin was the only professional weaver appearing in an Acadian census, in 1671.[113] In 1685 de Meulles wrote that there were weavers, plural, in the colony, the trade being passed down through the generations, but these weavers must have been combining time at their looms with other work as no professionals in the trade are recorded after Martin's death.[114] The group of deportees that settled at Belle-Ile-en-Mer in 1765–66 had strong reputations as weavers, and were given looms by the French government in order to ply their skills in "tissu acadien."[115]

Spinning and weaving locally produced fibres to supplement imported fabrics and keep their households in textiles, Acadian women turned the products of their farms and flocks into warm wool and heavy linen. The technology they had allowed for simple patterns, but the amount of work it took to generate even the simplest of textiles – to go from sheep to shawl – is impressive no matter how decorative the end result. Somewhere between the late seventeenth century and the 1760s, Acadian weaving had developed a distinctive character that was both identifiable to others and desirable as a commodity.

Conclusions

Examining the tools of textile production can tell us useful things about Acadian dress, and about the culture surrounding their production methods. Even the missing items such as looms and spinning wheels have left traces behind in their absence. The presence of sewing tools outdoors leads to an exploration of the idea of work spaces, turning textile production and maintenance into activities that blur the boundaries between the household and the community. The pins, awl, and bodkin give us the most specific information about garment styles of any of the tools, while the spindle whorl and distaff speak more clearly about local textile production. The delicate pins found at the Melanson site suggest that residents were wearing lightweight fabrics, possibly linen caps and fichus for the women and girls. The awl and rings may have been used together to place eyelets on bodices or breeches, lacing plackets confirmed by the presence of a bone bodkin. The simplicity of the bodkin and plain nature of the scissors at Melanson contrast to the silvered scissors and snips found at Beaubassin, suggesting a difference in the way femininity was being constructed and presented in the various communities. This may relate to differences in audience: that is, for whom the display was being created.

Many comments on Acadian productivity appear in letters from both French and British officials. The letters called Acadians indolent, the writers' ire primarily directed at Acadian men for leaving the uplands uncleared and unfarmed to the satisfaction of British administrators.[116] In 1690, Vincent Saccardy, the engineer general for the French crown in Canada, complained about Acadian clearing of the marshlands over the uplands, calling out both the small number of available labourers and their general work ethic.[117] Governor Jacques-François de Monbeton de Brouillan wrote on arrival in 1701 that he had discovered the Acadians of Minas to be living "en vrais républicains, ne reconnaissant ni autorité royale ni justice" – as true republicans, recognizing neither royal authority nor justice – an expression of frustration at a people chafing under imperial control.[118] Later, Richard Philipps, governor of Nova Scotia from 1717 to 1749, described them as "rather a pest, and incumbrance than of an advantage to the Country, being a proud, lazy, obstinate and untractable people, unskilful in the methods of agriculture … they have not in almost a century, cleared the quantity of 300 acres of Woodland. From their Corn and Cattle they have plenty of Dung for manure, which they make no use of, but when it increases so as to become troublesome, then instead of laying it on their Lands they get rid of it by removing their Barns to another spot."[119] Women's work is mentioned only in positive praise for their industry, but there may be an issue of perception at play. Swelling demographics suggest that the number of workers available for farm labour in Acadia had increased, even considering the general distaste for hiring outside servants and hands.[120] Gloria Main has posited a transition point in the colonial consumer economy around 1715, when there was less need for unskilled labour on the farms, freeing up men and women alike to specialize in non-farming occupations.[121] The availability of more hands meant time for activities that some considered luxuries.

Prior to the 1750s, the word "luxury" referred almost entirely to the unearned use of elite goods by those of lower status. Concerns revolved around the blurring of social boundaries, much as concerns in previous centuries about the poor usurping the clothing of the rich led to sumptuary legislation.[122] Rising access to consumer goods and non-subsistence items in the early consumer revolution of the eighteenth century confounded pre-existing categories of those who could afford elite goods and those who could not, an entanglement that changed the meaning behind women's use of luxury sewing tools. Embroidery and sewing scissors found at some Acadian settlements – Melanson, Beaubassin, Belleisle, and among the Acadian residents at French Fortress Louisbourg – indicated that Acadian women were also engaging in this kind of symbolic negotiation.

Women's leisure at Beaubassin and Belleisle may have taken the form of genteel pursuits, changing from subsistence sewing and weaving to embroidery and fancy-work during the day. They sewed and spun in spaces with the potential for social engagement, buying and using decorative tools as a means of displaying further pride in their work. These items expressed multiple messages about industry and skill, but also identification with a particular socio-economic status. This maps onto the ways in which fancy-work was associated with aristocracy for European women. The prevalence of embellished tools at Beaubassin indicates the growth of a new, local social stratum differentiating themselves and triggering anxious commentary from officials concerned about a subtle usurpation of authority.[123] This incorporation of activities marked as genteel, by women called peasants, may have contributed to a certain amount of cognitive dissonance for those looking in. An easy way to reconcile that dissonance would have been to name those luxury activities indolence, or laziness, rather than gentility.

Fancy-work and the attendant idealized domestic femininity stands in contrast to the descriptions of simple Acadian farmers given by English travellers, who saw "clothes pitched on with pitchforks," and the practical reuse of English "scarlet duffil" recycled into homespun skirts.[124] They did whitework and embroidered with colourful silks, spun fine threads with light spindles and wove textiles in domestic settings. Silk lace was imported in quantity, but cotton and linen lace may have been made locally.[125] The fancy embroidery scissors and the silks and ribbons found in Jeanne Thibodeau's sewing equipment, and with Marie Savoie and Marguerite Blanchard at Belleisle, indicate ways in which the women defined themselves through the use of luxury tools. The geometric stylings on the hafts of the decorated embroidery scissors mirror the simple geometry of weaving and stitching, crosses, curves, and squares turning both handles and fabric into works of art.[126]

The social importance of decorative work is doubly underlined in the scissor design, a privileging of artistic expression. The sizes of scissors represented in the

assemblages may hold further answer to the compelling question of "why so many?":
the snips found in quantity at Acadian sites correspond generally with the number
of young women living in their mother's households. Girls would learn sewing at
their mother's knees, beginning with simpler tasks such as hemming and sewing long
seams. A young woman's textile skills were of paramount importance, the ability to
"weave a web of cloth" considered as fundamental to the proper running of a household as a young man's abilities in carpentry and farming.[127] Their sewing kits included
thimbles, needles, and pins, and needed only a single pair of smaller scissors for com-
pletion. Sitting at the fire and on the front stoops of their houses with their mothers,
aunts, and sisters, the girls of Acadia learned the skills they would need for their own
households and gave their communal labour to both household needs and fancy-work.

Imagine, for a moment, the widow Dugas in Louisbourg, sitting on her stoop in
summer or the hearth on a winter's evening, surrounded by her daughters and step-
daughters – sisters, stepsisters, and half-sisters ranging in age from eight to seventeen
and all connected in some way to the major families of Acadia. There they sit, sharing
their hopes for the future, linen for a trousseau golden and warm upon their laps, their
needles flickering in the fire's glow. We can add others to this cozy group. Louisbourg
was home to a network of related Acadian women: Anne le Borgne de Belleisle, first
married to the merchant Jean Baptiste Rodrigue, lived kitty-corner to the widow Dugas;
we might add her to the gathering, along with Joseph's cousin Marguerite Dugas and
her children. Jeanne Thibodeau fits neatly into this network of related women as well,
her brother Michel married to Joseph's first cousin Marie-Agnes Dugas.[128] Based on the
physical evidence, we might even project so far as to include Mme de la Vallière, the
French neighbour across the street, in whose house the matching scissor handle was
found. Evidence of connection and exchange persists even outside of the settlements,
the networks of women keeping their community bonds significant and, even inside the
French fortress, strengthening their growing sense of a new Acadian identity.[129]

The items owned in each settlement were similar in many respects, the Dutch
thimbles, plain steel needles, and copper pins the same imported items used across
the colonies. The differences can be most strikingly seen in the scissors and the needle
cases, items meant to be seen in the context of sewing work and otherwise. Finely
pointed and decorated on the handles, silver-plated or steel, scissors played an important role in Acadian women's structuring and consideration of their roles as women
and providers. Distinct – and yet not entirely divided – from the scissors used by the
women round her, Jeanne Thibodeau's covered scissors reveal something about her
preferred leisure activity alongside her beliefs about her place in Louisbourg society.

The scissors found at the Melanson settlement, on the other hand, tell us that this is not the only force at play. The pairs of scissors found there are plain by comparison to those seen at Belleisle and Louisbourg, with undecorated hafts and clean blades, and no maker's mark or inlay to distract the eye. And yet we know from various censuses that the Melansons were among the wealthiest landowners in Acadia, so the simplicity of the scissors was not due to lack of funds. The settlement was flourishing in 1707, cultivating seventeen arpents of land among six family groups.[130] Basque considers the Melansons to be one of the elite families, or at the very least one of the most locally connected, and analysis of socio-economic differences between the "elite" Acadian families and the poorer settlements found limited differences in the kinds of goods owned.[131]

This difference is heightened when we compare the situation in Belleisle, where the clothing was more rustic, but the sewing equipment fancier. This dichotomy disturbed cultural expectations associated with European gentility, which paired elite femininity with leisure sewing. The disparity between social presentation and coded activity between the women in the banlieue and those in the marsh would have been a source of tension. It was the kind of mismatch that may have increased the general perception of Acadians as moving away from the manners and mannerisms that were so much a part of Continental French social understanding. It is that growing distance from imperial expectation and changes in social cues that suggests a forming perception change, and more justification for those on the outside to begin to see Acadian culture as something *other*. And it is a very short distance at times from "other" to "suspicious."

Fibres and Fabrics

They are in everything good artisans; There's nothing which they cannot
do; And by a hundred different needs inspired, They make the things they
lack ... thus by Their industry, their nakedness is veiled.[1]

— — — — — —

THE GLOBAL TEXTILE TRADE following 1500 saw a steady flow of goods from east
to west, and the fashion shifts that resulted from that broadening of trade networks
impacted Acadia. The specific entanglements of textiles – their physical qualities,
social meanings, and their enmeshment in a web of interdependent exchanges extending beyond the Atlantic world – expanded the range of possibilities for Acadian
clothing. Modern portrayals often show us an Acadia of striped wool skirts and coarse
homespun linen, and popular history overviews do not cover the full range of options
in the region. Wool and linen were certainly mainstays, but local leathers and imported silks and cottons also played surprisingly important roles in Acadian wardrobes.
The Acadian connection to the full breadth of the Atlantic marketplace can be seen in
their textiles, more markers of their participation in the global world of goods.

Interpretation of textile collections gained academic traction beginning in the
1970s, with rising interest in domestic lives and the relatively silent presence of
women in the standard historical narrative. Linda Baumgarten, Joanne Eicher, Ann
Smart-Martin, and Adrienne Hood, among others, engaged with collections and new
theoretical frameworks to design methods for extracting information about societal
values and patterns of behaviour from clothing and textiles.[2] Later scholars elaborated
on those frameworks, bringing in aspects of other disciplines including literary analysis, reconceptualizations of geography, economy, privacy, comfort, and luxury, in
order to understand the vital role textiles have played in the creation of personal and
psychological spaces.[3] The collision between sociological and curatorial approaches in

the discipline led to work that attempted to bridge the two, resulting in a framework for dress studies that was more encompassing than its theoretical predecessors.[4]

In this chapter, we will trace those connections and ideas about textiles, the subtextual understandings the Acadians brought with them during colonization, those they acquired in their new context, and the ways in which those understandings shaped dress choice in Acadian settlements. Colours and dyes, tactile sensations, the ways in which different fabrics aged, frayed, and felted, and the cultural tensions between imported fabrics and homespun all contributed to the types of garments into which yardage was made and the messages those garments could send. The transformative potential of textiles was mirrored in their socio-cultural uses, cloth used as trade good, symbolic gift, a centring force for a community, and an extension to the body.[5] Combinations of textiles created visual transitions that generated new meaning as they blurred the lines between the familiar and the unknown.

CLOTH OF ALL KINDS was an absolute necessity for colonial life, and descriptions of the kinds of textiles in use in Acadia appeared primarily in probate inventories and traders' manifests. The five major fibres of Western pre-industrial civilization – linen, hemp, wool, cotton, and silk – all found homes in Acadian fashion systems next to leathers and furs, though the stories they tell there are different than those of the same textiles found in Paris or London. Objects change meanings as they change contexts, and the presence of Indonesian cotton in Port Royal meant something quite different than the use of French silks in Louisbourg. The biographies of the different fibres and weaves, the hands they passed through, and the reactions of consumers and onlookers to the end results all play a vital role in understanding Acadian relationships with the fabrics that clothed their world.

Fibres entered the weaver's studio with value judgments already placed upon them, symbolism embedded in the different types over centuries of production and trade. The staple length of fibres, their durability, the ways in which they absorbed and held dye, and the possible drapes of the different textiles made from them also created a set of constraints around how clothing could be made, and parameters determining how those garments would look. The physical qualities of different textiles deeply informed the cultural resonance that developed around each, even as the subtexts shifted and new interpretations and symbols were created. The different webs of meaning surrounding textiles for the Mi'kmaq and the Acadians collided and intertwined in complex ways, tensions and ambiguity triggering ripples in multiple directions.

Objects are changed by interactions with human beings, surfaces polished by our touch, impressed with the patina of human sweat and oils. Textiles are unique among objects because of the intensity with which our bodies impress themselves into the clothes we wear. Constrictive and rigid clothing changes the shape of the body inside it, and in return the bodies of the spinners, weavers, cutters, tailors, and wearers dictate the form and structure of the garments. The embodied impact of clothing is different from the messaging that is carried by furnishings, for example, or architecture. The intimate connection between clothing and the body is as intensely personal as the production and consumption of food; in the act of dressing, the flesh is consumed by cloth. As Mary Brooks describes, garments carry evidence of use in themselves, perspiration and scent impressing itself upon the clothes as traces of the dyes and particles of the fibres blend themselves with the wearer's skin.[6]

The human body first intertwined with textiles during the process of production. Threshers and sheep shearers wrestled raw materials with their shoulders and arms, using giant shears to cut away the raw wool and lighten the sheep's summer burden. Heavy mallets or brakes thudded against the ground or threshing floor to break the long, hard flax fibres. Whether using a wheel or a drop spindle, a seventeenth- and eighteenth-century spinner teased out the fibres with her fingers and, with linen, her saliva or drops of water smoothed the thread as she twisted it into being. Before the advent of the power loom, weaving similarly depended on the weaver's body to generate form, tension, and strength. The ways in which the weaver structured the warp, threw his shuttle, and beat down the weft all contributed to differences in the final product. Stretched, shaped, fulled, beaten, kneaded by hand or brushed to raise the nap, the finished textiles were cut to specific shape and size to fit individuals rather than standardized sizes.

Fabrics came in bales of dozens of aunes as well as in shorter lengths, and could be cut to size as is, or treated and manipulated to become something new. Acadian textile producers were aware of but not constrained by Continental styles, and Acadian buyers unravelled red wool yardage, using the resulting yarn as weft threads for striped homespun.[7] Reworking the materials that had been produced by European bodies, they unmade imported textiles, incorporated dyestuffs from their local environment to recolour plain fabrics, and ultimately re-marked the warps and wefts with body rhythms of their own.

A weave was as much a declaration of the identity of the weaver as of the wearer. Weavers, once finished their apprenticeships, would adjust the weaves and setts they had learned by rote: using five shots of white instead of four on a common stripe pattern, or adjusting the colour balance to a preferred palette. As much as their bodies played with the rhythm of the loom, the weavers' tastes and individual styles were displayed along with their prowess on the bodies of their customers and families. Imported wools and knitted silk stockings in Beaubassin would have stood out against the homespun striped wools made by familiar weavers, or the *indiennes* and silk gowns worn in Louisbourg. Holland linen was used for fancy cuffs and caps, or made into shirts worn underneath homespun, and leather and wood were turned into moccasins and clogs suitable for the marshes and muddy ground.

While no textiles from the pre-deportation era have been recovered so far, there are similarities between the weaving of Acadian refugees from Louisiana communities and examples from those in Canadian communities from the eighteenth and nineteenth centuries that suggest a common origin. A consistent pattern of alternating stripes appears in post-deportation weaves in multiple parts of the Acadian diaspora. Another consistent feature noticed by weaving expert Dorothy K. Burnham is the so-called "barberpole twist," a manipulation of two weft threads, one dark and one light, spun together to create a visibly twisted stripe.[8] A survey of surviving French wool samples from early eighteenth-century sources shows that stripes were popular, but none display the same use of barberpole twist in the weft, or the same pattern of mirrored stripes seen in Acadian weaving.[9] As the technique appears in weaving styles consistent across Acadian diaspora groups who had endured minimal contact with one another since the deportation, it stands to reason that the barberpole twist was something developed by Acadian weavers after leaving France, but prior to the deportations. This may be the design innovation that helped define the distinctive "tissu acadien" produced in Belle-Ile-en-Mer in the 1760s.[10]

The ratio of imported goods to homespun used in Acadia varied throughout the century of occupation. Higher quantities of basic textiles were purchased early in the settlements' histories, before land could be cleared and flax farmed in great enough quantity, and before flocks of sheep were established to provide wool. In 1670, despite having a local production economy robust enough to supply Quebec with 6,000 lbs of salted beef, Acadians still needed to import textiles and pre-made clothing, some of which was sent by Intendent Jean Talon as part of the exchange for the meat.[11]

Linen and wool were the primary textiles in use in colonial Acadia. Some of that fabric was locally produced, but contrary to some contemporary reports, not all.

Local production was supplemented with imported textiles, some of which were of better quality than those which Acadians were able to produce. The proportion of locally made textiles to imports varied over the course of Acadian history. The first few decades would have been clothed almost entirely by imported fabrics, especially prior to the introduction of sheep. Later, wool and flax were both exported from Acadia in enough quantity to be recorded by colonial officials, even as wool textiles and linens continued to be imported from around the Atlantic.[12] Cotton and silk could not be produced locally with any success thanks to the climate and short growing season. Cotton was imported from India, France, and, later, from the West Indies, and while attempts at sericulture had been made in New England from 1616 until the nineteenth century, most ended in failure. Silk brought in by French traders nevertheless enjoyed a place on Acadian bodies in a number of different forms, from ribbons and laces, to velvets and damasks, to luxurious knitted stockings (see the section on Silk in this chapter). Textile trade networks connected the globe in the early modern period, trade routes in Asia facilitating the exchange of cotton and silk for spices and dyes. These materials made their way into the West, bolts of fabric arriving in Europe carrying the aesthetics, scents, and cachet of the distant East. Chintzes and indiennes appear in Louisbourg inventories in large quantities, a link between Acadia, France, and southern India's Coromandel Coast, a centre for textile production. Through Boston trade, Acadia could access silks, more Indian cottons, and fine worsted wools. In the 1680s, trader Henri Brunet brought yards of fine Holland linen; the East India Companies imported woollens and cottons; and silk ribbons, thread, and accessories came in through Acadian and Boston-based merchants.[13]

The environment played an important role in Acadian choices, the harsh, wet winters in Mi'kma'ki very different than those of their home provinces in western France. The clothing worn in expanding Acadia would have resembled that of France to a greater degree in those first years, but even then, local resources must have had an effect on the overall look. With familiar plants unavailable and imported dyestuffs limited and expensive, settlers would have been forced to turn to local flora to find materials to use for dyeing. One likely route for that education was through contact with Mi'kmaw wives of early settlers, or from trading partners living close by. Even intermittent and occasional contact may have taught Acadian dyers about local resources like goldthread (yellow dye), alder bark (tan/brown), marsh bedstraw (red), yew (green), and hemlock (tan/grey).[14]

Fashionable styles of fabrics changed quickly, shifts in weight and colour of which settlers were certainly aware. A 1733 letter from a trader to Mme Péré, a fashionable French businesswoman in Louisbourg with family connections to Acadia, confirms that those living in and around the town were aware of the changes in Continental fashion, even though their access was limited.[15] The distance between the metropole and the colonies was enough to create lag between the emergence of a new fashion in Paris and its arrival in Louisbourg, but generally that lag was a matter of months rather than years. Pierre Joubert, Mme Péré's French agent, writes to her with his apologies at not being able to find the specific red and white floral damask she had requested. He sends a different green damask instead, "of the latest style, the one that is now worn in France."[16] The weeks the textile would take to come across the Atlantic would not be enough to make Mme Péré's daughter's trousseau out of step with contemporary style.

The heavy fabrics of the baroque gave way to the new draperies and light colours that typified the rococo in the eighteenth century, a new pastoralism demanding light, airy, and above all, nature-inspired design.[17] Florals were popular in Louisbourg, many of the most fashionable fabric lengths and garments, described in the probate inventories as "a [sic] fleur" or "avec fleurs."[18] Goods that travelled through Minas, however, were more often checked or striped. From the limited evidence available, Acadians in the Minas basin settlements seem to have embraced the stripes and squares that subverted as well as complemented the nature that surrounded them. Set against the lush greens and blues of the lakes and forests, the vibrant reds and golds of ginghams and wools made splashes of colour against the fields. In the city – and likely in both the banlieue settlement of Melanson and the trading hub of Beaubassin, where European clothing accessories show up more frequently – the sinuous florals of the eighteenth-century fabric designers brought them back to nature. If, as Naomi Griffiths argues, French officials wanted their colonies to be the reflection of the best of what the empire had to offer, the alterations to costume made by the Acadians in response to both their new environment and different access to materials would have been a blow to imperial pride.[19] This may be one of the reasons for early French travellers' somewhat disparaging commentary on Acadian dress – that it no longer looked like the high fashion of France but was becoming a style all of its own.

Weaving and Production

Acadian weavers had barn-frame looms, though equipment shortages were reported in the 1670s in a supply request to Quebec for looms made there.[20] Archaeology has yet to turn up any evidence relating to those looms, but smaller finds such as scissors, pins, and thimbles open up a window onto Acadian production techniques.[21]

The only professional weaver listed on the Acadian censuses was Mathieu Martin (ca 1636 – ca 1724), resident of Belleisle.[22] Martin does not appear to have married and had no children, nor any recorded apprentices, and following his death in 1724, no other Acadian is listed as a professional weaver. A second option for locally produced textiles appeared in the form of the itinerant weaver, a familiar figure in colonial New England and one for which there is some evidence later in the Acadian story. For a fee, the weaver would set up his reed and harness on a family's loom with the warp threads already wound onto the warp beam, removing the need for him to build a portable frame.[23] He would weave with a weft provided by the household, cut off the woven textile at the agreed-upon length, and then carry the remainder of his warp on to the next client. A surviving nineteenth-century reed and harness belonging to Acadian weavers Wilfred and Charles Boudreau, currently in a private collection, is still strung with a cotton warp. Wool and linen would have been more likely for local production in the seventeenth and early eighteenth centuries.[24]

Acadian households were weaving for themselves by 1686, as the Bishop of Quebec Jean-Baptiste de la Croix de Chevrières de Saint-Vallier described during his tour of the region.[25] This would have been a recent development, as looms were among the badly needed supplies sent to Acadia from Quebec in 1671.[26] These weavers were not yet all women, Vallier's description referring to men among the group as well.[27] His commentary about the manufacture of "coarse homespun of inadequate quantities" likely correctly reflects the status quo in 1686 when the Acadian settlements were new and poorly provisioned, but that status quo would not last. Once the land was cleared for farming and herds of sheep introduced to the region, Acadians harvested, spun, and wove their own linen and wool. They had a system of division of labour and work sharing within kin groups that undoubtedly extended into textile production as deeply as they relied upon it for maintaining the marsh dykes. Surette's maps of Acadian homesteads in the Beaubassin region show closely related kin groups living in close proximity, holdings expanding outward as subsequent generations claimed new lands on the outskirts of their current farmsteads.[28] Shared labour was an extremely efficient way of processing fibres and threads into textiles, as the productivity of at least five or six carders and spinners was necessary to supply one full-time weaver.[29]

The fashion for light-coloured plain silks in France in the early 1700s could be replicated on the old two-shaft looms used in French backwaters and the colonies, but the shiny, smooth satins and sateens required more complex machinery – five or more shafts at minimum.[30] The basic tabby weave of the two-shaft looms found complexity in stripes and checks, and in pattern bands made by changing colours in the weft. The maximum fabric width on the two-shaft looms was defined by the arm span of the weaver, with textiles generally woven in widths of 27, 36, or 45 inches.[31] Heavy, two-man looms were used elsewhere to try and increase that maximum width, but the major innovation that allowed for increased width of yardage, the flying shuttle, was only patented in 1733 and did not enter into widespread use until the 1760s.[32]

Contemporary accounts from writers like Villebon and Dièreville describe Acadian women making much of their families' clothing at home, processing and weaving flax and wool, but not whether the women worked together or in solitude, more during one season than another, or even the general rhythms of their day.[33] During the seasons when materials were readily available, the daylight lingered longer and travel between homesteads and settlements was easiest, but fabric production would by necessity happen throughout the year. A nineteenth-century description of Acadian traditions in and around Chéticamp describes a communal event similar to those noted in earlier writings:

> When the warm days of summer began, everyone sheared their sheep. Then, outdoors, in large cauldrons, the wool was boiled, to wash it. After drying in the sun, it was teased so that it would be easier to card. It was then ready for the carding bee. Neighbourhood women and other friends were invited with their carding combs and their aprons. With ten or twelve carders, the wool was soon done. After a few hours of work, and a lot of gossip, the wool piled up in front of each carder in soft rolls ready to be spun.[34]

Communal and intergenerational work appears in the customs of Louisiana Acadians as well, where textile crafts were passed on to children by older female relations. Grandmothers were particularly important in this transmission of skills and behaviours in multi-generational communities, which fits with the descriptions offered in contemporary and later sources.[35] Inheritance traditions in Acadia often included elderly parents giving their sons their land and house as their abilities to work the land and livestock dwindled. Many of these properties were deeded to the next generation in return for the promise of lifetime maintenance, which included enough cloth annually – likely wool – to be made into a new outfit.[36] The same behaviours are present in all the communities surrounding the Acadians both temporally and geographically, two distinct diaspora groups (post-deportation Chéticamp and Louisiana) engaging in the same patterns of activity.

Domestic weavers relied on the efforts of daughters and younger women in the community for the hundreds of hours of labour needed to spin thread and warp the looms. As with women in New England villages, the young women of affiliated families would move back and forth between households sharing domestic labour.[37] The exchanges made as part of this communal labour, different from the guild system of vertical transmission of knowledge from master to apprentice, made creative synergy more likely. Gossip and news – sometimes one and the same – were passed on during these meetings, keeping households engaged socially and politically with the world around them. As Acadian weaving shifted from the professional into the domestic sphere, the patterns and methods learned from other women in the community reified themselves, inspiration begetting inspiration, forming distinct styles unknown elsewhere.[38]

Textile Seals and Inventories

Artifacts related to textile production and sale survive in the archaeological context of the Maritimes where the textiles themselves do not. While spindles, distaffs, and scissors can teach us about local production, the lead textile seal gives us physical evidence of the presence of imported fibre goods. Seals were stamped lead discs used as identification tags for merchandise that passed through various European hands, marking quantities, weights, original manufacturer or licensed importer for tax and export duty records. Prior to the Industrial Revolution cloth was produced in a cottage industry, where workers with their own looms would take in raw materials and produce cloth for resale. Production consistency became a concern, leading to the introduction of this system to control for differences in quality.[39] Seals from bolts and bales of finished textiles appear at multiple colonial sites. Some of the coats of arms and company names marked on surviving seals can be identified, while others are more obscure.

To date, across these four sites, archaeologists have recovered a total of 107 lead seals.[40] Cathrine Davis's excellent recent study on French colonial seals identified ninety-one seals in Louisburg's archaeological collections, but none could be directly associated with a known Acadian context.[41] Of the sixteen seals from the other three sites, and two from nearby sites Pointe-aux-Vieux and Grand Pré, fourteen have enough information on them to attempt identification, and six are blank or include only a sequence of numbers.

FIGURE 3.1 • Textile seals, Blanchard house, Belleisle.

Intriguingly, two of the seals found at Beaubassin are silk seals from the city of Nîmes, the text around the outer edges identifying them as belonging to importers of silk stockings. Silk accessories, as with fancy embroidery scissors, carried connotations of status, and their presence at Beaubassin fits with other evidence of performative display in the region.[42] A third seal found at Beaubassin bears the royal seal and arms of the Compagnie des Indes, originally attached to écarlatines designated for the fur trade, and two others have the seal of the Sceaux de contrôle in the French city of Mazamet (figure 3.2). While Mazamet later became famous as a wool production centre, in the seventeenth and early eighteenth centuries it was better known as a site for dyeing and finishing the coarser woollen textiles commonly used for clothing items in North America, particularly among the voyageurs and habitants.[43]

The quantity of seals found at Beaubassin is high for a site of this size when compared with the small number of seals found to date at other Acadian settlements (see table 3.1), and the inclusion of a textile seal from the Compagnie des Indes is a strong suggestion of trade with the Mi'kmaq. Beaubassin was in an ideal location to become a hub for the fur trade, and textiles brought from New England and Louisbourg would have been exchanged with Mi'kmaw traders.[44] The Compagnie des Indes had the monopoly on the fur trade between 1719 and 1763, importing English strouds marked with their own seal. By the 1750s, the Compagnie was supplying between 1,000–1,200 pieces of cloth per year directly into the fur trade market. Indigenous buyers preferred wool to linens, sales of wool from Philadelphia traders outstripping linen at a ratio of three or four to one.[45] Jacques Bourgeois, the first French settler at Beaubassin, had

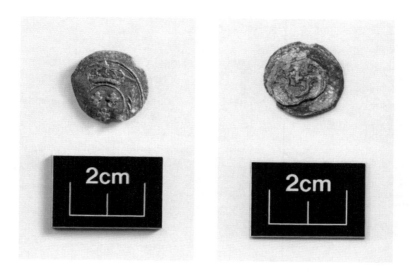

FIGURE 3.2 • Textile seal with the mark of the town of Mazamet, Beaubassin.

been trading with the Mi'kmaq of Chignecto for forty years before moving his family there. The Indigenous village of Oesgag, about 8 kilometres away as the crow flies, would have been a natural trading partner once he was fully settled.

The nature of travel between Acadia and other colonized areas, the relationships between Acadians and both Indigenous and settler groups, and their engagement with the natural environment all played major roles in the textiles they acquired and influenced how those textiles were used. The types of fabrics worn by Acadian women in Louisbourg are recorded in inventories, lists of belongings, creditors, and debts officially recorded post-mortem and, in one case, prior to a second marriage. Fashionable fabrics like *siamoises* and silk damasks appear in more than one inventory, alongside painted indienne chintzes, calico cottons, and inexpensive drugget wools. Personal inventories include wool and cotton, while shop inventories from Acadian merchants show velvets, silks, and lace available for sale in large quantities. The textile names recorded in those inventories can be difficult to interpret, changed often, and in many cases were different from those used today. Those names can sometimes help us identify a point of origin, as fabrics were often named for their place of manufacture but may also carry the name of their target market. Surviving swatch books from eighteenth-century textile producers preserve samples of the popular fabrics of the day as well as their prices, which make for useful cross-reference.[46]

TABLE 3.1 • Textile seals found at Acadian sites

Location	Quant.	Associated textile	Seal type
Beaubassin	2	Silk stockings	Single-disc lead seal, series C type,[1] NIMES / COL NEM
Beaubassin	2	Wool	Two-disc lead seal with stamped rivet, Controle de Mazamet
Beaubassin	1	Écarlatines (red wool stroud trade cloth) for use in the fur trade	Type A two-disc with rivet, stamped on one side with the French royal arms, on the other with the Arms of the Compagnie des Indes (French East India Company).[2]
Beaubassin	2	Unidentified	Numbers only / R + fleur de lys + unknown second letter, above a pair of feathers or stalks of wheat. The seal with the imagery is most likely a cloth worker's personal seal, with the R and unknown letter marking the owner's initials.
Beaubassin	3	Non-classifiable lead or copper fragments	
Belleisle	1	Unidentified	Two-disc lead seal with stamped rivet, overlapping ferns, 303.
Belleisle	1	Unidentified	Two-disc lead seal with stamped rivet, ostrich and branches image, border with fleur de lys and leaves. Possibly Mazamet / gallic cock. 4316 numerals in same style as Michilimackinac seal Type 1, Variety M, Figure 175d (Stone 285)
Belleisle	1	Unidentified	A two-piece seal, the number 302 scratched on one side. Obverse folded over, part of a crest visible, with ferns below and feathers or leaves visible under the fold.
Belleisle	1	Unidentified	Blank single-disc seal, attached with wire.
Melanson	1	Unidentified	Numbers only, round seal.
Grand Pré	1	Likely to be Écarlatines (red wool stroud trade cloth). Associated with English encampment ca 1755.	Type A two-disc with rivet, stamped on one side with the French royal arms, on the other with the Arms of the Compagnie des Indes.[3]
Pointe-aux-Vieux	1	Silk or lightweight wool	Two-disc lead seal with rivet, lion passant stamped on obverse, reverse blank. Badge of Lyons.
Total	18		

NOTES

1 "(1) Series A, two disks connected by a flange; (2) Series B, one disk with a flange; and (3) Series C, one disk, perforated to allow wire or cord to be passed through it." Adams, "Lead Seals from Fort Michilimackinac," 1.

2 Prinet, "Antoine Sabatier," 397; Wellington, *French East India Companies*, 21.

3 Prinet, "Antoine Sabatier," 397; Wellington, *French East India Companies*, 21.

Linen

Garments worn next to the skin were made almost exclusively from linen, as were shifts and shirts, kerchiefs and cravats, sheets, tablecloths, and napkins – a large percentage of the trappings of everyday life.[47] Linen's durability and the ease of washing and bleaching made it uniquely suited to those intimate roles. Linen fibres come from the flax plant, *Linum usitatissimum*. Flax is a hungry plant and requires fertile soil, ideally space that has never previously been used for growing flax, and the newly drained and cleared marshes and pastures around the Bay of Fundy were ideal for this purpose. Flax is most useful for fabric if harvested during flowering rather than later in its growth cycle, and common practice was to sow two plots – one to process into fibres, and a second, smaller plot to ripen and provide seed for the next year.[48] Roche estimates that approximately 60 per cent of rural French households were engaged in linen production in the seventeenth and eighteenth centuries, and based on the land-clearance records in early Acadian censuses, this figure can also be extended to Acadia.[49]

Expensive imported linen appeared on manifests from merchants serving Acadia throughout the colony's history. Trader Henri Brunet's logbooks from the later decades of the seventeenth century list sales of yards of "ollonne," or Holland cloth – fine European linen. Germany, Holland, Flanders, and France were the major linen exporters, the Dutch Holland linen of generally high quality. In 1673, Brunet delivered approximately sixteen yards to a customer near Fort Pentagouët, and more to Plaisance. He traded with Charles Melanson in Acadia, bringing his fine fabrics to the family's new settlement, and later that same year Brunet made a request to his sister to have more fabric shipped to him in Pentagouët by the first available vessel.[50]

Linen came in a wide range of qualities, with an equally wide range of prices. Margaret Spufford isolated ranges for basic linen in the late seventeenth century (1660–1705) as between 5.3–22 pence per yard, and Holland specifically ranging from 20.6–89.1 pence per yard.[51] The French aune was approximately equivalent to 0.71 yards, so doing the math shows that the Acadians Brunet served were buying fairly high-quality imported linen.[52] By comparison, Montreal's habitants purchased linen cloth of the quality normally associated with the fur trade: unbleached hemp, along with some bleached linens and *mélis* from the Indies.[53]

Production of linen increased in Acadia as the settlement grew: "Flax and hemp, also, grow extremely well, and some of the settlers of that region use only the linen, made by themselves, for domestic purposes."[54] Villebon confirmed this observation the same year: "As for the women they are always busy, and most of them keep their

TABLE 3.2 • Imported linen for sale in Acadia

Type	Price	Year	Location
White toile	20 s / aune	1750[1]	Louisbourg
"Bretagne"	30 s / aune	1750	Louisbourg
"Household linen"	36 s / aune	1750	Louisbourg
White toile	36 s / aune	1750	Louisbourg
Cambric	22 £ 10 s / piece (no lengths given)	1750	Louisbourg
"Toile de Bretagne"	30 s / aune	1754[2]	Louisbourg

NOTES

1 Notariat de l'Ile Royale, "Inventaire des biens meubles appartenant à Jacques Philipe Urbin Rondeau."
2 Notariat de l'Ile Royale (Greffe de Bacquerisse), "Inventaire des biens meubles appartenant à Marie Josephe Le Borgne de Belisle."

husbands and children in serviceable linen materials ... which they make skillfully from the hemp they have grown."[55] Frederick Cozzens quoted Abbé Reynal from the 1730s in saying, "Their usual clothing was in general the produce of their own flax ... with these they made common linens and coarse cloths."[56] Most descriptions of Acadian farming activities include the production of linen cloth as one of women's domestic chores, and early land grants along Baie Sainte-Marie stipulated that the grantees must cultivate "20 square rods of flax," one-eighth of an acre, as a condition of holding the land.[57] The six pounds of seed that could be planted in that amount of space would produce enough fibre flax annually for nine men's shirts.[58]

Correspondence from Mathieu de Goutin, lieutenant general for justice in Acadia, describes local flax production in the first decade of the eighteenth century as being so plentiful that it was one of the materials exported to Boston in return for iron, tools, and manufactured goods.[59] Purchase of linen from traders was not a matter of necessity by this point, but from a desire for something of finer quality, or with a different embedded significance. Descriptors of Acadian linen like "serviceable" and "common" do not suggest overly fine work, and it may be that the strain of flax grown in Acadia did not lend itself to more delicate fibres. While extraordinarily useful as a textile, linen is difficult to spin and to weave. Its "sticky" quality means that it takes more labour hours to process the same amount of fibre into yardage than for wool, for example, or cotton.[60]

Linen was an important symbol for the European body in colonial situations, serving as a marker of a particular conception of civilization and cleanliness derived from linen's unique cultural position as a second skin. Linen marked European-ness in a way that no other textile did, intricately bound up with early modern notions of bodily cleanliness and health. A person's health was understood to be directly related to the cleanliness and condition of the linen they wore, and the fineness of those linens was an indication of wealth and elite status.[61] The Mi'kmaq tended to be uninterested in linen, preferring water bathing for cleanliness and English wools for clothing, and so the purchase and use of fine linen by Acadians was one way in which Acadians could differentiate their communities.[62] Wearing linen, in shirts, bonnets, or elegant cuffs, was a means of reaffirming some aspects of Acadian visual culture as specifically elite and European.

Hemp

Hemp appears in contemporary references from 1670 onwards, often, but not always, in conjunction with flax and linen textiles.[63] Villebon's conflation of linen and hemp was not a matter of mistaken identity, but one in line with contemporary usage. Coming from the *Cannabis sativa* plant and growing up to eight feet tall, hemp produced long fibres, coarser than linen, that could be woven alone or mixed with linen, wool, or both to create a strong, durable textile. It did produce a greater yield in smaller spaces, however, making it an efficient crop associated more strongly with earlier homesteading. Inexpensive and commonly used, hemp did not carry the same elite messaging as fine linen. It implied European styles and bathing habits, but was not a status-generating textile like fine imported Dutch cloth.[64]

Contemporary accounts of hemp use differ from one another. Villebon describes the way hemp was grown and used in Acadia, and Régis Brun has confirmed that hemp seeds were imported to Acadia from France from the seventeenth century onward.[65] Delabat, on the other hand, complained that the Acadians in the St John River Valley were too lazy to make use of the local version of the resource: "The St. John River is a very convenient site for a large settlement, for commerce and for trade ... In certain places there is a great deal of wild hemp, which is said to be good for making cloth, but the settlers neglect it because of the effort it requires to go and get it."[66] Brook Watson, writing eight decades later, described hemp as being among the major textiles used in Acadia.[67] While hemp and flax were often conflated in documentation, *Cannabis sativa* seeds found in an Acadian well on the Oudy property on Prince Edward Island provide physical evidence of hemp use prior to the deportation.[68] Local hemp was also used by the Mi'kmaq, and seeds have been found at pre-contact and early-contact Mi'kmaw and

Maliseet sites.[69] The majority of the hemp grown and processed in the colonies became sail canvas, packaging goods for transport, and cordage for naval use. Some of Acadia's hemp was turned into clothing, including heavier working shirts and shifts, scarves, and fichus for casual wear. Hemp could not be bleached or dyed very easily, and the textiles made with it were not as colourful as those made from cotton, wool, or silk.[70]

Wool

Wool was the main fibre used for warm outerwear – jackets, cloaks, capes, practical skirts, and more. Wool gowns and robes were worn extensively in the medieval and early modern periods, with a linen layer commonly worn beneath to provide a barrier between wool and the skin. Accessories and other smaller garments were made from wool as well, including bonnets, mittens, and petticoats. We see higher use of wool in the rural settlements than in Louisbourg, where Acadian women wore more silk and cotton.[71] Stockings were often made from wool, though silk hose and hose made from wool with silk inserts or embroidery were available in both Louisbourg and Beaubassin (see above under Textile Seals and Inventories).

Between 80 and 90 per cent of the fabric imported into New France was wool, brought in from places like Normandy, Limbourg, and Paris.[72] English and French woollens had a distinctly different hand – that is, the softness, drape, and texture of the finished cloth.[73] English wool was described as superior due to its longer fibre staple, which could be used for flatter, more durable wools like worsteds, while French woollens were softer and often fuzzy to the touch, presenting an aesthetic that was more relaxed than crisp.[74] The general perception was that the English woollens were hardier and longer-lasting, accounting for their popularity among labourers and travellers:

> [P]eople praise them [French cloths] for their pliantness and easy wear; and though they are in reality greatly inferior to the English, many prefer them for this reason ... a very little beating brings the Cloth into a Body, and when finished it is soft, pliant, and very fit for wear ... They never crack, and the Looseness of the Woofe Thread rising from time to time, keeps them from wearing thread bare. Our [English] hard cloths are liable to grow bare at the seams; these never do, because they are less harsh. [French cloths] are fitter for gentlemen's service than for labouring people.[75]

Hard-wearing worsteds became closely associated with Indigenous and indigenized wardrobes, connections with the voyageurs and habitants continuing that movement of structured, plain-coloured wool cloth into a new intersectional space. The red strouds, or *écarlatines*, were of particular interest to Indigenous traders. The Compagnie des Indes had the monopoly on importing écarlatines to French territories between 1719 and 1763, the destination almost invariably Indigenous communities. The moisture-wicking qualities of the wool compared favourably to leather, and early introduction of deep indigo blue strouds earned these textiles quick integration into Indigenous wardrobes.[76] Though they could be purchased directly from English sources in British-occupied regions, French traders brought in smuggled strouds that had not been subject to English duties and could be sold for cheaper.[77]

Haliburton's description of the "coarse cloths" worn by Acadian men could mean that the Acadians were not adept at nor interested in weaving finer textiles, as has been the traditional interpretation, but could also be an assumption on his part that anything of higher quality must have been imported.[78] The shorter wool fibres used for the softer-napped, fuzzier woollen yarns required only carding, while the long fibres for the harder, less-fibrous worsteds were carded and then combed with different tools. Acadian women carded their wool but did not comb it, meaning the fleeces they prepared and the wool cloth they produced would have been softer, much closer in texture and appearance to French woollens than English worsteds. Woollens were made with a raised nap, the surface brushed to give a textured surface, and they draped around the body with more flow and less constructed stiffness. This difference could also easily account for some of the disparaging commentary made by English commentators about Acadian sloppiness of dress, as the soft flow of woollens with their raised surface created a more organic, less architectural silhouette than the straighter lines of crisp worsteds.[79]

In addition to woollens and worsteds, there were many named types of wool imported to Acadia from different points of origin, with their own unique appearances and uses. Druggets, tiretaines, and mazamet wools appear in inventories alongside silk-wool blend poplins and glazed calimancos.[80] The cheap woollens sold at 25s / aune, while the heavy cloak wools and plush velvets sold for 6£ / aune, a wide range of prices as well as qualities.[81] The number of inexpensive types of wool available suggests either that buyers valued imports over homespun, or that the colonies could not provide themselves with enough wool to cover the basics, or a combination of both (see chapter 1 under Allies and Smugglers).

TABLE 3.3 • Imported wool for sale in Acadia

Type	Price	Year	Location
Red cloth	3 s / yard	1691[1]	Port Royal
Red cloth	11 s 8 d / yard	1691	Port Royal
Blue cloth	11 s 8 d / yard	1691	Port Royal
Blue cloth	15 s / yard	1691	Port Royal
Serge	1£ 17 s 10 d / 2 pieces	1691	Port Royal
Red serge	—	1696/7[2]	Cape Sable
Segovie (likely segovienne, "a hairy twilled flannel," popular in the seventeenth century for upholstery)[3]	25 s / aune	1750[4]	Louisbourg
"Toile de brin commune"	25 s / aune	1750	Louisbourg
"Tortaine" (tiretaine – a coarse fabric made from all wool, or as a linsey/woolsey)	30 s / aune	1750	Louisbourg
Carises (Flemish serge)	30 s / aune	1750	Louisbourg
"Droguet de poitou" (narrow, lightweight wool or wool/silk blend)[5]	32 s / aune	1750	Louisbourg
Camlet (wool/silk/hair blend)	35 s / aune	1750	Louisbourg
Calmande (glazed/pressed wool)	38 s / aune	1750	Louisbourg
Estamine (lightweight worsted wool)[6]	40 s / aune	1750	Louisbourg
Dourgne	46 s / aune	1750	Louisbourg
"Ras de Marroq" (Moroccan Rash, one of the new draperies)	50 s / aune	1750	Louisbourg
Mazamet	55 s / aune	1750	Louisbourg
Papeline (wool/silk blend)	3£ 10 s / aune	1750	Louisbourg
"Panne Marron" (brown wool velvet)	5£ / aune	1750	Louisbourg
Grey "Gros drape" (heavier wool)	6£ / aune	1750	Louisbourg
Blue plush (wool velvet)	6£ / aune	1750	Louisbourg
Calimanco (pressed or glazed wool)	40 s / aune	1754[7]	Louisbourg
Brown drugget	40 s / aune	1754	Louisbourg
Brushed drugget	42 s / aune	1754	Louisbourg
Mazamet gase frisee (brushed-nap wool gauze)	50 s / aune	1754	Louisbourg
Sky blue papeline (wool/silk blend)	50 s / aune	1754	Louisbourg
"Bource"	3£ / aune	1754	Louisbourg
Poplin (lightweight wool/silk blend)	3£ / aune	1755[8]	Louisbourg

NOTES

1 "Invoice of Merchandise from Abraham Boudrot."
2 Welsteed, "Certificate by William Welsteed."
3 Montgomery, *Textiles in America*, 344.
4 Notariat de l'Ile Royale, "Inventaire des biens meubles appartenant à Jacques Philipe Urbin Rondeau."
5 Montgomery, *Textiles in America*, 226–7.
6 Ibid., 235.
7 Notariat de l'Ile Royale (Greffe de Bacquerisse), Inventaire des biens meubles appartenant à Marie Josephe Le Borgne de Belisle."
8 Notariat de l'Ile Royale, "Inventaire de la communauté de Marguerite Terriau, veuve de Pierre Boisseau."

Associated with hardy homespun and with local trade, single-colour wools were characteristic of lives lived at a distance from imperial control. The stripes and bar- berpole twists that developed in Acadian-woven wools created a new visual contrast to the solid strouds, as well as to the lightweight floral and checked cottons popular in wealthier settlements. The different textures of English and French woollens gave them different characters, rendering the garments made from them stiffer or softer, respectively, and the visible differences between types of wools and lighter garment fabrics like silk and cotton affected perceptions of Acadians both among themselves and from outside observers. In a period where access to many textiles was still legis- lated and there were strong associations between elite status and dress, rural Acadian use of cloth "fitter for gentlemen's service" would be enough to raise some eyebrows.[82]

Cotton

Cotton was a relatively new fibre for Western garments in the early modern period. Until the second half of the seventeenth century cottons were primarily employed for home decor, only becoming fashionable for clothing in the West around the 1660s. Cotton made steady inroads into European fashion following its introduction, thanks to its combination of durability and lightness, as well as properties that made dyes more colourfast.[83] At first adopted primarily by men, by the early eighteenth century in col- onies such as Montreal and Louisiana, cotton was predominantly worn by women.[84] Cotton's lightweight nature also made it a reasonable substitute for silk in some ap- plications, and the lighter, floatier styles of the rococo became more accessible as a result. That availability allowed for the fashions of the courts to spread more rapidly through the population.[85] Novelty played a large role in the popular adoption of cotton textiles, particularly indiennes, printed calicoes, chintzes, and other *toiles peintes*. By the years 1740–82, up to a quarter of European homes and wardrobes across all social levels included some cotton in dress or furnishings.[86]

Techniques of printing on cotton fabric entered France in the late seventeenth cen- tury via Armenian dyers who settled in Marseilles, who themselves had learned the techniques of colour-fast mordants and dyes from experts in Persia and the Levant.[87] French-printed calicoes were inferior, the European manufacturers' skills not equal to those of the talented painters in South Asia, and public interest in the high-quality original indiennes was viewed as a major threat. As a consequence of their rising popularity, the import of cottons was heavily taxed and finally banned in England,

Femme de Qualité en déshabillé détoffe Siamoise.

FIGURE 3.3 • *Femme de qualité en déshabillé d'étoffe Siamoise*, French, 1687. J.D. de Saint-Jean, *Recueil des modes de la cour de France*. Photograph © 2022, Museum of Fine Arts, Boston.

France, Spain, and Prussia between 1686 and 1721, leading in some cases to riots and assaults on women wearing Indian calicoes.[88] Cotton consumption was encouraged in the colonies, however, as the trade duties on cotton were a useful revenue stream, and the law against indiennes was rarely enforced in New France.[89] Textiles imported to North America from the various east India companies (EOC, VOC, CdI) originated in India and in China, even after the early seventeenth-century rise in attempts to replicate the prints in Europe. Cotton production in the West Indies – and the slave trade linked with it – rose only in the early eighteenth century; by 1700 cotton accounted for only 2–4 per cent of the value of plantation exports.[90]

Woven brocades and stripes had been a part of the European textile portfolio for centuries, the more complex patterns reserved for those who could afford the extra time needed by the weaver to set up the more complex patterns on their looms.[91] The major production advantage of cottons was that they could be easily block-printed with colour-fast repeating patterns, opening the doors to vibrantly embellished fabrics without the labour and materials costs of embroidery, hand-painting, or appliqués. These new colour-fast fabrics brought an astonishing fluidity of pattern to the scene. Floral sprigs and pale, curling lines writhed across dark backgrounds on Indian cottons, a colour palette that would soon be reversed under exporter pressure to appeal to European tastes.[92] Manufacturers also changed their large patterns to small repeats and borders better suited for European styles of skirts and gowns. Indiennes seem to have been worn mostly by women, and records from confiscated garments in France during the ban period show that the print fabrics were mostly being used for gowns, with the rest used for handkerchiefs, fichus, petticoats, and mantles.[93]

Cotton disrupted a textile system built around ideas of appropriate and inappropriate dress, centuries of sumptuary legislation restricting silks, furs, and other expensive textiles to the closets of the elites. As a new fibre, cotton began its reign from outside that system, arriving on the European fashion scene with no preconceived notions attached. Calicoes and indiennes entered European markets as luxury textiles, equivalent to silks and tinsels. They soon descended across socio-economic barriers, however, with the rising popularity of more affordable and locally made replicas and inferior imports. Ginghams and checks were lower-priced and lower-prestige styles, and striped variations like siamoises quickly became inexpensive and widely available.[94]

Siamoises were brightly striped fabrics inspired by the clothing worn by ambassadors from Siam to the court of Louis XIV in 1684 and 1686 (figure 3.3). Originally wool or silk, then a silk-cotton or linen-cotton blend, by the early eighteenth century siamoises were being made predominantly of inexpensive cotton.[95] Their patterning also evolved through the period, manufacturers in Normandy producing checked variations as well as a variety of stripes. With costs ranging between about 2£ 8s and 3£ 10s per aune, siamoises in Louisbourg were in the same price range as indiennes or even simple wool calamanco, and only twice the price of basic cotton ginghams (table 3.4).[96]

Seventeenth- and eighteenth-century changes to the markets for non-essential goods and the concomitant rise in consumption revamped the fashion system as well, engaging more non-elites in the creation and deployment of new fashions. Gingham fabrics entered Minas with Abraham Boudrot in 1693 – 26.5 yards of it in one shipment, which would have been enough for three full gowns or robes de chambre, or about five skirts. Marie Le Borgne de Belleisle carried checked gingham in her stock in Louisbourg in the 1750s. At 20s per aune, it was the least expensive textile that

TABLE 3.4 · Imported cottons for sale in Acadia

Type	Price	Year	Location
Gingham	3 s 3 d / yard	1691[1]	Port Royal
White cotton, unspecified	–	1696/7[2]	Cape Sable
Striped siamoise "en trois quartes"	48 s / aune	1750[3]	Louisbourg
Worked (embroidered) cotton	3£ / aune	1750	Louisbourg
"Bourg"	3£ 5s / aune	1750	Louisbourg
Striped siamoise	3£ 10 s / aune	1750	Louisbourg
Checked cotton (gingham)	20 s / aune	1754[4]	Louisbourg
"Indienne avarice"	40 s / aune	1754	Louisbourg
Striped siamoise "en sept huit"	50 s / aune	1754	Louisbourg
Striped siamoise "en cinq huit"	2£ 10 s / aune	1754	Louisbourg
Cotton, unspecified	3£ 8s / aune	1754	Louisbourg
Cotton, unspecified	3£ 10 s / aune	1754	Louisbourg
Cotton, unspecified	4£ / aune	1754	Louisbourg
Cotton, unspecified	5£ / aune	1754	Louisbourg
Cotton, unspecified	6£ / aune	1754	Louisbourg
Muslin, striped	8£ / aune	1754	Louisbourg
Muslin, plain	10£ / aune	1754	Louisbourg

NOTES

1 "Invoice of Merchandise from Abraham Boudrot."

2 Welsteed, "Certificate by William Welsteed."

3 Notariat de l'Ile Royale, "Inventaire des biens meubles appartenant à Jacques Philipe Urbin Rondeau."

4 Notariat de l'Ile Royale (Greffe de Bacquerisse), "Inventaire des biens meubles appartenant à Marie Josephe Le Borgne de Belisle."

she sold.[97] The term is associated today with picnic blankets and children's clothing, but gingham was also used to describe a lightweight tabby-weave cotton originating in India and Dutch-colonized Malaysia, presenting as a single colour with white stripes of equal narrow width.[98] The square version was becoming more popular in the mid-eighteenth century, and appears in Louisbourg records in Le Borgne's 1754 inventory entry of sixteen aunes of cotton, including "one quarter gingham or fabric with squares."[99] Two pieces of white cotton came in with Charles de La Tour, and, like many of the Indian cottons that arrived in Britain, these were similar in look to linens, though less expensive. If dyed locally, the dye would not have been as colour-fast as those applied by Indian master dyers.[100] In the Louisbourg inventories, Jeanne

Thibodeau, Anne Levron, and Marianne Benoist all owned gowns in "cottonade rayé" and "Indienne."[101]

Originating in India and South Asia, cotton textiles became a force to be reckoned with in the European textile market of the late seventeenth and eighteenth centuries. Although the textiles had been banned for decades in France, the colonies were untouched by the restrictions on indiennes and continued to import them for wear by both elites and non-elites. Commonly made in inexpensive blues and reds, imported cottons stood out against the soft drape of French woollens and the crisp rustle of light silks. The prices meant that the fabrics were accessible to at least the better-off among the settlers. Cotton woven in South Asia, painted through Armenian expertise learned in the Levant, adjusted to English and French tastes, and imported through French hands into Acadia, had already traversed more than a quarter of the way around the globe before it arrived in Le Borgne's storage room in Louisbourg. Acadian dressmakers then cut and styled the fabric into the gowns, jackets, kerchiefs, and mantelets that, when worn, wove all of those distant places and people into the visual landscape of Acadia.[102]

Silk

Silk was not worn with the same frequency or in the same quantities as wool and linen, but Acadians did enjoy the luxury. Silk ribbon, embroidery thread, and lace came to Annapolis through Port Royal traders like Abraham Boudrot, who also had siblings and connections among the early settlers in Beaubassin.[103] Lead seals at Beaubassin arrived attached to imported silk stockings, and one found at a daughter colony from Beaubassin, at Pointe-aux-Vieux on Prince Edward Island, suggests the possibility of silk yardage from Lyons.[104] Silk manufactured in cities like Lyons fed the Paris clothing market, which in turn exported local designs and styles to an international market already hungry for new designs. Inventories at Louisbourg include silk yardage of varying types and price points, as well as silk shoelaces, handkerchiefs, ribbons, shoes, hat trims, and lace. Unlike cotton, silk in one form or another appears on every Acadian inventory from Louisbourg.

Silk has a long history of association with wealth and with royalty, as well as with women. Silk was seen as effeminate in the Roman Empire, was used for dowries in ancient China, is *haram* (forbidden) for men under the rules of Islam except under very specific circumstances, and in medieval Europe was associated with the Saracens and with the feminized, orientalized east.[105] Women working with silk was a common literary trope in medieval French romances, often acting as a plot mover in terms of social mobility: the tradesman's daughter spins silk threads and catches the eye of a prince. Silk production in France was deeply embedded in the experience of the female.[106] Montreal inventories show a gendered split in the ownership of various textiles in the late seventeenth and early eighteenth centuries, with silk and cotton proportionally more likely to have been owned by women, wool and linen by men.[107] The silk stockings sold in Beaubassin and merchandise in Le Borgne's shop in Louisbourg cannot be attributed to a specific gender, though the link with feminine refinement, nobility of body and of rank, and of respectability and luxury continue to mark the textile in all its contexts.[108]

Too delicate and expensive to be worn for manual labour, silk was a conspicuous symbol of leisure, power, and status for those above a certain socio-economic line. While a well-cut suit or gown could be lined with linen on the inside, one needed visible facings and turnbacks of silk to be considered *of the mode*. Mediation through the early modern period and the relaxation of sumptuary laws reduced high-status associations with silk, as did the rising French interest in sericulture and associated increase in production and export. Silk, like cotton, was a disruptive textile – in silk's case, for its new availability to the lower ranks of society after millennia of reserve for the elite.[109]

Wide access to silk accessories and small garments like stockings expanded as silk lost its status marker, though silk yardage was not documented in Acadia in any quantity outside of Louisbourg.[110] Paris inventories from the same period show a much higher proportion of silk fabrics to cotton or wool across socio-economic levels.[111] In 1700, nearly 10 per cent of the garments listed in inventories for wage workers and domestic servants in Paris were made of silk and 12 to 15 per cent of the working poor in Paris owned at least one silk item, proportions that tripled by the end of the eighteenth century.[112] The silk ribbons sold in Port Royal and Louisbourg were likely of similar quality to those found in Boston from the same period: low-twist silk taffetas and grosgrain, which would have had a more matte finish than the high-gloss silk-satin ribbons worn by continental elite. Some of these ribbons would have been used for bodice trimming, others for shoe ties, seam bindings, and headdress trimmings, adding a luxurious edge to the appearance without the expense of a full gown.[113] Acadia and Montreal both followed a colonial pattern of silk use and ownership rather than a Paris one, with ownership of silk accessories far outnumbering that of silk garments.

TABLE 3.5 • Imported silk for sale in Acadia

Type	Price	Year	Location
Silk ribbon	8-10 £ / aune	1691[1]	Port Royal
Silk ribbon	4-10 £ / aune	1691	Port Royal
Cherry red taffeta	7£ 10 s / aune	1750[2]	Louisbourg
Blue taffeta	7£ 10 s / aune	1750	Louisbourg
Triple velvet plush	4£ / aune	1754[3]	Louisbourg
Pink taffeta	7£ 10 s / aune	1754	Louisbourg

NOTES

1 Consignment inventory, Abraham Boudrot, 1691.

2 Notariat de l'Ile Royale.

3 Notariat de l'Ile Royale (Greffe de Bacquerisse), "Inventaire des biens meubles appartenant à Marie Josephe Le Borgne de Belisle."

Louisbourg, as is often the case, was the exception. Acadian women living in the fortress owned silk gowns, as well as silk yardage kept both for sale and personal use. Each Acadian woman discussed here owned at least one silk gown, including eight-year-old Marianne Benoist, and all the adults owned more. Silk accessories also appear on these lists, though wool stockings appear more often than silk. The inventories for both Marie-Josephe Le Borgne's personal clothing and her retail operation showed more than a dozen yards of cherry-red and blue silk taffetas alongside her doubled-silk handkerchiefs and lace headdresses.[114] The emphasis on silk stands out when compared with descriptions of Acadians elsewhere wearing more wool. Louisbourg was a French fortress, the Acadians a distinct minority population, and their choice to wear more expensive textiles was connected with community aesthetics. Acadian wives of French officials integrated into French society to a certain extent, enough to travel and engage in French styles, and yet rejected wool in a greater proportion than the women from France and New France who lived around them (see table 5.3). Insecurity can sometimes lead to over-compensation, and the administrative hierarchy was not all fond of the marriages between French officers and Acadian women. The wives' embrace of silk and indiennes in higher proportions than their neighbours may have been an attempt at ownership of that difference, actively performing French-ness and elite sophistication at a highly visible level.

Leather and Fur

Some articles of clothing and accessories required more durable materials, and leather was an easily available option. Different kinds of leathers and furs appear in descriptions of Acadian goods, connected to trade with the Mi'kmaq that brought in pelts as well as sealskin and elk hides.[115] Clark's examination of Acadian herds found that Acadians were butchering low numbers of cattle, but seal leather, used by the Mi'kmaq and naturally waterproof, turned out to be extremely useful for items like footwear and bags.[116] Leather was used for shoes, belts, and harnesses, for women's stays, and for specialized trade wear like blacksmiths' aprons.[117] Louisbourg records include mention of leather in men's clothing, mostly for weather protection and heavier labour. Some men's vests at Louisbourg were made of leather, though it was not as popular as fabric options. Breeches could be lined with "skins," and for going out on the water, sailors and fishers required leather cloaks, aprons, or even mittens as protection from the elements.[118]

Hides suffer from the same problem of survivability as textiles, though some of the associated notions remain: harness buckles and shoe buckles have been found in abundance at Acadian archaeological sites (see chapter 4, under Shoes and Buckles). Buckles of varying materials, costs, and qualities were produced elsewhere and imported; not the case with the materials to which they attached. Skins and furs were sourced from the surrounding environment, at first by hunting and trading, and later, as osteological evidence suggests, by more extensive use of the cattle being ranched in Siknikt.[119] Acadians tanned their own leather, and cow bones were used for notions and decoration.[120] Marguerite Terriau from Louisbourg had four untanned ox hides in her probate inventory, either destined for trade or for future use as clothing, footwear, or accessories.[121]

The fur trade provided pelts of varying types especially after 1730, when cargoes of furs began to ship out from Port Royal with more regularity, and some of the goods remained in Acadian hands. Prior to that, the bulk of the fur trade was centred around the St John River Valley and the Boston to London route.[122] Indigenous trappers offered not only beaver pelts, in high demand in Europe, but many other kinds of pelts and tanned hides as well, as a price list from Bellenger's visit in 1583 describes:

1 Buff hides reddie dressed vpon both sides bigger then an Oxe,
2 Deere skynes dressed well on the inner side, with the hayre on the outside
3 Seal skynns exceding great dressed on the ynnerside

4 Marterns enclyning vnto Sables

5 Bevers skynes verie fayre as many as made 600 bever hattes

6 Otters skynnes verie faire and large

...

11 Luserns, which the frenche call Loupceruiers.[123]

Dièreville, in his travels around Port Royal, noted that both Acadians and Mi'kmaq were wearing sealskin moccasins in 1699.[124] By the later eighteenth century, Brook Watson described Acadian fur use as being even more encompassing: "[wool, flax and hemp, along] with furs from bears, beaver, foxes, otter, and martin, gave them not only comfortable, but in many instances, handsome clothing."[125] Bear fur was a surprising addition to the list, suggesting either misidentification or a new and greater comfort level with hunting large game. In some cases, small pelts such as martin and fox were used for trim on outerwear. A French fashion plate published in the periodical *Mercure Galant* in 1677 showed dressmakers of the time an example of how such trim could be applied to keep up with the latest styles (figure 3.4).

FIGURE 3.4 • Fashion illustration for the winter of 1677–78. Issued with the "Mercure Galant" Extraordinaire (supplementary) of January 1678.

FIGURE 3.5 • Detail, fashion plate from the *Mercure de France*, 1729, with muffs on both the lady and the gentleman.

This is high fashion in the truest sense, some aspects of which made their way across the Atlantic to Acadia. Marie Joseph Le Borgne had a petticoat in her inventory described as "jupon vair piqué," or a skirt made of spotted squirrel fur.[126] Spotted grey fur comes very close to the black-tailed ermine used in the *Mercure* fashion plate to trim the underskirt of the model's mantua. Accessories included muffs and hats, and muffs make a frequent appearance in fashion plates of the time. Requiring less tailoring than gloves and allowing more mobility than mittens, fur muffs worn on cords around the neck provided extra warmth for cold winters. They were impractical for work, however, making them a leisure-time fashion (figure 3.5). Beaver hats were sold in Louisbourg, though no identifiable hat buckles have yet been found at Acadian sites.

Available in quantity, even with the number of pelts sent out of the colonies for trade, furs and hides played a significant role in Acadian wardrobes. Soft against the skin, capable of repelling water and shedding condensed breath from around the face, furs made for excellent warmth layers as linings for other garments, including breeches, cloaks, and mantles. Leather was used for shoes, garments, and accessories, both for utilitarian items and for high-fashion embellishment. Drawing on local resources rather than the styles in fashion on the European continent, additions like bearskin and sealskin followed contemporary fashions in some respects, and in others – notably the type of fur being used – set them visually apart, adding a unique localized quality to Acadian wardrobes.

Dyes and Colours

Fashionable colours changed over the course of the seventeenth and eighteenth centuries, and regional tastes often conflicted. The lighter, softer colours popular in France in the mid-seventeenth century shifted to darker, more sombre tones with the rise of Mme De Maintenon, the deeply pious mistress of Louis XIV. By the 1720s the New England fashionable set preferred lighter, softer colours again, particularly in silks, and manufacturers imported those colours they deemed most likely to sell.[127] Contemporary descriptions of Acadian dress mention a wide range of colours, including reds and blues, but with little indication of how vibrant or subdued those tones might have been.

Conflicting evidence abounds about the colours and dyestuffs available to and used by Acadians during their tenure in Mi'kma'ki. Dyes including vermillion and indigo appear among the lists of trade goods brought to Minas and Louisbourg in 1681 and 1696, and the Mi'kmaq used a wide range of local dyestuffs.[128] Commentators like Watson and Brown, on the other hand, described a much more restrictive palette in Acadian dress, consisting only of black and green. Brown expanded on Watson's letters, including the assertion that Acadian use of those colours was restricted by age: "They had only two dyes, green and a grey black; both obtained from vegetable substances, & equally divided between the population; the green being appropriated to the young, and the grey black to the old."[129] That description is so at odds with the availability of local dyestuffs, however, that it must be treated as suspect.

The simplest colours to produce from natural botanical sources were oranges, browns, yellows, and blues. If the Acadians were limiting their clothing to grey, black, red, and green, that would have been a deliberate style choice, requiring extra effort, equipment, and expense to produce.[130] Colour-fast black dye was extremely difficult to produce prior to the invention of aniline dyes in the 1860s, however, and required processing of the black walnut (*Juglans nigra*), native to the east coast of North America, which produced a brown dye that could be turned black with the addition of iron as a mordant. The closest to black that could be easily obtained was spinning and weaving the wool from black sheep, which were rare among North American flocks.

Local Indigenous groups had red dyes made from local ochres recorded as far back as the 1580s, and were willing to sell them. Bellenger records "Diuers excellent Cullors, as scarlet, vermillion, redd, tawny, yellowe, gray and watchett [blue]" among the trade goods offered to Europeans in the sixteenth century.[131] Watchet blue may be the green of Watson's experience, though it is generally described as being a woad-based dye more along the blue end of the spectrum.[132] When processed with a copper mordant, however, such as inside a copper dye pot, the green hues could be intensified. Mi'kmaw dyers made extensive use of goldthread (*Coptis trifolia*), a type of buttercup native to Mi'kma'ki, to create a yellow or gold pigment that fixed easily to both plant and animal fibres.[133] Once Caribbean indigo became available in quantity, woad was quickly replaced by the more intense and colour-fast import.[134]

Documentation on dye techniques from the pre-colonial and colonial periods is sparse, but descriptions from Nicolas Denys and Father Leclerq in the seventeenth century, as well as Hudson's Bay botanist Andrew Graham, and Swedish-Finnish botanist Peter Kalm in the mid-eighteenth century, describe *tisavoyanne* both "jaune" (*Coptis trifolia*, or goldthread) and "rouge" (*Rubia tinctorum*, or madder) as dyes in use by both Indigenous groups and French Canadians.[135] Kalm describes what the language confirms – that "The French, who have learned this from them [the Indigenous peoples], dye wool and other things yellow with this plant."[136] "Tisavoyanne" is a French loanword from "t'ssawiaqan," a word of Mi'kmaw origin used to describe materials used for dyeing, pointing to French engagement with Mi'kmaw craftspeople on the subject.[137] Going on to describe the use of red, Watson claimed that "in order to obtain scarlet – of which they were remarkably fond – they procured the English scarlet duffil which they cut, teized, carded, spun, and wove in stripes to decorate the women's garments."[138]

Red has always been a difficult and expensive colour to obtain with natural dyes. Europeans were greatly interested in the possibility of obtaining new red dyestuffs from North America, with cochineal-derived scarlets being the most valued. Marsh bedstraw (*Galium tinctorium*), which the Mi'kmaq used as a red dye for porcupine quills, gave European visitors some hope for a new source similar to the Spanish-monopolized Brazilwood.[139] Vermillion (mercuric sulphide) was a valuable trade good for the fur trade, as well as an important component in pigments, sealing wax, and even cosmetics, used for cheek rouge; de La Tour imported a pound of vermillion to Acadia for sale in 1693, enough to dye more than ten pounds of wool.[140]

Contrary to the commentary about their simple wardrobes, the colours the Acadians chose to wear demonstrated their expertise with sophisticated dyestuffs and colourways. While no textiles survive to be explored, inventories from Louisbourg reveal that Acadian women owned pink, brown, and blue garments, striped fabrics and florals, and cream and white lace.[141] Accessories found at Beaubassin included green paste gemstones, and a blue glass paste stone was excavated at Belleisle (see chapter 4, under Buttons). Sleeve buttons and jewellery were not necessarily colour-coordinated with the overall outfits, but even so the colours of the stones themselves would have added some brightness to their ensembles.

Conclusions

The textiles worn in Acadia were a mixture of local and imported, coarse homespun and luxurious finery; the proportions of each differed by settlement. Many households did not make all their own textiles, despite having enough people available for the labour by the early eighteenth century. Men and women tended the gardens that grew the flax, and sheared the flocks of sheep for wool, preparing the fibres with their own hands for local use. They also engaged with local economies by purchasing from Acadian, French, and Indigenous traders, sending barter and trade goods moving through other hands. They participated in the Atlantic and global textile economies, cottons from Malaysia, China, and India clothing bodies already layered in Dutch linens and French silks. The admixture of local and imported textiles was heavier on the homespun than equivalent ownership in Montreal and among the habitants of Quebec, but the Acadian interest in silks, cottons, and fine linens appears to have been just as keen.

The lack of consistent records makes it impossible to track individual patterns of textile use over time, but the evidence we do have is enough to draw some general conclusions. Geography, the length of time for which a settlement had been established, the age, gender, occupation, and socio-economic status of the wearers all played roles in the types and quantities of textiles purchased, made, used, traded, and coveted across the settlements. Complete self-sufficiency was impossible in the early years of colonial settlement and undesirable later, while new and exciting textiles continued to be imported from overseas. Both internal and external trade networks flourished in the early eighteenth century. Traders like Marie Josephe Le Borgne and David Basset acted as conduits to the markets and manufacturers of France and New England, their commercial ties throughout Acadia and the Indigenous communities a welcome resource. Acadian settlers drew on those networks to access contemporary fashion and commercial goods, including luxury items like silks, calicoes, jewellery, and lace.

Once resource lines had been established for local products – flax, sheep for wool, and trade relationships for furs – some imported supplies began to take a back seat. Brunet brought in bolts of fine linen in the 1680s, but by the 1740s, Le Borgne carried only pre-made linen clothing, tablewear, and kerchiefs. Strouds and other basic woollens designated for the fur trade came in through the trading companies. Acadian weaving, making the most out of the solid two-shaft traditional looms, began to incorporate new striped designs possibly inspired by the imported striped siamoise cottons, though local weavers added their own unique twist. Some families never accumulated the necessary quantity of livestock to provide themselves with enough wool, or land on which to grow flax, and crops like hemp provided a solution. Others had far more than their own households could enjoy, encouraging a successful barter system along with farther-reaching trade. Family connections brought goods from Atlantic trade networks to even isolated Acadian settlements. Distance from the centres of European fashion caused delays in uptake but did not seem to lessen interest in fabrics in the latest styles.

Silk and cotton remained imports due to the impossibility of producing those fibres in the North Atlantic climate. They were not replaced with close substitutes, however, despite the availability of other textiles. Imported fabrics were the focus of interest because of their physical qualities – both lightweight and crisp, in line with airy rococo fashion – but also *because* they could not be homespun. Fascination for the delicate painted floral cottons and woven silks was based on their distant origins and the embodied labour of the Indian and Indonesian labourers who produced them. The appeal of distance and access to "the exotic" drove interest, to the point where French textile manufacturers were accused of spicing French-made silks with peppercorns to make them smell as though they had crossed the ocean in a spice trader's hold.[142] It was the connection with travel, the distance from the centre, and the social weight of the associated goods – the spices, and their association with the silk road and other orientalized images of decadent wealth – which made the difference.

The settlements also used textiles differently. Beaubassin residents imported silks and lace. A textile seal found at their daughter-colony of Pointe-aux-Vieux suggests that the families living there may have enjoyed silks from Lyons. The prohibitions against painted cottons in France did not have measurable impact on the use of indiennes in Acadia, except perhaps to encourage it. Acadian women at Louisbourg wore calico petticoats, kerchiefs, and mantelets that were forbidden to their Continental counterparts. The intensity of the vibrant patterns and colours linked Acadia to the combined visual languages of the west and east. Pattern, texture, and colour were a consistent theme through Acadian clothing. Checked and floral cottons were worn alongside striped woollen skirts in blues, greens, golds, and reds, worn with leather vests, moccasins, and fur-trimmed and lined petticoats and breeches. New dyestuffs were incorporated from local flora, and when the right colour dyes for their stripes were not readily available, Acadians could acquire English worsteds and unravel them for reuse. Red English wefts entwined with Acadian wool, sometimes passing through home-made linen and hemp warps grown from French seeds, or cotton warps brought up from the plantations of the south. Soft and draping Acadian woollens had the Atlantic world and the textures of France woven in with every pass of the shuttle.

Cost was a factor, as was individual taste and the embedded social codes and assumptions that came with the settlers from their home provinces. Age categories did not play as much of a role in dress choice as they do today, when categories of childhood, pre-teen, adolescence, and young adult all have their own schema. Prior to the rise of humanism in the late eighteenth century children wore smaller, sometimes simpler, variations of adult clothing, and young Marianne Benoist's inventory, folded in with that of her mother, Anne Levron, included dresses in wool, silk, and painted cottons like those of the adult women around her.[143] Gender was more of a determinant, with silk's connection to femininity also connected to notions of gentility. Everyone wore wool and linen, though women wore more linen and hemp, thanks to the kerchiefs, fichus, and fancy cuffs for their gowns.

Most importantly, the available evidence refutes the stereotype of doughty Acadians clothed only in practical homespun. Homespun wool and linen were important, of that there is no doubt, but a wide variety of textiles was available to Acadian buyers. Once the settlements were established, the fields planted, population increased, and the flocks reproducing, the settlers had some breathing room. They engaged in contemporary fashion, developed their own weaving styles that took advantage of local resources, and circumvented the sumptuary regulations that made certain luxury goods exclusive to the colonies. They trimmed their wools, cottons, and silks with silk ribbons, lace, furs, and beads. Those choices, in turn, determined the kinds of garments that could and would be made from the textiles and trimmings, laying the groundwork for what would come to be considered a particularly Acadian style.

Dress Accessories

They are remarkably fond of rosaries, crucifixes, agnus deis,
and all the little trinkets consecrated by religion, with which
they love to adorn their persons.[1]

— — — — — —

THE EDGES OF GARMENTS are marked spaces, the place where the second skin gives way to the first, and covered flesh to the naked. Accessories and decorations bridge that conceptual and physical gap – buttons closing the plackets and openings of jackets and breeches, buckles binding ribbons around hats and shoes around feet. Closures define the places where the body and the garment meet, and jewellery echoes those lines demarcating naked spaces of the human form. Thanks to the materials from which many accessories are made and the way in which they define those edges, they can also be used archaeologically to determine the types, shapes, and styles of the garments they originally graced. Buttons, buckles, and other metal accessories are associated with European clothing, while beads and copper tinkler cones were more often part of Indigenous dress. Strings of beads adorned necklines, pins and brooches closed kerchiefs, and shoe buckles separated European leather from Indigenous moccasins and fieldworkers' wooden clogs.

This chapter examines the buttons, buckles, aglets, hooks, and eyes associated with Acadian clothing, as well as the jewellery that Acadians owned and wore. I argue that a close examination of these items gives us a stronger sense of which garments were being worn, where, and sometimes by whom. Accessories also give us a window onto local values and status performance, the decorative elements themselves part of entangled systems of communication surrounding gender, age, and wealth. The types of accessories recovered at Acadian sites and listed in the Louisbourg inventories shows that Acadians actively participated in exterior markets and fashion systems, purchasing and wearing items that would not have looked out of place on the shoes of a Paris merchant, or the shirt cuffs of a New England magistrate. This material also expands our understanding of the developing Acadian fashion system – the means by which they invented and disseminated information about their changing social structure and group identity.[2]

Accessories and notions contain embedded cultural information as well as physical, and we can tease out world views from the pieces that remain. The designs of buttons and buckles spoke to social aspirations, as well as notions of embodied status and degrees of civility. Spurs were heavily linked to understanding of gender, and religious jewellery embodied Acadians' Catholic faith in physical form. Ideologies of gender, status, and connection to local spaces and the global community are encapsulated in the forms and styles of the small finds that populate archaeological sites and museum collections. Pewter, brass, iron, and glass articles have been excavated from all four sites, some still in association with the tools used to manufacture or attach them to clothing. Leather and fabric accessories such as belts and pockets can be known only in absentia, through the buckles and records left behind; others, like buttons, buckles, and some pieces of jewellery, are intact enough to be the focus of study. The ways in which accessories have been categorized and the meanings embedded within them present us with perhaps the best opportunity to test out the detangling process. If accessories and notions are specific enough in their meanings and uses, then we should be able to walk backwards from this assemblage to determine the garments on which they were originally worn.

Differences appear between the assemblages, and the accessories recovered from Beaubassin, the Melanson site, Belleisle, and the Acadian houses at Louisbourg add more evidence that wardrobe choices among the groups were not uniform. Their different social environments, major occupations, distance from colonial authority, and amount of engagement with non-Acadians all had impacts on clothing selection. The variations in local vernaculars demonstrate the ways in which Acadians were active participants in crafting a visual identity for themselves – one that incorporated contemporary mainstream European fashion as well as adjusted for the geographical, cultural, and micro-level social differences that made the settlements distinct.

Buttons

Buttons were a mainstay of men's clothing in the colonial era, women's clothes more often fastened together with pins or hooks and eyes. Beyond the basic function of attaching clothing to itself, a function also fulfilled by straight pins, buttons placed precious metals on clothing as a venue for the display of wealth and social status.

FIGURE 4.1 • *Portrait of Two Boys*, probably Joseph and John Joseph Nollekens, ca 1745.

The expense of the buttons on an outfit tended to correlate with the wearer's general wealth, though in the late seventeenth and early eighteenth centuries pewter buttons had not yet developed their cultural association with lower socio-economic status.[3] That would change by the late eighteenth century, when gold-coloured buttons became much more popular among those who could afford brass and gilt. Size categories, decorative elements, and choices between metal and cloth-covered button blanks speak to the income of the wearer, as well as give some indication as to the kinds of garments being worn.

Buttons are mobile, dropping off one garment and being repurposed for others, and it is very difficult to determine the original use for a single button found in isolation at a site.[4] In groups, however, we can learn more. The larger buttons needed to close coats can be separated archaeologically from the smaller buttons used for waistcoats and breeches, as well as the lightweight bone, thread, and wood buttons used for shirts and undergarments.[5] Fabric and thread buttons were popular through the medieval period and into the early modern. Scraps of material left over from garment

TABLE 4.1 • Button types found at four Acadian sites

	Melanson	Belleisle	Beaubassin	Louisbourg
Bone			2	11
Clay		1		
Copper alloy	17	2	3	49
Pewter	5		16	6
Wood				7
Other	2	1	2	2
Mixed materials	1			6

manufacture were used to create small fasteners, often wrapped around ball-shaped bone or wood button blanks. Most of these styles would not survive burial, leaving only the bone and metal buttons – and possibly some wood, in lucky circumstances – to be recovered later on. Metal buttons emerged during the sixteenth and seventeenth centuries, though fabric and thread-wrapped buttons remained an inexpensive option for the domestic producer.[6]

Bone, wood, fabric, and thread buttons could all be manufactured at home, and even pewter could be easily cast over a fire without specialized equipment thanks to its low melting point. Molten pewter would be poured into the carved depression of a button mould (figure 4.2) and then a wire shank attached, either while the metal was still liquid, or soldered into place after it cooled.[7] Decorative buttons could be moulded with the decoration included, or the metal could be cast as blanks and the decoration hand-tooled on as a finishing touch. Imported by traders and sold by haberdashers and merchants, the buttons found in Acadia bear a striking resemblance to others found in New England from the same time frame. Those found at the Ephraim Sprague House, for example, in Andover, Connecticut, included octagonal pewter buttons, both cast with decoration and hand-tooled, as well as a sleeve button set with a red paste gem. Ephraim Sprague and his family were farmers of the "middling sort," neither wealthy nor poor, heavily involved in community adjudication and leadership, and with a strong interest in keeping up appearances.[8] The same pewter buttons and buckles in Acadia would have been equally fashionable and associated with similar socio-economic status.

One simple style of button is the dorset button, a type of inexpensive linen or thread button made by wrapping thread around a horn or metal ring. Commercial

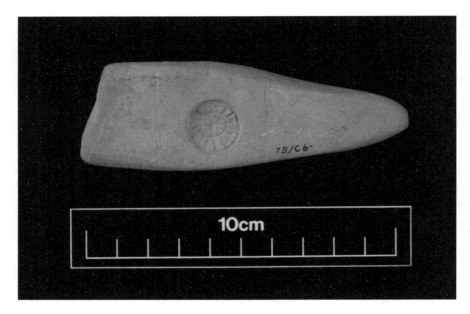

FIGURE 4.2 • Clay button mould for pewter buttons, Beaubassin.

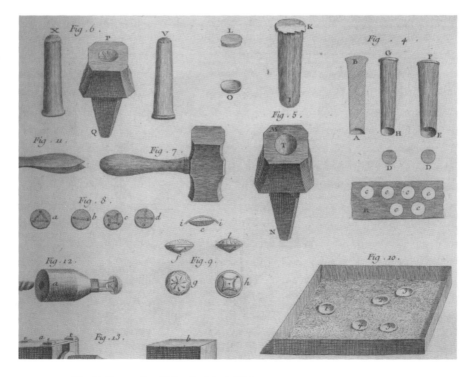

FIGURE 4.3 • The Button-maker, Diderot, plate 3. 1771.

FIGURE 4.4 • Detail, embroidered linen waistcoat with dorset buttons, British, 1740s.

dorset buttons were predominantly made with brass interior rings, but another interpretation of the lacing rings found at Beaubassin and Melanson (see figure 2.21) may
be as bases for home-made thread-wrapped buttons of this type. First appearing as
linen and horn combinations somewhere around 1680–1700 in Dorset, England, dorset
buttons were an inexpensive and easily made simple button variation that used far
less valuable metal than cast pewter or brass. Dorset buttons could be manufactured
domestically as well as purchased in large quantities and were used on lightweight
garments such as lace cuffs and collars, high-fashion calico gowns, or the turned-up
sleeve cuffs of mantuas (see chapter 5 under Gowns, Skirts, and Petticoats), as well as
shirts and underclothes. The wire ring version first appeared between 1720 and 1730,
and is rarely, if ever, properly identified at archaeological sites.[9]

Intended for fine linen shirts or for lightweight cotton casaquins and robes volante, dorset buttons indicate a sophisticated level of dressing more associated with urban environments. Whether worn on lace or muslin cuffs and collars, on shirts and jumps, or on the sleeves of cotton gowns and jackets, the potential use of dorset buttons may speak to a delicacy and economic security in some of the clothing worn at Beaubassin. The contemporary descriptions of Beaubassin Acadians wearing poor clothing in coarse homespun wool – textiles too heavy to be securely fastened by dorset buttons – does not match the archaeological evidence. Descriptions of Acadians in low-cost and homemade clothing also contradict what is known about the quantity of money moving through later Beaubassin through the ship sales, fur trade, and the presence of the Baie Verte portage, which gave travellers easy access to the Northumberland Strait. The evidence, as already seen in a few different ways, indicates the repeated wear of different styles of fashionable European-style clothing.

The button types found at the four Acadian sites were split along income lines and connections to the European metropoles. More brass buttons appeared at Melanson and Louisbourg than at Beaubassin and Belleisle. These were also the sites where reinforcing the appearance of European-ness would have been most socially import-ant, adding an extra meaning to the use of fancier pieces. If clothing is a conversation between wearer and observer, then the choice of dialect – deliberate or otherwise – changes the tone of that conversation. Choosing brass buttons and their military associations over pewter or cloth suggests that the wearer was engaging with specific understandings of power and prestige that were bundled with the conceits of French and English gentility. The image the wearer was trying to portray would shift based on the rest of their individual context, which is unfortunately missing for most of Beaubassin. At Melanson, at least, we can understand the presence of these accesso-ries as a symbol of belonging – both in terms of self-fashioning, and for the benefit of nearby authorities.

Beaubassin

Trader Charles de Saint-Étienne de La Tour, son of the Acadian governor of the same name, brought pewter buttons to sell at La Have in 1696. Buttons were also among the small goods readily available at Louisbourg, but the vast majority of the buttons found at Beaubassin were styles that could easily be made on premises. These were metal and bone and included a group of nine identical round pewter buttons of an appropriate size for the knee bands on breeches or the front of waistcoats. Three matching hollow-cast copper alloy buttons were also found, as was a bone disc likely to have been a

TABLE 4.2 · Beaubassin button breakdowns

Material	Size	Style	Quant.	Possible use
Bone	14 mm, 17 mm	Solid, flat	2	Shirt
Iron wire rings for thread buttons	12 mm	n/a	2	Shirt or lightweight cuffs/collars/sleeves
Copper	12 mm	Octagonal, paste gem	1	Sleeve button
Pewter	16 mm	Octagonal, flat, hand-etched	1	Sleeve button
Pewter	14-16 mm	Hollow, 2-part	9	Waistcoat or breeches
Pewter	13 mm	One piece, flat back.	5	Waistcoat or breeches
Pewter	14 mm	2-part, back only	1	Waistcoat or breeches
Copper alloy	12, 17, 20 mm	Hollow, 2-part	3	Coat, waistcoat/breeches – military
Pewter	18 mm		1	Coat

button blank (table 4.2). All of these were medium-sized clothing buttons, appropriate for sleeves, waistcoats, and breeches, made between 1700 and 1765. Some were found in an operation on the site hypothesized to be a storage area for trade goods.[10]

Pewter buttons were inexpensive and utilitarian, worn by people from all socio-economic classes. They were also less durable than buttons made from more precious metals, due to pewter's malleability and low melting point. Pewter melts at a temperature of 170–230°C, a temperature possible to achieve over a basic campfire as well as more energy-efficient household hearths. Button moulds for pewter were easily made by hand, with an example from Fort Lawrence providing a beautiful example of an unfinished half of a home-made mould of local stone, decorated with a design that would be raised on the finished button (figure 4.2). Many button styles were made this way, and a single mould could be reused dozens, if not hundreds, of times. The mould was found in relation to the British encampment at Fort Lawrence, but similar buttons and moulds have been found at sites across Western Europe and North America.[11]

The copper alloy buttons present a more incongruous grouping. The three examples are different sizes but identical in construction, plain on the face rather than stamped with motifs or insignia. The design is deceptively simple, and when new and polished the surface would have caught the light. Copper alloy buttons were most popular in the latter half of the eighteenth century, particularly from 1775 onward,

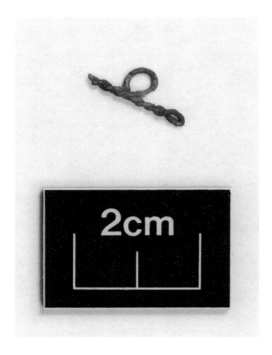

FIGURE 4.5 • Coiled iron wire finding, from Beaubassin.

FIGURE 4.6 • Man's conical silver toggle button, Malta, 1775–98.

when the fashion changed from silver-coloured buttons to gold-coloured ones.[12] There is no evidence of tin plating on these copper buttons, a technique commonly used to give the metal a silver hue. Brass buttons were used on French military uniforms in the first half of the eighteenth century despite not being in fashion in the civilian world, and similar two-piece domed copper alloy buttons have been found in association with other buttons from French uniforms in the French fort of St Louis in Old

FIGURE 4.7 • Bone button and bovine scapula, Beaubassin.

Mobile, Louisiana (occupied 1702–12) as well as at the British Fort Ligonier (1758–66).[13] A suit would have required matching buttons in all three sizes – small for pocket flaps or sleeves, medium for the waistcoat and breeches, and large for the coat front itself. Sleeve buttons found at Beaubassin (see Sleeve Buttons, below), confirm local interest in the fancier side of European clothing.

A twisted iron wire found in conjunction with fifteen fine straight pins bears a striking resemblance to a backing for a toggle-back button, a style typical of places like Malta (see figure 4.6). The toggle-style button would have been worn through doubled eyelets like a modern cufflink rather than being sewn to the body of a garment. The iron version is crudely made by comparison, but the size and shape are correct for a mid-eighteenth-century button backing, and the stratigraphy places it well within the period of Acadian occupation. It may be a home-made replacement for a lost backing, or a stronger backing for a locally cast pewter button. At least three men from Spain and Portugal are known to have settled in Acadia, marrying Acadian wives. Manoel (Emmanuel) Mirande, originally from Portugal, settled in Beaubassin late in the seventeenth century, and married into the Bourgeois family.[14] He would have brought his own sense of aesthetics and dress habits with him, and the presence of toggle-back buttons at Beaubassin, however crude, suggests that some of that Iberian sensibility may have found its way into the local vernacular.

Bone buttons were utilitarian rather than fashionable, predominantly used for men's trouser flies and shirt buttons. The two-hole drilled bone button recovered from Beaubassin would have been one of these, the drilled-hole versions the cheapest of the bone button types. This example was of a standard size for men's shirts.[15] The bone buttons at Beaubassin were made on site, the larger of the two found in conjunction with the scapula from which it had been recently carved.[16] The number of pieces found does not support an interpretation of large-scale button manufacturing, but rather work intended for personal or household use and made as needed.

Beaubassin was a trading hub with connections to New France, Indigenous communities, Louisbourg, and traders coming up the Bay of Fundy, so the issue was not one of lack of access. The presence of wood, bone, and home-made pewter buttons indicates a reliance on local materials alongside imported ones, an attitude that did not overly privilege external sources and fashions. Whether one chose to appear as a poor labourer entirely in homespun, or an analogue of a European nobleman in fine linen, silk hose, and jewelled sleeve links, or as someone who made the local landscape part of his clothing – each choice created a different impression of the person inside the clothes. This is different ground than the performative urban fashions of Louisbourg, or the practical realities at Belleisle, and would have created, for better or for worse, different relationships between the Beaubassin Acadians and their various neighbours.

Melanson

The buttons found at Melanson are similar in style and quality to those from Beaubassin, including the hollow copper alloy and flat pewter buttons also seen in New England and at Louisbourg. There are fewer home-made buttons in the assemblage, though this may well be a sampling distortion from the specific lots excavated. We see both fancy buttons and plain, sized for coats, waistcoats, and breeches. The button sizing suggests that there may be two suits represented in the assemblage, one with pewter buttons and another with copper alloy.

Copper alloy buttons were primarily imported to the colonies, though by the early eighteenth century button manufacturers were operating in New England. The plain styles that dominate at Melanson have many similarities to the buttons commonly used on the uniforms of the French navy, and identical examples have also been found at the British-owned Fort Stanwix (1758–81).[17] The buttons were not exclusive to military uniforms, certainly, but the rows of shiny metal down the fronts of coats evoked

TABLE 4.3 • Melanson button breakdowns

Material	Size	Style	Quant.	Possible use
Copper alloy	14 mm	Hollow, two-piece	2	Waistcoat or breeches
Copper alloy	18–19 mm	Hollow, two-piece	5	Coat or waistcoat
Copper alloy	21 mm, 24 mm, 29 mm	Hollow, two-piece	3	Coat
Copper alloy	unknown		5	
Iron	12 mm	Solid, domed, one piece	2	Waistcoat or breeches knee
Pewter	13 mm	Hollow dome	1	Waistcoat or breeches knee
Pewter	16–17 mm	Flat, cast shank	3	Waistcoat or breeches
Pewter	17 mm	domed	1	Sleeve, waistcoat, or breeches
Pewter	22 mm, 29 mm	Flat, plain	2	Coat
Wood and iron	unknown		1	
Unknown			2	

an aura of respectability. They also spoke to a kind of practical masculinity that had been in ascendance since the sixteenth century, and which would peak at the turn of the nineteenth. They embodied a swagger, a demonstration of power that called on the symbolism of militias, and a soldier's strength. Wearing this style of button was a personal identification with the ideas that it symbolized, calling attention to the clothing and to the fitness and gentility of the body inside it.

Belleisle

Only four buttons have been found at Belleisle: two of copper alloy, one of an unidentified white metal, and a fourth made from local clay. The large brass buttons are of military styling once again, though there are no markings on either to indicate an associated regiment. Like some of the brass buttons at Beaubassin and Melanson, these are plain and large, the right size for a man's coat.

The clay button blank presents an interesting conundrum for the archaeologist. The acidity in local soils destroys fabric, and it is the quality of the fabric or thread which once covered the blank that contains all the information about the cost of the button and the look to which it contributed. Fancy fabric buttons in gilt and brocades could be worn on matching waistcoats, and blanks covered with scraps of whatever wool or linen was on hand could be used for less visible or lower-status garments. On its own the button blank tells us little, except that fabric-covered buttons were being made on site.

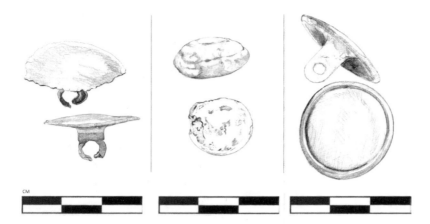

FIGURE 4.8 • Buttons, Belleisle.

TABLE 4.4 • Belleisle button breakdowns

Material	Size	Style	Quant.	Possible use
Copper alloy	27 mm	Class 1, Series A, Type 1, Variety A (Stone)	1	Coat
Copper alloy	24 mm	C1, SD, T1	1	Coat
Unknown, "white metal"[1]	u/k		1	Coat/waistcoat/breeches
Clay	15 mm	Biconvex cross-section	1	Shirt, waistcoat, breeches, gown sleeve

NOTE

1 Preston, "Excavations at Site BeDi-2," 9.

Belleisle's buttons are plain and utilitarian, similar to the simpler styles of buttons found at Melanson and Beaubassin. The plainest of the coat buttons and the clay button blank were both found at the Blanchard-Gaudet residence. The Blanchard family was relatively well off in the early eighteenth century, census records showing a thriving operation including six arpents of land and seventeen heads of livestock.[18] Any home-made and inexpensive buttons worn there were unlikely to be due to poverty or to lack of access to higher-quality items. The small sample size could easily be skewing perceptions, or the residents may have been able to take most clothing of value with them when they were deported. Or, if these four examples really are indicative of overall button use in Belleisle households, the farmlands may have inspired interest in a simpler dress idiom. This fits with the evidence from the heavier pins and plain buckles, a picture of a local culture that encouraged practicality, and less of a need to impress.

Louisbourg

The differences in the assemblage at Louisbourg lie partly in the quantity of evidentiary material recovered, and partly in the nature of that material. Most of what we know about buttons locally came from a shop inventory rather than archaeology, meaning that they were owned by an Acadian, or were briefly in the possession of an Acadian, but were not necessarily *worn* by Acadians. The inventories make an interesting distinction between buttons "pour habit" and "pour vente": buttons for clothes and buttons for sale.[19] The buttons listed as "pour vente" were valued at half the price of the buttons "pour habit," making it clear that the buttons "pour habit" were the larger, often fancier, coat buttons, while "pour vente" means that the buttons were of a common size that needed no further distinguishing description.[20] Coat buttons were normally listed separately from other buttons in inventories and merchants' ledgers, as the price points were higher.[21]

Copper alloy buttons dominate at Louisbourg over all other styles. The utilitarian bone and pewter buttons are evenly spread between the sites, with some of each appearing in each assemblage. The house of the widow Dugas was responsible for most of the wood buttons, though it is impossible to know to which of her two husbands the buttons originally belonged.[22] The buttons are appropriate for the types of men's clothing we would expect to see at Louisbourg in the first half of the eighteenth century: buttons for centre front openings, pockets, cuffs, and vents of fashionable breeches, coats, and waistcoats. And as at Melanson, there is a sense of performative gentility about the weighting toward brass buttons in the Louisbourg collections.

Le Borgne's trade activities provide ample reason for the vast quantities of buttons she kept in her store. Two hundred and forty of the "boutons dor" were valued at £4 / dozen and may have been plated with real gold in order to command such a high price; similar brass buttons in New England ledgers were more commonly sold for less than a pound per dozen.[23] This speaks to the higher standard of dress often seen in Louisbourg, and the purchasing power available to the French elite in the area.

TABLE 4.5 · Louisbourg button breakdowns

Material	Inventory	Artifact
Copper alloy		49
"Boutons dor"/copper alloy or gold plate[1]	324	
Pewter		6
Wood		7
Mixed		6
Hard paste porcelain		1
Bone		11
"Boutons dargent"/tinned or silver plate[2]	108	

NOTES

1 Notariat de l'Ile Royale (Greffe de Bacquerisse), "Inventaire des biens meubles appartenant à Marie Josephe Le Borgne de Belisle."

2 Notariat de l'Ile Royale (Greffe de Bacquerisse).

Sleeve Buttons

Some buttons were more decorative than others. A "green jewel" found at Beaubassin, set in a copper alloy setting with an s-curve hook, is a sleeve button – an early form of cufflink (figure 4.9). A matching jewel would be attached on the other end and the pair of buttons inserted into buttonholes on a sleeve cuff to keep it closed at the wrist, a style seen in many portraits of the period. The paste gem was made from molten leaded glass, poured into a mould that gave it a shape representing a popular contemporary gemstone cut, then set into a closed setting lined with a polished metal sheet that would help reflect the light. This particular example was moulded to look like an "old single cut," a square cut with faceted corners popular in the late seventeenth century.[24]

Sleeve buttons were flashy without being exuberant, a way to display awareness of the requirements of elite manners and the importance of clean, white linens, a strong signifier of European gentility. This was a marker of difference between European and Indigenous bodies in a way that the wool coats and even brass buttons were not. Donning a linen shirt and fastening the edges closed with sleeve buttons was a reaffirmation for the wearer that he was engaging with familiar forms of masculinity and gentility. Importantly, those looking at him would also be aware of that communication – the assertion that the wearer was choosing a specific form of self-expression that carried complex meaning.

FIGURE 4.9 • Sleeve button, green paste jewel in plated setting, Beaubassin.

FIGURE 4.10 • Detail, *Love in a Village*, Isaac Bickerton, 1767.

While other button types were used on a variety of garment styles, sleeve buttons were only ever worn with European-style linen shirts. They held collars and cuffs closed and provided a new location for decorative additions. Sleeve buttons could be worn singly at the neck or in pairs at the cuffs, closing off the ends of the body. If linen acted as a second skin, then the bright flashes of metal and coloured gems at the pulse points become piercings in that skin. They are non-contiguous and isolated, but when paired provide continuity across an entire outfit. Sleeve buttons are visually grounding, spots of punctuation that mark the beginnings and ends of private body space. In the grammar of clothing, they are the visual equivalent of full stops.

The round paste gem in a plated setting is typical of sleeve buttons from the late seventeenth to early nineteenth centuries, and the octagonal cut more frequently seen in the early eighteenth. The setting for the green Beaubassin sleeve button was plated, possibly with tin or silver, making it a striking piece of personal jewellery. Similar sleeve buttons were worn in New England, as almost identical versions have been found at the Ephraim Sprague house in Connecticut (1705–50 occupancy) and the Lake George region of New York.[25] One pewter sleeve button found at Beaubassin was a more sophisticated octagonal style, with a design hand-etched onto the front surface (figure 4.11). Copper alloy buttons were commonly hand-chased after being stamped

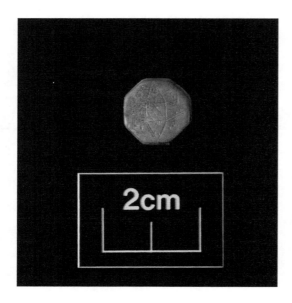

FIGURE 4.11 • Hand-etched button, Beaubassin.

out, as the process of hand-etching copper was cheaper than incorporating the design in the mould, and pewter buttons were similarly sometimes chased or die-stamped following the casting process. Octagonal sleeve buttons of this type were popular throughout North America during the colonial period, and examples have been found in colonial Williamsburg, colonial Harvard, and New Amsterdam.

A broken pair of copper alloy sleeve buttons were found at Melanson, in the infill that had been used to bury the corpse of a pig in the yard of Charles Melanson's house (figure 4.12). Small but finely made, each button is edged with a half-dozen tiny fleur-de-lys decorations barely 3 mm in length. Whether the sleeve buttons had been worn by someone working on refilling the grave, or they had broken and been lost in what became the infill dirt, is unknown. What can be said is that someone in the Melanson house wore fine white linen shirts cut in a European style, made with hand-worked buttonholes at the wrists to accommodate the link between the buttons. These sleeve buttons glinted and gleamed in the sun along with the brass buckles on his shoes, hat, and knees. The edges of the wearer's body were pinpointed with white lawn and shining metal, picking him out within a natural landscape of verdant greens and browns. Sleeve buttons confirm the use of linen shirts and attention to fashionable detail, confirming that at least some of the residents of Beaubassin and Melanson were keeping abreast of contemporary style.

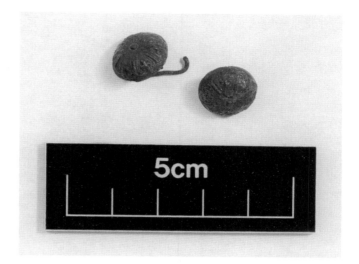

FIGURE 4.12 • Copper alloy sleeve buttons with fleur de lys details, Melanson.

Shoes and Buckles

Buckles were worn on several different types of garment, mostly men's clothing – hats, stocks, and breeches – and on almost all European-style shoes. Buckles replaced ribbon bows and latchet ties on leather shoes in the later seventeenth century, though they were not the only available option. Some less expensive shoes were still closed with ties or buttons, and some of the leather shoe straps found at Fort Beausejour had holes or slits cut in them for buttonholes.[26] The styles of shoe buckles worn by men and women were so similar and the range of styles so diverse that it is impossible to assign a particular gender to an isolated shoe buckle. Buckles evolved, beginning as small, simple fasteners cast in iron, copper alloy, or pewter. They became much more of a jewellery item over time, gaining in size, embellishment, and design complexity through the eighteenth century.[27]

Buckles were also used on other items of masculine-coded clothing. Knee buckles are associated with the breeches worn by men of European and colonial gentry, clothing so elite-coded that breeches fell out of use on the Continent shortly after the French Revolution in 1795.[28] Accessories are a tool for image creation, and some of the examples found in Acadia are of types that were intimately linked to conceptions of European gentility. The presence of knee buckles at a site reveals the presence of a man who dressed with an eye towards the fashions of the urban elite

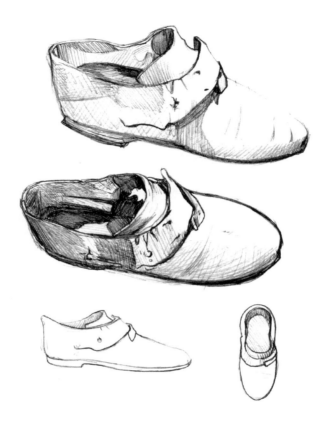

FIGURE 4.13 • Adult man's shoe, Grand Pré, dated ca 1720–30.

and found expression of his masculinity in that coding.[29] Brass spur buckles and decorated shoe buckles in particular both speak to a particularly Western European image of refined masculinity.

Shoes and boots underwent significant changes in this period. They were still made on straight lasts, with the leather moulded into left- and right-side shapes by the heat and pressure of the wearer's feet, and the uppers evolved through a series of different styles of decoration. Men's and women's shoe styles were similar, with small heels, high vamps, and latchets that fastened with some form of metallic buckle. Women's shoes became more important as a wardrobe item in the eighteenth century as skirts shortened and the feet became more visible. By the mid-eighteenth century, women's shoes had primarily cloth uppers, the foot encased in satins, brocades, and embroidered textiles. Leather and sabots were left for poor women, primarily the rural poor.

On the other hand, leather was the most common material for urban men's footwear in France, while the rural poor wore wooden sabots. The difference was not only price or comfort, but in conferred status. Sabots were intimately connected with the hierarchies of the ancien régime, conferring on the wearer a culturally constructed image of labouring masculinity. Associated with poor French farmers, the sabots would become a symbol of resistance during the Revolution at the end of the eighteenth century, and a target for British disdain for years before that.[30]

Contemporary chroniclers describe different forms of footwear worn by Acadians at different settlements. Dièreville described sealskin moccasins worn in the area around Port Royal, and De Muelles confirmed the use of so-called "sousliers sauvages," made from leather, which the Acadians tanned and worked themselves.[31] Robert Hale described wooden shoes he saw during his voyage through Acadia, as well as his surprise at the sight: "[20 June] 6 P.M. – Wee got up to the Gutt [entrance to the Annapolis harbor] & just after our Entrance 2 Frenchmen came on Board us, one of whom had Wooden Shoes on, the first that (to my remembrance) I ever saw."[32] De la Varenne's 1756 suggestion that the poor Acadians "go bare-footed in all weathers" is congruent with other descriptions of poorer Acadians, particularly those left "half-naked" by famine on Ile St-Jean, but only truly makes sense in the short-lived maritime summer.[33] In winters where the temperature could easily stay below zero degrees Celsius for weeks at a time, one wonders that a barefoot population would not be missing a great many toes to frostbite.

None of the contemporary commentators mention the presence of European-style leather or cloth shoes, perhaps to imply comparisons between the Acadians and the rural French labourers in their provinces of origin. Despite this gap in the written records, evidence across all four sites includes signs of regular use of European-style latchet shoes as well as moccasins and wooden sabots, while a spur buckle found at Melanson would have been worn only with leather boots. The intact man's shoe found at Grand Pré is a simple working man's shoe, with a minimal heel and rounded toe box (figure 4.13). The leather latchets across the instep are not visibly perforated, suggesting that they would have been worn with a simple chape-less buckle such as that seen in the centre of figure 4.14. Surviving moccasins found at Fort Beausejour (ca 1751–55) were closed with fine sewn pleats and a drawstring strap rather than a buckle. Those same moccasins show design details that are not standard to moccasins made for Mi'kmaw use, suggesting that they were made for – and possibly by – non-Indigenous wearers.[34]

Potential evidence of cross-cultural communication appears in some unexpected places, and the use of birchbark is one excellent example. Deveau describes the use of birchbark in the place of thatching as a notable local adjustment, and the utility of birchbark – something the Indigenous peoples knew very well – appears in other places as well.[35] In one exceptional example, birchbark was used for taking a pattern from an old shoe. The old shoe was then discarded along with the larger pattern, presumably after a larger version of the child's shoe had been constructed.[36] Using local resources to replicate European styles combines need and invention, though the process of shoemaking for heeled shoes is generally not something undertaken by amateurs. The process of making an eighteenth-century shoe required specialized tools and equipment, more so than the process of making soft-soled moccasins. Shoes were not difficult to come by, as the hundreds in Le Borgne's inventories make clear, with "escarpins communs" selling for £2 5s a pair in 1754. The effort to remake a pair with local materials, therefore, was less of a necessity and more of an interest in something that was not otherwise available for purchase.

Environmental requirements and exposure to other cultural groups can change dress decisions on a larger scale, French Canadian scouts adopting the woodland-appropriate clothing styles of Indigenous men, and Mi'kmaw leaders wearing European-style wool coats along with their leather leggings.[37] Through custom and practicality, shoe types inscribe a physical space for the wearer, demarcating the environment in which they work and the boundaries of their engagement with the world and their tasks. Without moccasins the woods became less hospitable, and a human presence in them an imposition. A letter written by Henry Bouquet to Brigadier General John Forbes from Loyalhanna, on 20 October 1758, describes the necessity of moccasins for use in the forested areas: "Our best woodsmen, accustomed to moccasins, cannot be used for lack of footwear. If it were possible to send 500 prepared skins from Philadelphia, these would be the means of providing them; and without moccasins, these men do not like to go into the woods."[38] They were practical footwear in the wet and the cold, easy to dry and to maintain in good condition, as Providence founder Roger Williams described in 1643: "Both these, Shoes and Stokins they make of their Deere skin worne out, which yet being excellently tann'd by them is excellent for to travell in wet and snow; for it is so well tempered with oyle, that the water cleane wrings out; and being hang'd up in their chimeny, they presently drie without hurt."[39] Wearing moccasins was an equivalent to wearing homespun woollens and linens, a sign that the wearer was engaging with the local environment rather than forcibly imposing European standards on colonial spaces.

Adding moccasins to the Acadian wardrobe meant adding convenience, but also created a new combination that stood apart from the rest: the riding boots worn with spurs at Melanson, the colonially styled outfits with latchet shoes in leather or cloth, or the Continental sabots that had come with the Acadians from France. Leather provided its own contradictions. When made one way into a European shoe it symbolized urban sophistication, and in another, it belonged to Indigenous lifeways. The contradiction was lessened for women due to the existing renegotiations of femininity in footwear. By the time shoe buckles were in ascendance, leather shoes on French women were deemed acceptable only for "les femmes de la campagne."[40] The blend of European and Mi'kmaw technology and knowledge involved in the process makes Acadian footwear a digression from colonial norms. These choices were also rooted in a specific geography, the combination of woollen skirts and breeches worn with moccasins placing Acadians into a category that was not Indigenous, nor fully colonial.

Combinations of Indigenous and European styles were more commonly found among those who lived at cultural intersections, adaptive choices enabling wearers to shift between identities more easily than would be possible without the use of dress as a social mediator. Diana DiPaolo Loren describes the settler body as a focal point of anxiety, a battleground on which tensions about colonial and Indigenous identity played out.[41] Charles Morris commented on cultural synthesis among the Acadians in his 1748 survey of the Chignecto region and Bay of Fundy. He described the Acadians he saw as:

> [T]all and well proportioned, they delight much in wearing long hair, they are of dark complexion, in general, and somewhat of the mixture of Indians; but there are some of a light complexion. They retain the language and customs of their neighbours the French, with a mixed affectation of the native Indians, and imitate them in their haunting and wild tones in their merriment; they are naturally full cheer and merry, subtle, speak and promise fair.[42]

Shifting identities between contexts was a negotiation skill, one that enabled those living at cultural crossroads to participate in multiple public and private spheres. That flexibility with what Loren calls "mixed dress," blending garments and decorative elements from settlements and Indigenous communities, appears elsewhere in Acadian clothing. We see it in the beads and materials used for embellishments, and the mixtures of homespun and imported textiles. This liminal state, this *in-between-ness*, carried through the spaces in which moccasins were predominantly used, the woods and the marshlands at the edges of Acadian settlement.

Beaubassin

Buckles were made with a lot of variation, so much so that a previous study found only one or two duplicates in a collection of over two thousand buckles.[43] Large shoe buckles appear more often later in the period than the smaller versions, as fashion encouraged the increasing size. Five buckles were found at Beaubassin, one pair and three singles, all of them in styles usually associated with shoes.

The presence of the chape – the piece that held the buckle to the strap, counter-balanced by the tongue – with a buckle makes it easier to date. One double-framed sub-circular buckle from Beaubassin has an intact stud chape (see figure 4.14, far right), a style that fell out of use around 1720.[44] The general dates of the brass shoe buckles in this assemblage match the span of time during which Beaubassin's population and prosperity increased. The large buckle in particular evokes power, reflected in the shape and size of the brass hardware, the visibility and bold engagement with fashion a claim on visual space.[45]

The similarities between this assemblage and those from middling-class households in New England demonstrate the Beaubassin Acadians' awareness of and interest in contemporary colonial and European fashion. Despite the distance between them, Beaubassin was in tune with prevailing New England menswear fashions in both materials and in style.

TABLE 4.6 • Beaubassin buckle breakdowns

Type	Description	Material	Size	Date range
Curved shoe buckle[1]	Shaped and scalloped		<2 cm	<1720
Oval shoe buckle (pair)	Curved and notched	Copper alloy	22 × 17 mm	1680–1720
Rectangular shoe buckle	3mm curve	Copper alloy	47 × 29 mm	1725–1740
Double framed sub-circular shoe buckle	Stud chape	Copper alloy	44 × 28 mm	1710–1720

NOTE

1 Shoe buckles post-1720 were more commonly over 45 mm long. Knee buckles were in this size range – under 30 mm – but were more common post-1730. Some shapes of buckle are more closely associated with knee buckles than shoe buckles, and a form of chape that resembles an anchor may be a sign of a knee buckle rather than one for shoes. See White, "Constructing Identities," 211, and "Buckles," Finds Recording Guides, *Portable Antiques Scheme*, last updated 5 February 2020, https://finds.org.uk/counties/findsrecordingguides/buckles/.

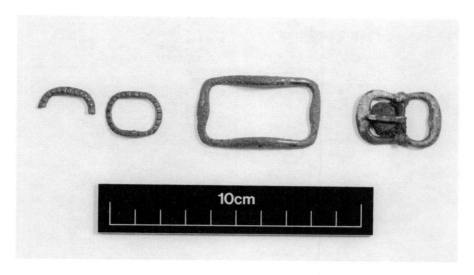

FIGURE 4.14 • Copper alloy shoe buckles, Beaubassin.

Belleisle

Pieces of five buckles have been found at Belleisle, four of the five originating at the Blanchard/Gaudet residence. The simple frames, rectangular shapes, and the drilled pin-terminal holes place the manufacturing date at around 1720–30, before the truly elaborate high rococo fashions turned to filigree and larger frames. The basic cross-hatching and scalloped edges seen here were common decorations throughout the period.

Primarily, the brass buckles confirm that someone in the household wore European-style leather shoes. Brass buckles would be appropriate for Sunday best for a farmer, in tune with but not overly luxurious by contemporary fashion standards. The multiple pairs and sizes at the Blanchard house fit with the family's general status in the community. They were among the wealthier members of the community in the early eighteenth century, with arpents of cultivated land and livestock listed at one and a half times those owned by the Savoies next door.[46] The shoe buckles, like the fancy embroidery scissors, suggest an outward projection of gentility. Sunday-best shoes and fancy-work scissors used in public spaces show sophistication in their attitudes towards display.

TABLE 4.7 • Belleisle buckle breakdowns

Type	Description	Material	Size	Date range
Rectangular shoe buckle	Curved to shape of instep along drilled axis.	Copper alloy	40 × 29 mm	1700–1740
Square-framed shoe or belt buckle	Similar to Whitehead 577, asymmetrical buckle. Broken.	Copper alloy	26 mm wide	1575–1700
Rectangular buckle	Identical to girdle buckle at Portsmouth, late 18th century.[1] Similar to Whitehead 645 (shoe buckle).	Copper alloy	32 × 21 mm	1690–1720 (Whitehead)
Portion of a buckle frame	Smooth, rounded edge and flat back. Decorated with cross-hatched motif.	Copper alloy	27 mm wide	u/k
Portion of a buckle frame	Part of a white metal buckle. Plain, with a small extension off one side. Possibly an attachment point for a hook.	Possibly pewter	19 mm × 22 mm (broken) – original 28 mm wide?	u/k

NOTE

1 White, "Knee, Garter, Girdle, Hat, Stock, and Spur Buckles," 249, Figure 15.

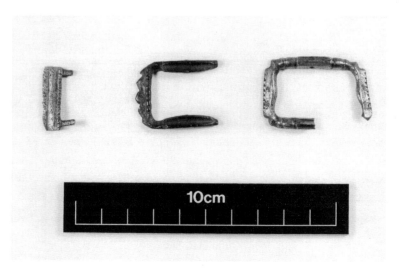

FIGURE 4.15
Buckles,
Belleisle.

FIGURE 1.5 • Trade silver buckle, Beaubassin.

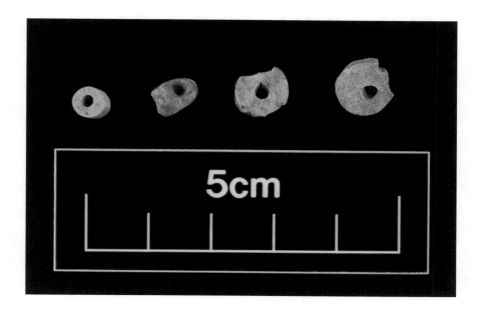

FIGURE 1.7 • Pipe stem fragments, possibly beads. Beaubassin.

FIGURE 2.2 • Plated scissors and snips found at Beaubassin.

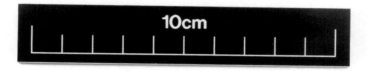

FIGURE 2.6 • Plated scissors, Beaubassin.

FIGURE 2.13 • Snips, Belleisle. Objects found together in the Blanchard house, unit A, level 1.

FIGURE 2.19 • Needle case, Louisbourg. Likely belonged to Anne Levron, Marianne Benoist, or Anne Jacau.

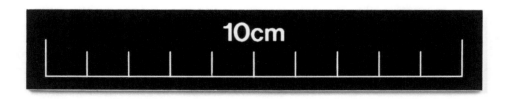

FIGURE 2.20 • Wooden and iron awl, Beaubassin.

FIGURE 3.1 • Textile seals, Blanchard house, Belleisle.

FIGURE 3.2 • Textile seal with the mark of the town of Mazamet, Beaubassin.

FIGURE 4.2 • Clay button mould for pewter buttons, Beaubassin.

FIGURE 4.7 • Bone button and bovine scapula, Beaubassin.

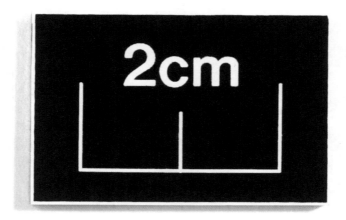

FIGURE 4.9 • Sleeve button, green paste jewel in plated setting, Beaubassin.

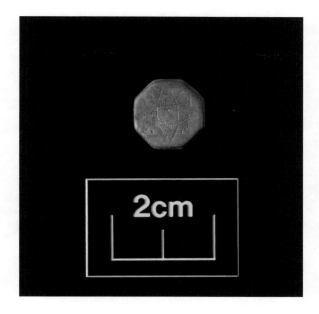

FIGURE 4.11 • Hand-etched button, Beaubassin.

FIGURE 4.12 • Copper alloy sleeve buttons with fleur de lys details, Melanson.

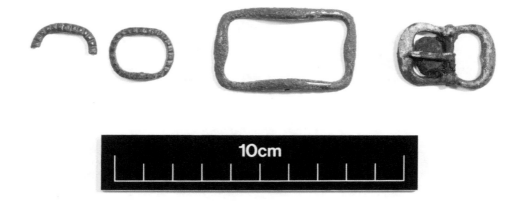

FIGURE 4.14 • Copper alloy shoe buckles, Beaubassin.

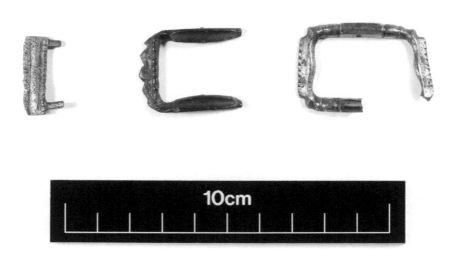

FIGURE 4.15 • Buckles, Belleisle.

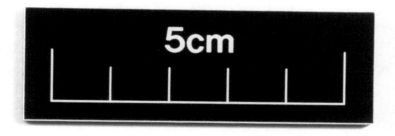

FIGURE 4.16 • Brass buckle, Melanson.

FIGURE 4.18 • Crucifix, Belleisle.

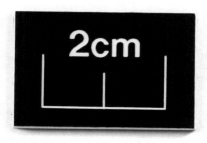

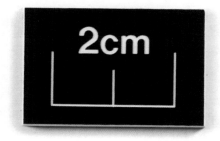

FIGURE 4.20 • Glass dove bead, Belleisle.

FIGURE 4.21 • Possible rosary beads, Beaubassin.

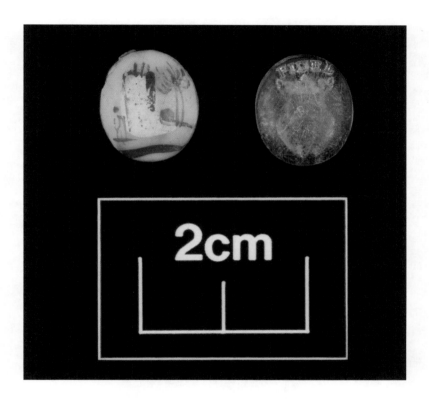

FIGURE 4.22 • *The Fidel Jewel*, Beaubassin.

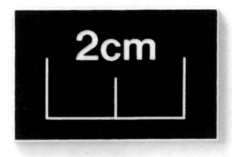

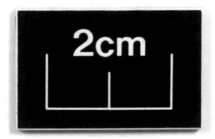

FIGURE 5.8 • Textile seal, single disc, obverse (top) and reverse (bottom), Beaubassin.
The text around the obverse side appears to read PIE----- ANH or ANK.

Melanson

Pieces of twelve different buckles were uncovered at Melanson, most from the house of Jean Charles Belliveau and Madeleine Melanson. Five were made of iron, and seven of copper alloy. Most of these were shoe or knee buckles, and the majority had simple surface embellishments or were cast in curved and decorative shapes. All of them are too early in style to be knee buckles for breeches, as those did not come into regular use until approximately 1735, and were not standard practice, replacing buttons entirely, until after 1750.[47] The early date also makes it possible for them to have been owned and worn by Belliveau prior to his death in 1707.

One fascinating buckle was discovered at Charles Melanson's house during the 1984 excavations (figure 4.16). The ornate copper-alloy buckle is approximately 32 × 29 mm, broken just past the crossbar, and displays the characteristic curves and rosettes of figure-eight–shaped buckles from the second half of the seventeenth or the early eighteenth centuries. Noël Hume identifies buckles of this type as small belt buckles, and a hobbyist source suggests horse harness buckles, while Whitehead and White reclassify them as spur buckles.[48] Rather than a leather strap, a cast metal pin terminating in a hook would hang from the crossbar, attaching to a loop on the spur arm. Identification of spur buckles missing the chape can only ever be tentative, but the shape, style, and size of this buckle are very similar to others in this category.

This buckle is likely to have been worn with a spur similar in style to the boot spur found in the trash pit at the Roma Site on Prince Edward Island, an eight-pointed star-shaped rowel on a simple U-shaped yoke with plain, undecorated arms and rectangular terminals.[49] Like the Melanson family, Jean Pierre Roma, founder of the Roma settlement, was culturally connected outside the Acadian community as the director of the La Compagnie de l'Est de l'Ile Saint-Jean.[50]

Spurs were worn predominantly by men in the seventeenth and eighteenth centuries both for riding and for status-related display. They were worn with boots rather than shoes, and buckle styles ranged from very simple iron trapezoids to moulded, stamped, and plated copper.[51] Cheaper iron spurs were part of the ironmongery sold by chapmen and peddlers alongside scissors, thimbles, whistles, and knives, while more expensive gilded versions could be custom-made or purchased at the jeweller. Spurs lost their connection with knighthood as they became civilian status symbols into the early modern period, but did not discard their gendered nature. Girded for war even in civilian dress, the wearers of spurs with decorative "spectacle buck-

TABLE 4.8 • Melanson buckle breakdowns

Type	Description	Material	Size	Date range
Oval buckle frame	Plain	Iron	37 × 25 mm	1690–1720[1]
Shoe buckle	Matches Whitehead 661, anchor chape.[2]	Iron (plated?)	40 × 30 mm	1690–1720
Double framed sub-circular spur buckle	For rowel-type spur. Matches buckle YORYM-BAC257 on finds.co.uk, and Whitehead 663.[3]	Iron (plated?)	24 × 15 mm	1690–1720
Rectangular, fragment	One corner only. Plain, flat. Cast rectangular or sub-rectangular buckle, possibly garter buckle.[4]	Iron	22 × 24 mm	ca 1570–1700
Belt or harness buckle[5]	Rectangular, pin and rollbar intact.	Iron	23 × 20 mm, pin 20 mm	–
Double framed sub-circular shoe buckle	Multipurpose spectacle buckle (Whitehead 303).	Copper alloy	37 × 28 mm, broken (orig ~ 50 × 30 mm)	ca 1550–1650
Small T-shaped fragment	See Whitehead 531–2 for closest options.	Copper alloy	19 mm × 8 mm	1620–1680?
Plain shoe or knee buckle	Curved fragment, one side, hole drilled for separate pin.	Copper alloy	31 mm long, 5 mm wide at hole	1660–1720
No details		Copper alloy	u/k	–
Spur buckle	Decorated with rosettes. Smaller version of Whitehead 444. Trilobe trefoil with fleur de lys.	Copper alloy	32 × 30 mm long (broken – original ~ 55 × 30 mm)	1600–1720
Shoe or spur buckle	Fragment, curved. Whitehead 560 or 563. (Central pin with asymmetrical loops).	Copper alloy	25 × 10 mm	1575–1700
Plain rectangular buckle	Bevelled edge. Whitehead 464.	Copper alloy	30 × 23 mm wide along broken side (est. orig. 0 × 50 mm?)	ca 1570–1700

NOTES

1 White, "Constructing Identities," 211.

2 Whitehead, *Buckles 1250–1800*, 101.

3 Ibid., 103 Also see https://finds.org.uk/database/artefacts/record/id/841980.

4 White, "Knee, Garter, Girdle, Hat, Stock, and Spur Buckles," 248–9, figure 14.

5 Type 5a from Fort Stanwix (ca 1758–1828). See Grimm, *Archaeological Investigation of Fort Ligonier 1960–1965*, 56.

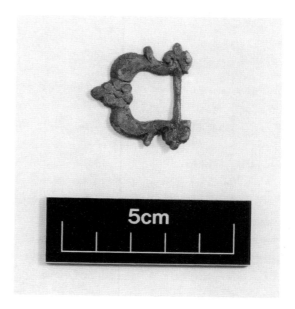

FIGURE 4.16 • Brass buckle, Melanson.

les" projected active masculinity and defined themselves through their visible – and audible – presence. The decoration and composition of the Melanson spur buckle suggests that it was part of dress wear rather than purely utilitarian farm equipment, a way to distinguish the wearer.

Charles and Pierre Melanson, the original founders of the settlement, had an English mother, and Charles Melanson's continuing attachment to the English was commonly known. Along with working to ensure the good favour of Boston magistrates, he also informed on local privateers and merchants to the English.[52] In return, the Melanson family and their allies were described by the English as being "aw'd by the Garrison [and] are the most, if not the only tractable Inhabitants in the province."[53] The relationship between Acadians and the British was certainly fraught at times, but co-operation and collaboration, as Griffiths points out, was crucial for the smooth functioning of the colony as a whole.[54] This close relationship, the Melansons' relative wealth and access to imports, and the settlement's close proximity to the official presence at the fort shaped their material culture. The Melanson association with British authorities at Fort Anne and in Massachusetts included shared values and a shared visual language of display. The Melansons expressed their understanding of what it meant to live within the banlieue through their visible engagement with elite English values.[55]

OBSERVERS' REPORTS INVARIABLY DESCRIBE Acadians as wearing either wood-
en sabots or leather moccasins, but the shoe found at Grand Pré and the buckles at
Beaubassin, Belleisle, and Melanson prove popular use of European-style leather
shoes. This difference between observation and evidence speaks to something interesting happening with self-presentation and perhaps deliberate choices of which items
were to be worn in front of whom. Melanson, with the family's complex relationship
with both the English and the French, and Beaubassin, where traders engaged with
merchants and traders from Indigenous cultures as well as New England, New France,
and Acadia, both revealed artifacts that suggest interest in fashioning community images in politically useful directions. The demarcation between work-related clothing
for potentially muddy or cold conditions and dress clothing for in town and possibly
Sunday finest shows a kind of flexibility already seen in other aspects of French settler adaptation to the Fundy marshes. Even at places like Belleisle, where the overall
vernacular was more local and further from that of the elite than Louisbourg, the
presence of brass buckles and buttons indicates the use of European-style clothing
including knee breeches and garters for stockings. Inventories of Acadian women in
Louisbourg include European-style shoes but make no mention of moccasins or sabots. These working shoes were not practical or fashionable on the cobbled streets of
the fort, but that did not prevent Acadians in Beaubassin from switching styles when
appropriate for their tasks and environment.

Other Closures

Different methods of fastening clothing have distinct effects on the garments and on
the body's movement inside them. Buttons fix edges semi-permanently; the buttons
themselves can be moved, but the buttonholes remain as a fixed puncture in the garment. Buttons themselves are solid and when placed at the fixed points of the buttonholes, they conform the fashion and the body inside to a shape set by the maker rather
than the user. This stabilized construction was a very European way to construct
masculine clothing, in opposition to the loose, draped, and more adaptable garments
worn by Mi'kmaw men.[56] The notion of the body as an amorphous construct in a state
of constant flux appeared across pre-modern Europe, often accompanied by anxiety

over the intersections of corporeality, stability, and gender. The changing body reflected the uncertain materiality of the world at large, and both required some form
of imposed control.[57]

Hooks and eyes could be found on everyone's clothing but were more closely associated with women's wear. The types of closures used affected the movement options
for the body inside the clothing, restricting some movements and permitting others.
Sleeves set in with pins required more caution when raising the arms and in rapid
movement than those that were laced on or sewn in, for example.[58] Embracing would
certainly require more forethought! The collection of closure options for women's
dress – lacing, hooks and eyes, and pins – create a freedom of choice that colonial
men's clothing had less of.

Lacing makes a woman's clothing more fluid, reactive to changes in her body shape
and comfort. Lacing a bodice closed creates subtle differences in a woman's silhouette
each time she dresses, sometimes compressing and sometimes embracing the body
inside of it. The cord length and tension are variable, quickly adjusted on a moment's
whim. Pinning garments, a very common method of arranging and attaching accessories and draperies to women's garments, makes outfits less stable. They become
temporary signposts, to be rearranged and recombined as mood and context determine.[59] This style of adjustment was an older one, associated closely with the working
poor and farm labour (see chapter 5, under Stockings). Men's garment closures, on the
other hand, emphasized conformity. Buttons and buckles replicated the same effects
each time a man put on his clothes. Lacing plackets in the back of breeches and waistcoats allowed some motion, but they were hidden as opposed to women's displayed
laces. This engendered a sense of trustworthiness in men's clothing in contrast to the
anxiety surrounding the body in women's wear. The guidelines that kept his clothed
silhouette consistent did not apply to her, and societal condemnation followed the
fluidly dressed women as a result.[60]

Contemporary commentary on Indigenous dress drew on the same narratives,
emphasizing anxiety about unrestrained leather tunics and leggings – button-free and
potentially amorphous: "As to their coats, these are large and broad. The sleeves are
not attached to the body, but are separate therefrom, and tied together by two thongs,
separated into equal parts by an opening which serves for the passing of the head.
One of these sleeves [falls to the] front, and covers only half of the arm; the other falls
behind, and clothes the entire shoulders."[61] Narratives about falsehoods perpetuating
themselves through dress permeated the popular written culture of early modern
Europe, with articles in publications such as the *Mercure de France* that fixated on the

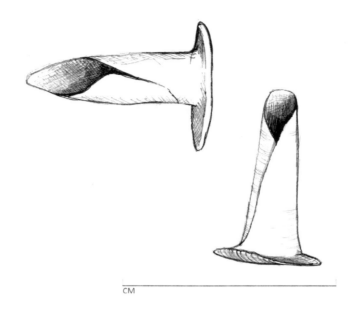

FIGURE 4.17 • Possible tinkler cones, Beaubassin.

fluid concealment of women's wear as the locus for tension over sexuality, freedom, concealment, and propriety.[62] Lessened formality in Acadian dress in some locations was a subject of discussion and derision for external commentators, that same fluidity a threat to the formal sartorial order.

Aglets and Tinkler Cones

Aglets were small items made from sheet metal, usually finely hammered copper, that was cut, wrapped in a cone, and pressed at the point to create an enclosed casing for the end of laces. Regulated by sumptuary law in multiple regions during the early modern period, aglets were a form of visible decoration on clothing and a place to display wealth and status; the presence of decorative aglets at a site therefore suggests the presence of garments of some value. Silver and gold aglets were forbidden to the common man of France, and copper aglets would be out of place on a working man's rough homespun smock.[63]

A pair of cones identified as aglets from Beaubassin are unfinished and crude (figure 4.17). These may have been lost in the middle of the manufacturing process, the bottom left uncompressed, but given the general size and shape were more likely intended as small tinkler cone-style decorations. Tinklers were associated with

Indigenous styles of dress and aglets with European clothing, though they could be deployed in similar ways. Aglets were attached to garments by pinching the wide end closed around a ribbon, while tinklers were attached via a strap passing through a small aperture at the narrow end.[64] A decorative aesthetic that included tinklers and aglets would have been recognizable to Europeans, making them an easy accessory to transition from one dress style to another. The tinkler cones found at Beaubassin were in association with a series of dress-related artifacts and notions, archaeological lot number 7B17E2 containing a sewing needle, four glass beads, a hook for a hook and eye closure, two pins, and a brass button, as well as the cones depicted in figure 4.17. The proximity of the cones to the other dressmaking elements suggests they may also have been intended for use on clothing – a sewing case spilled in the dirt, or a lost hussif with the fabric since decayed.

European settlers in other east coast colonies developed syncretic forms of dress that combined elements of European and Indigenous fashion systems, and a large number of tinkler cones found at Fort Michilimackinac have been definitively attributed to European (both French and British) as well as Indigenous use. Tinkler cones were likely worn by French and Indigenous residents at Fort St Joseph in conjunction with imported beads and metal buttons, and by residents of an early eighteenth-century European settlement in Texas.[65] The similarity of tinklers to decorative aglets, already part of the early modern European dress lexicon, also suggests the possibility of acceptance of the accessory with minimal cultural friction. Evidence of tinkler manufacture at French and British sites in the Great Lakes region confirms European use of tinklers on clothing, part of a blending of aesthetics between colonial settlers and Indigenous people in that contact sphere.[66] The presence of tinkler cones at Beaubassin does not definitively prove that they were regularly worn on Acadian clothing, but it would not have been a shocking aesthetic choice, nor one without precedent.

Hooks and Eyes

Hook and eye closures are more like buttons than lacing, in that they are sewn in place to create a fixed closure point on a garment. The usual method of overcasting hooks and eyes onto the surface of a garment, however, is much less permanent than cutting or piercing the fabric as for buttonholes or eyelets. A handful of iron wire hooks and eyes found at Beaubassin are standard for the type and time period, though hooks and eyes have retained the same shape from at least as early as the fifteenth century to the present day. This makes dating them all but impossible except through archaeological context.

The single eye found at Belleisle was 17 × 11 mm long, in line with standard sizes for the time. While Carolyn White's examinations of hooks and eyes from Portsmouth Point found brass was commonly used, Fort Michilimackinac's colonial assemblage was more than 90 per cent iron (13 brass : 139 iron), as were all the examples recovered from Acadian sites to date.[67] Hooks are more commonly found archaeologically than the corresponding eyes, as hooks were often paired with thread loops instead of metal eyes or bars as a lighter-weight option. While associated with women's dress, the presence of hooks and eyes is not diagnostically useful for garment types, as they could be used for men's coats and waistcoats as well as women's bodices and stomachers.[68]

Jewellery

Accessories shifted in and out of fashion over time as dress styles changed. Necklaces became more common as necklines descended through the eighteenth century, and knee buckles fell out of use as breeches became less popular. Shoe buckles increased in size and in decorative nature throughout the eighteenth century following their adoption in the late seventeenth, while pearls remained as popular – and expensive – as ever. The rise in manufacture of paste and glass gemstones in the eighteenth century helped to make costume jewellery more accessible to the rising middling class, and the larger quantities in circulation means that more examples of these wardrobe add-ons have survived in the archaeological record.

Jewellery counts as small finds, like buttons and buckles, the lines blurring between the categories of "practical" and "decorative." Jewellery, especially religious items like reliquaries and crucifixes, carries cultural symbolism as well as reflecting individual taste. Acadian jewellery was small and primarily religious in nature, and Catholic iconography is a constant theme even among the simplest pieces.[69] That simplicity does not necessarily mean they were inexpensive, however. Jewellery was a luxury item and was worn relatively sparingly in colonial settings, particularly among non-elites.

Jewellery was part of the Acadian vernacular, contemporary accounts describing their use of Catholic icons and pendants.[70] The sensory nature of the practice of Catholicism extended to the tactile with carved rosary beads and moulded glass pendants, imported reliquaries, and the simple brass crucifixes in a style popular across the European colonies. In addition to religious articles, some Acadian women were also wearing strings of beads, gold earrings, and finger rings set with both semi-precious and imitation stones. There were no silversmiths resident in Louisbourg at the time, and any fine jewellery, religious or otherwise, would have to have been imported.[71]

More secular jewellery appears in Louisbourg probate inventories than has been found at the other three sites. Marie Josephe Le Borgne de Belleisle had the most extensive jewellery collection on record for an Acadian woman, much of it secular in nature. The few items we do have from other locations were preserved by accident rather than by deliberate abandonment: broken pieces slipped between floorboards, glass beads trapped beneath the rubble of a housefire, and buried in infill. Even those are plainer in nature, with less inherent monetary value. More expensive examples and those with personal meaning may have been taken out of Acadia during the deportation, either by their owners or stolen by British soldiers. Nevertheless, those pieces that do remain give us at least part of the story.

Religious Jewellery

Acadia was served by French Catholic priests even while under British rule, their freedom of religion preserved in the treaties of the early eighteenth century. The priests assigned to Port Royal came from two distinct groups, the Récollet fathers and the Sulpician Order. The Récollet fathers, members of a French Franciscan order, served in Port Royal until 1720 and Louisbourg until 1756.[72] Other Catholic orders considered the Récollets too morally lax, particularly those from Brittany, and disdained their regular carousing with ship captains and fishermen. The departures of these priests shortly after the Treaty of Utrecht left an educational void for the children in Port Royal that was not refilled. Following the Récollet withdrawal from Port Royal in 1720, the area's Catholics were served instead by a series of Sulpician priests, likely from the seminary in Montreal. The order of Saint Sulpice had strong ties to Marian devotion, as well as a reputation that was quite the opposite from the more laissez-faire Récollets. Sulpicians were notoriously strict. They tended to be academics, doctrinally focused and strict in matters of morality, particularly sexuality and the roles of women. They did not take vows of poverty, and as with clergy in France, were supported by a voluntary – yet socially pressured – tithe of one-thirteenth of a parishioner's annual income.[73]

Religious life in the colonies followed the Roman Catholic church's precepts and the cycles of the feast days and holidays. Thirty-seven feast days and fifty-two sabbaths were to be annually devoted to religious practice, though the sheer number of days off may have encouraged settlers to work through some of the holy observances.[74] Abbé Petit described the Acadians around Port Royal as "inclined to piety" in 1686, despite having spent a decade and a half without spiritual leadership prior to his arrival.[75] They were not ascetically inclined, as a legal complaint from Beaubassin referred to local women coming to confession so decked out in lace and ruffles that their eyes could not be seen.[76] Mass was a social occasion as much as a religious one, an opportunity for families who would otherwise not see much of one another to reinforce connections. Even for those who preferred a quieter day of rest, mass was the central social event of the week, parishioners travelling 16 to 20 km from their homes to attend church in Port Royal in the 1680s.[77] Children acted as altar servers in the early days of Port Royal and were formally catechized, though formal religious education ended after the church was burned and clergy removed in 1690.[78]

The priests serving Acadian communities changed regularly, their attention often focused more on converting Mi'kmaw communities than on the French settlements. Port Royal alone saw twenty-three different Catholic priests stationed there between 1650 and 1755, with one – Abbé Durand in 1711 – even imprisoned in Boston for sedition.[79] The impact of this distance can be traced through parish records, in the number of infants baptized at home by the midwife or father of the child. As a result of the inconsistency Acadian Catholicism became a faith that was less reliant on the presence of a priest, centring more on the group and the individual. The visual aspects of their faith-based practices acted as a unifying force, identifying marks for a minority community.

Belleisle

Catholic devotional items have been found at Belleisle, including a brass crucifix and part of a glass dove. Both are detailed, the workmanship appropriate for small-run production of similar items, most likely through a lost-wax method of casting. Both clearly demonstrate not only the importance of religious faith, but the tangible reminders of that connection. Brass crosses and crucifixes were common in French colonial spaces as personal items of devotion, while elsewhere they were used primarily as trade goods.[80]

The Belleisle crucifix (figure 4.18) is the right size and style to depend from the bottom of a rosary or chaplet, and appears identical to examples found at Fort Michilimackinac in Michigan (1715–83) and the French colonial cemetery at the Moran Site in Harrison County, Mississippi (1717–23).[81] It is a standard Latin cross with cast images on both sides. On one side, the raised image depicts the mostly naked body of Jesus on the cross, a standard form generally known as the "corpus." The corpus has the partial letters "INRI" above his head, standing for the Latin phrase "Iesus Nazarenus, Rex

FIGURE 4.18 • Crucifix, Belleisle.

Iudaeorum," commonly seen on crucifixes across Europe. On both sides of the crucifix the figure's head is surrounded by a one-ring nimbus, or halo. The edges are defined by hashed decoration that emulates scrollwork. A skull rests under the corpus's feet, a common image used by the Jesuits to represent Adam's skull, and by extension original sin. Christ's blood dripping onto the skull symbolizes the washing away of sins, an event understood by Christians to have occurred at the crucifixion.[82]

The obverse shows the Christus Rex (Christ as King) archetype of Jesus. In this image, the figure is clothed and bearded. Similar imagery on other crosses of this type has been identified as the figure of the Virgin Mary, but the appearance of the beard in this figure requires different identification. The vestments are important to this form, combining the symbols of godhead and royalty.[83] The image is surmounted by the sacred heart, the holy dove, and flanked by the capital-letter texts "JESVS" and "MARIA." The figure's feet are consumed in flames, suggesting the parable known colloquially as the "harrowing of hell." In the tale, once crucified, Jesus descended into Purgatory or Hell itself to free the unbaptized righteous. This is the moment just prior to that resurrection, the Christus Rex figure hovering in a liminal stage between death and rebirth.[84]

The raised images complement each other, the duality conveying a clear message to the member of the Savoie household who originally wore it. The Corpus and Christus Rex tell the story of death followed by action, and in a motif particularly associated with the Counter-Reformation, Adam, symbol of humankind, goes from sinner to saved with a flip of the cross. The Harrowing of Hell is not purely biblical canon, only a handful of minor references appearing in the New Testament.[85] It found expanded form in the non-canonical gospels in the third century, but took on new resonance with the emergence of Purgatory as an important concept in medieval Catholicism.[86] Some English Protestants, already contemptuous of "papacy," were no more inclined to indulge the concept of Purgatory, seeing both the concept and the means of mitigation – good works in the name of the deceased and the recitation of funeral masses – as an elaborate scam intended to fleece the "poor Country People, being extreamly Simple and Ignorant."[87] Artwork regarding the Harrowing declined after the sixteenth century and the focus on the torments of Hell and Purgatory in French Catholicism declined in the mid-seventeenth, giving this piece a strong connection to this particular point in time.[88] The emphasis on new beginnings after hardship inherent in the story of the Harrowing would be likely to resonate with the early inhabitants of Acadia, their situation bringing fresh appeal to a story about moving on from a place of waiting to a new paradise.

Similar brass crosses have been found at other colonial sites including Fort Michilimackinac and Fortress Louisbourg, and the most common form of crucifix from the Fort Michilimackinac assemblage is this one – a single piece of cast brass with a raised graphic on one or both sides. Seven crucifixes of very similar style were found at the Fort, all with the same ridged edge, an identical corpus with INHS on the obverse, and a different image on the reverse.[89] All but one of the obverse images include Mary, the last showing an image of the Eucharist. Cherubs or angels appear at Mary's sides on three, and the words "JESUS" and "MARIA" on the arms of two.[90] No beads survive with the Belleisle crucifix to indicate the kind of rosary or chaplet with which it had been worn, but the in-progress rosary beads found at Beaubassin (see figure 4.21) suggest that making the chains of beads from local materials was an acceptable option.

The Louisbourg collection includes one cross attached to a beaded chaplet (figure 4.19), a third example of the same style of crucifix. This cross was found in a context that dates its loss to ca 1750–52. It bears a similar figure of the corpus on one side, without the INHS lettering. The obverse shows the Assumption of Mary, her head crowned, her feet on the globe, an angel or cherub at each arm of the cross symbolizing her rise

FIGURE 4.19 • Chaplet.

into heaven, and a possible fleur de lys on top.[91] The story of the Annunciation has a similar theme of redemption following suffering, and optimism associated with the resurrection. The presence of Marian references on the Louisbourg, Michilimackinac, and Belleisle crucifixes is common among late medieval and early modern Catholics, for whom the cult of Mary was an important part of worship.[92] Images of Mary appear on the reverse of crosses and reliquaries found in French regions, particularly in Brittany, the home of the Récollet order.

A glass bead in the shape of a dove made of white and blue glass was found in the same unit and lot at Belleisle as the crucifix (figure 4.20). The surviving fragment has a blue glass bead affixed to its breast, and traces of blue glass suggesting the original presence of similar beads on the undersides of both wings. The dove, a symbol for the Holy Spirit – one part of the Christian triune deity – appears on the crucifix as well, one of the more common symbols of the divine presence. The bird bead may have been part of a rosary, with portions of what appears to be a broken glass loop between the divisions of the tail. Suspended this way from a chain or at the base of a chaplet, the bead would have hung with beak downward, in the traditional posture of the Holy Spirit in Catholic imagery.

The blue glass drop on the belly area is not a common inclusion on dove images, and has multiple potential interpretations. It may represent a tear, a relatively common

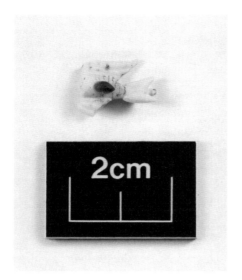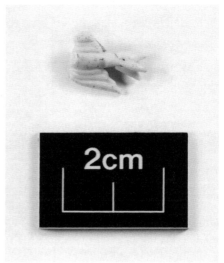

FIGURE 4.20 • Glass dove bead, Belleisle.

motif in Catholic art, as with the "gift of tears" attributed to some saints and mystics, the three glass droplets a sign of the Trinity, or drops of the water used in the ceremony of baptism.[93] Passages from the New Testament describe the Holy Spirit appearing as a dove at the baptism of Jesus, and water imagery may be connected to the dove in that respect.[94] Blue is also the colour traditionally associated with the Virgin Mary, which may have played a role in the glass artist's aesthetic choice.

The pieces were found close to the upper layer of the unit, suggesting they were lost during the deportation or shortly before. The dove and the crucifix may have been part of the same piece of devotional jewellery, or two separate items kept near each other – possibly in a jewellery case that has since decayed or been lost. If the dove was a part of the same rosary or chaplet as the crucifix, then it would most likely have been a marker bead or a pendant dangling off the other end of the single-string chaplet. Full rosaries included 153 plain beads, 15 marked beads, and a pendant, while the chaplets included only ten beads in total – making them more economical, and requiring less effort for a craftsman. The marker bead on the Louisbourg chaplet has a groove scored into it to distinguish it from the other beads, indicating the point at which one would turn back and complete another recitation of the prayers. This gives us a useful point of reference for scored beads found at Beaubassin.

Beaubassin

No crosses have emerged from Beaubassin, but that in no way indicates a lesser devotion to the material forms of Catholic worship. A series of glass beads that appear to have been designed or altered for the purposes of a rosary or chaplet are evidence of this. The context at Beaubassin has been disturbed by previous earthworks, so knowing how and where the beads were originally deposited on the site is impossible, though the combinations and some rarer types tell an interesting story.

Of the sixty-five beads of various styles found at Beaubassin (table 1.2), eight show signs of being part of a rosary or chaplet. Those signs include grooves carved into the surface to make a tactile marker, an elongated tab on one side of a glass bead to make it asymmetrical, or two holes drilled through the bead at 90° to turn it into a cross-piece to adjoin two separate chains (see figure 4.21, far right). Chaplets do not need a cross-piece, the pendants hanging from the bottom of a regular link, but full rosaries require one to complete the circle. Stone and wood beads were used for this purpose, and glass trade beads altered for the same.[95] Similar grooved beads were found at Fort Michilimackinac and have been identified as rosary beads designed either for local use or trade.[96]

A blue glass trade bead found with a partially drilled secondary cross-hole appears to have been intended as a cross-piece. Imported rosary beads were more commonly made of bone or ivory, and the unfinished glass beads at Beaubassin indicate local production for local use.[97] The proximity of the Mi'kmaw and Acadian communities in Siknikt and the pre-existing trade arrangements at Beaubassin also make it possible that these beads were intended for Mi'kmaw use. The elongated amber-coloured glass bead in particular is a style seen on rosaries made by and traded to Indigenous groups.[98]

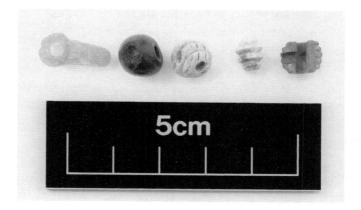

FIGURE 4.21 •
Possible rosary
beads, Beaubassin.

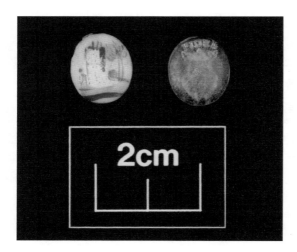

FIGURE 4.22 • *The Fidel Jewel,* Beaubassin.

A doubled glass pendant from Beaubassin is the most striking jewellery find to date, comprising two glass ovals, 14 × 10 mm, found back to back in the verdigris remains of what was once a copper setting (figure 4.22). One section is painted with an abstract image that appears to be a human form standing beside a tower or mill, with a wind-shaped spruce tree on the far side. The other is a clear, moulded glass bead of equal size with the transparent image of a doubled heart and the Latin word FIDEL surmounting the heart. This doubled heart image is a symbol found in the Sacré-Coeur de Vendée, a symbol seen on marriage jewellery and strongly associated with betrothal in the Poitou region of France.[99] The doubled hearts combine the Catholic symbols of the Sacred Heart of Jesus with the Immaculate Heart of Mary. The Immaculate Heart was a focus for religious fervour in northern and central France in the eighteenth century, connected particularly with the teachings of Louis Grignion de Montfort, a French priest (and later Catholic saint) who preached heavily on devotion to the Immaculate Heart prior to his death in 1716.[100]

Double-sided glass pendants appeared as religious devotional items in the early modern period, sometimes with painted miniatures set behind clear glass domes, other times used to preserve physical relics of saints. These pendants could be attached to the bottom of rosaries in place of a crucifix, or worn as separate pieces of jewellery. The fidel jewel falls in a category somewhere between these miniature reliquaries and moulded beads without drilled holes. Jewellery items found at archaeological sites are often broken or of low quality, small items that the original owners might have missed taking or not bothered to retrieve during an expedient exit. This piece represented significant expense, and was no doubt sorely missed. If the fidel jewel's design is related to Montfort and religion in the Vendée, as archaeologist and original finder Eric Tremblay suggests, then its presence in Beaubassin suggests that the inhabitants were keeping open communication with and were being influenced by trends and changes in the Poitou region.[101] Not only that, but they were also purchasing new and expensive pieces of personal adornment that spoke directly to their evolving religious values.

Religion and Religious Objects

Early modern Catholicism was not only spiritual in its expression but also grounded in and elevated by the physical. Items and vestments that were part of the holy service were imbued with a certain kind of divinity themselves, and objects of devotion played a prominent role in the display and enactment of faith. Raised embroidery on the vestments caught the light and drums and bells called Acadians to mass, while communion, incense, and choristers added taste, scent, and liturgical sound to the proceedings.[102] Robert Hale described the Acadian call to mass in 1731 as a public ritual incorporating all of the senses: "[there are] 2 Mais Houses or Churches, on one of which they hang out a Flagg Morning Evening for Prayers, to the other the Priest goes once a day only, Habited like a Fool in Petticoats, with a Man after him with a Bell In one Hand ringing at every door, a lighted Candle Lanthorn in the other."[103]

Textured rosary beads were designed to be touched and counted, soothed in the fingers and rubbed for comfort and a constant reminder of the presence of the divine. Many of the beads found at Acadian sites either were made from local materials or were imported and altered locally. The grooves and spirals carved into them, the unique drilling of the holes, and the presence of pendants all confirm the purpose of these beads for personal prayer. Large items of personal devotion were not commonly seen in inventories and wills in Louisbourg, but the small, portable items appear frequently.[104]

A letter from Louisbourg in 1756 described the Acadians as "remarkably fond of rosaries, crucifixes, agnus deis, and all the little trinkets consecrated by religion, with which they love to adorn their persons."[105] This is corroborated by physical evidence across Acadian archaeological sites. Beads found at Beaubassin show that while glass beads were being brought in for use and trade, locals were also repurposing older materials and crafting new ones on site. Crucifixes, beads, and other "trinkets" were not status-display objects in the economic sense. Most of them were inexpensive and of common types readily available in the colonial marketplace. Other pieces were hand-made, incorporating materials that were already an integral part of the visual landscape of Acadia. Sacred jewellery became the property of both public and private spaces, extensions of the bodies on which they were worn. Less intimate than linens, the brass and stone nevertheless took on body heat and were worn down by the repeated touch of fingertips. The half-drilled glass rosary beads give us a glimpse of a transient activity – the maker bent over at his bench, tiny auger and glass bead in hand, deft hands working to affect transformation without destruction. Possibly intended for himself or a family member, or a trading partner from the nearby Mi'kmaq settlement, his painstaking work transformed a currency and commodity into something sacred.

Secular Jewellery

Secular jewellery is evident at all the Acadian settlements examined here. A copper-alloy badge, a beaded choker, and sleeve buttons at Melanson, sleeve buttons at Beaubassin, and a blue paste gemstone found at Belleisle stand with gemstone and paste rings, earrings, and necklaces from the Louisbourg inventories as examples of Acadian interest in self-decoration. Glass beads were worn as strings of false pearls, a style popular in France since the sixteenth century. Short necklaces increased in popularity following the disappearance of the neck ruff from fashion. Contemporary portraits of elite women showed them with necklaces ranging from one strand to five, all of them worn with the open-necked robes à la française and square-necked mantuas that typified expensive women's dress of the time.[106] A series of glass beads found in Anne Bourg's cellar at Melanson was likely one of these short strings, consisting of white and black beads that would sit closely around the wearer's neck and maintain that fashionable line.[107] The short bead choker would have looked out of place worn with simple jackets and jumps, suggesting that Bourg's wardrobe likely contained at least one fashionable mantua or robe de chambre (see chapter 5, under Gowns, Skirts, and Petticoats).

A heart-shaped badge found outside the house of Anne Melanson is a unique piece (figure 4.23). The small metal object appears to be made from a copper alloy, has faint traces of decoration on one side, and two small triangles – one on each long edge – which may once have been folded over to close the badge around a belt, strap, or shoe latchet. Similar pewter badges have been recorded from other post-medieval sites and identified as lovers' tokens or pilgrims' badges, though any inscription that may once have been etched into this article is so worn that it cannot be read. Whether a gift from Melanson's second husband Alexandre Robichaud, a love token from a suitor to one of her daughters, or a religious object of devotion connected to the Sacré Coeur,

TABLE 4.9 • Jewellery in Acadia

Type	Location	Owner	Material	Price
Badge, heart-shaped	Melanson	Melanson/Robichaud	Pewter	
Bead choker	Melanson	Anne Bourg	Glass	
Brooch, ring	Beaubassin		Silver	
Crucifix	Belleisle		Copper alloy	
Decorative stud	Melanson	Bourg/Melanson	Glass	
Earring, 1	Louisbourg	Marie Josephe Le Borgne de Belisle	Silver and gold	7£ 10 s / ea
Earrings, 1 pair	Louisbourg	Marie Josephe Le Borgne de Belisle	Gold and silver	30£
Earrings, 2 pairs	Louisbourg	Anne Levron	Gold	~5£ / pair?
Fidel Jewel	Beaubassin		Glass and copper alloy	
Gem inset	Belleisle		Glass	
Necklaces, 2	Louisbourg	Marie Josephe Le Borgne de Belisle	Pearls	1£ 10 s / ea.
Pendant, dove	Belleisle		Glass	
Ring	Louisbourg	Anne Levron	Gold	~2£
Ring	Louisbourg	Marie Josephe Le Borgne de Belisle	Gold, silver, paste gem	9£
Ring	Louisbourg	Marie Josephe Le Borgne de Belisle	Gold, red gemstone	24£
Rings, 2	Louisbourg	Marie Josephe Le Borgne de Belisle	Gold, green topaz	100£
Sleeve button	Beaubassin		Plated copper alloy, glass paste	
Sleeve button	Beaubassin		Pewter	
Sleeve button	Louisbourg	Pierre Benoist	Copper alloy	
Sleeve button	Louisbourg	Joseph Dugas or Charles de la Tour	Copper alloy, glass paste	

Sleeve button	Louisbourg	Joseph Dugas or Charles de la Tour	Copper alloy
Sleeve button	Louisbourg	Joseph Dugas or Timothe Latapy	Copper alloy, glass paste
Sleeve button	Louisbourg	Cressonet dit Beausejour (<1742) or Jean-Baptiste Guion (>1737)	Glass paste
Sleeve buttons, 1 pair	Melanson	Bourg/Melanson	Copper alloy

the heart badge is an intriguing glimpse into the small objects of decoration that filled the jewellery boxes of Acadia.

False and real gemstones were worn alongside one another, and the loose blue paste stone from Belleisle suggests that someone in the Blanchard-Savoie household had at least one item decorated with the faux gems.[108] Marie Josephe Le Borgne de Belleisle had real pearls in her inventory, as well as four gold rings, two mounted with real topaz and two with paste gemstones. At some point shortly before her death Le Borgne sent a gold earring back to France for repairs rather than entrust the work to someone closer by. A local tinsmith or blacksmith might be able to do simple repairs, but their skills were apparently considered inadequate for the kind of work needed on a piece of fine jewellery.[109] Whether the repair work was being done by the original jeweller or simply a more trusted workman with strong connections across the Atlantic is unknown. Committing to that level of expense, however, shows that even the non-religious jewellery was important to Le Borgne's concept of herself as a successful cosmopolitan merchant.

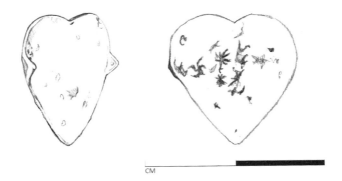

CM

FIGURE 4.23 • Heart-shaped badge, Melanson.

While many of the jewellery pieces found in Acadia were religious in nature, there were some not overtly associated with expressions of faith. Acadian women in both urban and rural environments were aware of contemporary trends in fashion jewellery and wore both real and fake gemstones alongside strings of beads and gold wedding rings. They wore items that connected back to their historic roots in France, fashions of the day, and those rooted in the economic and cultural realities of their own surroundings. Le Borgne's use of a jeweller in France particularly highlights the ongoing relationships maintained between some Acadians in the colony and artisans in the metropole, and the influences that the latter could still have on the former.

Conclusions

Small dress accessories and closures define the edges of garments and provide evidence for the kinds of garments worn under, beside, and around them. The presence of lacing rings, aglets, and the awl confirms that some garments were laced closed, and the hooks and eyes would have once belonged to jackets, waistcoats, or bodices that fit edge to edge. Leather and cloth shoes in European styles were worn in settlements alongside moccasins and sabots, suggesting variety in presentation. The moccasins and modified trade beads open a conversation about the potential for dress-related interchange between Acadian settlers and Indigenous groups.

Acadians at Beaubassin were engaged in processes of transformation, as indicated by the modified trade beads and reports of moccasin wearing, repurposing materials commonly associated with Mi'kmaw use for their own purposes. This cross-pollination or inspiration demonstrates the nature of the combination of two worlds of goods, beads intended to be commodities passed from European hands to Mi'kmaw, either coming back to rest with Acadians, or taking a detour in between to be modified into something new. The Acadians of Beaubassin may have modified European clothing with Indigenous fashion accessories, narrowing the style gap between themselves and the Mi'kmaq and widening that between Acadia and the formalized visuals of European civility. This developing fashion system was beginning to diverge from Continental and other colonial styles in important ways, and each settlement would continue to evolve with their own specific quirks until the disruptions of the deportation. The additions of trade beads and moccasins to the other garment types defined by the small finds – heeled shoes, buttoned waistcoats, and knee breeches, among others – was a part of a change away from Eurocentric notions of propriety, a shift that worried outside observers.[110]

The types of jewelled accessories worn indicated the socio-economic status of the owners and give us clues as to how their original owners had decided to present themselves. Shoe buckles and jewelled cufflinks in contemporary styles indicate that the Acadians of Beaubassin and Melanson were keeping up with styles worn both in other colonies and in fashion centres of Europe. The trade in gold- and silver-gilded buttons and the collections of copper alloy buttons in Louisbourg demonstrate what clothing looked like in a region heavily influenced by French fashion, with the buttons and spur buckles of the banlieue settlements following suit. The performative masculinity that accompanied horseback riding accoutrements like spurs intensified with the Melanson families' proximity to the seat of local political power. Religious articles made up a large part of the collection of decorative pieces, some of the intricate symbols of faith coming from Europe and reflecting the belief systems and popular religious beliefs of the Acadian families and their spiritual leaders. Others were typically colonial style, with Jesuit iconography and displays of redemption imagery. The rosaries and chaplets visually differentiated Acadians from British Protestants and provided a tangible connection to faith.

Acadians were neither removing themselves from the Atlantic network of goods or European styles of dress, nor committing to them exclusively. The pendants, beads, sleeve buttons, and buckles found on these sites all point toward the adoption and reworking of elite identity within a colonial context. While shifting their styles to accommodate the realities of their environment, they still maintained connection to changes in fashions and in philosophies from France. The messages in their accessories varied from site to site, more visible at Beaubassin than at Melanson or Louisbourg, while Belleisle reflected different priorities. The politics of living so close to the authorities at the forts and in the banlieue (French and English alike) required different dress choices than the trading hub on the isthmus, where maintaining good relationships with many different groups required a new kind of fluidity.

Garments

The wool of the sheep they raise is very good and the clothing worn
by the majority of the men and women is made of it … As for the women
they are always busy, and most of them keep their husbands and children
in serviceable linen materials and stockings which they make skillfully
from the hemp they have grown.[1]

— — — — — —

MAJOR CHANGES TOOK PLACE in women's and men's wardrobes alike in the
seventeenth century, the heavy opulence of the sixteenth century giving way to the
exuberance of the baroque and the fluttering delicacy of the rococo. This shift took
place in the colonies as well as in Europe, and Acadia was no exception. Fashion
changes followed the general shape of mainstream fashion, but with some subtle
and important differences. This chapter draws together evidence from previous
chapters to reconstruct the Acadian fashion system. That system includes the types
of garments worn, how outfits were put together, the ways in which those garments
related to the bodies they dressed, and the symbolic resonance of those choices – both
to the Acadians and to external observers.[2] Trace evidence suggests that Acadians in
different settlements chose different styles of dress, with varying levels of influence
from Continental European fashion. Some also drew upon accessories or materials
associated with Indigenous dress that sent specific signals, markers of belonging,
status, and identification.

Clothing bridges the gap between the personal and the social, individual choices existing within a system of contexts that define what is and is not appropriate.[3] Clothing
and adornment are languages through which people communicate personal, social,
religious, and economic information about themselves. These choices can be constrained by official factors such as sumptuary law, or social ones, such as community
shaming. Gender, economic status, marital status, religious affiliations, and more are

expressed in choices of clothing and accessories, and every human society has developed some commonly understood means of expressing all of those. The natural and social environments shape how human beings communicate through that visual language, and which dialect they "speak." An individual's choice of costume is personal communication within a broader, culturally imposed "grammar," an indicator of the levels of training and socialization required for the creation of a culturally approved personal appearance.[4] When expectations are subverted, consciously or otherwise, that approval can be withheld – sometimes with troubling results. Twentieth-century subcultures like the punk and hippie movements played with dress as subversion, consciously engaging with the expectations of the mainstream, as did *incroyables* and *merveilleuses* during the Directoire period in France.

No garments have survived from pre-deportation Acadia, so to uncover more about any expectations and subversions that may have been taking place there, we need to look elsewhere. Some details can be extrapolated from the archaeology, while others must be gleaned from comparisons with other groups for whom we do have visual records. Documentary sources for this chapter include written descriptions from travellers, contemporary images of others living near the Acadians, inventories on file at Louisbourg, and some sales records from merchants. Tailoring and dressmaking were skills commonly taught through apprenticeships and hands-on study, and textbooks containing instructions and cutting diagrams for garments did not become common until the nineteenth century. Painters and etchers in the Dutch Golden Age explored the lives of the working poor, though the very Continental fashions they portrayed were not always the same as those being worn in France or the colonies. Physical evidence includes textile seals, as well as pins, buttons, and buckles that can be associated with specific groups of people and styles of garments.

According to contemporary documentation, Acadians held on to older fashions longer than others in the years following their original settlement. The Sieur de Dièreville, who toured the Port Royal region in 1699–1700, noted that "[t]hey are in no way distinguished by new styles, And still wear hooded Capes," a fashion that had fallen out of favour in France around mid-century but remained popular in New England for its practicality in maritime weather.[5] The climate, the cost of access, distance between the colonies and Europe, the presence of new materials, and contact with Indigenous groups all influenced changes in colonial fashion. Beyond that, the roles that specific Acadians played in their communities and the position of those communities within the larger Acadian context also had an impact on which garments were worn, by whom, and when. Picking and choosing from available options,

Acadians in the four settlements moved between: rugged, utilitarian wear; high-end Paris-inspired gowns and suits; Indigenous-influenced shoes and decorations; and fashion with a distinctly local flair. Some may have deliberately code-switched, their clothing becoming a visual indicator of *Acadianité*.

In 1666, Charles II rejected the current French fashions of fussy petticoat breeches and yards of ribbon on men's clothing, advocating instead a Persian-inspired three-piece suit as an austerity measure.[6] France's fashions followed in short order, and a streamlined three-piece suit of knee breeches, waistcoat, and long, slim coat became the standard dress of the male middling classes and elite. Wealthy women wore gowns with long, smooth, boned bodices, over variations of hooped petticoats, which held their skirts out at the sides. Embroidery remained an integral form of decoration on garments, particularly depictions of plants and animals inspired by contemporary interest in botany and zoology. The snug bodices of baroque gowns gave way in the eighteenth century to the loose, floating robes à la française, looser gowns in pale colours with hidden lacings that relied on expensive or newer, lightweight textiles like silk, cotton, or the new woollen draperies to achieve the delicate, airy silhouettes that were in demand.[7]

The fancy ruffs of the sixteenth century vanished entirely by the middle of the seventeenth, replaced by pearl necklaces, falling collars, and cuffs of fine linen and lace. Stays as separate garments became less vital in women's wardrobes as bodices were more commonly made with integrated whalebone. Working women in France did not stiffen their bodices with boning, both due to the expense and the inconvenience of having the torso constrained during housework and other physical labour. The bodices shown on French working women in seventeenth- and eighteenth-century art are softer, supporting the body but curving with the wearer's natural shape. That softness had a negative connotation in English circles, especially throughout the early modern period. To be "loose" was to be uncontrolled, distancing oneself from the mores of polite society, while the upright, bound-in, and carefully precise body was a physical display of embodied privilege.[8] There is a strong difference here between France and England, where English working women did wear boned stays but laced them more loosely for ease of movement.[9]

Elegant silk gowns and slim knee breeches that closed with fancy buckles were markers of elite status and wealth. Labourers, artisans, and other non-elites tended to wear clothing that allowed more mobility. Those simpler styles followed fashionable silhouettes when possible, and those who could afford it would often have one or two outfits made in the most up-to-date styles, fashions they would have been exposed to through fashion plates. In the eighteenth century, knee breeches were coming to define a type of court masculinity that was connected in the popular mind with a corrupt and effete aristocracy typified by the excesses of the French court. This was in direct contrast to the more physical masculinity seen in the sailors and soldiers who were at the forefront of the expansion of empire.[10] In an interesting dichotomy, clothing fit for labour made a body seem loose, unpredictable, and uncouth, unfit for polite company, but it was the physical freedom provided by that same clothing that made both domestic labour and conquest possible.

The first arrivals of the French settlers in Sipekne'katik in the 1630s came at a time when elite French fashion included doublets and breeches, surface decoration in the forms of bows and ribbons, gold and silver lace and flowered embroidery, wide bucket-top boots, and full puffed sleeves. The fashions of the labouring classes – the farmers, blacksmiths, and merchants who joined the new settlement – were different than the handful of surviving high-end gowns and elegant portraits that we see in museums and galleries today. Jacques Callot's etchings and prints from the 1630s show a northeast France (Lorraine) with a very different visual landscape than the palace of Versailles. His subjects wear silhouettes that resemble those of the garments worn by the aristocracy, but with much more subdued surface treatments. The fabrics are plain, the styles simple, and women's heads are covered with folds of linen and lappet caps rather than lace. Bodices and jackets, occasionally quilted, with either attached or pinned-on sleeves, prevailed over whalebone-confined torsos.[11]

Labourers and the urban middling classes tended toward more practical garments, often in multiple pieces. Women's wear consisted of a skirt and jacket, or skirt and bodice combination, the practical skirts often ankle-length. Shorter skirts, with hems as high as ankle-length, displayed the shoes, making the feet more of a visual focus. The oldest extant Acadian garment is a skirt in the collection of the Nova Scotia Museum, dated to the early nineteenth century.[12] The banded, weft-faced tabby was woven from undyed white and black wool on a white cotton and linen warp and used the full width of the fabric, the single vertical seam sewn with hand-spun woollen thread. The cross-grain hang of the skirt, with the selvedge edge pleated into the waistband, creates a softer drape than if the wool had been cut into panels and sewn on the length of grain.[13] Considered a classic Acadian style, the shape and vertical stripes are closely associated with post-deportation communities and likely emerged in the later years of Acadian settlement. A fitted jacket (*casaquin*) with short basque and loose sleeves appears frequently in portraits of middle- and lower-status women of the early eighteenth century.[14]

FIGURE 5.1 • *Three Women, One Holding a Child.* Jacques Callot, 1634.

Loose knee- to ankle-length trousers appeared in the West as sailors' slops in the sixteenth century and continued to be a defining part of working men's wear until the late eighteenth. The use expanded to urban artisans and other lower-status men by the end of that century.[15] It was common for labourers in France to reserve fancy embellished clothing for leisure hours. As Restif de la Bretonne wrote of citizens of mid-eighteenth-century Paris:

> Monsieur Nicolas ... having spent the day at the printworks wearing labourer's clothes, put on a well-fitting cloat of ratteen, breeches of black drugget and white cotton stockings, took his handsome opera hat with the silk braid border under his arm, attached a smallsword with a steel hilt to his belt and, with hair curled and pomaded, walking on tip-toe in order not to dirty his patent leather shoes with their copper buckles, set off through the muddy streets ... the poorest working woman owns elegant (if inexpensive) outfits for wearing on high days and holidays.[16]

When they had access to the fashions of the metropole and reason to wear them, the fancier clothes associated with the urban wealthy took the forefront. All clothing in the seventeenth and eighteenth centuries was handmade, barring stockings, which were knitted on a semi-autonomous frame. A professional tailor could still make a full man's suit in about a week. If a deadline was tight, a woman's formal gown could be made in a day.[17] Some inexpensive garments were also available ready-made.

Merchants and milliners stocked items where precise fit was unnecessary, such as loose trousers and quilted petticoats.[18]

This was the fashion landscape that French settlers carried with them to the colonies. Once there, these fashions began to evolve in directions guided by the new settings. We have descriptions from outside observers to give us a starting point. Dièreville included a lengthy description of Acadian clothing at the end of the seventeenth century that has remained one of the standard images of the people: "[T]heir wool Is fashioned into Clothing, Caps and Socks. They are in no way distinguished by new styles, And still wear hooded Capes; their Shoes Of Elk and Seal skin are flat-soled And made for comfort."[19] The shoes he describes were certainly moccasins or moccasin-inspired designs, suitable for local ground conditions and easily made from local materials.

Robert Hale, who visited the province in 1731, remarked that Acadian women's clothes were "good eno" but they looked "as if they were pitched on with pitchforks & very often yr stockings [were] down about their heels." He also noted that the fashions were different than what he expected: "The women here differ as much in y r Cloathing (besides wearing of wooden Shoes) from those in New Engld as they do in Features & Complexion, w c is dark eno' by living in the Smoak in y e Summer to defend y m selves against y e Muskettoes, & in y e winter against y e Cold."[20] He did not describe specifics, however, and the general dishevelment he notes would likely have been the result of labouring lives. Farmers and labourers often wore their hose and stockings down around the knees for mobility purposes, a style that appears in illustrations in European manuscripts dating back to the high Middle Ages. Acadians would certainly not have shown up for mass in disarray, as we see from discussions of lace and silk-trimmed bonnets they wore in church, but practicality on the homestead is a far different thing. Rather than being a dispassionate description of his experiences, Hale's commentary makes a specific point regarding controlled and uncontrolled bodies – a train of thought that takes on greater resonance considering the ultimate British reaction to Acadian agency. The phrase "pitched on" adds an element of suspicion, as do his subsequent comments about smoke-darkened complexions. Hale draws subtextual parallels between Acadian bodies and Indigenous ones, categorizing them both as closer to a state of uncontrolled nature than the controlled lives of the presumably elegant European man.[21]

Similar connections between the Acadian and the Mi'kmaw fashion systems come from multiple writers, their prejudices explicit in texts like the 1686 orders from De Muelles for Acadian men living "a completely savage life [*sic*]" with Indigenous partners to return – alone – to the European settlements.[22] Andrew Brown even imagined physical transmutations among Acadians who lived in the settlements farthest removed from the political centres. He attributed the "vacuity" he perceived in the Acadian settlers to their proximity to Indigenous spaces:

It was likewise affirmed that in those families which had penetrated furthest into the [interior of the] forest, & had least opportunity of Social intercourse, the expression as well as the cast of the features bore a striking resemblance to those of the aboriginal inhabitants; even in cases where there was no intermixture of Indian blood. The muscles were equally relaxed. A similar air of vacuity spread over the countenance. And from this state of mutual repose, a stranger might have inferred either a stupid ignorance or an imperturbable apathy.[23]

Perceiving a link between the Mi'kmaq and the development of an Acadian clothing culture visibly different from that of the middling classes in France led to exaggerated descriptions of poor, uncivilized dress. De La Varenne's letters from Louisbourg in 1756 described Acadian men as being "commonly drest in a sort of coarse black stuff made in the country," a description of homespun wool either dyed dark shades or that had been spun from coloured fleece, though black sheep were relatively rare in non-specialized flocks.[24] We hear about black in Dernier's descriptions of Acadian preferences for black and red clothing, but the description does not match those from forty years later: Andrew Brown's story of green and grey-black, or Brook Watson's notes on striped black, green, and red textiles.[25] This may represent a difference pre- and post-deportation, as the fashions following the Acadian return from exile differed from what we now know about pre-1755 wardrobes.

Inventories from Acadian women in Louisbourg provide a rich textual source for their wardrobes. The location makes a difference, however, as their lives in French Louisbourg were markedly different than those of their farming cousins in Annapolis, or their trading-centre sisters in Beaubassin. Acadian women living in Louisbourg wore the clothes of the town, a group within a group that mostly assimilated into elite colonial French society. They ordered their clothing from France if they had the money to do so, purchased expensive textiles from local merchants, and owned approximately the same number of items of clothing as some of the wealthier fishermen in the region.[26] Unlike in rural Acadia, there is no indication that they used any materials or techniques introduced by the Indigenous population.[27] Acadians in Louisbourg were never able to completely shed their origins, however assimilated they may have appeared on the outside. They lived close together in a tight community, marked as socially different and less desirable due to their origins.

The documented wardrobes of some of these women – Anne Levron, Jeanne Thibodeau, young Marianne Benoist, Marie Josephe Le Borgne de Belleisle, and Marguerite Therrieau – as well as the clothes, accessories, and textiles that Le Borgne made available for sale, show another side of Acadia: that which survived even as it concealed. Acadian women living in the French fortress reaffirmed their identities in their actions and connections, as well as with subtle touches in their daily attire. Acadians living outside of Louisbourg had more freedom to play with their visual representation, directing external perceptions of themselves, their priorities, and their lifestyles through their clothing choices.

Shirts, Chemises, Corsets, and Bodices

Worn by everyone as the first layer against the skin for daywear and as the main article of sleepwear, the simple linen shirt was the most commonly owned item of clothing for those of European descent. Even the poor had multiple sets, the barest minimum one-to-wear and one-to-wash. Those in the middling classes owned many more, and inventories at Louisbourg included anywhere from twenty to fifty-two shirts.[28] Men's shirts and women's chemises were similar in construction, save for a triangular gore set into the skirt of the women's versions that added width for easier movement.[29] English chemises tended to be slimmer-cut, while French-cut chemises involved two gussets under each arm and were cut on the bias, which encouraged fluid movement of the textile around the body. Men's shirts had splits up the side seams and down the centre front, while women's chemises tended to have wide square or oval necklines designed to sit neatly within the fashionable necklines of the day. Women's sleeves, usually elbow length, were often rolled, and extra cuffs of fancier lace or muslin could be added to extend past the cuffs of the jacket or dress worn overtop. Men's shirt sleeves ended at the wrist, and the cuffs could be tied, buttoned, or held together with sleeve buttons. The majority of the shirts and chemises in the Louisbourg inventories were white or unbleached linen, with only a handful of examples of coloured or cotton versions.[30]

Over the chemise, women wore a supportive upper-body garment that came in a few varieties, the distinctions among which were not always clear – now or then. Contemporary writer T. Waller made tongue-in-cheek comments on the matter in

FIGURE 5.2 • French women in a less-structured jacket (E) and corps à baleine (A & B). From Garsault, *Art du tailleur*, 1769.

his description of bodice making and tailoring in his *General Description of all Trades* (1747): "There is a good deal of Difference between Stays, Jumps and Bodice, which I shall leave to the Women to settle between themselves."[31] Terms used by the French for this support garment included "corps" (body), "corps à baleine" (whalebone body, or stays), "corset," and "corselet," and the items themselves sometimes had multiple names – one particular piece called a corset in an inventory was later recorded as a corselet when it was sold.[32] Children wore unboned stays in styles similar to those worn by adults, to help "prevent deformities of the skeleton," a practice at least occasionally continued in the colonies.[33]

TABLE 5.1 · Louisbourg underpinnings

	Jeanne Thibodeau	Anne Levron	Marianne Benoist (age 8)	Marie Josephe Le Borgne
Bodices ("corps a femme")	–	3	–	–
Chemises	20	38	–	59
Corsets ("corsets a femme")	–	4	1	2
Waistcoats ("gillets pour femme")	–	9	–	–

Monique La Grenade suggests that a *corps* was stayed with whalebone, while a *corset* was a quilted undress garment without boning – contrary to the nineteenth-century use of the term.[34] No whalebone fragments or *corps à baleine* are listed in Acadian inventories or traders' manifests, and no evidence of the use of whalebone has been found at Acadian settlement sites. The corps listed in Acadian inventories, if boned, would have been set with something less expensive, like reeds or cording. Some of these boned or quilted garments included sleeves, becoming what we would more likely call a bodice today, and others included a matching stomacher pinned on to the front to disguise laces or other fastenings. Sometimes, particularly among working women, sleeves would be made as separate pieces and pinned or tied on overtop of the chemise sleeves to protect the linen during work. Most of these would have laced closed, allowing for the kinds of changes a woman's body underwent through frequent pregnancies and during breastfeeding.

Anne Levron owned nine old "vieux gillets pour femme," which were listed with her corps and corsets.[35] These utilitarian garments evolved from women's jackets of the sixteenth and early seventeenth centuries and became semi-undergarments, usually sleeveless, and were worn between the shift and the gown. Gillets could replace boned corps or soft, unboned corsets for informal wear for the middling and leisure classes. Levron's corps were valued at just under seven pounds each while her gillets were valued at one pound each, emphasizing the differences between fully tailored and possibly boned undergarments and the soft, inexpensive waistcoats.[36] There are no extant images of gillets in portraits or etchings, so what we know of them comes primarily from surviving examples, including two in the collections at Colonial Williamsburg. Often white, they supported the bust in the same general shape as boned bodices, but without the added pressure from whalebone. These garments were cut with wide, tabbed basques like those found on menswear, and could be quilted, embroidered, or

FIGURE 5.3 • Figured silk jumps with side lacing, possibly for maternity wear. French, ca 1730–80.

both.[37] The gillet appears to have been an east-coast oddity. No gillets appear in colonial women's inventories in Quebec between 1635 and 1760, while corsets and corps appear with some regularity after 1706.[38]

Levron had come to Louisbourg from Port Royal after her marriage to French officer Pierre Benoit circa 1715, when she was around the age of thirty or thirty-one.[39] She owned a much wider variety of undergarments than the other women whose inventories we examine here, including three corps and four corsets along with her gillets, suggesting frequent use of snug and structured bodices. These plain garments seem incongruous in Levron's inventory next to the silk and cotton gowns she also wore. If Levron's gowns were all a variation of the current *mode* of Paris, when did she wear her collection of gillets? Born in Port Royal and already in her thirties at the time of her marriage, she had years to accumulate an adult wardrobe before becoming an officer's wife with a different image to project. The combination of low- and high-end clothing in her wardrobe suggests that she had a use for both. Both her gillets and corps were described as "old," meaning they were worn and not in the best condition, so they were not sentimental pieces for display.[40] Rather, the fact that she kept the garments rather than sell them on the second-hand market or give them to one of her daughters indicates that she still had use for them. Wearing them for trips home, or for situations in which she did not need to be the Officer's Wife and could instead be simply *Anne Levron – Acadian*, explains why the simple underbodices would be important enough to keep.

Only one other woman in Louisbourg, Marianne Ponce, the widow Péré, had gillets in her inventory.[41] Péré was notably fashion-conscious and was Levron's contemporary, dying two years later in 1735. While she died a wealthy woman, thanks to her first husband's fishing concessions, she had grown up in the fishing community of Plaisance in Newfoundland. Péré's daughter Marie-Anne married into an Acadian family when she wed Charles de La Tour, son of Jacques de Saint-Étienne de La Tour and Lady Anne Melanson, in 1727.[42] Not Acadian herself but from similar rural roots and connected to one of the more prominent families in Acadia, Péré would have had reason to own a garment or two that would help her fit in with her new connections.

In an era when the body was barely understood, it became a locus of anxiety, particularly during the major cultural shifts that took place during the seventeenth and eighteenth centuries. Health was associated with balance, closed orifices, and stability, and the human body was naturally equipped with none of those. The female body in particular, with its constant changes and regular bleeding, was seen as an unstable collection of vapours and fluids.[43] Etiquette and protocol became powerful political tools in France in the period. The careful deployment of the body was belaboured in dance manuals, etiquette guides, and instructional texts for the bourgeoisie on how to remake themselves into gentility, a process that required multiple methods of restraint.[44] Moral uprightness was demonstrated by upright posture, signalling self-control in opposition to others' instability. Stays provided that structure and closed-off solidity, reforming the amorphous female body with all its bewildering changes into a far more predictable and consistent shape. In France, the boned bodice was associated with the aristocracy, while the majority of middling and working women preferred looser silhouettes.

Stays and stay lacing were less of a concern among working women in France than in England, where even the poorest women found stays desirable enough to inspire property crimes. In France and its colonies, however, the social pressure to wear stays was lessening by the beginning of the eighteenth century.[45] Only three corsets in Quebec inventories are described as boned and only two references to whalebone stays appear in the Louisbourg records, none associated with Acadian ownership.[46] Leather stays, on the other hand, provided more structure than cloth jumps, and leather was an easily obtained option. Leather could also be broken in over time. Forced through repeated wear, heat, and stretching to conform to the shape of the body inside it, leather made the final silhouette softer and more rounded than usually achieved with boned stays. Leather stays have been described in contemporary sources, and extant English examples remain in the collections at Colonial Williamsburg and the Worthing Museum and Art Gallery.[47] Unfortunately, of the corsets, corps, and bodices described in the Acadian Louisbourg inventories, only two descriptions include the textile: one made in cotton, and one in silk damask.[48]

Constrictive undergarments, even the unboned corsets and gillets, changed the shape of the torso and the bustline, turning a natural silhouette into a more rigid, planar, and controlled body type. This shaping was necessary for the fit of certain styles of gown worn primarily by the French elite, was unneeded for casual bodices, casaquins, and jackets, and added another visual layer of distinction between town and country. Each shape told a story about who the wearer was, and how she defined herself. The types of layers that went over the corps or corsets differentiated groups as well, each with a significance that extended beyond basic dress codes.

Gowns, Skirts, and Petticoats

Fashions in Acadia diverged from those of France by the 1670s, when the mantua, a long, slim, and casual one-piece gown, became standard wear for both urban and bourgeois women in Europe. Ninety per cent of Parisian women of all socio-economic statuses owned a mantua by 1700, a previously unheard-of democratization of style.[49] This change in fashion in France pops up in records from Louisbourg from the 1730s and 1740s in the form of the robe de chambre, which makes an appearance in Anne Levron, Marianne Benoist, and Jeanne Thibodeau's inventories.[50] The robe de chambre was a loose dress based on the banyan, a popular form of men's housecoat, itself based on kimono styles that had been brought to Europe by the Dutch East India Company (VOC). These dresses were often decorated with ribbon trim and included "*Echelles,* [which] is a stomacher lac'd or ribbon'd in the form of the Steps of a Ladder, lately very much in request."[51] The 138 yards of ribbon that Abraham Boudrot imported to Port Royal in 1691 and the "different small pieces of ribbons in all colours" that Le Borgne had available for sale in Louisbourg sixty years later suggests that ribbon-trimmed gowns like the mantua or robe de chambre were in fashion in both places at various times, as men's fashionable dress had abandoned ribbon bows in the 1660s.[52]

As with the corsets, corps, and gillets, terminology for gowns could be fluid. In 1670, Madame de Maintenon, mistress and wife to Louis XIV, described the robe de

TABLE 5.2 • Ensembles in Louisbourg

	Jeanne Thibodeau	Anne Levron	Marianne Benoist (age 8)	Marie Josephe Le Borgne
Apron	–	5	–	–
Gown ("robe")	4	1	–	10
Mantua/manteau ("robe de chambre")	1	5	3	–
Petticoat/skirt ("jupon")	9	11	–	14
Hooped petticoat	1	–	–	–

chambre as a gown "worn closed in front and widening in the shoulders," which could be altered from older styles.[53] The Duchess d'Orléans, on the other hand, considered mantuas and robes de chambre as being two different garments of similar type, and both distinct from housecoats, when she complained about their ubiquity at court in 1702: "I have never worn a robe de chambre nor a mantua, and have only one robe de nuit for getting up in the morning and going to bed at night."[54] In 1756, the Duke de Luynes noted that women of the French court had permission to wear the robe de chambre rather than full court dress, known as the *robe de cour*, in the days before the court moved to Fontainebleau or Compiègne.[55] In all cases, the robes de chambre were described as casual gowns for wear in public spaces.

Unlike the formal robe de cour for court dress, the robe de chambre could be worn either with or without supportive undergarments. Levron, who owned the majority of the corsets and corps in the inventories, was also the owner of the majority of the robes de chambre. Her inventory from 1733 included five of those, and one gown of indeterminate style. The robe de chambre and mantua were well embedded in French fashion by the 1730s and considered far more conservative than the new innovation of the 1720s: the hooped petticoat and the voluminous gowns it supported.[56]

The hooped petticoat that appears on Jeanne Thibodeau's inventory in 1741 is a rarity in Louisbourg. It is one of only three hooped underskirts appearing in local records, Acadian or otherwise. These petticoats, made from linen and reinforced with split cane to give them shape, appeared in French dress around 1720 and were used for supporting the sides of formal skirts. They were at their widest in the 1740s and 1750s before their popularity began to decline, the fashionable oval shape becoming fossilized court wear by the later decades of the century. A signal that the wearer was not required to perform manual labour and satirically associated by some with degraded

TABLE 5.3 • Textile use, main garments – percentage of wardrobes

	Jeanne Thibodeau	Anne Levron	Marianne Benoist (age 8)	Marie Josephe Le Borgne	Acadian women	Louisbourg women
Silk	57.1%	42.9%	33.3%	38.1%	42.2%	24.1%
Cotton	28.5%	42.9%	33.3%	33.3%	35.6%	43.8%
Wool	14.3%	14.2%	33.3%	–	8.9%	21.4%
Damask	–	–	–	28.5%	13.3%	10.7%
Number of garments	7	14	3	21	45	112

NOTE
Louisbourg numbers taken from La Grenade-Meunier, "Le costume civil à Louisbourg."

moral character and the concealment of pregnancy, hooped skirts broadened the wearer's visible silhouette, making her take up more physical, visual, and social space than normally allotted.[57] Thibodeau marked her transition from peasant to nobility with her belongings, wearing her new status in her hooped petticoat, silk gowns, and the scissors on her belt. She positioned herself visibly as a member of not only the French colonial elite, but as a participant in the styles preferred by the Continental powerful.

Unhooped petticoats and skirts ("jupons") blend together as a category. They would often be worn under front-opening gowns such as the robe de chambre, and sometimes worn on their own and paired with shorter jackets. High-fashion skirts cut on the length of grain in multiple narrow panels had multiple seams that both added bulk and lifted the fabric slightly away from the body. Post-deportation Acadian skirts were predominantly sewn on the cross-grain, the weft stripes vertical on the body, so that only one seam was required. The waist was either gathered into a waistband or folded over to make a channel and drawn in with a drawstring.[58] The silhouette difference between the two skirt styles was technically and visually significant.

Gowns worn at Louisbourg tended to be made of cotton or silk, a contrast to the wool skirts and bodices worn more often in the countryside. The raw numbers are so small, unfortunately, that the dataset is of limited statistical value. Additionally, some garments were excluded if the fibre content was not listed, or the trade name of the textile could not be identified. Nevertheless, some things do stand out as interesting. The woman with the largest wardrobe also had the most elite items, only wearing wool in her accessories (stockings). Even Le Borgne's cloaks were made of calico or gauze, certainly for fashion rather than protection from the elements. On the other

FIGURE 5.4 • Parisian textile merchants and their clients. All wear ruffled *manchettes* (cuffs) at the elbow, and the shopgirls wear bibbed aprons and short-sleeved casaquins. From Garsault, *L'art de la lingere*, 1771.

hand, the adult woman with the smallest wardrobe, Jeanne Thibodeau, had a much higher proportion of silk garments, suggesting that she chose to invest in fewer garments of higher value rather than purchase multiple pieces of cheaper stuff. That, combined with her hooped petticoat, paints a picture of a woman concerned with presenting herself in the grandest possible light.

Daniel Roche's study of Parisian wardrobes in the seventeenth century found that it was the up-and-coming merchants and artisans who had the highest proportion of fancy clothing in their inventories. The wealthiest had no need to blatantly display their wares, and the poorer group were unable to devote the money to the expense of maintaining luxurious clothing.[59] We can extend this theory into the eighteenth century at Louisbourg. The higher proportion of silk gowns worn by Acadian women living at the fortress may have been overcompensation for social prejudice toward their origins, a mark of incomplete assimilation into urban French cultural norms.

Louisbourg's gowns are accessible through documentation, but we must turn to trace evidence to build a case for the nature of the gowns, skirts, and petticoats being worn at the other settlements. The wire rings suggesting dorset buttons or lacing rings at Beaubassin and Melanson (see chapter 2, under The Sewing Awl, and chapter 4, under Buttons) suggest the presence of lightweight fabrics and unstructured gowns. The Fashion Museum in Bath has a robe volante in its collection dated between 1730 and 1739 with dorset cartwheel buttons on the sleeves, the thread worked over wire rings very similar to those found at Melanson and Beaubassin.[60] The lightweight robe volante was a competitor and successor to the robe de chambre, a loosely pleated gown made of lightweight silk or cotton that entirely concealed the body's shape. These gowns were far more formal than waistcoats and skirts, and the imported cottons and potential for dorset buttons suggest that such fancy, fashionable clothing was within reach of the wealthier households.

Any existing Acadian elite was not so socially stratified that they had to strictly maintain social status through clothing codes. Rather, many Acadians had access to a wider range of clothing in their wardrobes of differing levels of formality, which could be worn for different occasions. Calico and silk gowns were owned alongside practical wool skirts and stockings, fancy jackets and gillets giving women multiple options for levels of formality in dress.

Trousers and Breeches

Menswear for the era comprised a consistent list of pieces, though details changed with fashion trends. From the skin out, we begin with linen shirts, which could be plain or outfitted with fancy cuffs and collars; waistcoats that mimicked coats in cut and shape; either trousers or breeches to cover the legs, accompanied by stockings and shoes; and all of those covered by coats of varying shapes and lengths. Linen drawers were worn under both trousers and breeches, tied around the waist with a drawstring or sewn-in ties, and often tied at the knee. All of these garments were available in various levels of cost and formality. And as with women's outfits, the textiles used, the cut, fit, and choice of notions and accessories all changed the cost and the messaging inherent in each piece.

The two options for men's leg coverings – trousers and breeches – conveyed very different messages about status, occupation, and ambition. Trousers, derived from sailors' slops, were worn by the working class prior to the French Revolution, while knee-length breeches or *culottes* were worn by the elite. Breeches exposed the stockings and garters. The cuffs closed with both buckles at the knee band and buttons along the front placket, adding extra expense. Breeches were usually made of wool or leather, though some inventories also included linen breeches, which would have been worn in summertime.[61] Louisbourg inventories include leather breeches, good for durability and fit. Breeches closed at the front with a buttoned-fly opening or a fall-front placket. The latter style became more popular near the middle of the eighteenth century, as men's waistcoats shortened and more of the breeches became visible. Many breeches had pockets, "little bags set in the sides of the Breeches to put or carry any small thing in," cotton or linen linings, and sometimes elaborate trim.[62]

Breeches required careful tailoring and attention to proper fit, as the length was difficult to alter without removing the knee band and cutting them back. Lengthening breeches without visible patching and joins was a near-impossible task. Breeches were not as close-cut and body conscious in this period as they would later become, but their use already indicated the wearer's ability to consume fabric without consideration for reuse. More than that, buckled breeches and the snug hose worn beneath them reflected an aspirational masculinity that valued poise, careful manners, and a rejection of the rough lifestyles of labouring men.[63] The seventeenth- and eighteenth-century French concept of the *honnête homme* saw the rise of new ideals of masculine deportment, associated with civility, self-control, and unstudied refinement. Born from the Enlightenment, the *honnête homme* was as polished as he was unassuming, his carefully contained self-presentation associated with moral uprightness.[64]

Working men's trousers were straight-legged and worn long. They reached below the knee and sometimes down to the ankle, sometimes worn loose and at other times tucked into high boots or gaiters to keep them contained around the leg. They had evolved from sailors' slops as the leg coverings of labourers, sailors, and farmers, and were synonymous with physical work.[65] The simple shapes were more practical for farms, riding, and heavy work in situations where fancy wool or silk stockings could be snagged or otherwise ruined. Wearing long trousers or slops was distinctly lower-status in the early seventeenth century, as seen in the Sieur de Montmartin's 1615 condemnation of the fashion-conscious Remboth monks who dressed above their status and wore "the sleeues of their garments wide, their slops puft vp [as in, puffed full and girdled around the knee], and their gownes gathered thicke," in contravention of their vows of poverty.[66] A charity case supported by the Mennonite Church in Montgomery County, Pennsylvania, provided a pauper with a shirt and pair of long pants a year, while those employed and further up the social ladder were purchasing breeches.[67]

Trousers were inherently less expensive than breeches, requiring less fitting and fewer notions to close. Though buttoned fall-front closures were common, knee buckles and buttons were optional. Trousers could be worn with or without stockings, and when made of fabrics such as linen, usually reserved for intimate apparel, were much more casual in effect than silk breeches. Like women's waistcoats and skirts, trousers were the more economical option and could be re-hemmed and adjusted for another wearer more easily, making them practical for hand-me-downs. And as

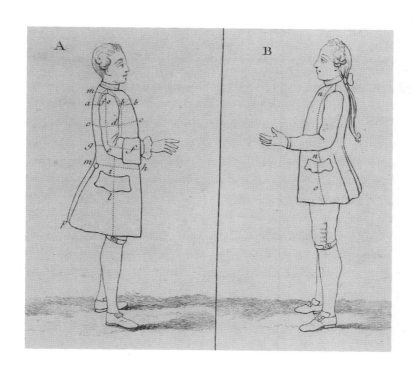

FIGURE 5.5
French man in a 1760s justaucorps (A), a waistcoat (B), and fall-front breeches (F). Garsault, *Art du tailleur*, 1769.

with petticoats, drawers, and other easily resized garments, trousers could be bought ready-made from milliners and merchants as early as the 1670s.[68]

Straight-legged trousers could be styled to look like breeches from a distance as with the Remboth monks, albeit without the use of buttons and buckles. Moses de la Dernier, an Acadian who survived the deportation and later wrote about his youth, described the men as wearing "Leg Bandages, Belts &c hanging in knots and bows."[69] Those leg bandages were not for first aid, but a type of trouser accessory that performed a function similar to gaiters – protection for the lower leg, particularly useful in snow or underbrush. Gaiters and leg wraps appear in seventeenth- and eighteenth-century images of farmers, sailors, and labourers, binding loose-cut trousers into a snug below-the-knee fit. This modification combined the practicality of trousers with the aesthetic of breeches, avoiding the expense of brass buckles and matching buttons.

The wool and linen are long gone, so discovering trousers and breeches in the archaeological record relies on the presence of buttons and buckles. Only one reference to breeches appears in the Louisbourg Acadian inventories, in a combined listing for Pierre Boisseau and his wife Marguerite Terriau. The 1755 inventory describes a stack of old, worn-out clothes found in a basket in Boisseau's house, including his coats, waistcoats, and breeches.[70] While buttons and buckles are much more closely associated with masculine clothing than with women's garments, the details are less diagnostic than could be hoped. Finding buttons at a site, even if they are all similar in size and style, does not guarantee that they were used on the same outfit, or had even been attached to a garment in the first place. Buttons are small and easily lost, reclaimed, and re-attached to new garments to replace those lost elsewhere, making associations more difficult. Buckles are somewhat more useful when it comes to garment identification, as knee buckles for breeches are usually smaller than those for shoes or hats, flat rather than convex, and sometimes oriented vertically rather than horizontally, the bar running between the short sides.[71]

The presence of knee buckles and smaller fancy buttons on a site means that breeches were likely being worn there, an important indicator of the presence of European and colonial elite fashion. Military dress naturally comes with fancy buttons as well, but since none of the buttons found at these four sites included regimental markings, it is unlikely that even the plain brass buttons were directly associated with military uniform even as the wearers tangentially engaged with that aesthetic. The small knee buckles and buttons found at Melanson and Beaubassin suggests that some of the men there were wearing breeches, an important sign of intentional identification with the urban powerful. This is predictable for Melanson, the settlement within the banlieue of Port Royal. It also fits with the evidence for silk stockings at Beaubassin, and the fine linens that would have been worn with the sleeve buttons discussed in chapter 4.

Jackets, Coats, and Accessories

Coats and outerwear for men came in a few shapes and styles. The *justaucorps*, or jacket, was knee-length and collarless, displayed fancy pocket flaps, and closed with a row of buttons down the centre front. A semi-formal to formal coat, worn with breeches and a waistcoat, it took the stylistic place of today's suit jacket. The collared version was called the *volant*, or frock coat. Often worn over the justaucorps as an overcoat, this version did not have pockets. In *The Academy of Armory*, Holme describes some informal jackets including a slim-cut "street-bodied coat," worn over a kind of waistcoat known as a "cheat," or "chate," since only the front was made of expensive fabric while the unseen back was "no such thing" – the panels that would not be seen, made of a cheaper fabric.[72] Other descriptions include loose coats that extended to the thighs with a slit up centre back for mobility.[73] Many working men wore shorter, hip-length versions of the justaucorps or volant, both for ease of mobility and reduced cost in fabric. Any of these styles could be worn with wood buttons, fabric-covered buttons, pewter, or brass buttons, depending on the wealth and aspirations of the wearer.

An overcoat similar to the riding coat described in Holme occasionally appears in records at Louisbourg, described as a "surtout," or an over-all.[74] This was probably cut to the same pattern as a justaucorps or frock coat but wider and longer, and worn over other coats during colder weather. *Redingottes*, or riding habits, were a recent English fashion and did not appear in the Acadian inventories. Cloaks and mantles, lacking sleeves, would have been the simplest forms of outer garments to make and to alter, but the extra fabric was inconvenient to wear during work and cloaks were uncommon. Illustrations of Newfoundland fishermen seen on a 1715 map of North America show the men wearing hooded coats, the hoods apparently at least edged with fur, and aprons – likely canvas – with bibs pinned up underneath their chins to protect their clothing (figure 5.6). Leather aprons, called *barvells* in New England, were common safety wear for fishermen as well as blacksmiths.[75]

Outerwear for women in Louisbourg was restricted to *mantes* and *mantelets*, two types of sleeveless outer garments cut in similar styles. The mantes, or mantle, hung

TABLE 5.4 • Outerwear and accessories in Louisbourg

	Jeanne Thibodeau	Anne Levron	Marie Josephe Le Borgne
Mantelet	–	5	6
Mante	1	–	2
Shoulder scarves ("mouchoirs de col")	6	–	13
Steinkirk	2	–	–
Hat ("chapeau")	–	–	1
Bonnet	1	14	14
Indoor cap ("toquet")	–	–	8
Cap ("miramions")	–	–	4

longer, below the waist, and the mantelet was cut short and covered only the shoulders and upper torso. Mantles were "a round thing made of any stuff, having a round hole in the middle, and so is cut through to the hole, which being put about the neck hangs round about the wearer: which according to the fashion, is large or little, faced or laced," not unlike a poncho.[76] While tailoring manuals and descriptions from the time discuss women's riding habits and other fitted outer coats, none of these appear – even on Le Borgne's store inventory.

Thibodeau had a single mantle in her probate inventory, consistent with the small size of her wardrobe as a whole. Levron owned five of "various stuffs" while Le Borgne owned eight, many of which were in fashion fabrics rather than textiles that would provide warmth. This may relate to Le Borgne's role as living advertisement for her shop and her wares, but it also speaks directly to perceptions of desirability. Wool cloaks were certainly more practical in Nova Scotia winters, but only one of Le Borgne's eight mantles was made of wool. The others were deeply impractical but highly fashionable, made from gauze, satin, damask, and three in varieties of Indian calico cotton. The lightweight textiles made them useful for sun protection in the summer and for modesty over low-cut necklines, but of little use in a rain or snowstorm.

Calico had a significance far beyond its surface appearance (see chapter 3, under Cotton). The French bans on calicoes and chintzes did not extend to the colonies, making this one of the few realms where the colonies had more access to a fine commodity than did Paris. Using calicoes and chintzes for outer layers created a display that called attention to itself, an addition of an eastern aesthetic to the Louisbourg streetscape as pointed as wearing Indonesian gingham in Port Royal. Le Borgne was easily able to afford higher-end textiles, but for those whose budgets for luxuries had to be stretched slightly, wearing a mantelet made from imported luxury textiles rather than homespun or heavy wool was more of a statement. Warmth and protection from the weather were relegated to other places, to the fur-trimmed or lined petticoats and breeches, as well as the large numbers of hats and gloves that appear for sale in Le Borgne's shop.

Whether made of cotton, wool, or fur, hooded capes, shawls, scarves, and mantelets all used similar methods of closure. Those included buttons, often with a loop or a twist of cord serving in place of a buttonhole, but clasps appeared less frequently as cloaks fell out of fashion. Pins and brooches were used for garments like shawls where versatility was important, allowing the wearer to unpin and reconfigure the garment at will – to cover the head in case of inclement weather, for instance, or to turn a shawl into an impromptu baby swaddle or basket. The pins used for these were heavier, longer, and thicker than dressmakers' pins, and some of this type have been found at Belleisle and Beaubassin.[77] The long pins in the assemblage may indicate shawls or heavier wool mantles in use. Lighter-weight pins, if not used for dressmaking, would have been used for securing linen layers in fichus or headdresses.

Linen accessories like aprons, head linens, and fichus defined the edges of the garments they bordered, softening the sharp hems and cuffs, gentling the transition between outer garment and skin. More than just the visuals of conspicuous consumption, the fine linen used for falling cuffs, delicate shawls, and headdresses bridged the boundaries between the private and the public realms. Neckcloths served the same purpose, with variations worn by both men and women. Cravats and kerchiefs came into fashion in the late 1600s, with the advent of coats without collars, and consisted of a length of linen tied under the chin with a knot or bow.[78] All of these linen accessories could be pinned in place with fine pins or knotted to keep them secure. We have no descriptions of Acadians in the settlements wearing linen cravats, but steinkirks, a particular style of linen neck cloth, appear in Thibodeau's probate inventory alongside six *mouchoirs de col*, kerchiefs for the collar. Le Borgne also owned twenty-two of these collar kerchiefs – commonly called fichus – in fine muslin and *coton des Indes*.

Steinkirks were similar to a cravat in that they were constructed out of a length of plain linen, but were styled in deliberate *dishabille*. A short-term fashion fad, they also help with dating the movement of fashion trends between Paris and Louisbourg. Steinkirks first appeared as a fashion in 1692 following the Battle of Steenkerque, as Voltaire's history describes: "The men at that time wore lace-cravats, which took up some time and pains to adjust. The princes having dressed themselves in a hurry,

FIGURE 5.6 • Newfoundland fishermen, detail from *This map of North America, according to ye newest and most exact observations*, 1719.

FIGURE 5.7 • Detail from Diderot, vol. 4, Third section: Foundries. Plate III: Forges, Third Section, Clay Mold.

threw these cravats negligently about their necks. [After the battle] The ladies wore handkerchiefs made in this fashion, which they called *Steinkirks*."[79]

What began as an adjustment to men's fashion quickly entered women's fashion, as cravats were already being worn with masculine-coded garments like riding habits. The steinkirk moved from the equivalent of sportswear to city dress and was a gender-neutral accessory. The steinkirk transcended socio-economic barriers as well, worn by artisans, merchants, and labourers through the years of its ascendance. Stocks began to replace the steinkirk in men's fashion around 1720, the twisted kerchief slowly fading out of fashion, and by 1741, the year of Thibodeau's death, the style was out of fashion among French and English gentry. It remained a fashion for the middling class, and images of artisans still wearing the steinkirk exist from France in 1748.[80]

Aprons were part of domestic and leisure costume for women, only the fineness of the fabric and type of embellishment distinguishing fancy show pieces from the workaday casual. Many gowns and skirts were paired with matching aprons in the inventories, and the fabrics used to make those articles indicate whether a particular apron was a functional or a decorative piece. Aprons made of silk taffeta were not designed for wear in kitchens or stillrooms, while those made of linen or serge were less likely to be worn with a silk gown for church or holiday festivities. Many aprons of the time were made with bibs, while some only came as high as the waist. Bibbed aprons did not yet have shoulder straps, and were worn pinned to the front of the gown or bodice with tinned or brass straight pins.[81]

Aprons for men, on the other hand, marked the wearer by profession, a signal that became codified in the butchers' blue apron in the nineteenth century.[82] The same style of apron worn in Herman Moll's line drawing of Newfoundland fishermen can also be seen on the French foundry workers in Diderot's trades encyclopedia, though those would have been made from fire-resistant hide rather than canvas or oiled linen (figure 5.7). Straight pins were used to fix the bibs of these aprons to the wearer's shirt front, and some of the heavier pins found on sites may signal the use of these protective garments.

Stockings and Pockets

Stockings of some form were required articles of clothing in the European wardrobe, the uncovered leg considered an exposure too intimate for the public sphere. This was a contrast to Indigenous dress, which often included leggings but not the same cultural mandate against exposed skin.[83] The well-fit stocking under knee-length breeches was a sign of gentility, signifying the ability to afford fine silk stockings or wool ones made precisely to fit. The tumbled-down, perhaps hand-me-down unfitted sock was a look associated with poverty and the "uncivilized."

Stockings in the mid-seventeenth to mid-eighteenth centuries were knee-high and often knitted. They could be made of any of the natural fibres (linen/hemp, cotton, silk, or wool), in varying weights. Often white but available in a range of colours including green, blue, "poppy red," and pink, stockings were often chosen to coordinate with the outfit.[84] They were fabricated with clocks – elaborate patterns sitting over the instep and ankle – and tied on at the knee with separate garter bands that were themselves often beautifully embroidered. After 1656 the hosiery frame became available in France, speeding up production time for stockings and making them both more widely commercially available and less expensive. Knitted stockings declined as a status symbol as a result, and the specialized silk stockings became more desirable.[85] Most early frame-made stockings were in silk, with hand-knitting the preferred technique for woollen ones until the technology was more refined. In 1700, Louis XIV restricted stocking production to eighteen cities in an effort to impose quality control, and Canada became a major outlet for Orléans hosiery in particular.[86] Wool stockings were manufactured in Beaubassin, both for local use and for export. By 1743, knitters in the settlement were producing enough pairs that merchant Zacharie Richard's cargo included thirty to forty pairs of woollen socks made in "laccadie" and intended for sale elsewhere.[87]

Nîmes became a centre for hosiery production in France, with more than two thousand knitting frames active in the city by the late 1720s.[88] Though it began with the production of wool stockings, manufacturers soon turned to the more profitable silk market, especially through the second quarter of the eighteenth century. By 1750, hosiery brought an estimated five million livres per year to the city of Nîmes, and hosiery traders were making sales around the Atlantic.[89] Two lead seals found at Beaubassin are single-piece textile seals, stamped on both sides. This type of seal would have been attached with a cord to the goods it marked, rather than stapled through the edge of the textile itself (figure 5.8). The COL NEM markings and crocodile image found on both are the marks of the Colonia Nemauensis, the old name for the city of Nîmes. These particular seals include the name of the provider surrounding the border on the obverse side and are of a style used for imports of silk stockings rather than yardage. Similar seals for Pierre Larnac, a trader, and David Baumer, a Nîmes manufacturer of silk stockings, are described in Geoff Egan's extensive report on the British Museum's collection of seals.[90]

FIGURE 5.8 • Textile seal, single disc, obverse (left) and reverse (right), Beaubassin. The text around the obverse side appears to read pie----- anh or ank.

As stockings were manufactured without gendered differentiation in design, the sex of the wearer of a specific stocking can only be guessed at based on size. Abraham Boudrot's manifest included twelve pairs of men's stockings, but de La Tour's similar cargo is described only as "Two dozen halfe stockins" of indeterminate size, colour, and style.[91] From the price (two pounds, one shilling for twelve pairs), Boudrot's cargo was most likely knitted wool. Silk stockings brought through regular trade were four or five times more expensive than wool ones, ranging between twelve and seventeen shillings a pair in colonial regions. Stockings and hosiery were small goods transported and often sold informally by sailors, however, as convenient, lightweight items that could fit in personal sea chests and be sold for profit free of taxation or import duties.[92] A sailor in Sicily in 1688 found silk stockings selling there for about six shillings a pair, making them very profitable to smuggle out for later resale.[93] Part of clandestine trade as well as formal import and export channels, untagged stockings connected the bodies of the wearers to the smugglers moving through Fundy waters, and from them back to profit-seeking sailors hoarding the luxury goods from the silk mills of Italy and France in their salt-stained sea chests.

Thibodeau had stockings in her inventory in Louisbourg, but Levron did not. Bare feet would have been inconceivable at the time, however, not only for reasons of fashion or modesty, but for blister protection in shoes, and for warmth in the winter. The omission must be understood as an aberration – or perhaps, an indication that her stockings were taken by someone prior to the inventory being made. Roche points out that items went missing from Parisian probate inventories for a variety of reasons, including division between heirs prior to the inventory being taken; the items being out on loan at the time of the owner's death; items excluded from the household goods due to conditions surrounding personal effects in the marriage contract; or the items having been sold.[94] Any of these are possible in this case. Straddling the line between utilitarian necessity and luxurious extravagance, stockings of all sorts were among the more personal and intimate garment types in circulation.

A similarly intimate accessory, pockets were solely women's wear. They were separate items of clothing, one or two fairly large pouches tied around the woman's waist with a lace. Working women kept their pockets accessible, wearing them over their skirts or tucked under their aprons for easy access. With more formal dress, pockets were often worn beneath a woman's skirts and close to her skin. Whether nestled under the apron or accessed through slits in the gown, skirt, and petticoats, pockets were a private and intimate space on the body, safe from pickpockets, purse snatchers, and other thieves.[95] Pockets were available ready-made. They were also easily and often made at home, either out of fabric remnants left over from garment making or new linen embroidered for that purpose.[96] Both Thibodeau and Le Borgne had pockets in their inventories, and the collection of sewing tools found in Anne Bourg's midden at Melanson suggests that a pocket or hussif of hers met its end there among the refuse.

Made of cotton or linen, pockets were often decorated with fancy embroidery. These were used for carrying personal grooming and work items, from bodkins and earspoons – and bodkins *with* earspoons – to keys, scissors, buttons, and needle cases. Women carried their money in them, as records of stolen or lost pockets document, as well as small valuables: "D[r]opp'd … a pair of white fustian pockets, in which was a silver purse, work'd with scarlet and green S.S. In the purse there was 5 or 6 shillings in money; a ring with a death at length in black enamell'd, wrapp'd in a piece of paper; a silver tooth pick case; 2 cambrick handkerchiefs, one mark'd E.M. the other E5D; a small knife; a key and pair of gloves, and a steel thimble. &c."[97] Thibodeau's pockets would have held her sheathed embroidery scissors, the sheath preventing the sharp scissors from poking through the pocket's fabric. As much as buttons and spurs were visible constructions of masculinity, pockets were a concealed means of constructing feminine identity. Pockets gave women a private, autonomous space on the body, one whose design and whose contents were entirely within her own control.[98]

Hair and Headdress

Hair styles, hats, and headdresses are as much a part of wardrobe as shoes and shawls, though not as frequently discussed in the primary sources on Acadia. The most thorough description of Acadian headdress comes from a hundred years after the deportation, and Frederick Cozzens's nineteenth-century prose was both romanticized and likely heavily influenced by Longfellow's fictional *Evangeline*:

> From the forehead of each you see at a glance how the dark mass of hair has been combed forward and over the face, that the little triangular Norman cap might be tied across the crown of the head. Then the hair is thrown back again over this, so as to form a large bow in front, then re-tied at the crown with colored ribbons. Then you see it has been plaited in a shining mesh, brought forward again, and braided with ribbons, so that it forms, as it were, a pretty coronet, well-placed above those brilliant eyes and harmonious features. This, with the antique kirtle and picturesque petticoat, is an Acadian portrait.[99]

The braided coronets and bows Cozzens described are anachronistic and far more in tune with 1850s and 1860s North American hairstyles, those in fashion at the time of Cozzens's writing, than the fashions of the seventeenth-century French.

We have only two contemporary descriptions of pre-deportation Acadian hairstyles: one from a protest from a religious dispute in Chignecto, and the other from a note from de la Varenne regarding the headdress of women at Louisbourg. The complaint lodged by a group of Acadian women against Abbé Claude Trouvé in 1690, then priest at Beaubassin, charged that he had refused to grant them absolution following confession because they were wearing lace and ribbon. His response was that he needed them to wear caps where he could see their eyes, suggesting some form of frilled headdresses or overly decorated bonnets were at the heart of the dispute.[100] Lace was a status symbol in the seventeenth and eighteenth centuries, becoming more affordable in later years, but usually worn by the lower orders only in small quantities.

The church was the physical and social centre of the community, providing a focal point for gatherings and for in-group tensions. Attending mass was a chance to see and be seen in your best dress. Sundays were the time to wear European-style leather shoes with fancy buckles, lace bonnets and lappets, crucifixes, jewels, and beads. Residents at Beaubassin would have been regularly exposed to fashion trends thanks to the relatively constant movement of people between Port Royal, Beaubassin,

Louisbourg, France, and New England, and had access to materials through regular trade. Some of the women of Beaubassin – socially powerful enough to challenge their local priest and confident in their success when they did – wore lace to church and vocally defended their right to do so.

The other surviving description, from De la Varenne, concerns a kerchief as the main headdress for Acadian women at Louisbourg: "The women are covered with a cloak, and all their head dress is generally a handkerchief, which would serve for a veil too, in the manner they tied it on, if it descended low enough."[101] The basic linen cap of the early eighteenth century was a variation on the medieval coif and often trimmed with bands of bobbin lace. Long lace bands known as lappets could be hung from that border, either left to drape down the back or be pinned up to the cap. Working-class women from France wore a similar type of cap with the lappets pinned up on the top of the head, as seen in the 1738 engraving of the oyster seller (figure 5.9). Small brass pins called "short whites" were standard for this use, the same style and size used for pinning fichus and aprons in place. Short whites were found at all the Acadian sites (see chapter 2, under Pins).

A tall confection of lace and ribbon called a fontage was popular among aristocratic women in the late seventeenth century in Europe, though inventories in colonial North America suggest that it was far less popular in the colonies outside of concentrated urban areas.[102] Louisbourg inventories contained fancy collars, cuffs, and bonnets alongside expensive fontages and yards of handmade lace. The differences between the descriptions of plain kerchiefs at Louisbourg and lace bonnets at Beaubassin could be due to any one of a handful of factors – daily wear contrasted with Sunday best, winter versus summer wear, or poor compared to rich. Perhaps De la Varenne saw what he wanted to see, assuming that the Louisbourg ladies he saw wearing high lace fontages and gold-edged bonnets were French, rather than Acadian wives of French officers.

We have no hats or wigs left behind to give a clear image of Acadian men's headwear, and there are no identified hat buckles among the Acadian finds to suggest the use of beaver hats. Images from nearby colonies and French seafarers show a range of other options. Hats worn by the lower orders were usually felt or wool, round or slightly square-crowned, with a medium-width brim. The brimmed hats could be pinned up on one, two, or three sides, or worn with the brim down. For working on the water, knitted caps like the Monmouth cap were popular from the sixteenth century onwards.[103] Wigs, while common within most socio-economic strata by the latter half of the eighteenth century, do not show up in the Acadian archaeological

FIGURE 5.9 • Lappets up: *Oyster Seller*.
Anne Claude Philippe de Tubières,
comte de Caylus, 1738.

FIGURE 5.10 • Lappets down: *Mrs Faber*.
John Faber Jr, after Thomas Hudson,
mid-18th century.

record, descriptions, or inventories. The most common archaeological sign of wig use is the ubiquitous wig curler, a double-bulbed ceramic stick that could be heated. The hairdresser would then wrap the wig hair around the heated curler and let it set. Wig curlers of this type have been found at other colonial sites, including Louisbourg, but none directly associated with Acadian households. The high count of wig curlers found at sites where wigs were certainly worn suggests that the lack of curlers at a site – or fragments thereof – is a strong indicator that wigs were not worn there.[104]

The non-use of wigs is as revealing as the use of curlers and wigs would be. Wigs in this period were heavily entrenched in notions of status and financial success. Part of the same group of luxury consumer items as jewelled sleeve buttons and lace trim, wigs played a large role in the performance of European masculinity.[105] Wigs on men began as courtly wear in the seventeenth century and trickled down to everyone else by the eighteenth, becoming less expensive as more wig makers were employed. Variations flooded the market, some styles even associated with specific professions. The lack of wig wearing in Acadia would have been a choice, not a question of money or of access, as wigs were available for purchase in Louisbourg. Le Borgne's store inventory included bags of hair that were likely being sold for wig making, and for stuffing the bag wigs and false queues worn at the fortress.[106] And while wigs had problems with frizz and general unruliness in wet weather, those drawbacks did not prevent wig wearing in Louisbourg or Montreal.[107]

By the mid-eighteenth century wig wearing had become common in small villages and towns across France and the colonies. Bag wigs in particular were common wear among male residents of New France and Louisbourg.[108] Women's hair was normally natural but enhanced, and wigs were worn only in contexts where masculinity was incorporated in their performance of a variation of feminine style, as with riding habits.[109] Wigs as part of the genteel wardrobe were part of the conceptualization of bodily control that pervaded ideas of appropriate behaviour. The wig was replacement hair, part of the culture of artifice that placed barriers between man and nature. The natural body, in this mindset, was unruly and required taming – skin covered with powders, flesh constrained by corsetry, movement refined by etiquette and protocol. Natural hair was seen as uncouth and a sign of not only poverty but deliberately uncivilized behaviour. This is a prejudice that still surfaces today, aimed at naturally tightly curled hair among non-white ethnicities.[110] By rejecting wigs, Acadian men marked themselves as more "natural," behaviour correlated in the common opinion with incivility and the common man.

Acadian women, whose hair was worn bound up underneath linen caps, did not face the same kind of negative stereotyping. Their use of lace caps occasionally stood out as incongruous and inappropriate, however, because of the mixed messages their headdresses were sending. It was becoming difficult to tell: were the Acadians poor, physically exposed with their ankles and hair uncovered, and entirely too integrated into this liminally settled space, as some descriptions would have it? Or were they Europeans of the middling class with lace fripperies and silk ribbons, fine linen cuffs, and jewelled buttons? The incongruity of the styles extended outsiders' discomfort, reinforcing perceptions of Acadians as a new and emerging culture with their own dress vernaculars.

Conclusions

Determining which garments were worn and by whom requires extrapolation from a wide evidence pool. Primary source documents and the archaeology do not always agree, and a lot relies on our ability to interpret the patterns of small finds in their contexts. Written descriptions from the seventeenth and eighteenth centuries describe Acadians as poor and rustic, while the probate inventories and small finds show us that those living in settlements like Beaubassin and Melanson engaged with elite European clothing culture. Other evidence points to simple clothing, worn simply.

How can we reconcile all of this into a larger picture of the Acadian fashion system?

We can be sure of some things. Despite the time and distance between Acadia, Canada, New England, and France, Acadians displayed interest in contemporary fashion. Materials available to them that were not easily or legally available elsewhere gave them something of an advantage fashion-wise, such as the cotton indiennes popular among Acadian women in Louisbourg. The different settlements also appear to have different priorities. While subject to similar weather conditions and with similar materials available, the social and political needs of each settlement were different, and that variety of experience was reflected in their clothing. The clothes worn by Acadian women in Louisbourg came the closest to the styles of metropolitan France of anything Acadians wore. Even then, aspects of their upbringing shaped their choices – in their rejection of the rural fashion for wool skirts and bodices, and in acceptance, such as Anne Levron's simple waistcoats and the surviving fragments of knitted wool stockings.[111] When they moved into the urban centre, Acadian women embraced styles like the hooped petticoats that were impractical for the marshes and fur-trading hubs of Annapolis and Siknikt.

Beaubassin, the richest archaeological deposit excavated to date, shows evidence of wardrobes that included a little bit of everything. The inhabitants there were probably code-switching, wearing European fashions when necessary for political display, or for special occasions and Sunday best. Elements of Mi'kmaw dress come through else-where, in the local leathers and furs, and the repurposing of trade beads for decoration on their own clothing. The red stripes of which Acadians were fond can be seen in Mi'kmaw clothing and adornment as well, a colour with deep cultural significance.[112] Homespun and basic wool were inexpensive and functioned as protective wear in the winter as well, potentially, as protection against people. If Acadians presented them-selves to outsiders as poor and not worth attacking, it may have bought them some space, while in the background their trading economy boomed. Their geographical position and ability to meet others on their own visual level both contributed to their success as middlemen.

Evidence of European clothing surfaced at Melanson alongside bead necklaces and fancy status items. The ability to engage with government officials on symbolic sarto-rial ground would have been more useful in earlier years, waning as political relation-ships soured. The fashions of nearby Belleisle are more difficult to determine because of the lack of personal notions that have been uncovered at the site. We do have the spindle whorl indicating the use of homespun wool; the embroidery scissors, which prove embellishment beyond the most basic; and pins used to keep aprons, collars, cravats, and sleeves in place as part of the controlled and tidy body.

On the one hand, the lack of constraining garments and artifice in hair and wig made the Acadians stand apart from the fashionistas of the empires that surrounded them. By comparison with the carefully controlled bodies of the eighteenth century, some later Acadians were believed to be rough and rustic, their clothes seemingly "tossed on."[113] All of this led to assumptions regarding their social standing and socio-economic abilities. Robert Hale's descriptions of poverty and sparse belongings in Acadian houses in Beaubassin perpetuate this imagery and have become something of the standard by which Acadian homesteads were viewed, despite physical evidence to the contrary. Perhaps the answer lies in shifting expectations for the display of material wealth. The burgeoning consumer economy that grew alongside the Industrial Revolution influenced the methods by which Europeans demonstrated wealth and status, turning clothing from a method of displaying power and allegiance to a way in which power could be created. In the French ancien régime, constrained and constrictive clothing demonstrated a person's moral integrity and manners. The looser, less-controlled bodies of the Acadians, who nonetheless wore buckled shoes, with clean linens and fine silks against their skin, confounded attempts to place them into either category.

On the other hand, by the middle of the eighteenth century, formal clothing and impressive wigs were coming to define the artifice that philosophers such as Rousseau were in the process of rejecting. The eighteenth century was an era both of masking and of intense curiosity in what lay below the mask. Moralists appealed to the natural body and environment as inherently superior, while manufacturers worked at making artificial hair that could not be differentiated from the natural. The wigless, trouser-wearing Acadian became, in this world view, a more *authentic* man. That authenticity eventually became romanticization, until all that was left in the collective memory of the Acadians were their farms and domestic lives. Uncovering the truth means digging up the remnants of the fancy clothes that they also kept in their wardrobes, reflections of a consumer market to which the Acadians were not strangers.

Assembling the Puzzle

Once viewed simply as mere artifacts, cloth and clothing are now
recognized as culturally constructed commodities with complex symbolic
properties, transmitting purity and pollution, linking past and present,
transforming through belief.[1]

— — — — — —

MATERIAL CULTURE IS IDEOLOGY MADE PHYSICAL, a system of symbols reflecting core beliefs about the order of the world and the values of the community. A culture's world of *things* can be read, and when given the appropriate context, interpreted to give us glimpses into that society's priorities and beliefs and the entanglements they create. Dress is one of the most intimate spheres of material culture, and clothing design and daily choice go far beyond the individual. Daily dressing decisions rely on an immense weight of contextual information that we process both consciously and subconsciously. The environment, access to materials and goods, pressures from elite style setters, contact with other groups and their encoded signals, and explorations of gender and age roles all contribute to what we think of as "fashion sense," on both individual and societal levels. We display our assumed identities literally on our sleeves, using conscious and subconscious encoded messages within different modes of dress to communicate to others how we see ourselves – and our place in the world. Those choices intersect with politics, encoding messages about the social and physical body, loyalties, economy, and identity. Dress is part of this vast interconnected web of relationships that brings meaning to non-verbal communication. The multitude of ways in which we cover our bodies is a defining feature of human culture, the creation of a second, social skin layered on top of the intimate messiness of biology.[2] We project our own ideas of a person onto their choice of dress, making the body into a site of contestation and tension: is the wearer being perceived the way she wishes to be perceived, or are her signals being read through a different lens?

The environments in which people exist are fundamental to the methods by which they internalize and display these concepts. Dress can be used to control, mitigate, and redefine the edges of the body, and the physical aspects of some forms of dress, such as corsetry or wooden clogs, change how a person engages with the rest of the world.[3] Temporal, geographical, and cultural context also matter. The modern business suit carries different weight today than the 1980s power suit with its wide shoulder pads and narrow skirts, or the Victorian frock coat and vest – and we would make very different assumptions if we saw someone wearing either of those outfits on a modern-day subway train.

Identity as defined by dress is also malleable, since clothes can be removed and changed. The early modern concept that the internal self could be shaped by external appearance struggled against the belief that that outward appearance reflected internal morality and health. If outward appearance could be changed, and if that action in turn changed the inner self of the wearer, how could anyone's deportment and demeanour be used to gauge their worthiness? This pair of core beliefs around dress caused further consternation when European fashion systems butted up against one another, and then against those of groups in the New World. Understanding dress as a form of communication gives us new insight into previously obscured connections and perspectives. The results invite us to reimagine how we might consider Acadia, and the Acadians.

Imperial interests have always included clothing, and control over self-expression through dress has been a persistent part of the colonial project. Imperial interest in the sartorial creation of and control over Acadian bodies, already perceived as being different than French bodies in New France and the Indigenous bodies of Mi'kma'ki, generated a new tension for colonial authorities at the intersection of style and function. The evolving social spaces of Acadia encouraged the creation of new clothing styles and the adoption of local ones better suited to the environment. The resulting differences from European dress were appropriate to their new context and worked as a means of navigating the complicated intersections of imposed control and local priorities.[4]

Despite the practicality of the shorthand, speaking about the fashion of "the Acadians" as a monolith is incorrect. What we have seen is that differences evolved between the settlements that in turn reflect the differences in local contexts: the rural and urban environments, the settlements' distance from the centres of imperial control, and the level of engagement different groups of Acadians had with non-Acadian neighbours and guests. The data also suggest that we need to re-evaluate evidence from primary documentary sources. Some of the poor, humble farmers from the seventeenth- and eighteenth-century descriptions wore more elaborate and higher-status clothing than observers have led us to believe, raising questions of bias, intent, and audience. We see that residents in all the settlements had interest in and paid attention to luxury goods in different ways, especially in the realm of sewing. Leisure activities associated with luxury continued the process of blurring social boundaries and distinctions between elite and non-elite families.

France's fashion system in the seventeenth and eighteenth centuries equated physical manners with gentility, and used dress as a means of differentiating and separating the social castes. Core beliefs in Britain during the same time period placed a high moral value on physical control over the human body, and status for both was read through the lens of appearance. The creation of the dressed body in provincial Poitou was necessarily different from the performance of a settler identity in North America, and the changes were embodied in the distinctions between the wardrobes of the Acadian women in Louisbourg and the artifacts found at Beaubassin. The admixture of the Acadian experience and the expectations of civility expressed through the modes of contemporary European fashion can be seen in some of the Beaubassin and Louisbourg artifacts, echoed in items found at rural Acadian sites. Construction of a new political identity that was neither French, English, nor Indigenous allowed Acadians to move between all those worlds, mobility made possible by their manipulation of fashion norms.

The mixed style of dress that emerged in Acadian settlements was an indication of the early development of a new and unique fashion system, as successive generations of settlers moved further away from their French origins. Notwithstanding other influences, that system would still have been deeply rooted in the cultural milieu of seventeenth-century rural southwestern France. Despite all the changes in their lives over the course of the turbulent seventeenth and early eighteenth centuries, Acadians still lived within a Eurocentric, Christian-dominant culture – they were not going to discard everything they knew about clothing and textiles to begin entirely from nothing. What they did, as evidence shows, was to adjust their behaviours within the constraints of their pre-existing entanglements.[5] Some variations used local materials to reproduce known styles, such as carving glass trade beads for use as rosary spacers, while others were added that filled new needs, such as sealskin moccasins for travelling in the forest or local furs for winter warmth.

The low levels of surviving evidence mean we can only sketch out a few individual wardrobes with certainty, but enough remains in the physical and documentary record that we can draw out some larger trends. Acadians across the settlements had access to imported goods and took advantage of that – in some decades more than others, depending on the state of war or peace and levels of military activity in the major seaways. Acadians living within Fortress Louisbourg developed a different dress style from those living in Beaubassin, who appear to have been dressing subtly differently again from those living near Annapolis. Those small regional variations carried information that would have read clearly to contemporary observers.

Connections between France and Acadia changed over the course of the settlements' histories. Trade continued, even though it took different forms and different routes following the handover to the British in 1713, and some Acadians maintained correspondence and exchange with the European continent. The ease of access to New England compared with the long travel times between the Bay of Fundy and New France played a major role in the preferencing of Boston trade over that with Quebec or Montreal. If the Chignecto canal had been built as proposed, that relationship may well have tilted more in favour of goods coming in from the Northumberland Strait. As it was, however, the easier two-day sail between Boston and Port Royal, as well as the kinship ties between Acadians and Huguenot merchants, ensured that New England fashions played a larger role in the Acadian visual landscape than they otherwise would have.

The British takeover brought a new tension into the system. Dress standards were already different enough between France and England that French-based styles – including differences like softer, easily draped wools and less structured bodices – attracted derisive commentary from the English. Further differences, like decorative motifs and techniques learned from the Mi'kmaq, encouraged imperial anxiety over social and bodily control.[6] Confusion erodes trust, which was in short supply to begin with, and that may have played a role in imperial attitudes towards Acadians as a group. If Acadians no longer looked like French farmers, they were also not on the way to becoming English ones. Their syncretic mix of aesthetics, incorporating fashions common to New England as well as suggestions of Indigenous styles, made them even less predictable than before.

Religious identity is one of the fields that set the Acadians apart from others in the region. As French Catholics their faith made them a target of derision and violence from English Protestants, as annoyed comments about their clergy and their rites appear throughout colonial documents of the period. And yet they maintained strong visible connections to that same religious identity, seen in the reports of Acadian women in their lace and ribbon finery for mass, the religious jewellery, and the importance they placed on displaying their faith. These pieces were not ostentatious, but quiet, visible tools to use in daily worship and spiritual life.

Internally, the communal aspects of shared domestic labour point towards a reinforcement of women's socio-political power. Quilting and carding bees became venues through which community bonds and reciprocal labour exchanges were reinforced, and uneven access to materials like fleeces may have encouraged a barter and labour-exchange secondary economy within the settlements.[7] Developing their own sensibilities, Acadian agency caused concern for imperial authorities. The role of Acadia as first a direct extension of the French empire and then as a potential breadbasket for the British colonies was thrown into dispute as Acadian politics changed and their visual vocabulary emphasized their growing differences. Externally, trade practices displayed sophistication. Acadian merchants traded with New England investors and contacts, supplied goods to Louisbourg, and marked social and gender roles with luxury tools and adornments. Acadians in different settlements engaged with the changing economy of the Atlantic world and were in the early stages of developing their own claims on culture and adornment in the midst of it all.

The Banlieue: Melanson

Physically closest to the seat of first French and then British power in Acadia, the Melanson families had strong personal and political connections to both regimes. Evidence from excavated houses and middens in the forms of brass buckles, buttons, decorated spur buckles, and bead chokers confirms their use of European-style clothing and footwear. The chronology available from the early destruction of parts of the site show that this was not a late-coming trend for them, but a style choice that persisted throughout the first half of the eighteenth century. Wearing fashionable clothing was likely a reaction to the centrality of the region and the presence of a power centre within a few kilometres. The clothing vernacular of the region would have been inspired by fashions at Port Royal, fed by merchants who did business with Port Royal, and in return communicated that sense of regional belonging back to Port Royal.

Materials from the Melanson site support the narrative sketched out by the documentation and interpersonal politics – that some members of the Melanson family worried about the appearance of belonging. That belonging in turn made it less important for them to display other signifiers that were a normalized part of European fashion. The large collection of plain scissors indicates that sewing work took place at the settlement, but the focus was not on the luxury levels of the tools. Prestige goods at Melanson were wearable: the badges, beads, sleeve buttons, and fine-wire pins for delicate linens defined the edges of garments that would not have looked out of place among the middling classes in Paris.

While the difference in the numbers of artifacts recovered from the different sites makes direct comparisons difficult, the materials we do have from Melanson suggest a different outlook on fashion than at the next-closest site – the settlements on the Belleisle Marsh. The Melansons who lived in those residences that have been excavated wore clothing that marked them as reasonably but not extravagantly well off, attuned to current fashion, and following contemporary gender norms. There is little evidence of Indigenous influence on dress styles, and no direct evidence of moccasins or sabots, though we may assume that some form of practical footwear was in use for farming and labour. Some of the men at Melanson wore buckled breeches, and women wore laced jackets and bodices. Some may have worn robes de chambre like their cousins at Louisbourg, suggested by their access to imported cottons and the shape of a necklace designed for low necklines. They wore linen fine enough to justify delicate pins and copper sleeve buttons, and accessorized with eye-catching decorations and strings of glass beads that resembled high-fashion pearls. Overall, the Melanson aesthetic was likely in line with that of the Fort; all the better to maintain clear lines of communication and the appearance of tractability.

The Marsh: Belleisle

Farther away from the interference and politics of the Fort than Melanson, the residents of the Belleisle marsh had less contact with outsiders to concern themselves with. We have much less physical evidence of dress from this settlement than the others, which requires some caution in interpretng those materials as an assemblage. What evidence that does remain of dress and textile use at Belleisle suggests a more practical mindset in play. Plain buttons and heavier pins are of the right size for coarser fabrics, while the buckles are generally simpler and smaller than those seen elsewhere. The Savoie and Blanchard families appear to have engaged in more practical and less demonstrative styles of dress than the Melanson families, more in line with the needs of a farming community.

Of all the settlements examined here, Belleisle comes the closest in terms of dress to the archetypes of the rural farmers that appear in older texts. Dièreville's descriptions of the residents of Port Royal and the surrounding regions included out-of-date fashions and sealskin moccasins, observations congruent with the heavier pins and plain buttons found at Belleisle. Clark's assertion, on the other hand, that the residents of Annapolis outside of the banlieue were living unsophisticated lives devoid of status signalling, is incorrect.[8] Trade and contact with Port Royal and Louisbourg as well as Boston brought in decorated scissors and jewellery, woollens, silk ribbons, painted cottons, and potentially silk or velvet yardage as well. The spindle whorl found on site confirms that one of the residents of the Savoie house was spinning delicate threads, though whether those wool threads were intended for weaving lightweight woollens, sewing, embellishment, or a combination of all those activities is unknown.

Men's dress at Belleisle appears to have consisted of trousers and waistcoats, with woollen stockings for everyone – possibly worn down around the knees at times, for comfort. Women were probably wearing gillets, woollen bodices, and skirts. By the eighteenth century some of those skirts were likely woven in a vertically striped style with a twisted weft that was developing into a distinct regional design. Shirts and headdresses, perhaps even aprons, would have been made of coarser linen and hemp, with finer textiles and adornments reserved for Sundays. Textual references suggest the use of sabots and sealskin moccasins as at Beaubassin, with the added option of European-style leather shoes with latchets, ribbon ties, or buttons.

The presence of decorative snips at the Savoie/Blanchard house does point to Marie Savoie and Marguerite Blanchard embroidering items like pockets, as personal adornment was accomplished through items that also had some practical or religious use. The fancy scissors would have hung from the women's waists or been tucked in their hussifs or pockets. The decorated crucifix and embellished beads also found among the remains of their homestead served as physical manifestations of their Catholic faith. The way this community connected was through shared labour, land records revealing many plots worked by collectives of two, three, or more men, sometimes related and sometimes not; the dykes were maintained through similar practices.[9] Textile manufacture and clothing production worked the same way, creating a series of public spaces populated by Acadian women, their pride and identity resting in the works of their hands.

The Fortress: Louisbourg

Marie Josephe Le Borgne de Belleisle had a very different life in Louisbourg than Lady Anne Melanson, or Marie Breau *dite* Vincelotte from Belleisle, but the threads that bound them all together remained strong. The social context of Louisbourg – a handful of Acadians living in the middle of a bustling French port and garrison

– was different from the small settlement farming and fishing life of Annapolis, which was much more removed from European influence than either the fortress or the Melanson settlement. The locations of the settlements themselves influenced the ways in which Acadians dressed, both in terms of daily life and in the types of pressures that surrounded them. Those in residence at Louisbourg were most heavily influenced by the fashions of France, and had greatest access to higher-status materials, garments, and accessories. The urban lifestyle enjoyed by successful merchants and officers' wives removed the need for environmental adaptations like moccasins, and encouraged the purchase of status-bearing materials like silk and indiennes.

The Acadians with long-term residence at Louisbourg were primarily women, wives of French officers and other notables. Their probate inventories suggest that they had integrated most of the way into colonial French urban society, but a few anomalies remain. The plain gillets and wool skirts suggest an attachment on at least one woman's part to simpler rural styles, while another's extravagant hooped petticoats defined a high-status silhouette. The mantua or robe de chambre was the most popular style early on, while later gowns included yards of imported Indian cottons unavailable to those still living in Paris. The styles that Anne Levron, Jeanne Thibodeau, and their friends wore would have been impractical for farm work, and there is no indication that the women at Louisbourg spent any time wearing sabots or moccasins. Brass buttons and decorative sewing equipment found in the Acadian houses at Louisbourg speak to this differentiation as well. The men wore coats, waistcoats, and breeches like the other men around them; fancy stockings, hats, and leather shoes were all available from Acadian traders as well as local producers.

Life in Louisbourg would have been one of almost-fitting-in, the dress styles similar, but Acadian tastes – as much as can be surmised from such a small sample size – leaning toward the silks, velvets, and imported painted cottons. Perhaps it was a sign of over-compensation, attempts to more fully erase the social stigma of coming from a rural background, or perhaps it was carrying over the colourful aesthetics of home. Accessories including pockets and gold jewellery completed the outfits. Items such as Le Borgne's France-made earrings were symbols of their connections to contemporary continental fashions. Slightly out of step from the mainstream, but overall assimilated, Acadians in Louisbourg were the group most closely affiliated with the contemporary French fashion system.

The Trading Hub: Beaubassin

Living outside of the radius of easy imperial control, the Acadians of Beaubassin were able to use that relative lack of interference to begin constructing a new identity for themselves.[10] The large number of dress-related artifacts discovered at Beaubassin, combined with the surviving documentation, gives us the strongest evidentiary base of all the sites examined here. That evidence indicates that Acadians at Beaubassin combined homespun linen and wool with imported textiles, wore moccasins, sabots, and European-style buckled shoes, decorated themselves with both home-made and imported religious and secular jewellery, and kept lines of trade open in multiple directions despite Britain's and France's best efforts at suppression and control. They may also have engaged with a colonial tendency to interweave Indigenous styles with European dress and choose which versions of dress to wear based on who was around to see them.

By 1750, Beaubassin was on its way toward developing its own vernacular of dress. Local production of linen and wool was supplemented by imported textiles. At first this was a necessary supply stream while they ramped up local resources, and later became a means of acquiring luxuries that they were unable to produce themselves: high-end linens, silk, vermillion, indigo, and cotton. Eventually the textile trade expanded and Beaubassin became an export site, engaging in the economy as small-scale hosiery producers. Beaubassin was also a hub for trade into nearby Mi'kmaw communities. While distant from the Atlantic coast, the settlement was by no means isolated physically, economically, or culturally. The inhabitants of Beaubassin engaged in sophisticated trade practices with a wide range of partners and took advantage of their location at the entrance to the Chignecto Isthmus to facilitate that trade.

Accessories, ribbons, lace, and silk tell another big part of this story. The presence of items like jewelled sleeve buttons and brass shoe buckles confirms the regular use of Continental fashion through at least the 1720s and 1730s. The awl and snips for making eyelets confirm that they were actively constructing and recreating fashionable garments alongside homespun skirts and variations on moccasins. Buttons – both locally made and imported – buckles, lacing rings, and hooks and eyes alongside the possibilities of decoration with tinkler cones, pipe-stem beads, and local dyes suggest a transitional space where new signifiers emerged. The traditional symbolism attached to these items changed either as new entanglements were added, the wearer's identity shifted, or both.

The tools used for clothing-related tasks are the means by which women at Beaubassin engaged with ideals of gender. The plated scissors and embroidery snips speak both to the regular practice of fancy-work and to the level of social prestige associated with women who performed this work. Women engaged in heavy domestic labour in Beaubassin and also in the kind of activities and dress choices more closely culturally associated with elite ladies of leisure. Embroidery in this period transitioned into a craft for these women, the means through which wealthy girls were inculcated into a very specific ideal of femininity. Farm women engaging in silk embroidery flipped that script.

Even with some aspects of the context of dressing nebulous at best, we can still paint an image of a hub society around which the wheel of northeastern trade turned. The Acadian gentleman of Beaubassin wore his jewelled and engraved sleeve buttons on his fine holland shirt alongside homemade dorset buttons. His homespun wool breeches were offset by imported silk stockings and brass shoe buckles. He and his wife wore moccasins one day and European leather shoes the next. They carried rosaries with spacers carved from glass trade beads, and pendants imported from France. She spun everyday linen from homegrown flax and wove it for shifts to wear beneath her striped wool skirts and gingham cotton gowns. And she also tied French silk ribbons and lace into her headdress. Settlers at Beaubassin had interest in elegant clothes, in silks and in brass shirt buttons, and they could access the goods as well as the capital with which to acquire them. Drugget and mazamet woollens entered the settlement as trade goods as well as rugged cloth for outerwear and coats, while tin- or silver-plated sewing tools spoke to the pride of those who could display them in their sewing kits. Jewels were given as love pledges, and the fidel jewel was a reminder to its owner both of their faith in general and the specific version of Catholicism that came with them from southwestern France. Migrants from other regions settled in both Beaubassin and Louisbourg, bringing their own sensibilities and aesthetics to add to the mix. European glass and ceramics completed the furnishing of homes described by travellers as being poverty-stricken and without resources, a contradiction that inspires questions about display and intent.

Conclusions

A variety of influences shape human decisions about what to wear, and the messaging contained with those clothing choices changes with time and as context shifts. Geography, climate, environment, religion, social pressures, age, and gender all make a difference, as does access to both raw materials and finished products. The combinations of context, people, and dress create what Roche called a clothing system, a new dialect of a visual language.[11] Each human society has a fashion system, and some of the most innovative things happen in the spaces where they collide. In order to understand a clothing system, the parts of that system need to be identified. This presents a problem for researchers looking at Acadia, as there are no extant garments or textile samples remaining. Extrapolating from what has survived is the only available option: finding the edges and details of the original wardrobes from the clues they left behind. Even in situations where portraiture and sketches are non-existent, bringing the context and second-degree artifacts into play can give us a sense of what was taking place. In this case, examination of the physical evidence has highlighted places where biases and assumptions exist in the written primary sources and in previous interpretations of those sources.

The Nova Scotia Acadians were neither direct copies of French villagers, nor were they fully independent exceptions from the culture of the Atlantic world. They maintained many aspects of their original fashion system, and over time, differences began to emerge between settlements. Groups were in the process of developing their own vernaculars, altered by different levels of exposure to imperial power, social expectation, and trade opportunities. They were neither isolated nor self-sufficient, and engaged frequently with the Atlantic marketplace, as well as the global network of goods. The changes in Acadian dress had a measurable impact on the reactions of outside observers, governors, and travellers unsettled by Acadian "demi-republican" disregard for imperial authority.[12] To French onlookers, Acadians were drawing too heavily on local materials and styles and drifting away from appropriate colonial fashions; for the British, the soft wools, less-structured bodices, and Catholic devotional jewellery made them too visually French to be trusted. Acadian bodies became unruly subjects in need of further control.

Sleeve buttons, silk stockings, and brass buckles suggest that many Acadians were clothing-proud. The striped weaves, finely spun thread, and high-effort dye colours typical of Acadian weaving show the effort and planning they put into what outside observers denigrated as "coarse stuff." Acadian weavers developed their own unique weaves and techniques, inspired by contemporary textiles like siamoises. The visual simplicity of Acadian weaving makes it easy for the casual observer to underestimate the skill level required to produce their signature textiles. The plain tabby weaves were a restriction of the style of their looms, and the creativity they explored in combinations of imported and local dyes made up for any technical limitations. Their interest in stripes was connected to mainstream fashion of the era but enjoyed unique local expression. The dyes they used and colours they achieved, including creative work-arounds like unravelling and reworking red wool yardage, show a willingness to make the extra investment to acquire dramatic and locally resonant colours that diverged from current urban fashion.

Despite some structural similarities between Acadia and the settlers' villages of origin, Acadian culture prior to the deportation was deviating from the cultures of their provinces of origin. Acadian spaces began as imperial projects and as early testing grounds for what French-ness could look like in a new environment. What happened instead was the creation of a cultural dialect, a *francophonie* modified in reaction to the new logistics of life at a distance from the metropole. The changes meant that Acadian society no longer aligned with the categories and estates of the ancien régime, which in turn confused external observers. The systemization of knowledge going on in the contemporary sciences led to focus on categories – in humankind as well as natural science – and uncertainty was a source of tension. Changing the meanings behind signifiers of gentility and civility changed the messages being sent and received, seen most vividly in the construction of womanhood.

Clothing at this stage was less about personal taste than it was about communicating understanding of one's role in society, the notion of appropriate dress feeding into the "culture of appearances" that was so important at the time.[13] The evidence for clothing in Belleisle suggests a farming community more concerned with practical dress. At the same time, the sewing tools found there show us that some of the women at Belleisle were spending time on embroidery and fancy-work, leisure sewing activities that were generally associated with gentility. The sewing tools at the Melanson site, on the other hand, are numerous but simple. Middling class affectations appeared instead in their worn accessories – spur buckles and fancy cufflinks. The means by which Acadian households were signalling their social status and engagement with the world of goods were variable and inconsistent, not aligning with overarching expectations. The tension between expectations and apparent reality that arose as a result may be behind some of the contemporary commentary regarding lazy or indolent Acadians. Villebon, Dièreville, and others saw what appeared to be labourers of the third estate engaging in leisure activities and wearing some articles of higher-status clothing, and understood the behaviour behind this to be a sign of sloth, social climbing, or at best a distraction from more appropriate tasks, when the reality was more of a reshuffling of priorities.

Selections from four archaeological assemblages and six inventories open a window into the daily lives of Nova Scotia Acadians in the late seventeenth and early eighteenth centuries. While broad details of marriages and land ownership give us some insight into the web of interpersonal networks that made up their social world, the collections of tools and accessories shed some light on how they saw themselves and their relationships with others. The connections created by domestic labour sharing bound female community members closer than blood ties alone. Reciprocal labour arrangements gave each participant a direct investment in the welfare of new families, and intergenerational work gave women a space to tell stories and histories, and to communicate values and beliefs to the children working with them. That bond across the generations was reinforced by the familial support seen in marriage contracts that included living space, and the ante-mortem transfer of farm properties from living parents to younger children.[14] The communal activities of fancy-work, plain work, and fibre processing made a foundation for a strong community. The tight bonds of communication, idea transmission, and intergenerational, cross-familial labour sharing created a sense of identification as a distinct group with responsibility towards one another, a group that was both insular and self-regenerating. The recovered textile tools are physical confirmation of the processes of connection and exchange that fuelled these strong networks, the Acadians' growth as a self-identifying community of kin, and ultimately a tight and bounded cultural community of their own.

The wider literature on Acadia has seen much debate regarding Acadian participation and agency in the wider transatlantic world. Introducing clothing and display as a source of evidence brings the possibility of bridging that gap and adds new perspective to that discussion. Acadians at all the settlements, however rural, understood and engaged with contemporary European and colonial fashions to some degree. Imported fabrics, tools, and jewellery brought in by traders from ports along the eastern seaboard and across the ocean marked Acadia's deep and abiding connections outside its geographical borders. Daughters and sons moved from thriving settlements to establish new ones and carried the vertices of those kinship diagrams with them, merchant relatives drawing new lines and entanglements with each trip back and forth between homestead and birthplace. Beaubassin exported linen and hosiery for other markets, while households brought in fashion items both for local use and for trade. It is also clear that in some areas, that fashion was changing based on local influence and materials. Sealskin moccasins, trade bead rosaries, tinkler-style aglets, and local dyes made inroads into the aesthetic, particularly in settlements like Beaubassin, where engagement with the Mi'kmaq was more frequent.

Despite being depicted as coarse farmers innately at risk of sliding away from Europe's civilizing influence, many Acadians were holding on to portions of their European identity with relative ease. At the same time, however, some were incorporating elements of Indigenous dress into their wardrobes – moccasins, red stripes, tinkler cones, and glass beads. They became embodiments of the tensions between three fashion systems, entangling their bodies with the big questions of empire and identity. These demonstrations of "intertwined lines of identity" forged a new kind of space at the intersection of colonial and Indigenous lives, negotiating for a concept of Acadian-ness that would remove them from Atlantic politics.[15] Visiting commentators described Acadian dress as crude and simple, an image at odds with materials found on site. It may be the distinctive addition of the homespun wools and linens that created that impression, materials that were not being produced in any major quantity in New France at this stage.[16] Acadian wardrobes incorporated soft woollens instead of hard-wearing worsteds, used no rigid body shaping, included both homemade buttons and imported fancy brass ones, and incorporated new furs and leathers with their own special properties. Acadians wore indiennes, lace headdresses, and gold, but also owned wooden sabots and laced their bodices with bone bodkins instead of silver. The amount of variety in their wardrobes and the creativity with which they incorporated other materials puts the lie to descriptions of barefooted, kirtled poverty that have become so much a part of their narrative.

Dress comprises signs and signifiers, a communication medium used to create and navigate expressions of social, political, and environmental identity. Clothing choice was as much a negotiation between spheres as were treaties and alliances. The European self transmuted into something far more connected to the land they farmed and the spaces they claimed for themselves. Acadians lived complex lives at the intersections of multiple material cultures, from which they picked and chose the pieces best suited to their new existences. They neither held firmly to the culture and materials brought over from France, nor were they solely dependent on the work of their own hands and the products of their new environment. The webs of connections and interlinkages that the Acadians knew prior to resettlement collided with those of Mi'kma'ki, the entanglements reweaving across space, time, and *thing* to create a vibrant tapestry all their own.

Notes

Introduction

1 Hon. Brook Watson to the Reverend Andrew Brown, 1 July 1791, cited in Hannay, "The Acadian French," 133.

2 The Debert site in Colchester County, Nova Scotia, is the oldest recorded habitation site in Atlantic Canada, and has been dated ca 11,000–10,500 BP. See Canadian Museum of History, "Gateway to Aboriginal Heritage – The Debert Palaeo-Indian National Historic Site."

3 See, for example, Saccardy's complaints about the lack of cleared uplands and Acadian focus on the marshlands. "Le Sieur Saccardy: Description de la baye de Chedabouctou, description du Port Royal, 3 January 1690." MS-6-24, William Morse Collection, Dalhousie University Archives.

4 Kawamura, *Doing Research*, 27, 89; Georg Simmel, in Taylor, *Establishing Dress History*, 44.

5 Entwistle, *The Fashioned Body*, 133; also see Brown, *Foul Bodies*; White, "To Ensure That He Not Give Himself Over to the Indians."

6 Hebdige, *Subculture*, 17–18.

7 Hodder, "Material Entanglement," 1–5. See also Hodder, *The Meanings of Things*; Thomas, *Entangled Objects*; Jordan, "Colonies, Colonialism, and Cultural Entanglement," 31–49; Hodder, "Wheels of Time," 175–87; Hodder, *Studies in Human–Thing Entanglement*; Der and Fernandini, *Archaeology of Entanglement*.

8 I use "thing" here in italics to indicate the definition as used in entanglement theory, in the hopes of providing clarity.

9 Hodder, *Entangled*, 42–4, 101.

10 Ibid., 94–7.

11 Der and Fernandini, *Archaeology of Entanglement*, 11.

12 Brun, *Les Acadiens avant 1755*, 2003.

13 Hodson, *The Acadian Diaspora*, 20.

14 Gwyn, *Excessive Expectations*, 16–17; Reid, "Pax Britannica or Pax Indigena?," 175–6.

15 Clark, *Acadia*, 166; de Saint-Père, *Une colonie féodale*, 308.

16 Collins, "The Economic Role of Women," 442.

17 Griffiths, *Migrant to Acadian*, 182–3; Basque, "Family and Political Culture," 61–2.

18 Loren, "Social Skins," 173; Roche, *The Culture of Clothing*, 370–5.

19 Loren, "Social Skins," 176; See also White, "To Ensure That He Not Give Himself Over to the Indians," 111–49; Ferris, Harrison, and Wilcox, eds, *Rethinking Colonial Pasts through Archaeology*.

20 Roche, *The Culture of Clothing*, 92–4.

21 See Stone, *Fort Michilimackinac, 1715–1781*; White, *Buckles from Seven Sites*, and White, *Constructing Identities*.

Chapter One

1 Denys, *Description and Natural History*, 123.
2 Griffiths, *From Migrant to Acadian*, 238, 260; Coleman, "Acadian History in the Isthmus of Chignecto"; Bumsted, *Land, Settlement, and Politics*; Ross and Deveau, *The Acadians of Nova Scotia*; White, *Dictionnaire Généalogique*; Barriault, "Famille DesRoches," 51–160.
3 Kennedy, *Something of a Peasant Paradise?*, 17, 26, 103–4.
4 Payne, MacDonald, and Campbell, *The Greater Gulf*, 6.
5 Paul, *We Were Not the Savages*, 72–3, 83; Griffiths, *Contexts of Acadian History*, 23–5; Patterson, "Indian–White Relations in Nova Scotia," 25.
6 Kennedy, Peace, and Pettigrew, "Social Networks across Chignecto"; Griffiths, *From Migrant to Acadian, 1604–1755*, 172, 434–5.
7 Ricker, *L'sitkuk*, 4.
8 Miller, "Aboriginal Micmac Population," 117–18; estimates for the total Mi'kmaq population across all of Mi'kmak'i have gone as high as 200,000. See Ricker, *L'sitkuk*.
9 Lewis, "Pre-Contact Fish Weirs," 27, 29–30; Ricker, *L'sitkuk*, 3, 17.
10 McKenzie, "Reassembling the Greater Gulf," 18; Joudry, "Puktewei," 22; Paul, *We Were Not the Savages*, 18; Berneshawi, "Resource Management and the Mi'kmaq Nation," 118.
11 Joudry, "Puktewei," 48–9, 50, 54; also see Stewart, *Forgotten Fires*. Where this would come into conflict was against the European desire for logging – wood was a major export and important resource, and burns to clear forest undergrowth caused consternation. See Hinke, "Report of the Journey of Francis Louis Michel from Berne, Switzerland, to Virginia, October 2, 1701–December 1, 1702," 113–41 for a contemporary description. Rather than the misconception that the Mi'kmaq passed through their lands without leaving agricultural marks, it is vital to understand the arrival of the settlers as the arrival of a new form of agriculture that competed with long-standing local practice.
12 See Joudry, "Puktewei," 71; Lescarbot, *Histoire de la Nouvelle France*, vol. 3, 252; Martin, "European Impact," 8; and Ricker, *L'sitkuk*, 7, 8.
13 Thwaites, *The Jesuit Relations*, vol. 3, 75–7; Bourque and LaBar, *Uncommon Threads*, 85–6.
14 Denys, *Concerning the Ways of the Indians*, 8–9; Thwaites, *The Jesuit Relations*, 74; Bourque and LaBar, *Uncommon Threads*, 82.
15 Lescarbot, *Histoire de la Nouvelle France*, 212; Graham, *Observations on Hudson's Bay*, 135–8.
16 Denys, *Concerning the Ways of the Indians*, 9.
17 Ibid., 34–5; Ricker, *L'sitkuk*, 8–10; Paul, *We Were Not the Savages*, 39; Lescarbot, *Histoire de la Nouvelle France*, vol. 2, 45–6, 247.
18 Paul, *We Were Not the Savages*, 54; Wicken, "Mi'kmaq Decisions," 90; Wicken, "Re-Examining Mi'kmaq–Acadian Relations," 95; Lennox, *Homelands and Empires*, 77, 127–8, 152.
19 Peace, "Two Conquests," 45–6; "General Census Taken in the Month of November 1708 of All of the Indians in Acadia Who Reside on the East Coast, and Those of Pintagouet and of Canibeky" (Census, 1708), Extrait G.1, 466-1., Library and Archives Canada.
20 Peace, "Two Conquests," 93–4, 102; Dickason, *Canada's First Nations*, 169–70; Griffiths, *Contexts of Acadian History*, 24–5. See also Christine Bear, "Elizabeth Warren Scandal Highlights Lack of Indigenous Data in DNA Banks," CBC, last updated 16 November 2018, https://www.cbc.ca/news/technology/indigenous-dna-research-1.4896440.

21 Kennedy, Peace, and Pettigrew, "Social Networks across Chignecto"; Wicken, "Re-Examining Mi'kmaq–Acadian Relations," 103.

22 Alexander, "Afterword," 485.

23 Jordan, "Colonies, Colonialism, and Cultural Entanglement," 32.

24 Wicken, "Re-Examining Mi'kmaq–Acadian Relations," 105, 108; Paul, *We Were Not the Savages*, 82–3.

25 Griffiths, *From Migrant to Acadian*, 65–6. Other non-French settlers came from England, Ireland, Portugal, and Belgium.

26 Kennedy, *Something of a Peasant Paradise?*, 18–19; Chiasson and Landry, "History of Acadia," Griffiths, *From Migrant to Acadian*, 531.

27 Shears, "Examination of a Contested Landscape," 60; Griffiths, *From Migrant to Acadian*, 290–1; Clark, *Acadia*, 204.

28 Hon. Brook Watson to the Reverend Andrew Brown, 1 July 1791, in Hannay, "The Acadian French," 133. Some details of the description are suspect, as Acadian houses were not log houses in the early years, but the point regarding shared labour nevertheless remains.

29 Clark, *Acadia*, 161, 176; Dièreville, *Voyage du Port Royal de l'Acadie*; Griffiths, *From Migrant to Acadian*, 175; C.A. Brasseaux, "Acadian to Cajun: History of a Society Built on the Extended Family," posted 9 August 1999, https://www.medschool.lsuhsc.edu/genetics_center/louisiana/keynote_brasseaux_p.htm (site discontinued).

30 Griffiths, *From Migrant to Acadian*, 124 for an estimate of six to seven children, while Clark, *Acadia*, 202–3, gives an estimate of 5.5–6.

31 Marcy, "Fertility of Historical Populations," 314; Tommaselli et al., "Complete Breastfeeding and Lactational Amenorrhoea," 253; Hynes, "Demography of Port Royal," 15.

32 Coleman, "Acadian Social Life," 24.

33 Clark, *Acadia*, 202; Offen, *The Woman Question in France*, 51; Collins, "The Economic Role of Women," 442; "Rescensement du Port Royal a l'accadie de l'année 1707" (Census, 1707), Dépôt des papiers publics des colonies; état civil et recensements: Série G1: Recensements et documents divers: c-2572, Library and Archives Canada.

34 Morris, "Breif Survey of Nova Scotia [*sic*]." 1748. MG 18 vol. F.4–F.10. Library and Archives Canada.

35 Dunn, Ross, and Wallace, "Looking into Acadie," 38; Crépeau and Dunn, "The Melanson Settlement," 3; White, *Dictionnaire Généalogique*, vol. 1, 562. The "Melanson" surname appears to have originated with brothers Pierre and Charles, with no obvious source. All Acadian Melansons are descended from these two.

36 Dunn, Ross, and Wallace, "Looking into Acadie," 33; Dunn, "History of the Melanson Settlement," 59, 70.

37 Marie died in Boston in 1722. She evidently moved there on marriage, as all her children were born in Boston; M.C. Rosenfield, "BASSET, DAVID," in *Dictionary of Canadian Biography* (University of Toronto/Université Laval, 2003), http://www.biographi.ca/en/bio/basset_david_2E.html. This biography identifies his wife as the daughter of Pierre Melanson, rather than that of Charles le père. Basque, "Family and Political Culture," 52; White, *Dictionnaire généalogique*, 78–9.

38 Basque, "Family and Political Culture," 52, 53; Crépeau and Dunn, "The Melanson Settlement," 3; Rosenfield, "BASSET, DAVID."

39 Governor's Order in Relation to Sheep, *N.S. Arch. II*, 194–5.

40 Dunn, "History of the Melanson Settlement," 27; White, *Dictionnaire généalogique*, 97, 1147; Crépeau and Dunn, "The Melanson Settlement," 3.

41 Dunn, "History of the Melanson Settlement," 17–18.

42 Ibid., 39, 41; White, *Dictionnaire généalogique*, 1156.

43 Delaney, "La reconstitution d'un rôle des passagers du Pembroke," 5. See especially footnotes 4 and 5.

44 Dunn, "History of the Melanson Settlement," 65.

45 Lavoie, "Beaubassin Revisited," 196.

46 Christianson, "Belleisle 1983," 7.

47 Bleakney, *Sods, Soil, and Spades*, 5.

48 Lescarbot, *Histoire de la Nouvelle France*, 314–16, 321, 355.

49 Morse, *Acadiensia Nova*, 144, 146, 150; Christianson, "Belleisle 1983," 8.

50 Lavoie, "Un nouveau regard," 78–80; Christianson, "Belleisle 1983," 7; Hody, "BLANCHARD, GUILLAUME," *Dictionary of Canadian Biography*. Blanchard's house is the feature designated House 1 in the 1984 excavation.

51 See Lavoie, "Belleisle Nova Scotia"; Hynes, "Demography of Port Royal," 6; Lavoie, "Un nouveau regard," 82; White, *Dictionnaire généalogique*, vol. 1, 146, 152.

52 White, *Dictionnaire généalogique*, vol. 1, 152–3. Marguerite died at the age of thirty-four in 1757, and Marie Savoie at age eighty-six on 10 February 1767. See also Vital Records of Duxbury, Massachusetts, 415. (Marie Savoie as "Mary Savory").

53 Desan, "Making and Breaking Marriage," 3; Hynes, "Demography of Port Royal," 7.

54 Lavoie, "Un nouveau regard," 78, 82; "Rescensement du Port Royal à l'accadie de l'année 1707."

55 White, *Dictionnaire généalogique*, 1376, 1378, 1458, 1460–1, 1521.

56 Lavoie, "Belleisle Nova Scotia," 267.

57 Kennedy, Peace, and Pettigrew, "Social Networks across Chignecto."

58 Jordan, "Colonies, Colonialism, and Cultural Entanglement," 36.

59 Hale, "Journal of a Voyage to Nova Scotia."

60 Cadillac, *Extracts from a Memoir*, 6:89

61 Trueman, *The Chignecto Isthmus*.

62 Nadon, "The Isthmus of Chignecto," 10. Various dates given for the founding include 1671 (Arsenault), 1672 (Annual Report of the Beaubassin and Fort Lawrence Public Archaeology Experience), and post-January 1673 (Nadon).

63 Faragher, *A Great and Noble Scheme*, 72. Faragher flags certain locations, such as Butte à Roger and Butte à Mirande, as having been named for well-known Irish and Portuguese immigrants.

64 "The Acadians and the Creation of the Dykeland 1680–1755," *The Landscape of Grand Pré*, accessed 7 May 2022, http://www.landscapeofgrandpre.ca/the-acadians-and-the-creation-of-the-dykeland-1680ndash1755.html.

65 Macdonald and Clowater, "Natural Ecosystem Connectivity," 11; Lavoie, "Archaeological Reconnaissance," 4.

66 Cadillac, *Extracts from a Memoir*, 6:89.

67 July 1720, Phillipps to Craggs, in Akins, *Selections*, 37; 23 November 1741, Mascarene to Lords of Trade.

68 de Meulles, "Recensement fait par de Meulles ... 1686"; "Rescensement du Port Royal à l'accadie de l'année 1707." 1686: 236 cattle, 111 sheep, 189 hogs. 1707: 510 cattle, 500 sheep, 328 hogs.

69 Lavoie, "Belleisle Nova Scotia, 1680–1755," 35–6; Coleman, "Acadian Social Life," 14.

70 de Meulles, "Mémoire concernant Beaubassin."

71 Brebner, *New England's Outpost*, 116.

72 John Nelson (nephew of Thomas Temple) and Jacques Bourgeois (mill builder in Beaubassin, funded by Nelson). See Hodson, *The Acadian Diaspora*, 29; and Daigle, "Nos amis les ennemis," 104.

73 Brun, *Les Acadiens avant 1755*, 84, 92.

74 Journal of Colonel John Winslow, *Collections of the Nova Scotia Historical Society*, 164.

75 Griffiths, *From Migrant to Acadian*, 392; Coleman, "Acadian History in the Isthmus of Chignecto," 3.

76 Lavoie, "Archaeological Reconnaissance," 4.

77 Lavoie, "Beaubassin Revisited," 1, as per Cormier, "Bourgeois, Jacques," in *Dictionary of Canadian Biography*, 1969, 98; Nadon, "The Isthmus of Chignecto," 9. Bona Arsenault dates this to 1671 but Bourgeois was present at a meeting in Port Royal in 1673, possibly making his move later than originally assumed.

78 Kristmanson, "Archaeology at Pointe-Aux-Vieux, Part 1," 22; Lavoie, "Beaubassin Revisited," 1.

79 Nadon, "The Isthmus of Chignecto," 9; Lavoie, "Beaubassin Revisited," 1; de Meulles, "Recensement fait par de Meulles … 1686," 33.

80 de Meulles, "Mémoire concernant Beaubassin."

81 White, *Dictionnaire généalogique*, 1199. Mirande had previously been living in Quebec, leaving in 1675 after one Catherine Basset, a woman with whom he "had been keeping company," was expelled from the city due to her bad reputation. See White, *English Supplement to the Dictionnaire*, 255.

82 de Meulles, "Recensement fait par de Meulles," 1686.

83 Personal communication with Sara Beanlands, October 2018. See also Tremblay, "A Typological Analysis of the Stone Pipes of the Isthmus of Chignecto, Eastern Canada."

84 "General Census Taken in the Month of November 1708," Library and Archives Canada.

85 Wicken, "Tall Sails and Tall Tales," 231–2.

86 Kennedy, Peace, and Pettigrew, "Social Networks across Chignecto," 16, 18.

87 Clark, *Acadia*, 212.

88 Schmeisser, "The Population of Louisbourg," 38, 44.

89 Johnston, "The People of Eighteenth Century Louisbourg," 150–61; Johnston, "From Port de Peche to Ville Fortifiee," 4, 10; Schmeisser, "The Population of Louisbourg," 8.

90 Wood, *The Great Fortress*, 3–6; Johnston, *Religion in Life at Louisbourg*, 5.

91 Dunn, Ross, and Wallace, "Looking into Acadie," 37; Johnston, "Un regard neuf," 155–72.

92 White, *Dictionnaire généalogique*, vol. 2, 1509; Jonah and Tait, "Filles d'Acadie," 28–9.

93 Dunn, "Louisbourg – Block 2," 70–1.

94 Donovan, "Slaves and Their Owners," 3; Cipolla, *Foreign Objects*, 17–18.

95 Notariat de l'Ile Royale, "Inventaire de la communauté de Marguerite Terriau, veuve de Pierre Boisseau."

96 Jonah, "Unequal Transitions," 111; White, *Dictionnaire généalogique*, 1030.

97 Wood, *The Great Fortress*, 7–8; Dunn, Ross, and Wallace, "Looking into Acadie," 30–1.

98 Morris, "Breif Survey of Nova Scotia [sic]," 257–8; Deveau, "Preliminary Report," 62–3.

99 Reid, "Acadia and the Acadians," 26–31.

100 Germain le père's son François Xavier married Marie Josephe Richard, another granddaughter of Sansoucy, and Marguerite Richard (the widow Dugas)'s second cousin. René Blanchard le fils married François's sister Marie. White, *Dictionnaire généalogique*, vol. 2, 1458.
101 The Abbé Raynal, as described in Haliburton, *An Historical Statistical Account*, vol. 1, 196.
102 Turgeon, "Material Culture and Cross-Cultural Consumption," 87, Borck and Mills, "Approaching an Archaeology of Choice," 42–3.
103 Harper, "'Copper Kettle' Burials," 11–36; Fisher and Loren, "Embodying Identity in Archaeology," 225–30.
104 Ships from France or England could take a month or more to make a single crossing, with instances of ships delayed over three months due to bad weather on the crossing. Times generally ranged between 40–100 days, with some outliers on either side depending on wind and weather. See Proulx, *Between France and New France*, 54 (54–70 for longer discussion); Macdonald, "Ships of War," 119–35. From the Bay of Fundy to Quebec City is approximately 2,000 km by ship, up and around Cape Breton. Making a high estimate of a speed of 10 knots, the shortest time such a trip would take would have been between five days to a week, depending on the winds. The approximately 490 km between Port Royal and Boston was a straight line that could be navigated in less than two days.
105 Governor Simon Bradstreet, 1680. Dow, *Massachusetts Bay Colony*, 150.
106 Cipolla, *Foreign Objects*, 17–18.
107 de Meulles, "Voyage of Monsieur de Meulles," 110; Dièreville, *Voyage du Port Royal*, 175; Kalm et al., *Voyage de Pehr Kalm au Canada en 1749*, 569; Balvay, "Tattooing," 3–4.
108 Anishanslin, *Portrait of a Woman in Silk*, 53–4, 216.
109 Webster and Villebon, *Letters, Journals and Memoirs*, 128.
110 Ibid., 132. Minas, 27 October 1699.
111 Cozzens, *Acadia*, 295.
112 Brown, "Removal of the French Inhabitants of Nova Scotia by Lieut. Governor Lawrence & His Majesty's Council in October 1755," transcribed in Beanlands, "Annotated Edition of Rev. Dr. Andrew Brown's Manuscript," 180.
113 Translation by author, from de Meulles, "Mémoire concernant Beaubassin."
114 Rygiel, "The Homespun Economy," 178.
115 Hood, *The Weaver's Craft*, 120–3.
116 "Recensement Fait par de Meulles … 1686"; "Rescensement Du Port Royal à l'accadie de l'année 1707." Jean did the best of them all, with twenty sheep, while poor Guillaume struggled along with two.
117 Rygiel, "'The Homespun Economy,'" 53.
118 "Estat des Habitans de Port-Royal," 1693, Library and Archives Canada.
119 Hood, *The Weaver's Craft*, 133–4.
120 "Invoice of Merchandise from Abraham Boudrot, Massachusetts Archives; Welsteed, "Certificate by William Welsteed," Suffolk County Court.
121 "An Act to Prevent the Exportation of Wool out of the Kingdoms of Ireland and England," *Statutes of the Realm*, vol. 7, 524–8; also see Daigle, "Nos amis les ennemis," for more on illegal and legal trade in early Acadia.
122 Coleman, "Acadian History in the Isthmus of Chignecto," 116–17; Daigle, "Nos amis les ennemis," 97.

123 Daigle, "Nos amis les ennemis," 79–80, 116.

124 "De Meulles au roi", 1684, F3 II, 200. Cited in Daigle, "Nos amis les ennemis," 102.

125 Webster and Villebon, *Letters, Journals and Memoirs*, 46, 56, 175, 194.

126 de Meulles, "Voyage of Monsieur de Meulles." "Il vient tous les ans dans ce lieu une barque anglais au mois d'avril, qui leur apporte le reste de leurs petites necessities, qu'ils achètent pour des pelleteries qu'ils ont en des sauvages."

127 Desgoutins, "Résumé d'une Lettre de Mathieu de Goutin."

128 "Governor's Letter-Book, Annapolis, 1719–1742," in *A Calendar of Two Letter-Books*, 69.

129 "Nova Scotia Archives Commission Book, 1720–1741," in *A Calendar of Two Letter-Books*, 201.

130 Faragher, *A Great and Noble Scheme*, 103–4; Griffiths, *Migrant to Acadian*, 177; Griffiths, *Contexts of Acadian History*, 29.

131 Kennedy, Peace, and Pettigrew, "Social Networks across Chignecto," 9. Many of the arguments in this section were refined and expanded thanks to conversation with Charles Burke at Parks Canada, and the chapter has been greatly enhanced by his contributions.

132 de Meulles, "Mémoire concernant Beaubassin."

133 Brun, *Les Acadiens avant 1755: Essai*, 101 Arrivees, f. 155, 157; also see Hodson, *The Acadian Diaspora*, 29.

134 Report by M. Tiberge, Agent of the Acadia Trading Company, 30 September 1695, in Webster and Villebon, *Letters, Journals and Memoirs*, 141–2.

135 Summer 1695, Tibierge, in Webster and Villebon, *Letters, Journals and Memoirs*, 141–2.

136 Coleman, "Acadian Social Life," 31.

137 Ibid., 32.

138 "MGII, Nova Scotia A" vol. 11, 211.

139 "MGII, Nova Scotia A" vol. 20, 125.

140 See logs from Henri Brunet (1690s), and the letter books of Peter Faneuil (1716–1739) in particular, as well as Whitmore and Appleton, *Report of the Record Commissioners*, vol. 14, 162–3.

141 "Billet de Zacharie Richard, de Port-Royal, En Faveur de Minet, Pour Marchandises Reçues, 1743; Enregistré à La Requête de Mme Mullot (Julienne Minet)"; Brun, *Les Acadiens avant 1755*, 101.

142 Dechêne, *Habitants and Merchants*, 80. Welsteed, "Certificate by William Welsteed." Note that this Charles de La Tour was the son of the more famous Charles de Saint-Étienne de La Tour and Jeanne Motin.

143 25 September 1715. MGI, CIIA, vol. 35, 203. Also see Coleman, "Acadian Social Life," 34–5; Zoltvany, "BÉGON DE LA PICARDIÈRE, MICHEL," in *Dictionary of Canadian Biography*.

144 From Mr de Brouillan, governor of Cape Breton, to Doucette. Louisburg, 21 July 1718. Colonial Records, N.S., vol. II., quoted in Richard, *Acadia*, 110–11.

145 Brun, *Les Acadiens avant 1755*, 100 F1965, Laborde, 2046, 17-06.

146 Landry, "Culture Matérielle et Niveaux de Richesse"; Brun, *Les Acadiens avant 1755*, 100–1.

147 Landry, "Culture matérielle et niveaux de richesse," paragraph 52.

148 Johnston et al., *Louisbourg: An 18th Century Town.*

149 Archives nationales, Archives des colonies, CIIB v 5 folio 392.

150 Little, *The State of Trade*, 20–2.

151 Surette, *Atlas*, vol. 1, 12; Nadon, "The Isthmus of Chignecto," 9; Griffiths, *From Migrant to Acadian*, 208.

152 Lavoie, "Un nouveau regard," 86–8.
153 Pierre-Georges Roy, ed., "Lettre de Talon Au Ministre Colbert (11 Novembre 1671) Rapport de l'archiviste de La Province de Québec Pour 1930–1931," 164. Translation by author.
154 "Invoice of Merchandise from Abraham Boudrot."
155 Ordoñez and Welters, "Textiles from the Seventeenth-Century Privy," 82.
156 Welsteed, "Certificate by William Welsteed." Other materials included in the cargo were axes, fishing hooks, cooking ingredients, and rum.
157 "Invoice of Merchandise from Abraham Boudrot."
158 The banlieue was a three-mile range around the Fort, as defined by Vetch in 1611 and Delabat's map in 1708. See "Polie des habitans de la bans lieux du Fort Du Port Royal speciffie famile par famille du 25 October 1710" (25 October 1710), Library and Archives Canada.
159 Griffiths, *From Migrant to Acadian*, 157.
160 "Charles Melanson to the Governor Stoughton," 5 February 1696, Mass. Archives II, 587.
161 Deveau, "Preliminary Report," 16.
162 Lavoie, "Belleisle Nova Scotia," 42.
163 Morris, "Breif Survey of Nova Scotia [sic]," 4; Pothier, "GAUTIER Dit Bellair, JOSEPH-NICOLAS," in *Dictionary of Canadian Biography*; Coleman, "The Acadians at Port Royal," 47; Griffiths, *Migrant to Acadian*, 292, 342–3.
164 Griffiths, *Migrant to Acadian*, 342; Pothier, "GAUTIER Dit Bellair, JOSEPH-NICOLAS."
165 Pothier, "GAUTIER Dit Bellair, JOSEPH-NICOLAS"; Crowley and Pothier, "DU PONT DUVIVIER, FRANÇOIS," in *Dictionary of Canadian Biography*; Crowley and Pothier, "DU PONT DUVIVIER, JOSEPH," in *Dictionary of Canadian Biography*.
166 Mascarene to Lords of Trade, 23 November 1741, "MGI, Nova Scotia A" (Microfilm, n.d.), CIIA, Nova Scotia Provincial Archives, Nova Scotia A, vol. 25, 135.
167 Jonah, "Unequal Transitions," 111.
168 Ibid., 115, 116–17.
169 Notariat de l'Ile Royale, "Inventaire des biens meubles appartenant à Jacques Philipe Urbin Rondeau."
170 White, *Dictionnaire généalogique*, 1180.
171 MacMechan, *Original Minutes of His Majesty's Council at Annapolis Royal*, 396.
172 "Recensement de l'Ile Royale et de l'Ile Saint-Jean Dressé par Le Sieur de La Roque en 1752" (Census, 1752), Dépôt des papiers publics des colonies; état civil et recensements: Série GI: Recensements et documents divers: C-4582, Library and Archives Canada; Notariat de l'Ile Royale, "Inventaire des biens meubles appartenant à Jacques Philipe Urbin Rondeau."
173 Lennox, *Homelands and Empires*, 103.
174 Wicken, "Tall Sails and Tall Tales," 93–4, Map 7; Morse, *Acadiensia Nova*, 147.
175 Lennox, *Homelands and Empires*, 123–4, 128; Kristmanson, "Archaeology at Pointe-Aux-Vieux." Also see discussions in Kennedy, *Something of a Peasant Paradise?*, 8; Mi'kmaw names were omitted from transcribed registers: Kennedy, Peace, and Pettigrew, "Social Networks across Chignecto," 11.
176 See discussions in Jones and Stallybrass, *Renaissance Clothing and the Materials of Memory*; Roach-Higgins and Eicher, "Dress and Identity"; White, "Constructing Identities"; Richardson, "Domestic Objects"; Richardson, "Havying Nothing upon Hym"; White, "To Ensure That He Not Give Himself Over to the Indians."

177 See *An Indian Woman and Child of Pomeiooc,* John White, 1585. Woman with tattoos or painted marks carrying gourd vessel, child carrying contemporary English doll. Watercolour over graphite, touched with white © The Trustees of the British Museum; Ulrich, "Cloth, Clothing, and Early American Social History," 39–48; Loren, "Social Skins"; Loren, "Threads: Collecting Cloth"; DuPlessis, "Cottons Consumption."

178 Le Clercq, *New Relation of Gaspesia.*

179 Daigle, "Nos amis les ennemis," 90.

180 Coleman, "Acadian Social Life," 30; BAC-LAC MG 1 CIID, 3-1, 192, 194.

181 Karklins, *Trade Ornament Usage,* 14; Washburn, "Symbol, Utility, and Aesthetics," 201.

182 Pelletier, "From Animal Skins to Polyester," 205; LaBar-Kidd, "Indian Trade Silver," 14, 38.

183 Miramichi in the northwest "used the mark of a man with a bow and arrow drawn, done in bead-work on the clothes and marked on to the canoes" in Le Clercq, *New Relation of Gaspesia,* 39; Harper, Clouette, and Harper, *Highways to History,* 47.

184 Karklins, "Beads from Fort Beausejour."

185 Loren, *Archaeology of Clothing,* 5; Kristmanson, "Archaeology at Pointe-Aux-Vieux, Part 2," 33; Epstein and Prak, eds, *Guilds,* 210–11.

186 Loren, "Social Skins," 183–4.

187 Grimm, *Archaeological Investigation of Fort Ligonier,* 49.

188 Karklins, "Clay Pipe-Stem Beads," 18–19.

189 Turgeon, "Material Culture and Cross-Cultural Consumption," 97, 103.

190 "Lettre de Vaudreuil et Bégon au Conseil de Marine," 17 October 1722, f. 273–273v, Library and Archives Canada.

191 Dechêne, *Habitants and Merchants,* 79–81.

192 Personal communication with Jonathan Fowler, 7 December 2018. Identification of lead seal performed by author. The Grand Pré seal, however, was found in an area more likely associated with the British encampment than Acadian activity.

193 Hocquart à Mss. les directeurs generaus de la Compagnie des Indies, 17 October 1737, BAC-LAC, MGI-CIIA. Microfilm reel number C-2392 f. 289v-291.

194 Hale, *A Compleat Body of Husbandry,* 304; Preston, *Texture of Contact,* 54–5.

195 Proulx, *Between France and New France,* 154.

196 Carlos and Lewis, "Exchange among Native Americans," 24–5.

197 Gottmann, "French-Asian Connections," 542; Wellington, *French East India Companies,* 69.

198 Preston, *Texture of Contact,* 54–5.

199 Lennox, *Homelands and Empires,* 103–4; Hauser, "Jesuit Rings," 5.

200 DuPlessis, "Defining a French Atlantic Empire," 8–9.

201 Tilley, *Handbook of Material Culture,* 20–1.

Chapter Two

1 Schreiner, *From Man to Man,* 13.

2 Beaudry, *Findings,* 5–6.

3 Parker, *The Subversive Stitch,* 2–3, 11; Beaudry, "Stitching Women's Lives," 149–50.

4 Parker, *The Subversive Stitch,* 113; Beaudry, *Findings,* 71.

5 Parker, *The Subversive Stitch*, 81–82; Crowston, *Fabricating Women*, 129–31; Beaudry, *Findings*, 85; also see Beaudry, "Artifacts and Personal Identity," 218–19.

6 Appadurai, *The Social Life of Things*, 5; Kopytoff, "The Cultural Biography of Things," 65.

7 Kopytoff, "The Cultural Biography of Things," 65; Smyth, "When We Talk about Scissors," 293–307.

8 Daniels and Wright, *Joseph Wright*, 13; Joseph Wright, *Portrait of a Woman*, ca 1770, Metropolitan Museum of Art.

9 Parker, *The Subversive Stitch*, 10.

10 Shovlin, "Cultural Politics of Luxury," 576–7, 578.

11 The term used for Guillaume Trahan in the description on the passenger list from the St Jehan, however, "marechal de trenchant," may refer more closely to the maintenance of existing tools rather than training in the manufacture of new ones – "edge-tool worker" rather than blacksmith. Stephen A. White, "RE: [AFC] From Stephen A. White – Some Corrections to John Farragher's Book," e-mail, ACADIAN-FRENCH-CANADIAN-L *Archives*, 18 April 2010.

12 Brack, *Registry of Maine Toolmakers*, 13; Beaudry, *Findings*, 119.

13 Welsteed, "Certificate by William Welsteed."

14 Beaudry, 119; Rees, Tool and Trades History Society, and Gales & Martin, *A Directory of Sheffield*. Thirty-nine are listed as manufacturers of "fine scissors," and the remaining forty-eight of "common scissors"; Smyth, "When We Talk about Scissors," 295–6.

15 Anon., *The Workwoman's Guide*, 15; Fader, "Marine Archaeology," 15.

16 Beaudry, *Findings*, 133.

17 Stone, *Fort Michilimackinac, 1715–1781*, 161–2.

18 See definitions of sizes and uses in Arminjon et al., *Objets civils domestiques*, 580.

19 Cowgill, Neergaard, and Griffiths, *Knives and Scabbards*, 1:58.

20 Tinning or plating of iron involved sprinkling an iron surface with tin filings and applying heat, a process known in some form in Europe for hundreds of years. Jope, "The Tinning of Iron Spurs," 37.

21 Dunn, Ross, and Wallace, "Looking into Acadie," 27 (figure 38). Also see Crépeau and Dunn, "The Melanson Settlement."

22 Cameron, "Anthony Christian and the French Plating Trade."

23 Crowston, *Fabricating Women*, 129–30.

24 Noël Hume, *A Guide to Artifacts*, 267, 268, figure 87, #2.

25 Nadon, "Field Journals," 68-57–405.

26 Ibid., 68-57–405.

27 Personal communication, Marc Lavoie, 20 August 2017.

28 Parker, *The Subversive Stitch*, 11.

29 Brebner, *New England's Outpost*; Jones, "From Frontier to Borderland"; Smith, "Acadia's Outpost."

30 White, *Dictionnaire généalogique*, 1437. Also see Louisbourg in-house report written by Donald Harris, 1982. This is a third man of the same name, son of Jacques de Saint-Étienne de La Tour.

31 Harris, "Louisbourg – In-House Report on Site Histories."

32 Ibid.

33 Mandel, *Scissors*, 5. Further physical analysis will hopefully answer this question.

34 Noël Hume, *A Guide to Artifacts*, 269. See item 2L31Q22-3.

35 Jonah and Tait, "Filles d'Acadie, femmes de Louisbourg," 40.

36 Lavoie, "Belleisle Nova Scotia," 50–2.

37 Lavoie, "Un nouveau regard sur le monde acadien," 78–9.

38 Though it is uncertain whether this was Pierre Blanchard (Gougeon), Guillaume's son, or Pierre Blanchard (Savoie), Guillaume's grandson through René. Order for Road Making, Mascarene, 12 May 1740, and Order to Deputies to Enquire, Mascarene, 2 June 1740. In MacMechan, "Nova Scotia Archives Commission Book, 1720–1741," 235, 240. This was probably Pierre Blanchard (Gougeon), by virtue of ages – the elder Pierre was forty-five in 1740, making him a long-term adult member of the community, while his nephew Pierre was only twenty-seven; White, *Dictionnaire généalogique*, 147, 152.

39 Basque, "Family and Political Culture," 61–2; Johnston, "Call of the Archetype," 73; Jonah and Tait, "Filles d'Acadie," 24; Kennedy, *Something of a Peasant Paradise?*, 13.

40 Clark, *Acadia*, 212.

41 Lot 1C7, as per inventory from primary investigator Marc Lavoie. Lot contained twenty-four bone fragments and six clay shards, including the edge of a plate.

42 Christianson, "Belleisle 1983," 52.

43 Noël Hume, *A Guide to Artifacts*, 269.

44 Anon., *The Workwoman's Guide*, 15.

45 Lavoie, "Un nouveau regard," 84.

46 Crépeau and Dunn, "The Melanson Settlement," 10.

47 See Moroni's painting *The Tailor* (1565–1570), and Francesco Cossa's *Allegoria del mese di Marzo* (ca 1470), for example.

48 Noël Hume, *A Guide to Artifacts*, 268. For images of these artifacts from Bourg's collection, see Dunn, Ross, and Wallace, "Looking into Acadie," 27, figure 38.

49 White, *Dictionnaire généalogique*, 99–100.

50 Desan, "Making and Breaking Marriage," 3–4.

51 Caplan, "Yvon LeBlanc," 59. As per *Acadians in Gray*, the daughters were: Angelique (1727 – eighteen in 1745. d. at twenty in 1747, in Grand Pré), Jeanne (1731 – fourteen years old in 1745), Marie Charlotte de Saint-Étienne (1728 – seventeen years old in 1745), Louise Francoise de Saint-Étienne (1730 – fifteen years old in 1745), and Anne & Jeanne-Charlotte (twins b. 1737 – eight years old in 1745).

52 Personal communication, Marc Lavoie, 20 August 2017.

53 Heldman and Grange, *Excavations at Fort Michilimackinac*, 68; Adams, *Artisans at Louisbourg*, 58.

54 Parker, *The Subversive Stitch*, 15.

55 Caroline Duroselle-Melish, "A Pin's Worth: Pins in Books," *Folger Shakespeare Library*, posted 4 August 2015, https://collation.folger.edu/2015/08/a-pins-worth-pins-in-books/.

56 Beaudry, *Findings*, 29; Centre des Archives d'Outre-mer [CAOM], G2, vol. 197, dossier 151. Pin-papers, which allowed pins to be sold in small and less expensive packets, are generally described as not having come into common use until about 1785, but Jeanne Thibodeau's probate of 1741 includes a listing for six packets of pins.

57 See the excellent typology put together by Beaudry, *Findings*, 22–8.

58 Caple, "The Detection and Definition of an Industry," 253.

59 Interview with Charles Burke, Parks Canada, 13 December 2017.

60 Caple, "The Detection and Definition of an Industry," 248.

61 Laser ablation tests done at the University of New Brunswick confirm that these pins were originally tinned, and not of local origin. They are most likely home-repair jobs of imported pins from the same source as the others.

62 Boutilier and Christianson, "'Clothing Artifact Group,' in Belleisle 1983," 52–3.

63 Belleisle, 2004 dig, as per inventory from primary investigator Marc Lavoie.

64 Noël Hume, *A Guide to Artifacts*, 255–6.

65 Holmes, *A History of Thimbles*, 53, 55; Groves, *History of Needlework Tools*, 37; Beaudry, *Findings*, 94–6.

66 Holmes, *A History of Thimbles*, 23.

67 Ibid., 39.

68 Noël Hume, *A Guide to Artifacts*, 256–7; Beaudry, *Findings*, 112–13.

69 Holmes, *A History of Thimbles*, 55.

70 Ibid., 43, 56, 67, 138.

71 Hill, "Thimbles and Thimble Rings," 85.

72 Beaudry, "Stitching Women's Lives," 150.

73 McKenney, "That 'Bossy Shield,'" 5, 11.

74 Hon. Brook Watson to the Reverend Andrew Brown, 1 July 1791, cited in Hannay, "The Acadian French," 132–3; Clark, *Acadia*, 183; Griffiths, *From Migrant to Acadian*, 175.

75 Holme, *The Academy of Armory*, 91.

76 Brass thimbles cost between a half-penny and a penny. McKenney, "That 'Bossy Shield,'" 7.

77 Ibid., 2.

78 Noël Hume, *A Guide to Artifacts*, 256.

79 Beaudry, *Findings*, 111.

80 Boutilier and Christianson, "'Clothing Artifact Group,' in Belleisle 1983," 53; Beaudry, *Findings*, 52.

81 Christianson and Crépeau, "Home and Hearth."

82 Noël, "Inventory of Archaeological Records," 22, 25.

83 Feature 12, event 8. See field notes by Andrée Crépeau, as well as summary in Noël, 38.

84 Lot 17B2E3. See field notes, as well as summary in Noël, "Inventory of Archaeological Records," 35–6.

85 Burman and Denbo, *Pockets of History*, 23–4.

86 Jonah and Tait, "Filles d'Acadie," 23–4.

87 Beaudry, *Findings*, 77–9.

88 Ibid., 98.

89 2L81K9-7; also see Groves, *History of Needlework Tools*.

90 Hill, "Thimbles and Thimble Rings," 85.

91 Stone, *Fort Michilimackinac, 1715–1781*, 159; Spector, *What This Awl Means*, 31–2.

92 For shoemakers' awls, see Diderot, "Shoe and Boot Making," *The Encyclopedia*, vol. 3. For Eastern Dakota awl handles, see Spector, *What This Awl Means*, 31.

93 Awl 7B12V4.4 and snips 7B12V4.02. The almost-identical object catalogue numbers indicate that these artifacts were discovered in the same stratigraphical layer (Lot 4) of suboperation V.

94 Stone, *Fort Michilimackinac, 1715–1781*, 158–9.

95 "I wear a buckle behind and you have made eyelet holes for strings only and no cloth straps for the buckle." 1745. Eland, *Purefoy Letters*, 315–16.

96 Holme, *The Academy of Armory*, 94; Blanco et al., *Clothing and Fashion*, 331.

97 Mary Beaudry's investigation of court cases brought forward about bodkins revealed that they were all instigated by women, implying deeper emotional connection and identification with the bodkin among women than among men. Beaudry, "Bodkin Biographies," 95, 105; Beaudry, *Findings*, 82, 84.

98 Beaudry, "Bodkin Biographies," 96; Huey, "The Archaeology of 17th-Century New Netherland," 106–7.

99 Baumgarten, *What Clothes Reveal*, 149, 152–3.

100 Deveau, "Preliminary Report," 73–4; Walton, *The Story of Textiles*, 14–15.

101 Grömer, "Efficiency and Technique," 110–12, 114.

102 Christianson, "Belleisle 1983," 54.

103 Hale, *A Compleat Body of Husbandry*, vol. 3, 306; Beaudry, *Findings*, 139, 140–2. Inventories in Salem, Massachusetts, from the mid-seventeenth century show that of twenty-nine households that had spinning wheels listed, fourteen had more than one wheel in their possession, some defined specifically as "linen wheels." Beaudry, *Findings*, 140–2.

104 Rogers and Rogers, *A History of Agriculture*, 750; Dickson, *Old World Colony*, 206.

105 Files provided by Parks Canada and the museum at Fort Beauséjour.

106 Earle, *Home Life*, 175, 198.

107 French neutrals were living in a house that was commandeered as part of a movement around smallpox hospitals, 22 February 1764. "The following is an Inventory of the Things which were found in Mr. Gordons House, lately Occupied by the Robertsons and other French Neutrals"; Whitmore et al., *Records Relating to the Early History of Boston*, vol. 20; Dièreville, *Voyage du sieur de Dièreville en Acadie*, 85–6, 96, 118.

108 Ulrich, "Wheels," 6, 9–10.

109 Personal communication with master weaver Lesley Armstrong, July 2018.

110 Burnham, *The Comfortable Arts*, 54.

111 Whittle and Hailwood, "The Gender Division of Labour," Section VII.

112 Bythell, Duncan. "Hand-Loom Weavers," 346.

113 "Familles établies à l'Acadie, Census, 1671, Library and Archives Canada.

114 De Meulles, "Mémoire concernant Beaubassin," 43.

115 Deveau, "Preliminary Report," 202.

116 Clark, *Acadia*, 158–60 Also see Dièreville; Perrot, AC, CIID-2 (1), 40–1, 1686; Webster and Villebon, *Letters, Journals and Memoirs*, 132–3.

117 Le Sieur Saccardy: Description de la baye de Chedabuctou, description du Port Royal, 3 January 1690. MS-6-24, William Morse Collection, Dalhousie University Archives.

118 Brouillan to Minister, 6 October 1701. Nova Scotia Archives. RGI vol 3 doc 6, reel 15, 218.

119 Letter from Governor Philipps to the Lords of Trade, 3 August 1734. Printed in Akins, *Selections*, 102.

120 Hynes, "Some Aspects of the Demography of Port Royal, 1650–1755," 7–8; also see Jonah and Tait, "Filles d'Acadie," 30, on servants.

121 Main, "Gender, Work, and Wages," 62.

122 Shovlin, "Cultural Politics of Luxury," 576–8; see also Hunt, *Consuming Passions*.

123 For a much older take on the notion that Acadians were recreating/creating a form of European gentility for themselves, see Rameau de Saint-Père, *Une colonie féodale*, 112.

124 Hale, "Journal of a Voyage to Nova Scotia," 234; 1 July 1791. Hon. Brook Watson to the Reverend Andrew Brown. Original transcription by W.B. Tobin, Esq. in Hannay, "The Acadian French," 133.

125 A complaint filed against the parish priest at Beaubassin described how Abbé Claude Trouvé had refused to grant absolution to several local women after confession, as they were wearing lace and ribbon. NA, MGI, CIID, VOL.2, "Mémoire de l'acadie, nouvelle angleterre, nouvelle hollande et virgine par le sieur de Cadillac," fols. 147-152, 1692. Also see "Invoice of Merchandise from Abraham Boudrot."

126 Prown, "The Truth of Material Culture," 14.

127 Hon. Brook Watson to the Reverend Andrew Brown, 1 July 1791, in Hannay, "The Acadian French," 133.

128 Jonah and Tait, "Filles d'Acadie," 29; White, *Dictionnaire généalogique*, 562.

129 Jonah and Tait, "Filles d'Acadie," 44.

130 Crépeau and Dunn, "The Melanson Settlement," 7.

131 Basque, "Family and Political Culture," 61–2; Jonah and Tait, "Filles d'Acadie," 26.

Chapter Three

1 "Ils sont en tout bons ouvriers / Il n'est rien dont ils ne s'acquittent / Cent besoins divers les excitent / A se donner ce qu'ils n'ont pas ... Enfin leur nudité par leur travail se voile." Dièreville and Fontaine, *Voyage du sieur de Dièreville*, 47–8. Translation from "Relation of the Voyage to Port Royal in Acadia or New France," 96.

2 See, for example, Bowden, "Wool Supply and the Woollen Industry." Also see Burnham and Burnham, *Keep Me Warm One Night*; Burnham, *The Comfortable Arts*; Ames and Schlereth, *Material Culture*; Baumgarten, *Eighteenth-Century Clothing at Williamsburg*; Hood, "Material Culture and Textiles: An Overview"; Hood and Ruddel, "Artifacts and Documents in the History of Quebec Textiles"; Ruddel, "Domestic Textile Production in Colonial Quebec, 1608–1840"; Miller et al., *Approaches to Material Culture Research*; Roach-Higgins and Eicher, "Dress and Identity"; Martin, "Makers, Buyers, and Users"; Lemire, *Dress, Culture and Commerce*.

3 A very small sample of the kind of work produced in this phase includes: Brooks, *Textiles Revealed*; Jones and Stallybrass, *Renaissance Clothing and the Materials of Memory*; Bolton, "Classifying the Material"; Rygiel, "Thread in Her Hands"; Hood, *The Weaver's Craft*; B.S. Capp, *When Gossips Meet*; Beaudry, *Findings*; Parker, *The Subversive Stitch: Embroidery and the Making of the Feminine*; Lemire, *The Force of Fashion in Politics and Society*; Riello, "The Object of Fashion"; Hayward, "Crimson, Scarlet, Murrey and Carnation: Red at the Court of Henry VIII."

4 Küchler and Miller, *Clothing as Material Culture*, 1–2; Lemire, "Draping the Body and Dressing the Home."

5 Bragdon, "Our Strange Garments," 112.

6 Brooks, *Textiles Revealed*, 1–2.

7 Hon. Brook Watson to the Reverend Andrew Brown, 1 July 1791, cited in Hannay, "The Acadian French."

8 Burnham, *The Comfortable Arts*, 54.

9 Richelieu, "Echantillons d'etoffes et toiles des manufactures de France recueillis par le Marechal de Richelieu, Tome IV" (1737), Recueil. Collection Richelieu. Echantillons de

tissus, Bibliothèque nationale de France; Pennautier, "Enchantillon de drap du XVIIIme siecle" (Textile sample book, ca 1740), Accession Number: 156.415 EC4 F, Metropolitan Museum of Art.

10 Deveau, "Preliminary Report," 202.

11 Roy, ed., "Lettre de Talon au Ministre Colbert (11 November 1671)," Rapport de l'archiviste de la province de Québec pour 1930–1931.

12 Desgoutins, "Résumé d'une lettre de Mathieu de Goutin."

13 Berlekamp, "The Textile Trade in Boston," 5. Brunet, "Voyages of Henri Brunet"; Welsteed, "Certificate by William Welsteed"; "Invoice of Merchandise from Abraham Boudrot to André Taneuil."

14 AMEC Environment & Infrastructure, "A Mi'kmaq Historical and Ecological Knowledge Review," figs. 2–7.

15 Pierre Joubert, "Pierre Joubert's Bill to Mme Péré" (10 April 1733), G2, vol. 195, doss. 83, Library and Archives Canada.

16 Pierre Joubert's bill to Mme Péré. Nantes, 10 April 1733. N.A., Overseas section, G2, vol. 195, doss. 83. The colour of the replacement damask is not mentioned in the letter but does appear in Mme Péré's probate inventory. See "Procès Verbal de levée de scelle et inventaire faits chez la d'Ile Peré" (9 June 1735), vol. 194, doss. 80, Louisbourg.

17 Anishanslin, *Portrait of a Woman in Silk*, 189.

18 Notariat de l'Ile Royale (Greffe de Bacquerisse), "Inventaire des biens meubles appartenant à Marie Josephe Le Borgne de Belisle."

19 Griffiths, *Migrant to Acadian*, 197.

20 "Lettre de Talon au ministre Colbert," 1671, in Clark, *Acadia*, 164.

21 No evidence for looms has yet been uncovered at Beaubassin, though documentary and logical evidence informs us that they must have existed. Looms could be relatively easily broken down and rebuilt from existing timber, the construction not requiring a huge amount of specialized expertise. The element of the loom that was valuable and required specialized knowledge was the reed, a section of carefully spaced vertical dividers used to separate out the threads of a warp and beat down the weft once a shot had been passed through the warp shed. These could be made of wood, river reed, or metal, or a combination of materials. While not easily broken down, reeds were removable and small enough to be packed and transported even during a hasty evacuation scenario. The larger equipment was also of practical use, and anything remaining may have been either removed by the incoming British or French officers or put to the torch.

22 "Familles établies à l'Acadie. Abrégé envoyé de Québec à Colbert par Le Sieur Randin, 8 Novembre 1671."

23 Itinerant weavers were invariably male in this period, considering the need for solitary travel through often inhospitable terrain.

24 Earle, *Home Life*, 213; Hood, *The Weaver's Craft*, 16.

25 Têtu and Gagnon, *Mandements, lettres pastorales et circulaires*, 217. "[N]ecessity has given them [Acadians] the industry to make some fabrics and coarse textiles, but they cannot make enough to dress everyone."

26 Roy, ed., "Lettre de Talon au Ministre Colbert (11 Novembre 1671) Rapport de l'archiviste de la province de Québec pour 1930–1931," 164.

27 As can be seen in footnote 42 of Saint-Vallier's description: "la nécessité leur a donné l'industrie de se faire quelques toiles et quelques étoffes grossières, mais *ils* ne peuvent en fabrique assez pour se vêtir tous." ([N]ecessity has given them [Acadians] the industry to make some fabrics and coarse textiles, but they cannot make enough to dress everyone.) Emphasis of the masculine plural added.

28 Surette, *Atlas*, vols. 1 & 2.

29 Hood, *The Weaver's Craft*, 15–16.

30 Oelsner, *A Handbook of Weaves*, 25; Daumas, ed., *A History of Technology*, 606.

31 Diderot and Gillispie, *Encyclopedia of Trades and Industry*, vol. 9, plate IV: Tailor of Suits, Fabrics and Measuring Tools; Hood, *The Weaver's Craft*, 90.

32 Daumas, *A History of Technology*, vol. 3, 601.

33 Griffiths, *Migrant to Acadian*, 176; Webster and Villebon, *Letters, Journals and Memoirs*, 128, 132.

34 Chiasson, *Chéticamp*, 2nd ed., 245–6. Translation mine. "Les 'écarderies' [French maritime regionalism] – Quand les chaleurs de l'été commençaient, chacun tondait ses brebis. Puis, dehors, dans de grands chaudrons, on faisait bouillir la laine, pour la nettoyer. Après l'avoir fait sécher au soleil, on l'écharpait pour pouvoir la carder plus facilement. Elle était prête pour l'écarderie. Les femmes voisines et d'autres amies étaient invitées avec leurs écardes et leur tablier. À dix ou douze écardeuses, la laine passait vite. Après quelques heures de travail, où la jasette avait sa grande part aussi, la laine s'amoncelait devant chaque écardeuse en boudins soyeux prêts a filer."

35 Louisiana State Museum and Musée du Nouveau Monde, *L'amour de maman*, 20, 23.

36 Lavoie, "Les aboiteaux acadiens," 76; Jonah and Tait, "Filles d'Acadie," 26. "10 aulnes of fine cloth, three barriques of flour, a fattened pig, a side of beef, and two pots of brandy." 10 aunes: variable definition but somewhere around 10–12 yards, would have been enough for a jacket and skirt, or a full man's suit of breeches and jacket.

37 Hood, *The Weaver's Craft*, 16, 76; Ulrich, "Wheels," 11–12. Also see Ulrich, *A Midwife's Tale*.

38 Burnham, *The Comfortable Arts*, 54.

39 Adams, "Lead Seals from Fort Michilimackinac, 1715–1781," 31.

40 Two others have turned up at Grand Pré, in the Minas Basin, and at Pointe-aux-Vieux on Prince Edward Island. New Brunswick assemblages have not yet been surveyed for similar seals.

41 Davis, "Threads across the Atlantic," 84–5.

42 Including lace headdresses, jewelled buttons, and other decorative accessories for more formal European clothing. See chapter 4 in this volume, under Dress Accessories. For seals, see Egan, *Lead Cloth Seals*, 346, fig. 46. A similar seal has been found on Prince Edward Island by a private collector. See entry at http://www.bagseals.org/gallery/main.php?g2_itemId=35108.

43 Adams, "Lead Seals from Fort Michilimackinac," 46–7; White, "To Ensure That He Not Give Himself Over to the Indians." For hooded overcoats on voyageurs, see dress article for Quebec women wearing skirts from mazamet wool at the same time; Beaudoin-Ross, "'À La Canadienne' Once More," 69.

44 "Memoire on the Present State of the Province of Acadia," July 1697, in Webster and Villebon, *Letters, Journals and Memoirs*, discusses furs traded into Boston that had been taken from Beaubassin, Minas, and Port Royal. See also Gwyn, "The Miíkmaq, Poor Settlers," 69–70.

45 Adams, "Lead Seals from Fort Michilimackinac," 48–9. Brown, *Foul Bodies*, 71.

46 See particularly the extensive collections of fabric swatches collected and compiled for Louis François Armand de Vignerot du Plessis, 3rd Duke of Richelieu, in the 1730s. Richelieu, "Echantillons d'Etoffes et Toiles"; Pennautier, "Enchantillon de Drap du XVIIIme siècle"; also see Beck, *The Draper's Dictionary*; Johnson and Rothstein, eds, *A Lady of Fashion*.

47 Dolan, "The Fabric of Life," 19.

48 Hale, *A Compleat Body of Husbandry*, vol. 3, 117–18, 122; Ejstrud et al., "From Flax to Linen," 9.

49 Roche, *The Culture of Clothing*, 265.

50 Dunn, "History of the Melanson Settlement," 8. The goods he brought to the Melansons included corsetry, hats, and shoes. Brunet, "Voyages of Henri Brunet," 82, 149, 188.

51 Dolan, "The Fabric of Life," 32.

52 Abbé Reynal, quoted in Cozzens, *Acadia*, 295.

53 Dechêne, *Habitants and Merchants*, 80; DuPlessis, "Consumer Revolution," 150.

54 Webster and Villebon, *Letters, Journals and Memoirs*, 128.

55 Ibid., 132. Villebon's conflation of flax and hemp was a common one for the time. See under Hemp, below.

56 Cozzens, *Acadia*, 295.

57 Deveau, "Preliminary Report," 25.

58 Ejstrud et al., "From Flax to Linen," 12, 44, 52–7. An experiment at the University of Denmark estimated that 10.5 km of hand-spun linen thread was required to make a shirt for a slim man. Production of linen requires months, much of which is spent waiting for the crop to grow and then for the retting process to finish, a procedure in which flax stalks are laid out on the ground or in water to begin decomposition and make it possible to separate the fibres. A drying pit and a series of tools (breakers, scutching knife and board, hackle) were needed to complete the processing. If linen processing was taking place on site, we should expect to see some of these reflected in the archaeological record.

59 De Saint-Père, *Une colonie féodale*, 314; Pothier, "GOUTIN, MATHIEU DE."

60 Verbal communication, master weaver Lesley Armstrong.

61 Brown, *Foul Bodies*, 6–7, 26, 30.

62 DuPlessis, "Defining a French Atlantic Empire," 9; Brown, *Foul Bodies*; White, "To Ensure That He Not Give Himself Over to the Indians," 120, 129.

63 Roy, ed., "Lettre de Talon au Ministre Colbert (11 November 1671)," Rapport de l'archiviste de la province de Québec pour 1930–1931, 164; Webster and Villebon, *Letters, Journals and Memoirs*, 132.

64 Dolan, "The Fabric of Life," 204–6.

65 Leonard, "Archaeobotanical Remains," 28.

66 Morse, *Acadiensia Nova (1598–1779)*.

67 Hon. Brook Watson to the Reverend Andrew Brown, 1 July 1791, cited in Hannay, "The Acadian French," 132–3.

68 Leonard, "Archaeobotanical Remains," 26, 28.

69 Whitehead, "Plant Fibre Textiles from the Hopps Site: BkCp-1," 2–3.

70 Dolan, "The Fabric of Life," 50–1, 212, 214.

71 La Grenade-Meunier, "Le costume civil à Louisbourg."

72 Dechêne, *Habitants and Merchants*, 79.

73 White, *The Middle Ground*, 125.

74 Ryder, "Medieval Sheep and Wool Types," 24.

75 Hale, *A Compleat Body of Husbandry*, vol. 3, 307.

76 Racette, "My Grandmothers Loved to Trade," 70–1.

77 Hon. Cadwallader Colden to Governor Clinton, 8 August 1751, in Brodhead, Fernow, and O'Callaghan, *Documents Relative to the Colonial History of the State of New-York*, vol. 6, 740–1.

78 Cozzens, *Acadia*, 140.

79 Hale, "Journal of a Voyage to Nova Scotia."

80 Notariat de l'Ile Royale, "Inventaire des biens meubles appartenant à Jacques Philipe Urbin Rondeau"; Notariat de l'Ile Royale (Greffe de Bacquerisse), "Inventaire des biens meubles appartenant à Marie Josephe Le Borgne de Belisle."

81 Ibid.

82 Hale, *A Compleat Body of Husbandry*, vol. 3, 307.

83 Riello, *Cotton*, 113, 126.

84 DuPlessis, "Cottons Consumption," 233–4.

85 Douglas, "Cotton Textiles in England," 30–1.

86 Riello, *Cotton*, 115.

87 Jacqué, *Indiennes*; Parthasarathi, *Why Europe Grew Rich*, 91; Daumas, *A History of Technology and Invention*, 637–8.

88 Crosby, "First Impressions," 19–20, 119; Lemire, *Cotton*, 51–6. See particularly France's Edict of 26 October 1686 and England's Calico Acts of 1700 and 1721.

89 Riello, *Cotton*, 145; Davis, *Threads*, 46.

90 Riello, *Cotton*, 191.

91 Riello, "Asian Knowledge," 4–5.

92 Douglas, "Cotton Textiles in England," 34.

93 A.N. F12, 1403. "Etoffes des Indes, Année 1705, Année 1706," reprinted in Crosby, "First Impressions," 70.

94 Lemire, *Cotton*, 33, 36; Crosby, "First Impressions," 27, 29; Riello, *Cotton*, 127, 129.

95 Thepaut-Cabasset, "Fashion Encounters," 165–6, 168–9; Montgomery, *Textiles in America*, 347.

96 Notariat de l'Ile Royale, "Inventaire des biens meubles appartenant à Jacques Philipe Urbin Rondeau"; Notariat de l'Ile Royale (Greffe de Bacquerisse), "Inventaire des biens meubles appartenant à Marie Josephe Le Borgne de Belisle."

97 Notariat de l'Ile Royale (Greffe de Bacquerisse), "Inventaire des biens meubles appartenant à Marie Josephe Le Borgne de Belisle."

98 Tortora and Johnson, *Dictionary of Textiles*, 261.

99 "seize aunes, un quart Gingan ou toille a Carreau." Notariat de l'Ile Royale (Greffe de Bacquerisse), "Inventaire des biens meubles appartenant à Marie Josephe Le Borgne de Belisle."

100 Welsteed, "Certificate by William Welsteed"; Lemire, *Cotton*, 41.

101 "Rayé," meaning striped. Beck, *The Draper's Dictionary*, 272–3; "Procès verbal de levée des scelles et inventaire des meubles et effets de la succession de deffunte Dame Jeanne Thibaudo, Veuve Degoutin"; "Inventaire après décès de Dame Anne Levron, à la requête de son mari, Pierre Benoît, Enseigne d'une Compagnie de La Marine."

102 French Archives Nationale – from Crosby 59. A.N. F12, 1403. "Estat des etoffes des indes trouvées chez les marchands de Paris suivant les proces verbaux des commissaires qui en ont fait la visitte, 13 aoust, 1700."

103 White, *Dictionnaire généalogique*, 185; "Invoice of Merchandise from Abraham Boudrot to André Taneuil"; Daigle, "Nos amis les ennemis," 217.

104 Jim Day, "Great Find on P.E.I.," Lifestyles, *Guardian*, 5 September 2014, https://www.the guardian.pe.ca/lifestyles/great-find-on-pei-109459/.

105 Purdie and Cichon, eds, *Medieval Romance, Medieval Contexts*, 57; Mahallati, "Women in Traditional Sharī'a," 8. The hadiths against men wearing silk in Islam allow for men to wear silk into battle as psychological warfare against the opposing forces, or when sick, reaffirming the gentle, nurturing, and feminine attributes of the fibre. See also Hunt, *Consuming Passions*, 233.

106 Vasile, "The Gender of Silk," 105–6. See especially the discussions of women and silk production in Burns, *Sea of Silk*.

107 DuPlessis, "Consumer Revolution," 149–50.

108 A number of sumptuary laws forbade sex workers and other "common lewds" from wearing silk. See Hunt, *Consuming Passions*, 242–5, 247.

109 Hunt, *Consuming Passions*, 370; Lemire, *Cotton*, 35–6.

110 DuPlessis, "Consumer Revolution," 151.

111 Coclanis, *The Atlantic Economy*, 81.

112 Sewell, "Empire of Fashion," 91; Coclanis, *The Atlantic Economy*, 81.

113 Ordoñez and Welters, "Textiles from the Seventeenth-Century Privy," 82, 86.

114 Notariat de l'Ile Royale, "Inventaire des biens meubles appartenant à Jacques Philipe Urbin Rondeau."

115 D.B. Quinn, "The Voyage of Étienne Bellenger to the Maritimes in 1583: A New Document," *Canadian Historical Review* 43, no. 4 (1962): 341–2.

116 Clark, *Acadia*, 243. Whitehead, *Elitekey*, 11; Dièreville, *Voyage du Port Royal*, 103; Quinn, "The Voyage of Étienne Bellenger to the Maritimes in 1583," 334.

117 Lynn Sorge-English has examined surviving leather stays in English contexts, in Lynn Sorge-English, *Stays and Body Image in London*, 167.

118 La Grenade, "Le Costume civil à Louisbourg au XVIIIᵉ siècle," fig. 5, 68–9.

119 Kennedy, *Something of a Peasant Paradise?*, 37.

120 de Meulles, "Voyage of Monsieur de Meulles," 112; Dièreville, *Voyage du Port Royal*, 103.

121 Notariat de l'Ile Royale, "Inventaire de la communauté de Marguerite Terriau, veuve de Pierre Boisseau."

122 Gwyn, "The Miíkmaq, Poor Settlers," 69–70.

123 Quinn, "The Voyage of Étienne Bellenger to the Maritimes in 1583," 341–2.

124 Dièreville, *Voyage du Port Royal*, 103.

125 Hon. Brook Watson to the Reverend Andrew Brown, 1 July 1791, in Hannay, "The Acadian French," 132–3.

126 Notariat de l'Ile Royale (Greffe de Bacquerisse), "Inventaire des biens meubles appartenant à Marie Josephe Le Borgne de Belisle."

127 Peter Baynton to Walter Nisbet, 2 June 1725, Peter Baynton Ledger and Letter Book, 1721–26, Ms. 907, Historical Society of Pennsylvania, referenced in Anishanslin, *Portrait of a Woman in Silk*, 189.

128 "Invoice of Merchandise from Abraham Boudrot" (26 April 1691), XXXVII 93, Massachusetts Archives; William Welsteed, "Certificate by William Welsteed," 12 January 1696, Suffolk Court Files XXXVIII, 3007, 9th paper, Suffolk County Court.

129 Hon. Brook Watson to the Reverend Andrew Brown, 1 July 1791, in Hannay, "The Acadian French," 132–3; Brown, "Removal of the French Inhabitants of Nova Scotia," transcribed in Beanlands, "Annotated Edition of Rev. Dr. Andrew Brown's Manuscript," 180.

130 Ferreira et al., "Historical Textile Dyes," 329.

131 Quinn, "The Voyage of Étienne Bellenger," 334–5, 341–2.

132 Watchett blue was a bluish-green colour that faded quickly, a blue that Chaucer used as a synonym for untrustworthiness in the Miller's Tale as far back as the late fourteenth century. See Linthicum, *Costume in the Drama*, 16.

133 Northern Woodlands, "Local Color: Finding Wild Sources for Dye in the Forest / Autumn 2009," *Center for Northern Woodlands Education*, last accessed 11 December 2017, https://northern-woodlands.org/articles/article/local_color_finding_wild_sources_for_dye_in_the_forest.

134 Brun, *Les Acadiens avant 1755*, 84. In 1743, Pierre LeBlanc of Minas sold his 70-tonne boat to Pierre Aubry, a dealer from Martinique, for 66 barrels of rum @ 80 pounds a barrel, 50 barrels of molasses @ 50 pounds per barrel, and 200 pounds of indigo @ 4 pounds per pound. F1973, A.C. G3, Louisbourg, Notariat, Carton 2058, 1743, no. 15-16; Notaire, Louisbourg, Laborde, Carton 2046, 7.

135 Denys, *Concerning the Ways of the Indians*, 9; Kalm, *Travels into North America*, vol. 3, 14–15; Le Clercq, *New Relation of Gaspesia*, 95–6.

136 Kalm, *Travels into North America*, vol. 3, 161.

137 Haberlin et al., "Migmaq/Mikmaq Online Talking Dictionary Project," accessed 16 October 2018, https://www.mikmaqonline.org/; Kalm, *Travels into North America*, vol. 3, 160; Graham, *Observations on Hudson's Bay*, 137; Also see the editor's note on Le Clercq, *New Relation of Gaspesia*, 89: "metasiamogol, which means 'brightly or vari-coloured clothes.' The word, curiously enough, is said to persist among the Canadian French."

138 Hon. Brook Watson to the Reverend Andrew Brown, 1 July 1791, in Hannay, "The Acadian French."

139 AMEC Environment & Infrastructure, "A Mi'kmaq Historical and Ecological Knowledge Review," figs. 2–7.

140 Cardon, *The Dyer's Handbook*, 35; Welsteed, "Certificate by William Welsteed."

141 Notariat de l'Ile Royale (Greffe de Bacquerisse), "Inventaire des biens meubles appartenant à Marie Josephe Le Borgne de Belisle,"; Notariat de l'Ile Royale, "Inventaire des biens meubles appartenant à Jacques Philipe Urbin Rondeau."

142 A.N. F12, 1403. 'Mémoire d'Anisson au Conseil de Commerce," cited in Crosby, "First Impressions," 68.

143 "Inventaire après décès de Dame Anne Levron, à la requête de son mari, Pierre Benoît, Enseigne d'une Compagnie de La Marine."

Chapter Four

1 De la Varenne and Donovan, "A Letter from Louisbourg, 1756," 124.

2 McCracken, "The Fashion System," 136.

3 White, "Constructing Identities," 152, 246–7.

4 Lindbergh, "Buttoning down Archaeology," 53.

5 Sleeve buttons tend to be between 13–17 mm. We don't see buttons much smaller than 12 mm used for clothing at this date, while buttons used for waistcoats and breeches were

larger, in the 14.5–19.5 mm range. Coat buttons were the largest of all, at 18–35 mm. See White, "Constructing Identities," 251, 681–4.

6 Noël Hume, *A Guide to Artifacts of Colonial America*, 88; White, "Constructing Identities," 244–5.

7 Loren, *Rethinking Colonial Pasts*, 259.

8 See Harper, Clouette, and Harper, *Highways to History*; Harper, "Historical Archaeology," for more on the Sprague house.

9 Lindbergh, "Buttoning down Archaeology," 51.

10 White, "Constructing Identities," 274. Interview with Charles Burke, Parks Canada, 13 December 2017.

11 Harper, "Historical Archaeology," 9–16.

12 Galle, "Costly Signaling," 32.

13 Gums, "Earthfast (Pieux En Terre) Structures at Old Mobile," 19; Type 5 button, Grimm, *Archaeological Investigation*, 59, 61, 64.

14 White, *Dictionnaire généalogique*, 1198–1200.

15 Ferris, "Buttons I Have Known," 99–100; White, "Constructing Identities," 617; Lindbergh, "Buttoning Down Archaeology," 51.

16 Conversation with Charles Burke, June 2018.

17 Fort Stanwix, Casemates, and Cannonballs. Archeological Investigations at Fort Stanwix National Monument. *National Parks Service*, https://www.nps.gov/parkhistory/online_books/archeology/14/chap4.htm.

18 "Recensement Fait Par de Meulles, Intendant de La Nouvelle-France, de Tous Les Peuples de Beaubassin, Rivière Saint-Jean, Port-Royal, Isle Percée et Autres Costes de l'Acadie, s'y Étant Luy Même Transporté Dans Chacune Des Habitations Au Commencement de l'année 1686"; "Rescensement Du Port Royal a l'accadie de l'année 1707"; Lavoie, "Un nouveau regard," 77–8.

19 Notariat de l'Ile Royale (Greffe de Bacquerisse), "Inventaire des biens meubles appartenant à Marie Josephe Le Borgne de Belisle"; Notariat de l'Ile Royale, "Inventaire des biens meubles appartenant à Jacques Philipe Urbin Rondeau."

20 Notariat de l'Ile Royale (Greffe de Bacquerisse), "Inventaire des biens meubles appartenant à Marie Josephe Le Borgne de Belisle." The "boutons d'argent" (likely tinned or pewter rather than actual silver) were valued at 1£ / doz. "pour vente" and 2£ / doz. "pour habite," while the "boutons d'or" (likely brass) were valued at 2£ / doz. "pour vente" and 4£ / doz. "pour habite."

21 White, "Constructing Identities," 252.

22 Dunn, "Louisbourg – Block 2," and internal reports from Louisbourg curator.

23 McCullough, *Money and Exchange*, 129. Nova Scotia currency was pegged to that of Massachusetts after 1746, suggesting that Louisbourg pricing can be reasonably directly compared with merchants' books from elsewhere in the region. White, "Constructing Identities," 255–6.

24 White, "Constructing Identities," 366, 371.

25 A copper sleeve button almost identical to the Beaubassin button with a dark blue paste gem was found in the Lake George region and is now in a private collection in Cooperstown, New York.

26 Rahman, "Boots and Shoes from Fort Beausejour," 29.

27 Whitehead, *Buckles 1250–1800*.

28 Roche, *The Culture of Clothing*, 139–40; Waugh, *The Cut of Men's Clothes*, 55, 116.

29 White, "Knee, Garter, Girdle, Hat, Stock, and Spur Buckles," 246.

30 Morin, *Manuel du bottier*, 139; Riello, *A Foot in the Past*, 33.

31 Dièreville, *Voyage du Port Royal*; Wicken, *Mi'kmaq Treaties on Trial*, 47. De Meulles, "Mémoire Concernant Beaubassin," 112 PAC, MG I, CIID, vol 2-1.

32 Hale, "Journal of a Voyage to Nova Scotia."

33 De la Varenne and Donovan, "A Letter from Louisbourg, 1756," 124.

34 Rahman, "Boots and Shoes from Fort Beausejour," 37–9, 42.

35 Deveau, "Preliminary Report," 22.

36 Erskine, "The French Period in Nova Scotia," 23–4; Racette, "My Grandmothers Loved to Trade."

37 Denys, *Concerning the Ways of the Indians*, 9; Baumgarten, *What Clothes Reveal*, 68, 71–4; Bourque and LaBar, *Uncommon Threads*, 86–9. Also see Racette, "My Grandmothers Loved to Trade."

38 Henry Bouquet, letter from Bouquet to Forbes, Loyalhanna, 20 October 1758. Stevens et al., *The Forbes Expedition*, 582.

39 Williams, *Language of America*, 120.

40 An eighteenth-century French commentator, quoted in McNeil and Riello, "The Material Culture of Walking," 180.

41 Loren, "Social Skins," 184; Loren, *Archaeology of Clothing*, 9.

42 Morris, *Brief Survey of Nova Scotia*, 1748.

43 White, "Constructing Identities," 186.

44 Ibid., 220.

45 Fisher and Loren, "Embodying Identity in Archaeology."

46 "Rescensement du Port Royal a l'accadie de l'année 1707."

47 White, "Knee, Garter, Girdle, Hat, Stock, and Spur Buckles," 244–5.

48 Noël Hume, *A Guide to Artifacts*, 85, figure 12, #2; White, "Constructing Identities," 235, 239; Whitehead, *Buckles 1250–1800*, 81–2.

49 Korvemaker, "Archaeological Excavations at the Roma Site," 126–7.

50 Ibid.; Coleman, "The Roma Settlement at Brudenell Point."

51 White, "Constructing Identities," 419, 429; Rivers-Cofield, "A Guide to Spurs of Maryland and Delaware," 43, 46.

52 Daigle, "Nos amis les ennemis," 151–2.

53 Little, *The State of Trade*, 54–5.

54 Griffiths, *Migrant to Acadian*, 323.

55 Daigle, "Nos amis les ennemis," 151.

56 Fisher and Loren, "Embodying Identity in Archaeology."

57 Scott and Barbezat, *Fluid Bodies and Bodily Fluids*, 2–3.

58 Tiramani, "Pins and Aglets."

59 Pellegrin, "Le genre et l'habit," paras. 21–3.

60 Ibid., paras. 16, 21–23; Jones, "Repackaging Rousseau," 947–8.

61 Le Clercq, *New Relation of Gaspesia*, 93–4

62 See the satirical article "Modes" in the May 1726 edition of *Mercure de France*. *Tome X, Janvier-Juin 1726*, 251–4 (946–59, original); also see *Mercure de France*. *Tome XXI, Juillet-Décembre 1731*, 99–102 (1932–2002 in original), which discusses the ballet *Empire de la mode*, a production that contrasted unstable women's fashions with stable men's fashions.

63 Louis XIII, *Déclaration, portant règlement reforma sur la reformation des habits*, 5. Also see Tudor Royal Proclamations Volume II: The Later Tudors 1553–1587 (Greenwich, 15 June 1574, 16 Elizabeth I), 386, for English legislation. English sumptuary law was repealed in 1604 by James I, so the ban on aglets no longer applied in the English-controlled colonies.

64 Bourque and LaBar, *Uncommon Threads*, 88; Hayward, *Dress at the Court of King Henry VIII*, 353; Majewski and Gaimster, *International Handbook of Historical Archaeology*, 217; Walder, "A Thousand Beads to Each Nation," 379.

65 Loren, *Archaeology of Clothing*, 29–30; Stone, *Fort Michilimackinac, 1715–1781*, 133–4; Loren, "Dress, Faith, and Medicine," 147.

66 Walder, "A Thousand Beads to Each Nation," 136.

67 White, *American Artifacts of Personal Adornment*, 75; Stone, *Fort Michilimackinac, 1715–1781*, 81.

68 White, "Constructing Identities," 307–8.

69 Kristmanson, "Archaeology at Pointe-Aux-Vieux, Part 2," 34; and personal communication with Marc Lavoie, August 2017.

70 De La Varenne and Donovan, "A Letter from Louisbourg, 1756," 115.

71 Adams, "Artisans at Louisbourg," 19–20.

72 Comeau, *The Oldest Parish in Canada*, 14; Johnston, *Religion in Life at Louisbourg*, 31–3; Nova Scotia Archives, "The Registers of St. Jean-Baptiste, Annapolis Royal, 1702–1755," Nova Scotia Archives – An Acadian Parish Remembered, 24 June 2003. Father Petit, priest to Port Royal between 1676–1693, was from the Quebec seminary, not the Récollet order.

73 Kauffman, "The Sulpician Presence," 678, 681; Johnston, *Religion in Life at Louisbourg*, 44; Casgrain, *Les sulpiciens et les prêtres des Missions-étrangères en Acadie*.

74 Johnston, *Religion in Life at Louisbourg*, 18; Crowley, "The Inroads of Secularization," 20. If they did, they were not alone. Officials at Fortress Louisbourg ordered construction crews to keep working on the fortifications through Sundays and feast days in 1742 and 1756. AN, Colonies, CIIB, vol. 24, fols. 37–40v., Duquesnel et Bigot, 30 October 1742; vol. 36, fols. 130-133v., Prévost, 11 August 1756.

75 Louis Petit, "Abbé Petit to Monsignor Vallier," 22 October 1685.

76 BAC-LAC, MGI, CIID, vol 2, fols. 147–52, 1692.

77 Abbé Louis Petit to Monsignor Vallier, 22 October, 1685, quoted in Bernard, *Le drame acadien depuis 1604*, 165.

78 Abbé Petit to Monsignor Vallier, 22 October 1685, quoted in Bernard, *Le drame acadien depuis 1604*, 165–6. Also see Letter from Vallier to the Bishop, 1686, and from Sister Chausson to Quebec, 27 October 1701; Comeau, *The Oldest Parish in Canada*, 10, 12–14.

79 Kuusisto, "Priests and Parish Organizations in Acadia," 39–42; Micheline D. Johnson, "DURAND, JUSTINIEN," in *Dictionary of Canadian Biography*; Nova Scotia Archives, "The Registers of St. Jean-Baptiste, Annapolis Royal, 1702–1755."

80 Letter from Father Pierre Biard to the Reverend Father Provincial, at Paris. Port Royal, 31 January 1612. In Thwaites, *The Jesuit Relations*, vol. 2, 98–9. Kerr, "An Analysis of Personal Adornment at Fort St. Joseph," 47.

81 Stone, *Fort Michilimackinac*, 120–2, plates 53–5, figure G; Danforth et al., "Archaeological and Bioarchaeological Investigations," 128.

82 Webber, *Church Symbolism*, 143, 381.

83 Ibid., 102.

84 Hulme, *The Middle-English Harrowing of Hell*, x; Tingle, *Purgatory and Piety*, 83; Hall, *Dictionary of Subjects and Symbols*, 100.

85 1 Peter 3:19–20, which speaks of Jesus preaching to "the imprisoned spirits." Catholic Catechism adds Ephesians 4:9, "[Christ] descended into the lower parts of the earth."

86 Kerr, "An Analysis of Personal Adornment at Fort St. Joseph," 47. See also various translations of the Gospel of Nicodemus (the Acts of Pilate), ca 4th century. Part two of the book is written from the point of view of two souls freed during the Harrowing.

87 A.F., *The Travels of an English Gentleman*, 158. Also see 155–60 overall.

88 Tingle, *Purgatory and Piety*, 83; Hall, *Dictionary of Subjects and Symbols*, 100.

89 Stone Series A, Type 2, Stone, *Fort Michilimackinac*, 119–20.

90 Stone, *Fort Michilimackinac*, 120, Figure 53, C–H.

91 Karlis Karklins, Fortress Louisbourg database record for item 4L56L9-2, entered May 2000. Identification of the globe may be incorrect – the image could also be that of the skull as seen on previous examples.

92 Tingle, *Purgatory and Piety*, 26.

93 See Piroska Nagy, "Religious Weeping as Ritual in the Medieval West," *Social Analysis: The International Journal of Social and Cultural Practice* 48, no. 2 (2004): 119–37.

94 Matthew 3:13–17, Mark 1:9–13, Luke 3:21–2.

95 The black/navy blue beads are of a type designated IIa6, nine of which were found on site.

96 Stone, *Fort Michilimackinac*, 116–17, figure 52.

97 Stone, *Fort Michilimackinac*, 88, 114.

98 Conversation with Charles Burke, Parks Canada, 15 December, 2017.

99 Beaudoin and Lacouloumère, "Le Coeur Vendéen," 607–12. Personal communication and 2013 presentation by Eric Tremblay, archaeologist who discovered the jewel at Beaubassin. With many thanks to Mr Tremblay and Parks Canada archaeologist Charles Burke for the introduction to this fascinating artifact. For more on the Fidel Jewel, see Eric Tremblay, *Sacré-Coeur de Vendée*, 2013.

100 De Montfort, *Secret of the Rosary*, trans. Mary Barbour; Séguy, "Millénarisme et 'Ordres Adventistes,'" 23–48; Thelagathoti, *The Mystical Experience*.

101 Tremblay, "Beaubassin 2: Sacré-Coeur de Vendée."

102 Letter from Sister Chausson to Quebec, 27 October 1701, quoted in Johnston, *Religion in Life at Louisbourg*, 12.

103 Hale, "Journal of a Voyage to Nova Scotia," 232.

104 Crowley, "The Inroads of Secularization," 17–19. Of eighty-six wills examined from Louisbourg, only 7 per cent showed ownership of larger religious items (basins, icons, wall-mounted crucifixes, etc.) other than books or jewellery.

105 De La Varenne and Donovan, "A Letter from Louisbourg, 1756," 115.

106 Dirlam, Misiorowski, and Thomas, "Pearl Fashion through the Ages," 67–8. Also see, for example, *Portrait of a Noble Girl*, 17th century, circle of Pierre Mignard I (French, 1612–1695); *Portrait of a Lady Carving a Tree* (French School, 17th century); *Marie de Rabutin-Chantals, Marquise de Sévigné*, Claude Lefèbvre, ca 1665.

107 Crépeau, "Lot Summaries Melanson 17B: 17B2."

108 Christianson, "Belleisle 1983," 54.

109 Notariat de l'Ile Royale (Greffe de Bacquerisse), "Inventaire des biens meubles appartenant à Marie Josephe Le Borgne de Belisle."
110 Vila, "Elite Masculinities," 19.

Chapter Five

1 Webster and Villebon, *Letters, Journals and Memoirs*, 128, 132.
2 An explanation and basic methodology for defining fashion systems has been laid out in Roche, *La culture des apparences*, 34–5.
3 Roche, *The Culture of Clothing*, 34–5; Scholz, *Body Narratives*, 17–18; Rosenthal, "Cultures of Clothing," 473.
4 Entwistle, *The Fashioned Body*, 133.
5 Baumgarten, *What Clothes Reveal*, 14. Also see Dièreville, *Relation of the Voyage to Port Royal*, 96. Plates in the Mercure Galant from 1678 and onwards no longer show hooded cloaks as desirable fashion items.
6 *The Diary of John Evelyn*, 18 October 1666, vol. 2, 26–7.
7 Pennautier, "Enchantillon de drap du XVIIIme Siecle"; Edwards, *How to Read a Dress*, 34; Delpierre, *Dress in France*, 10–11.
8 Steele, *The Corset*, 13, 27; Crowston, *Fabricating Women*, 34–5.
9 Sorge-English, *Stays and Body Image*, 165–7, 211.
10 On the subject of masculinities, see Lemire, "A Question of Trousers"; and Kuchta, *The Three-Piece Suit and Modern Masculinity*.
11 Crowston, *Fabricating Women*, 31–2. There is extremely minimal evidence of whalebone use in New France, even among the moneyed elite. See La Grenade-Meunier, "Le costume civil à Louisbourg," 15.
12 Burnham, *The Comfortable Arts*, plate 55.
13 Ibid., 78.
14 Delpierre, *Dress in France*, 14; Roche, *The Culture of Clothing*, 144.
15 Lemire, "A Question of Trousers," 3, 7–8.
16 De la Bretonne, *Monsieur Nicolas*.
17 Baumgarten, *What Clothes Reveal*, 25.
18 Lemire, "A Question of Trousers," 4, 9.
19 Dièreville, *Voyage du Port Royal*, 96.
20 Hale, "Journal of a Voyage to Nova Scotia," 199.
21 White, "To Ensure That He Not Give Himself Over to the Indians," 112–13.
22 De Meulles, "Voyage of Monsieur de Meulles," 109; Perrot, "Relation de l'acadie envoyée par le Sr. Perrot," 9 August 1686.
23 Brown, "Removal of the French Inhabitants of Nova Scotia," transcribed in Beanlands, "Annotated Edition of Rev. Dr. Andrew Brown's Manuscript," 167.
24 Varenne and Donovan, "A Letter from Louisbourg, 1756," 124.
25 De la Dernier: Public Archives of Canada, MG 21, E5, 19071, 338.
26 Landry, "Culture matérielle et niveaux de richesse." Probate inventories for Acadian Jeanne Thibudeau, Anne Levron, and Marie Bourg show wardrobes ranging from twenty-five to forty items. Centre des Archives d'Outre-mer [CAOM], G2, vol. 197, dossier 151; CAOM, G3 2042

256 *Notes to pages 187–93*

1754, 21 June; Centre des Archives d'Outre-mer [CAOM], G2, vol. 182, 986–1009, Inventaire après le décès de dame Anne Levron, 19 December 1733.

27 La Grenade-Meunier, "Le costume civil à Louisbourg," 55.

28 "Procès verbal de levée des scelles et inventaire des meubles et effets de la succession de Deffunte Dame Jeanne Thibaudo, Veuve Degoutin"; "Record of the Sale after Death of the Possessions of Pierre Lambert" (6 April 1756), Id. vol. 205, doss. 393. Fortress Louisbourg terminology was not consistent between English and French and men's and women's wear. For the sake of clarity, the linen undergarment worn by men will be termed a "shirt," and the women's the French "chemise."

29 Diderot and Gillispie, *Encyclopedia of Trades and Industry*, sec. Supplement III, 751.

30 La Grenade, "Le costume civil à Louisbourg au XVIIIᵉ siècle," 113, 114, 117–18; La Grenade-Meunier, "Le costume civil à Louisbourg," 12–13.

31 Waller, *A General Description of All Trades*, 25.

32 La Grenade-Meunier, "Le costume civil à Louisbourg," 14.

33 See the "petit corps" worn by Marianne Benoist, listed in "Inventaire après décès de Dame Anne Levron, à la requête de son mari, Pierre Benoît, enseigne d'une Compagnie de la Marine."

34 La Grenade-Meunier, "Le costume civil à Louisbourg," 14. The terminology issue is a complex one. The term "corset" for boned, shape-altering garments did not enter the English lexicon until ca 1795. The term "corset" appears in French use much earlier, as seen in Anne Levron's inventories in 1733, though it is not certain at all whether or not the French "corset" was a whalebone-stiffened garment as corsets would become in the nineteenth century.

35 "Inventaire après décès de Dame Anne Levron, à la requête de son mari, Pierre Benoît, enseigne d'une Compagnie de la Marine."

36 Ibid., 1328 #10.

37 Baumgarten, *What Clothes Reveal*, 148–9.

38 Tomczyszyn, "Papers of the Past," 215.

39 "Estat des habitans du Port-Royal, leurs familles, terres en valleur, bestiaux et fusils" (Census, 1700).

40 Ibid., "neuf vieux Gillets pour femme."

41 "Procès verbal de levée de scelle et inventaire faits chez la d'Ile Peré."

42 Notariat de l'Ile Royale, "Contrat de mariage entre Charles Saint-Étienne, Sieur de La Tour, né en Acadie, fils de défunt Jacques Saint-Étienne, Sieur de La Tour et de Dame Anne Melançon, et Demoiselle Marie Perré, Fille de Feu Antoine Perré, de son Vivant Marchand à Louisbourg, et de Marianne Ponce."

43 Rublack and Selwyn, "Fluxes: The Early Modern Body," 2.

44 See texts including Antoine de Courtin, *Nouveau traité de la civilité*, and Nicolas Faret, *L'honnête homme*.

45 Steele, *The Corset*, 26, 28; Roche, *The Culture of Clothing*, 172–3. On stays and the lower orders in England, see Sorge-English, *Stays and Body Image in London*, 165–78.

46 La Grenade-Meunier, "Le costume civil à Louisbourg," 15; Tomczyszyn, "Papers of the Past," 215–16.

47 Sorge-English, *Stays and Body Image in London*, 52–4.

48 Notariat de l'Ile Royale (Greffe de Bacquerisse), "Inventaire des biens meubles appartenant à Marie Josephe Le Borgne de Belisle."

49 Crowston, *Fabricating Women*, 37, 41; Roche, *La culture des apparences*.

50 La Grenade found only two other robes de chambre among other Louisbourg inventories and was uncertain as to the type of gown indicated by the terminology. La Grenade-Meunier, "Le costume civil à Louisbourg," 23.

51 John Dunton, *The Ladies Dictionary*, 10.

52 "Invoice of Merchandise from Abraham Boudrot to André Taneuil," Notariat de l'Ile Royale, "Inventaire des biens meubles appartenant à Jacques Philipe Urbin Rondeau."

53 Waugh, *The Cut of Women's Clothes*, 62.

54 Quoted in ibid., 112–13; Roche, *La culture des apparences*, 121.

55 Waugh, *The Cut of Women's Clothes*, 117.

56 Crowston, *Fabricating Women*, 51–3; Waugh, *The Cut of Women's Clothes*, 68, 115.

57 Baumgarten, *What Clothes Reveal*, 64; Waugh, *The Cut of Women's Clothes*, 114–15; Crowston, *Fabricating Women*, 54–5.

58 Burnham, *The Comfortable Arts*, fig. 55. Nova Scotia Museum, Halifax, accession # 8031.

59 Roche, *The Culture of Clothing*, 105.

60 A robe volante was a "floating gown," a loose-bodiced dress popular in the first half of the eighteenth century, worn for casual entertaining. The other use for the rings could be as reinforcements for eyelet holes, a theory supported by their proximity to a sewing awl when found.

61 Copeland, *Working Dress*, 58:xv.

62 Holme, *The Academy of Armory*, 96.

63 Lemire, "A Question of Trousers," 7–8.

64 Vila, "Elite Masculinities," 19–20.

65 Copeland, *Working Dress*, 58.

66 D'Avity, *Estates, Empires, and Principallities*, 1200–1.

67 Hood, *The Weaver's Craft*, 120.

68 Spufford, *Reclothing of Rural England*, 124.

69 Public Archives of Canada, MG 21, E5, 19071, 338.

70 Notariat de l'Ile Royale, "Inventaire de la communauté de Marguerite Terriau, veuve de Pierre Boisseau."

71 White, "Constructing Identities," 224; Also see Whitehead, *Buckles 1250–1800*.

72 Holme, *The Academy of Armory*, 96.

73 Ibid., 96.

74 "Procès verbal de vente des effets de feu François Gassot" (19 August 1752), Section Outre-Mer, Série G2, Vol. 201, Dossier 251, Archives de la Marine; Roche, *The Culture of Clothing*, 135.

75 Copeland, *Working Dress*, 30.

76 Holme, *The Academy of Armory*, 95–6.

77 Anishanslin, *Portrait of a Woman in Silk*, 181. See artifact BEDi:2-2473, Nova Scotia Museum.

78 Holme, *The Academy of Armory*, 97; Waugh, *The Cut of Men's Clothes*, fig. 7.

79 Voltaire, *The Age of Louis XIV*, vol. 1, 214.

80 Lester and Oerke, *Accessories of Dress*, 215–16; Copeland, *Working Dress*, 9.

81 La Grenade-Meunier, "Le costume civil à Louisbourg," 23.

82 Copeland, *Working Dress*, 81.

83 Ricker, *L'sitkuk*, 15; Bourque and LaBar, *Uncommon Threads*, 59–60.

84 Letter from the firm of Bousquet & Cie, 1733, cited in Sonenscher, "The Hosiery Industry of Nîmes and the Lower Languedoc in the Eighteenth Century," 152.
85 Fairchilds, "The Production and Marketing of Populuxe Goods," 233, 235.
86 Dechêne, *Habitants and Merchants*, 356n86. Also see Lefebvre, *Études orléanaises*.
87 "Billet de Zacharie Richard, de Port-Royal, en faveur de Minet, pour marchandises reçues, 1743; Enregistré à la requête de Mme Mullot (Julienne Minet)"; Brun, *Les Acadiens avant 1755*, 101.
88 Smith, "Learning Politics," 499.
89 Sonenscher, "The Hosiery Industry of Nîmes," 142, 152; Smith, "Learning Politics," 529.
90 Egan, *Lead Cloth Seals*, 102, plate 346; Elton, *Cloth Seals*, 289.
91 "Invoice of Merchandise from Abraham Boudrot to André Taneuil"; Welsteed, "Certificate by William Welsteed."
92 Lemire, "Men of the World," 298–9.
93 Barlow, "Journal of Edward Barlow," vol. 1, 158.
94 Roche, *The Culture of Clothing*, 86, 88.
95 Groves, *History of Needlework Tools*, 68.
96 Burman and Denbo, *Pockets of History*, 14–15.
97 *Mist's Weekly Journal* (London), 22 May 1725.
98 Auslander, "Deploying Material Culture," para. 5.
99 Cozzens, *Acadia*, 55–6.
100 Dunn, Ross, and Wallace, "Looking into Acadie," 40.
101 Varenne and Donovan, "A Letter from Louisbourg, 1756." Veil, in this context, means a hair covering of the sort previously seen on wired hoods, rather than a face covering.
102 Staples and Shaw, *Clothing through American History*, 246.
103 Buckland, "The Monmouth Cap," 23–37.
104 Muraca et al., "Small Finds," 5–6.
105 Ibid., 6.
106 Notariat de l'Ile Royale (Greffe de Bacquerisse), "Inventaire des biens meubles appartenant à Marie Josephe Le Borgne de Belisle"; Donovan, *Cape Breton at 200*, 21.
107 White, *American Artifacts of Personal Adornment*, 215–16.
108 Donovan, *Cape Breton at 200*, 18–19, 20.
109 Mays, *Women in Early America*, 50.
110 Kwass, "Big Hair," 652, 653; Morgan and Rushton, "Visible Bodies," 41.
111 Louisbourg curator's spreadsheet, item # 2L80H9-10.
112 Bourque and LaBar, *Uncommon Threads*, 61.
113 Hale, "Journal of a Voyage to Nova Scotia," 234.

Chapter Six

1 Kawamura, *Doing Research in Fashion and Dress*, 96.
2 Loren, "Social Skins," 173.
3 Shukla, "The Study of Dress and Adornment," 4.
4 See Loren, *Archeology*, 23, and Loren, "Social Skins," 175, for more discussion of doxies and praxies in colonial spaces.
5 Hodder, *Entangled*, 170.

6   Loren, "Social Skins," 173.
7   Lawes, *Women and Reform*, 47. See the work of Laurel Thatcher Ulrich, particularly *The Midwife's Tale*, on the growth and role of the female-led domestic economy in colonial contexts.
8   Clark, *Acadia*, 212–13.
9   Lavoie, "Un nouveau regard."
10 Jordan, "Colonies, Colonialism, and Cultural Entanglement," 36.
11 Roche, *The Culture of Clothing*, 45–6.
12 Brouillan to Minister, 6 October 1701. Nova Scotia Archives. RG1 vol 3 doc 6, reel 15, 218.
13 Roche, *The Culture of Clothing*, 377–8.
14 Lavoie, *Archéologie au marais de Belle-Isle*, 79.
15 White and Beaudry, "Artifacts and Personal Identity," 213.
16 Ruddel, "Domestic Textile Production," para. 20.

Bibliography

Archival Collections

Archives des Colonies: Série CIIA. Correspondance générale; Canada. Library and Archives Canada.

Archives des Colonies: Série CIID. Correspondance générale; Acadie. Library and Archives Canada.

Colonial fonds, Centre des archives d'outre-mer, France.

Dépôt des papiers publics des colonies; état civil et recensements: Série GI: Recensements et documents divers: C-2572. Library and Archives Canada.

Dépôt des papiers publics des colonies; état civil et recensements: Série GI: Recensements et documents divers: C-4582. Library and Archives Canada.

Dépôt des papiers publics des colonies; notariat: MG 1 G3. Archives coloniales – Fonds des Colonies. Library and Archives Canada.

Great Britain. Colonial Office: Nova Scotia and Cape Breton, Original Correspondence reel C-9119. Library and Archives Canada.

Nova Scotia Archives, Halifax, Nova Scotia.

Series Collections: Research (Interpretations). Historical Resources. Fortress of Louisbourg Archives, Parks Canada.

Series Collections: Research (Louisbourg). Historical Resources. Fortress of Louisbourg Archives, Parks Canada.

William Inglis Morse Collection: MS-6. Archives and Special Collections, Dalhousie University Libraries.

Books and Articles

Adams, Blaine. "Artisans at Louisbourg." Parks Canada. Department of Indian and Northern Affairs, August 1972.

Adams, Diane L. "Lead Seals from Fort Michilimackinac, 1715–1781." Master's thesis. Mackinac Island, MI: Mackinac State Historic Parks, 1989.

Akins, Thomas B. *Selections from the Public Documents of the Province of Nova Scotia.* C. Annand, 1869.

Alcega, Juan de, and J.L. Nevinson. *Tailor's Pattern Book, 1589: Facsimile.* New York: Costume & Fashion Press, 1589.

Alexander, Rani T. "Afterword: Toward an Archaeological Theory of Culture Contact." In *Studies in Culture Contact: Interaction, Culture Change, and Archaeology,* edited by James G. Cusick, 476–95. Carbondale: Southern Illinois University, 1998.

Allen and West. *The Taylor's Complete Guide, or, A Comprehensive Analysis of Beauty and Elegance in Dress ... / the Whole Concerted and Devised by a Society of Adepts in the Profession.* Printed for Allen and West, 1799.

AMEC Environment & Infrastructure. "A Mi'kmaq Historical and Ecological Knowledge Review of the Gaetz Brook Property." Dartmouth: Nova Scotia Department of Natural Resources, 2013.

Ames, Kenneth L., and Thomas J. Schlereth. *Material Culture: A Research Guide*. Lawrence: University Press of Kansas, 1985.

"An Act to Prevent the Exportation of Wool out of the Kingdoms of Ireland and England into Forreigne Parts and for the Incouragement of the Woollen Manufactures in the Kingdom of England. 10 W. III. c. 16 (1699)." In *Statutes of the Realm*, 7: 1695–1701, 524–8. British History Online, 1820.

Anishanslin, Zara. *Portrait of a Woman in Silk: Hidden Histories of the British Atlantic World*. New Haven, CT: Yale University Press, 2016.

Anon. "A Description of the Ceremonial Proceedings at the Coronation of Their Most Illustrious, Serene, and Sacred Majesties, King James II and His Royal Consort Queen Mary Who Where [*sic*] Crowned at Westminster-Abby, on Thursday the 23th. of April, 1685." 1685. Wing / D1154; Reel position: Wing / 1685:15. Bodleian Library.

Anon. *Hic Mulier: Or, the Man-Woman and Haec-Vir: Or, the Womanish-Man*. Exeter, England: The Rota at the University of Exeter, 1973.

Anon. *The Workwoman's Guide: Containing Instructions to the Inexperienced in Cutting out and Completing Those Articles of Wearing Apparel, &c. Which Are Ususally Made at Home: Also, Explanations on Upholstery, Straw-Platting, Bonnet-Making, Knitting, &c.* London: Simpkin, Marshall, 1838.

Appadurai, Arjun, ed. *The Social Life of Things: Commodities in Cultural Perspective*. Cambridge [Cambridgeshire]; New York: Cambridge University Press, 1986.

Arminjon, Catherine, Nicole Blondel, André Chastel, Francis Salet, and Inventaire Général des Monuments et des Richesses Artistiques de la France. *Objets civils domestiques: vocabulaire*. Paris: Imprimerie Nationale, 1984.

Auslander, Leora. "Deploying Material Culture to Write the History of Gender and Sexuality: The Example of Clothing and Textiles." *Clio. Women, Gender, History*, no. 40 (15 April 2015).

Avity, Pierre d'. *The Estates, Empires, & Principallities of the World Represented by Ye Description of Countries, Maners of Inhabitants, Riches of Prouinces, Forces, Gouernment, Religion; and the Princes That Haue Gouerned in Euery Estate*. London: Printed by Adam: Islip; for Mathewe: Lownes; and Iohn: Bill, 1615.

Balvay, Arnaud. "Tattooing and Its Role in French–Native American Relations in the Eighteenth Century." *French Colonial History* 9, no. 1 (9 July 2008): 1–14.

Barlow, Edward. "Journal of Edward Barlow," 1703 1659. JOD/4. National Maritime Museum, Greenwich, London.

Barriault, Marcel. "Famille DesRoches." *Cahiers de la Société Historique Acadienne* 37, no. 2–3 (September 2006): 51–160.

Basque, Maurice. "Family and Political Culture in Pre-Conquest Acadia." In *The "Conquest" of Acadia, 1710 Imperial, Colonial, and Aboriginal Constructions*, edited by John G. Reid, 48–63. Toronto: University of Toronto Press, 2004.

Baumgarten, Linda. *Eighteenth-Century Clothing at Williamsburg*. Williamsburg, VA: Colonial Williamsburg Foundation, 1986.

– *What Clothes Reveal: The Language of Clothing in Colonial and Federal America : The Colonial Williamsburg Collection*. Williamsburg, VA: Colonial Williamsburg Foundation in association with Yale University Press, New Haven, 2002.

Beanlands, Sarah J. "Annotated Edition of Rev. Dr. Andrew Brown's Manuscript: 'Removal of the French Inhabitants of Nova Scotia by Lieut. Governor Lawrence & His Majesty's Council in October 1755.'" Master's thesis, Saint Mary's University, 2010.

Beaudoin, M., and G. Lacouloumère. "Le Cœur Vendéen (Bijou Populaire Ancien)." *Bulletins et Mémoires de La Société d'anthropologie de Paris* 5, no. 4 (1903): 607–12.

Beaudoin-Ross, Jacqueline. "'A La Canadienne' Once More: Some Insights into Quebec Rural Female Dress." *Dress* 7, no. 1 (1981): 69–81.

Beaudry, Mary C. "Bodkin Biographies." In *The Materiality of Individuality: Archaeological Studies of Individual Lives*, edited by Carolyn L. White, 95–108. New York: Springer, 2009.

– *Findings: The Material Culture of Needlework and Sewing*. New Haven, CT: Yale University Press, 2006.

– "Stitching Women's Lives: Interpreting the Artifacts of Sewing and Needlework." In *Interpreting the Early Modern World: Transatlantic Perspectives*, edited by Mary C. Beaudry and James Symonds, 143–58. Boston: Springer, 2011.

Beck, S. William. *The Draper's Dictionary : A Manual of Textile Fabrics: Their History and Applications*. London: The Warehousemen & draper's journal office, 1882.

Berlekamp, Linda Baumgarten. "The Textile Trade in Boston: 1650–1700." Master's thesis, University of Delaware (Winterthur Program), 1976.

Bernard, Antoine. *Le drame acadien depuis 1604*. Montreal: Les Clercs de Saint-Viateur, 1936.

Berneshawi, Suzanne. "Resource Management and the Mi'kmaq Nation." *Canadian Journal of Native Studies* 17, no. 1 (1997): 115–48.

"Billet de Zacharie Richard, de Port-Royal, en faveur de Minet, pour marchandises reçues, 1743; Enregistré à la requête de Mme Mullot (Julienne Minet)." Louisbourg, 15 July 1743. Amirauté de Louisbourg à La Rochelle (R12063-4-X-F). Library and Archives Canada.

Blanco, José, Patricia Kay Hunt-Hurst, Heather Vaughan Lee, and Mary Doering, eds. *Clothing and Fashion: American Fashion from Head to Toe*. 4 vols. ABC-CLIO, 2015.

Bleakney, J. Sherman. *Sods, Soil, and Spades: The Acadians at Grand Pré and Their Dykeland Legacy*. Montreal and Kingston: McGill-Queen's University Press, 2004.

Bolton, Lissant. "Classifying the Material: Food, Textiles and Status in North Vanuatu." *Journal of Material Culture* 6, no. 3 (2001): 251–68.

Borck, Lewis, and Barbara J. Mills. "Approaching an Archaeology of Choice: Consumption, Resistance, and Religion in the Prehispanic Southwest." In *Foreign Objects: Rethinking Indigenous Consumption in American Archaeology*, edited by Craig N. Cipolla, 29–43. Tucson: University of Arizona Press, 2017.

Bourque, Bruce J., and Laureen A. LaBar. *Uncommon Threads: Wabanaki Textiles, Clothing, and Costume*. Augusta: Maine State Museum, 2009.

Boutilier, Brenda, and David J. Christianson. "'Clothing Artifact Group,' in Belleisle 1983: Excavations at a PreExpulsion Acadian Site (Belleisle BeDi-2)." Halifax: Nova Scotia Museum Publications, 1983.

Bowden, P.J. "Wool Supply and the Woollen Industry." *Economic History Review* 9, no. 1 (1956): 44–58.

Brack, H.G. *Registry of Maine Toolmakers : A Compilation of Toolmakers Working in Maine and the Province of Maine Prior to 1900*. Davistown Museum, 2008.

Brasseaux, C.A. "Acadian to Cajun: History of a Society Built on the Extended Family." Presented at the Community Health Event Genetics of the Acadian People, McNeese State University in Lake Charles, LA, 9 August 1999.

Brebner, John Bartlet. *New England's Outpost: Acadia before the Conquest of Canada*. New York: Columbia University Press, 1927.

Bretonne, Nicolas-Edme Rétif de la. *Monsieur Nicolas ou le coeur humain dévoilé*. 16 vols. Paris: Publié par lui-même, 1794.

Brodhead, John Romeyn, Berthold Fernow, and E.B. (Edmund Bailey) O'Callaghan. *Documents Relative to the Colonial History of the State of New-York : Procured in Holland, England, and France*. Albany, NY: Weed, Parsons, 1853.

Brown, Kathleen M. *Foul Bodies: Cleanliness in Early America*. New Haven, CT: Yale University Press, 2009.

Brun, Régis. *Les Acadiens avant 1755: Essai*. Moncton: Self-published, 2003.

Brunet, Henri. "Voyages of Henri Brunet," 1673. Collection Clairambault, vol. 864. BAC-LAC Microfilm reel C-4594, MG 7 IA5. Bibliothèque nationale de France / Library and Archives Canada.

Buckland, Kirstie. "The Monmouth Cap." *Costume* 13, no. 1 (1 January 1979): 23–37.

Bumsted, J.M. *Land, Settlement, and Politics on Eighteenth-Century Prince Edward Island*. Montreal and Kingston: McGill-Queen's University Press, 1987.

Burman, Barbara, and Seth Denbo. *Pockets of History: The Secret Life of an Everyday Object*. Chester: Arts and Humanities Research Council, 2006.

Burnham, Dorothy K. *The Comfortable Arts: Traditional Spinning and Weaving in Canada*. Ottawa: National Gallery of Canada, 1981.

Burnham, Harold B., and Dorothy K. Burnham. *Keep Me Warm One Night: Early Handweaving in Eastern Canada*. Toronto: University of Toronto Press in cooperation with the Royal Ontario Museum, 1972.

Burns, E. Jane. *Sea of Silk: A Textile Geography of Women's Work in Medieval French Literature*. University of Pennsylvania Press, 2009.

Bythell, Duncan. "The Hand-Loom Weavers in the English Cotton Industry during the Industrial Revolution: Some Problems." *Economic History Review* 17, no. 2 (1964): 339–53.

Cadillac, Antoine Laumet de Lamothe. *Extracts from a Memoir of M. de La Mothe Cadillac, 1692, Concerning Acadia and New England, from the Archives of Paris*. Translated by James Robb. Boston: n/a, 1859.

Cameron, Peter. "Anthony Christian and the French Plating Trade in Eighteenth-Century London." *Journal of the Antique Metalware Society* 20 (June 2012): 264–71.

Caplan, Ronald. "Yvon LeBlanc, Architect Fortress of Louisbourg." *Cape Breton's Magazine*, 1 August 1983.

Caple, C. "The Detection and Definition of an Industry: The English Medieval and Post Medieval Pin Industry." *Archaeological Journal* 148, no. 1 (1991): 241–55.

Capp, B.S. *When Gossips Meet: Women, Family, and Neighbourhood in Early Modern England*. Oxford: Oxford University Press, 2003.

Cardon, Dominique. *The Dyer's Handbook: Memoirs of an 18th Century Master Colourist*. Oxford; Philadelphia: Oxbow Books, 2016.

Carlos, Ann M., and Frank D. Lewis. "Exchange among Native Americans and Europeans before 1800: Strategies and Interactions." Paper presented to the CNEH Conference, Banff, Alberta, 26–8 October 2012.

Casgrain, Henri-Raymond. *Les sulpiciens et les prêtres des Missions-étrangères en Acadie: (1676–1762).* Quebec: Pruneau & Kironac, 1897.

Cartier, Jacques, Henri Michelant, and Alfred Ramé. *Relation originale du voyage de Jacques Cartier au Canada en 1534: Documents inédits sur Jacques Cartier et le Canada (Nouvelle Série).* Paris: H. Michelant et A. Ramé, 1867.

Chiasson, Anselme. *Chéticamp: histoire et traditions acadiennes.* 2nd ed. Moncton: Éditions des Aboiteaux, 1962.

Christianson, David J. "Belleisle 1983: Excavations at a PreExpulsion Acadian Site (Belleisle BeDi-2)." Halifax: Nova Scotia Museum Publications, 1984.

Christianson, David J., and Andrée Crépeau. "Home and Hearth: An Archaeological Perspective on Acadian Domestic Architecture." *Canadian Folklore Canadien* 17, no. 2 (1995): 93–109.

Clark, Andrew Hill. *Acadia: The Geography of Early Nova Scotia to 1760.* Madison: University of Wisconsin Press, 1968.

Clark, John, ed. *The Medieval Horse and Its Equipment, c. 1150–c. 1450.* Boydell Press, 2004.

Coclanis, Peter A., ed. *The Atlantic Economy during the Seventeenth and Eighteenth Centuries: Organization, Operation, Practice, and Personnel.* Columbia: University of South Carolina Press, 2005.

Coleman, Margaret. "Acadian History in the Isthmus of Chignecto." Manuscript Report Series 29. Ottawa: National Historic Parks and Sites Branch, 1968.

– "Acadian Social Life." Manuscript Report Series 80. Ottawa: National and Historic Parks Branch, 1968.

– "The Acadians at Port Royal." Manuscript Report Series 10. Ottawa: National Historic Sites Service, Dept. of Indian Affairs and Northern Development, September 1969.

– "The Roma Settlement at Brudenell Point, Prince Edward Island." Occasional Papers in Archaeology and History No. 1. Ottawa: National and Historic Parks Branch, 1974.

Collins, James B. "The Economic Role of Women in Seventeenth-Century France." *French Historical Studies* 16, no. 2 (1989): 436–70.

Comeau, Jean Ambroise. *The Oldest Parish in Canada.* Yarmouth, NS: Lawson Publishing, 1962.

Copeland, Peter F. *Working Dress in Colonial and Revolutionary America.* Westport, CT: Greenwood Press, 1977.

Courtin, Antoine de. *Nouveau traité de la civilité qui se pratique en France parmi les honnêtes gens. Nouvelle édition, revue, corrigée & de beaucoup augmentée par le même auteur.* De la Boutique de feu M. Josset a Paris Chez Louis Josse, à la Couronne d'Epines et Charles Robustel, au Palmier. ruë Saint Jacques, 1712.

Cowgill, J., Margrethe de Neergaard, and N. Griffiths. *Knives and Scabbards.* Woodbridge: Boydell Press, 2008.

Cozzens, Frederic S. *Acadia, or, A Month with the Blue Noses.* New York: Derby & Jackson, 1859.

Crépeau, Andrée. "Lot Summaries, Melanson." Melanson, NS: Parks Canada/Parcs Canada, 1985. Parks Canada.

Crépeau, Andrée, and Brenda Dunn. "The Melanson Settlement: An Acadian Farming Community (ca. 1664–1755)." Ottawa: Environment Canada, Parks Canada, 1986.

Crosby, Gillian. "First Impressions: The Prohibition on Printed Calicoes in France, 1686–1759." PhD dissertation, Nottingham Trent University, 2015.

Crowley, Terry. "The Inroads of Secularization in Eighteenth-Century New France: Church and People at Louisbourg." *Canadian Catholic Historical Association Historical Studies* 51 (1984): 5–27.

Crowston, Clare Haru. *Fabricating Women: The Seamstresses of Old Regime France, 1675–1791.* Durham, NC: Duke University Press, 2001.

Daigle, Jean. "Nos amis les ennemis: relations commerciales de l'Acadie avec le Massachusetts, 1670–1711." PhD dissertation, University of Maine, 1975.

– ed. *L'Acadie des Maritimes: études thématiques des débuts à nos jours acadiennes.* Moncton: Chaire d'études acadiennes, Université de Moncton, 1993.

Danforth, Marie Elaine, Danielle N. Cook, J. Lynn Funkhouser, Matthew Greer, Heather Guzik, Amanda R. Harvey, Barbara T. Hester, Harold W. Webster, Jr, and Ronald Wise, Jr. "Archaeological and Bioarchaeological Investigations of the French Colonial Cemetery at the Moran Site (22HR511), Harrison County, Mississippi." Excavation Report. Biloxi: Mississippi Department of Marine Resources, July 2013.

Daniels, Stephen, and Joseph Wright. *Joseph Wright.* Princeton, NJ: Princeton University Press and Tate Gallery, 1999.

Daumas, Maurice, ed. *A History of Technology & Invention; Progress through the Ages.* New York: Crown Publishers, 1970.

Davis, Cathrine. "Lead Seals from Colonial Fort St. Joseph (20BE23)." Honours thesis, Western Michigan University, 2014.

– "Threads across the Atlantic: Tracing the European Origins of Eighteenth-Century Imported Cloth in New France Using Lead Seal Evidence from Three French Colonial Sites." Master's thesis, Université Laval, 2018.

Dechêne, Louise. *Habitants and Merchants in Seventeenth-Century Montreal.* Translated by Liana Vardi. Montreal and Kingston: McGill-Queen's University Press, 1993.

Delaney, Paul. "La reconstitution d'un rôle des passagers du Pembroke." *Cahiers de la Société Historique Acadienne* 35, no. 1–2 (2004): 4–75.

de la Roque. "Census by the Sieur de La Roque, 1752." In *Report on Canadian Archives, 1905. Part 2,* 40:3–172. Public Archives of Canada, 1906.

Delpierre, Madeleine. *Dress in France in the Eighteenth Century.* Yale University Press, 1998.

Denys, Nicolas. *Concerning the Ways of the Indians (Their Customs, Dress, Methods of Hunting and Fishing, and Their Amusements).* Nova Scotia Museum, 1672.

– *The Description and Natural History of the Coasts of North America (Acadia).* Toronto: Champlain Society, 1908.

Der, Lindsay, and Francesca Fernandini. *Archaeology of Entanglement.* Walnut Creek, CA: Left Coast Press, 2016.

Desan, Suzanne. "Making and Breaking Marriage: An Overview of Old Regime Marriage as a Social Practice." In *Family, Gender, and Law in Early Modern France,* edited by Suzanne Desan and Jeffrey Merrick, 1–25. University Park: Pennsylvania State University Press, 2009.

Deveau, J. Alphonse. "Preliminary Report on Source Material Re Acadians before 1755: For Education Media Services." Manuscript compilation. Halifax, 1980. FC 2043 P74. Nova Scotia Provincial Archives.

Dickason, Olive Patricia. *Canada's First Nations: A History of Founding Peoples from Earliest Times.* Toronto: McClelland & Stewart, 1992.

Dickson, David. *Old World Colony: Cork and South Munster, 1630–1830.* Madison: University of Wisconsin Press, 2005.

Diderot, Denis, and Charles Coulston Gillispie. *Pictorial Encyclopedia of Trades and Industry: Manufacturing and the Technical Arts in Plates, Selected from L'Encyclopédie; Ou, Dictionnaire raisonné des sciences, des arts et des métiers, of Denis Diderot.* Dover Pictorial Archive Series. New York: Dover Publications, 1959.

Diderot, Denis, and Jean Le Rond d'Alembert. *The Encyclopedia; Selections [by] Diderot, D'Alembert and a Society of Men of Letters. Translated, with an Introd. and Notes, by Nelly S. Hoyt [and] Thomas Cassirer.* Translated by Nelly S. Hoyt and Thomas Cassirer. Indianapolis, IN: Bobbs-Merrill, 1965.

Dièreville, Sieur de. *Relation du voyage du Port Royal de l'Acadie, ou de la Nouvelle France: dans laquelle on voit un détail des divers mouvemens de la mer dans une traversée de long cours: la description du païs, les occupations des François qui y sont établis, les maniéres des differentes nations sauvages, leurs superstitions, & leurs chasses: avec une dissertation exacte sur le castor.* Amsterdam: Chez Pierre Humbert, 1710.

Dièreville, Sieur de, and L. Urgèle Fontaine. *Voyage du sieur de Dièreville en Acadie.* Quebec: A. Côté., 1885.

Dirlam, Dona M., B.E. Misiorowski, and Sally A. Thomas. "Pearl Fashion through the Ages." *Gems and Gemology: Quarterly Journal of the Gemological Institute of America* 21, no. 2 (Summer 1985): 63–78.

Dolan, Alice Claire. "The Fabric of Life: Linen and Life Cycle in England, 1678–1810." PhD dissertation, University of Hertfordshire (United Kingdom), 2016.

Donovan, Kenneth. *Cape Breton at 200: Historical Essays in Honour of the Island's Bicentennial, 1785–1985.* University College of Cape Breton Press, 1985.

– "Communities and Families: Family Life and Living Conditions in Eighteenth Century Louisbourg." *Material Culture Review / Revue de la culture matérielle* 15 (6 June 1982).

– "Imposing Discipline upon Nature: Gardens, Agriculture and Animal Husbandry in Cape Breton, 1713–1758." *Material Culture Review / Revue de la culture matérielle* 64 (June 6, 2006).

– "Slaves and Their Owners in Ile Royale, 1713–1760." *Acadiensis: Journal of the History of the Atlantic Region / Revue d'histoire de la région atlantique* 25, no. 1 (1 October 1995): 3–32.

– "Slaves in Île Royale, 1713–1758." *French Colonial History* 5, no. 1 (May 17, 2004): 25–42.

Douglas, Audrey W. "Cotton Textiles in England: The East India Company's Attempt to Exploit Developments in Fashion 1660–1721." *Journal of British Studies* 8, no. 2 (1969): 28–43.

Dow, George Francis. *Every Day Life in the Massachusetts Bay Colony.* Boston: Society for the Preservation of New England Antiquities, 1935.

Dunn, Brenda. "Acadian Architecture in Port-Royal." *Heritage/Patrimoine* 5, no. 3 (Summer 2002): 10–13.

– *A History of Port Royal/Annapolis Royal, 1605–1800.* Halifax: Nimbus Publishing, 2004.

– "History of the Melanson Settlement: An Acadian Settlement." Parks Canada Agency, 2007.

– "L'inventaire de La Veuve Plemarais, 1705." *Les Cahiers, Journal of La Société Historique Acadienne* 25, no. 1 (1994): 27–37.

Dunn, Brenda, Sally Ross, and Birgitta Wallace. "Looking into Acadie: Three Illustrated Studies." Curatorial Report 87. Halifax: Nova Scotia Museum Publications, November 1998.

Dunton, John. *The ladies dictionary, being a general entertainment of the fair-sex a work never attempted before in English*. London: Printed for John Dunton, 1694.

DuPlessis, Robert S. "Cottons Consumption in the Seventeenth- and Eighteenth-Century North Atlantic." In *The Spinning World: A Global History of Cotton Textiles, 1200–1850*, edited by Giorgio Riello and Prasannan Parthasarathi, 227–46. OUP/Pasold Research Fund, 2011.

– "Defining a French Atlantic Empire: Some Material Culture Evidence." In *Fleuves, rivières et colonies: La France et ses empires (XVIIᵉ–XXᵉ siècle)*, edited by Mickaël Augeron and Robert DuPlessis. Les Indes savantes, 2010.

– "Louisbourg – Block 2." In-house report. Researching the Fortress of Louisbourg National Historic Site of Canada / Recherche sur la Forteresse-de-Louisbourg lieu historique national du Canada. September 1971.

– "Was There a Consumer Revolution in Eighteenth-Century New France?" *French Colonial History* 1 (2002): 143–59.

Earle, Alice Morse. *Home Life in Colonial Days*. New York: Macmillan, 1917.

Edwards, Lydia. *How to Read a Dress: A Guide to Changing Fashion from the 16th to the 20th Century*. Bloomsbury Academic, 2017.

Egan, Geoff. *Lead Cloth Seals and Related Items in the British Museum*. London: Department of Medieval and Later Antiquities, British Museum, 1994.

Ejstrud, Bo, Stina Andresen, Amanda Appel, Sara Gjerlevsen, and Birgit Thomsen. "'From Flax to Linen.' Experiments with Flax at the Ribe Viking Centre." Esbjerg: Ribe Viking Centre, University of Southern Denmark, 2011.

Eland, G., ed. *Purefoy Letters, 1735–1753*, vol. 2. London: Sidgwick & Jackson, 1931.

Elton, Stuart F. *Cloth Seals: An Illustrated Guide to the Identification of Lead Seals Attached to Cloth*. Oxford: Archaeopress Archaeology, 2017.

Entwistle, Joanne. *The Fashioned Body: Fashion, Dress and Modern Social Theory*. Cambridge, UK: Malden, MA: Polity Press ; Blackwell Publishers, 2000.

Epstein, Stephan R., and Maarten Roy Prak, eds. *Guilds, Innovation, and the European Economy, 1400–1800*. Cambridge; New York: Cambridge University Press, 2008.

Erskine, John S. "The French Period in Nova Scotia A.D. 1500–1758 and Present Remains: A Historical, Archaeological and Botanical Survey." Wolfville, 1975.

Fader, Gordon. "Marine Archaeology Offshore Digby Neck, Bay of Fundy." Halifax: Atlantic Marine Geological Consulting, March 2005.

Fairchilds, Cissie. "The Production and Marketing of Populuxe Goods in Eighteenth-Century Paris." In *Consumption and the World of Goods*, edited by John Brewer and Roy Porter, 229–48. London: Routledge, 1993.

"Familles établies à l'Acadie. Abrégé envoyé de Québec à Colbert par le Sieur Randin, 8 Novembre 1671." Census, 8 November 1671. Dépôt des papiers publics des colonies; état civil et recensements: Série GI: Recensements et documents divers: C-2572. Library and Archives Canada.

Faneuil, Peter. "Peter Faneuil Papers, 1716–1739. Letterbook (Business), 1737–1739," 1739 1737. H234, Volume F-4, Mss:766 1712-1854. Baker Library Historical Collections, Harvard Business School.

Faragher, John Mack. *A Great and Noble Scheme: The Tragic Story of the Expulsion of the French Acadians from Their American Homeland*. New York: W.W. Norton, 2005.

Faret, Nicolas. *L'honnête homme. Ou, L'art de plaire à la cour*. Strasbourg: Welper, 1664.

Ferreira, Ester S.B., Alison N. Hulme, Hamish McNab, and Anita Quye. "The Natural Constituents of Historical Textile Dyes." *Chemical Society Reviews* 33, no. 6 (2004): 329–36.

Ferris, Neal. "Buttons I Have Known." *Studies in Southwestern Ontario Archaeology*, Occasional Publications of the London Chapter, OAS, 1 (1986): 98–106.

Ferris, Neal, Rodney Harrison, and Michael Vincent Wilcox, eds. *Rethinking Colonial Pasts through Archaeology*. Oxford University Press, 2014.

Fisher, Genevieve, and Diana DiPaolo Loren. "Introduction: Embodying Identity in Archaeology." *Cambridge Archaeological Journal* 13, no. 2 (2003): 225–30.

Fowler, Jonathan. "Archaeology in Nova Scotia: 2013/14 News." *Nova Scotia Museum*, 2014.

– "The Minas Environs Project: 2nd Annual Report, 1999–2000." Manuscript Report. Heritage Division: Nova Scotia Department of Communities, Culture and Heritage, 2000.

Fowler, Jonathan, and Earle Lockerby. *Jeremiah Bancroft at Fort Beauséjour and Grand-Pré*. Kentville, NS: Gaspereau Press, 2013.

France. *Lettres patentes du Roi, concernant les manufactures. Données à Marly le 5 mai 1779*. De l'Imprimerie du Roi, 1779.

Franquelin, Jean Baptiste Louis. "Carte geralle du voyage que Monsr. DeMeulles Intendant de la Justice Police et Finances de La Nouvelle France a fait par ordre du Roy et commencé le 9ᵉ Novembre & finy le 6ᵉ Juillet 1686 ensuivant comprenant toutes les terres de l'Accadie, Isle Du Cape Breton, Golfe & Riviere St. Laurens depuis La Riviere St. Georges Limittes de La Nlle. France et de la Nouvelle Angletere jusqu'a la Ville de Quebec." Quebec: s.n., 1686.

Galle, Jillian E. "Costly Signaling and Gendered Social Strategies among Slaves in the Eighteenth-Century Chesapeake: An Archaeological Perspective." *American Antiquity* 75, no. 1 (January 2010): 19–43.

Garsault, François-Alexandre-Pierre de. *L'art de la lingere*. Paris: De L'Imprimerie, L.F. Delatour, 1771.

– *Art du tailleur: contenant le tailleur d'habits d'hommes, les culottes de peau, le tailleur de corps de femmes & enfants, la couturière & la marchande de modes*. Paris: De L'Imprimerie, L.F. Delatour, 1769.

"General Census Taken in the Month of November 1708 of All of the Indians in Acadia Who Reside on the East Coast, and Those of Pintagouet and of Canibeky." Census, 1708. Extrait G.I, 466-I. Library and Archives Canada.

Graham, Andrew. *Andrew Graham's Observations on Hudson's Bay, 1767–91*. Edited by Glyndwr Williams. London: Hudson's Bay Record Society, 1969.

Griffiths, N.E.S. *Contexts of Acadian History, 1686–1784*. 2nd ed. Montreal and Kingston: McGill-Queen's University Press, 1992.

– *From Migrant to Acadian: A North American Border People, 1604–1755*. Montreal and Kingston: McGill-Queen's University Press, 2005.

Grimm, Jacob L. *Archaeological Investigation of Fort Ligonier 1960–1965*. Pittsburgh: Carnegie Museum Institute, 1970.

Grömer, Karina. "Efficiency and Technique – Experiments with Original Spindle Whorls." British Archaeological Reports, International Series, 2005.

Groves, Sylvia. *The History of Needlework Tools and Accessories*. 2nd ed. London: Country Life Books, 1966.

Gums, Bonnie L. "Earthfast (Pieux En Terre) Structures at Old Mobile." *Historical Archaeology* 36, no. 1 (2002): 13–25.

Gwyn, Julian. *Excessive Expectations: Maritime Commerce and the Economic Development of Nova Scotia, 1740–1870.* Montreal and Kingston: McGill-Queen's University Press, 1998.

– "The Mi'kmaq, Poor Settlers, and the Nova Scotia Fur Trade, 1783-1853." *Journal of the Canadian Historical Association* 14, no. 1 (2003): 65–91.

Hale, Robert. "Journal of a Voyage to Nova Scotia Made in 1731: By Robert Hale of Beverly." *The Essex Institute Historical Collections* 42 (July 1906): 217–33.

Hale, Thomas. *A Compleat Body of Husbandry. Containing Rules for Performing, in the Most Profitable Manner, the Whole Business of the Farmer and Country Gentleman.* Vol. 3. 4 vols. London: S. Crowder, 1758.

Haliburton, Thomas Chandler. *An Historical Statistical Account of Nova Scotia in Two Volumes: Illustrated by a Map of the Province, and Several Engravings.* 2nd ed. Vol. 1. 2 vols. Halifax: Published for Joseph Howe, and Sold by C.H. Belcher, Robert Scholey, London, and Oliver & Boyd, Edinburgh, 1829.

Hall, James. *Dictionary of Subjects and Symbols in Art.* London: John Murray, 1989.

Hannay, James. "The Acadian French." In *Collections of the Nova Scotia Historical Society*, edited by W. B. Tobin, 1:129–60, 1881.

– *The History of Acadia, from Its First Discovery to Its Surrender to England.* St John, NB, Printed by J. & A. McMillan, 1879.

Harper, J. Russell. "Two Seventeenth Century Micmac 'Copper Kettle' Burials." *Anthropologica*, no. 4 (1957): 11–36.

Harper, Ross K. "Historical Archaeology on the 18th Century Connecticut Frontier: The Ways and Means of Captain Ephraim Sprague." *Museum of the Fur Trade Quarterly* 41, no. 2 (2005): 9–16.

Harper, Ross K., Bruce Clouette, and Mary G. Harper. *Highways to History: The Archaeology of Connecticut's 18th-Century Lifeways.* Newington: Connecticut Department of Transportation in cooperation with the Federal Highway Administration. 2013.

Harris, Donald. "Louisbourg – In-House Report on Site Histories." Parks Canada and Fortress Louisbourg, 1982.

Hauser, Judith Anne. "Jesuit Rings from Fort Michilimackinac and Other European Contact Sites." Master's thesis, Western Michigan University, 1982.

Hayward, Maria. *Dress at the Court of King Henry VIII.* London: Routledge, 2007.

Hebdige, Dick. *Subculture: The Meaning of Style.* New Accents. London: Routledge, 1981.

Heldman, Donald P. and Roger T. Grange, Jr. *Excavations at Fort Michilimackinac: 1978–1979. The Rue de la Babillarde.* Mackinac Island State Park Commission, Mackinac Island, Michigan, 1981.

Hill, Erica. "Thimbles and Thimble Rings from the Circum-Caribbean Region, 1500–1800: Chronology and Identification." *Historical Archaeology* 29, no. 1 (March 1995): 84–92.

Hinke, William J. "Report of the Journey of Francis Louis Michel from Berne, Switzerland, to Virginia, October 2, 1701–December 1, 1702." *The Virginia Magazine of History and Biography* 24, no. 2 (April 1916): 113–41.

Hoad, Linda. "Louisbourg – Block 3, Lots A & B." In-house report. Researching the Fortress of Louisbourg National Historic Site of Canada / Recherche sur la Forteresse-de-Louisbourg lieu historique national du Canada, June 1971.

Hodder, Ian. *Entangled: An Archaeology of the Relationships between Humans and Things*. Malden, MA: Wiley-Blackwell, 2012.

– "Material Entanglement." In *The Encyclopedia of Archaeological Sciences*, 1–5. American Cancer Society, 2018.

– *The Meanings of Things: Material Culture and Symbolic Expression*. London/Boston: Unwin Hyman, 1989.

– *Studies in Human-Thing Entanglement*. Stanford, CA: Ian Hodder, 2016.

– "Wheels of Time: Some Aspects of Entanglement Theory and the Secondary Products Revolution." *Journal of World Prehistory* 24, no. 2 (2011): 175–87.

Hodson, Christopher. *The Acadian Diaspora: An Eighteenth-Century History*. New York: Oxford University Press, 2012.

Holme, Randle. *The Academy of Armory, or, A Storehouse of Armory and Blazon Containing the Several Variety of Created Beings, and How Born in Coats of Arms, Both Foreign and Domestick: With the Instruments Used in All Trades and Sciences, Together with Their Their Terms of Art*. Chester: Printed for the Author, 1688.

Holmes, Edwin F. *A History of Thimbles*. London: Cornwall Books, 1985.

Hood, Adrienne. "Material Culture and Textiles: An Overview." *Material Culture Review / Revue de la Culture Matérielle*[Online] 31, no. 1 (Spring 1990).

– *The Weaver's Craft: Cloth, Commerce, and Industry in Early Pennsylvania*. Philadelphia: University of Pennsylvania Press, 2003.

Hood, Adrienne D., and D.T. Ruddel. "Artifacts and Documents in the History of Quebec Textiles." In *Living in a Material World: Canadian and American Approaches to Material Culture*, edited by Gerald L. Pocius, 55–91. St John's: ISER Books, Memorial University of Newfoundland, 1990.

Huey, Paul. "The Archaeology of 17th-Century New Netherland since 1985: An Update." *Northeast Historical Archaeology* 34, no. 1 (2005): 95–118.

Hulme, William Henry. *The Middle-English Harrowing of Hell and Gospel of Nicodemus*. London: Pub. for the Early English Text Society by K. Paul, Trench, Trübner, 1907.

Hunt, Alan. *Governance of the Consuming Passions: A History of Sumptuary Law*. London: Palgrave Macmillan, 1996.

Hynes, Gisa I. "Some Aspects of the Demography of Port Royal, 1650–1755." *Acadiensis: Journal of the History of the Atlantic Region / Revue d'histoire de la région atlantique* 3, no. 1 (1973): 3–17.

"Invoice of Merchandise from Abraham Boudrot to André Taneuil," 26 April 1691. XXXVII 93. Massachusetts Archives.

Johnston, A.J.B. "The Acadian Deportation in a Comparative Context: An Introduction." *Journal of the Royal Nova Scotia Historical Society; Halifax* 10 (2007): 114–31.

– "The Call of the Archetype and the Challenge of Acadian History." *French Colonial History* 5, no. 1 (2004): 63–92.

– "The People of Eighteenth Century Louisbourg." In *Aspects of Louisbourg: Essays on the History of an Eighteenth-Century French Community in North America*, edited by Eric Krause, Carol Corbin, William A. O'Shea, 150–61. Sydney, NS: University College of Cape Breton Press: Louisbourg Institute, 1995.

– "From Port de Peche to Ville Fortifiee: The Evolution of Urban Louisbourg 1713–1858." In *Aspects of Louisbourg: Essays on the History of an Eighteenth-Century French Community in North America*, edited by Eric Krause, Carol Corbin, William A. O'Shea, 3–18. Sydney, NS: University College of Cape Breton Press: Louisbourg Institute, 1995.

– "Preserving History: The Commemoration of 18th Century Louisbourg, 1895–1940." *Acadiensis: Journal of the History of the Atlantic Region / Revue d'histoire de la région atlantique* 12, no. 2 (1983): 53–80.

– "Un regard neuf sur les Acadiens de Île royale." *Les Cahiers de la Société Historique Acadienne* 32, no. 3 (2001): 155–72.

– *Religion in Life at Louisbourg, 1713–1758*. Montreal and Kingston: McGill-Queen's University Press, 1984.

Johnston, A.J.B., Kenneth Donovan, B.A. Balcom, and Alex Storm. *Louisbourg: An 18th Century Town*. Halifax: Nimbus Publishing, 1991.

Jonah, Anne Marie Lane. "Unequal Transitions: Two Métis Women in Eighteenth-Century Île Royale." *French Colonial History* 11 (2010): 109–29.

Jonah, Anne, and Elizabeth Tait. "Filles d'Acadie, Femmes de Louisbourg: Acadian Women and French Colonial Society in Eighteenth-Century Louisbourg." *French Colonial History* 8 (2007): 23–51.

Jones, Ann Rosalind, and Peter Stallybrass. *Renaissance Clothing and the Materials of Memory*. Cambridge, UK; New York: Cambridge University Press, 2001.

Jones, David R. "From Frontier to Borderland: The Acadian Community in a Comparative Context, 1605–1710." *Journal of the Royal Nova Scotia Historical Society* 7 (2004): 15–37.

Jope, E.M. "The Tinning of Iron Spurs: A Continuous Practice from the Tenth to the Seventeenth Century." *Oxfordshire Architectural and Historical Society*, 1956, 8.

Jordan, Kurt A. "Colonies, Colonialism, and Cultural Entanglement: The Archaeology of Postcolumbian Intercultural Relations." In *International Handbook of Historical Archaeology*, edited by David Gaimster and Teresita Majewski, 31–49. New York: Springer Science + Business Media, LLC, 2009.

Joubert, Pierre. "Pierre Joubert's Bill to Mme Péré." Nantes, 10 April 1733. G2, vol. 195, doss. 83. Library and Archives Canada.

Joudry, Shalan. "Puktewei: Learning from Fire in Mi'kma'ki (Mi'kmaq Territory)." Master's thesis, Dalhousie University, 2016.

Kalm, Pehr, Jacques Rousseau, Guy Béthune, and Pierre Morisset. *Voyage de Pehr Kalm au Canada en 1749*. Montreal: CLF, 1977.

Kalm, Peter. *Travels into North America: Containing Its Natural History, and a Circumstantial Account of Its Plantations and Agriculture in General, with the Civil, Ecclesiastical and Commercial State of the Country, the Manners of the Inhabitants, and Several Curious and Important Remarks on Various Subjects*. Vol. 3. Translated by Johann Reinhold Forster. London: The Editor, 1771.

Karklins, Karlis. "Beads from Fort Beausejour, New Brunswick." Research Bulletin. Ottawa: Parks Canada, July 1981.

– "Clay Pipe-Stem Beads in North America." *Northeast Historical Archaeology* 45 (2016): 18–22.

– *Trade Ornament Usage among the Native Peoples of Canada: A Source Book*. Ottawa: Intl Specialized Book Service, 1992.

Kauffman, Christopher J. "The Sulpician Presence." *Catholic Historical Review* 75, no. 4 (1989): 677–95.

Kawamura, Yuniya. *Doing Research in Fashion and Dress: An Introduction to Qualitative Methods.* Oxford, UK; New York: Berg, 2011.

Kennedy, Gregory. *Something of a Peasant Paradise? Comparing Rural Societies in Acadie and the Loudunais, 1604–1755.* Montreal and Kingston: McGill-Queen's University Press, 2014.

Kennedy, Gregory, Thomas Peace, and Stephanie Pettigrew. "Social Networks across Chignecto: Applying Social Network Analysis to Acadie, Mi'kma'ki, and Nova Scotia, 1670–1751." *Acadiensis: Journal of the History of the Atlantic Region / Revue d'histoire de la région atlantique* 47, no. 1 (9 May 2018): 8–40.

Kerr, Ian. "An Analysis of Personal Adornment at Fort St Joseph (20BE23), An Eighteenth-Century French Trading Post in Southwest Michigan." Master's thesis, Western Michigan University, 2012.

Kidd, Kenneth, and Martha Kidd. "A Classification System for Glass Beads for the Use of Field Archaeologists." Occasional Papers in Archaeology and History. Canadian Historic Sites, 1 January 2012.

Kopytoff, Igor. "The Cultural Biography of Things: Commoditization as Process." In *The Social Life of Things*, edited by Arjun Appadurai, 64–91. Cambridge: Cambridge University Press, 1988.

Korvemaker, E. Frank. "Archaeological Excavations at the Roma Site, Brudenell Point, P.E.I., 1968–1970." National Historic Sites Service. Parks Canada / Parcs Canada, 1980.

Krause, Eric, Carol Corbin, and William A. O'Shea, eds. *Aspects of Louisbourg: Essays on the History of an Eighteenth-Century French Community in North America.* Sydney, NS: University College of Cape Breton Press: Louisbourg Institute, 1995.

Kristmanson, Helen. "Archaeology at Pointe-Aux-Vieux." *The Island Magazine*, Fall/Winter 2009.

– "Archaeology at Pointe-Aux-Vieux, Part 1." *The Island Magazine*, Spring/Summer 2015.

– "Archaeology at Pointe-Aux-Vieux, Part 2." *The Island Magazine*, Fall/Winter 2015.

Küchler, Susanne, and Daniel Miller, eds. *Clothing as Material Culture.* Oxford, UK; New York: Berg, 2005.

Kuchta, David. *The Three-Piece Suit and Modern Masculinity: England, 1550–1850.* Oakland: University of California Press, 2002.

Kuusisto, Kathy Moggridge. "Priests and Parish Organizations in Acadia, 1604–1755." Research paper (unpublished), 1976. MG 1, Vol. 2858, #14., Kathy Moggridge Kuusisto Collection, Nova Scotia Archives.

Kwass, Michael. "Big Hair: A Wig History of Consumption in Eighteenth-Century France." *American Historical Review* 111, no. 3 (2006): 631–59.

La Grenade-Meunier, Monique. "Civil Costume at Louisbourg: 1713-1758 Men's Costume." Fortress of Louisbourg Report. Parks Canada and Fortress Louisbourg, March 1972.

– "Le costume civil à Louisbourg: 1713–1758 le costume feminin." Fortress of Louisbourg Report. Ottawa: Direction des parcs nationaux et des lieux historiques, Parcs Canada, 1971.

– [Monique La Grenade] "Le Costume Civil à Louisbourg au XVIIIᵉ Siècle." Université de Montréal, 1974.

LaBar-Kidd, Laureen Ann. "Indian Trade Silver as Inter-Cultural Document in the Northeast." Master's thesis, University of Delaware (Winterthur Program), 2000.

Landry, Nicolas. "Culture matérielle et niveaux de richesse chez les pêcheurs de Plaisance et de l'Île Royale, 1700–1758." *Material Culture Review / Revue de la culture matérielle* 48, no. 1 (6 June 1998). Accessed 22 March 2023. https://journals.lib.unb.ca/index.php/MCR/article/view/17803.

Landry, Nicolas, and Nicole Lang. *Histoire de l'Acadie*. Sillery, QC: Septentrion, 2001.

La Roque, Antoine de. *Mercure de France. Tome X, Janvier-Juin 1726*. Genève: Slatkine Reprints, 1968.

– *Mercure de France. Tome XXI, Juillet-Décembre 1731*. Genève: Slatkine Reprints, 1968.

Lavoie, Marc. "Les aboiteaux acadiens: Origines, controverses et ambiguïtés." *Port Acadie: Revue interdisciplinaire en études acadiennes* 13 (2008): 115–45.

– "Les Acadiens et les 'Planters' des Maritimes: Une étude de deux ethnies, de 1680 à 1820." PhD thesis, Université Laval, 2002.

– "The Archaeological Reconnaissance of the Beaubassin Region in Nova Scotia and New Brunswick." Halifax, Nova Scotia: Council of Maritime Premiers – Maritime Committee on Archaeological Cooperation, 1986.

"Beaubassin Revisited: History and Archaeology." In *Proceedings of the 2003 Spring Heritage Conference*. Amherst, Nova Scotia, 2003.

– "Belleisle Nova Scotia, 1680–1755: Acadian Material Life and Economy." Curatorial Report 65. Halifax: Nova Scotia Museum Publications, 1987.

– "Un nouveau regard sur le monde acadien avant la Déportation. Archéologie au marais de Belle-Isle, Nouvelle-Écosse." In *Rêves d'Amériques: regard sur l'archéologie de la Nouvelle-France / Dreams of the Americas: Overview of New France Archaeology*, edited by Christian Roy and Hélène Côté, 70–95. Quebec: Association des archéologues du Québec, 2008.

Le Clercq, Chrestien. *New Relation of Gaspesia: With the Customs and Religion of the Gaspesian Indians*. Translated by William F. (William Francis) Ganong. Toronto: Champlain Society, 1910.

Lemire, Beverly. *Cotton*. Oxford; New York: Bloomsbury Academic, 2011.

– "Draping the Body and Dressing the Home: The Material Culture of Textiles and Clothes in the Atlantic World, c. 1500–1800." In *History and Material Culture: A Student's Guide to Approaching Alternative Sources*, edited by Karen Harvey, 89–105. Routledge, 2017.

– *The Force of Fashion in Politics and Society: Global Perspectives from Early Modern to Contemporary Times*. The History of Retailing and Consumption. Farnham, Surrey, UK: Ashgate, 2010

– "'Men of the World': British Mariners, Consumer Practice, and Material Culture in an Era of Global Trade, c. 1660–1800." *Journal of British Studies* 54, no. 2 (April 2015): 288–319.

– "A Question of Trousers: Seafarers, Masculinity and Empire in the Shaping of British Male Dress, c. 1600–1800." *Cultural and Social History* 13, no. 1 (2 January 2016): 1–22.

Lennox, Jeffers. *Homelands and Empires: Indigenous Spaces, Imperial Fictions, and Competition for Territory in Northeastern North America, 1690–1763*. Toronto: University of Toronto Press, 2017.

Leonard, Kevin. "Archaeobotanical Remains from a Mid-18th Century Acadian Well in Prince Edward Island National Park – Greenwich (15F2C)." Unpublished report, prepared for Rob Ferguson. Archaeoconsulting, 7 February 2010.

Lescarbot, Marc. *Histoire de la Nouvelle France Relation dernière de ce qui s'est passé au voyage du sieur de Poutrincourt en la Nouvelle France depuis 10 mois ença*. Project Gutenberg, 1612.

Lewis, Roger J. "Pre-Contact Fish Weirs: A Case Study from Southwestern Nova Scotia." Master's thesis, Memorial University of Newfoundland, 2006.

Lindbergh, Jennie. "Buttoning Down Archaeology." *Australasian Historical Archaeology: Journal of the Australasian Society for Historical Archaeology* 17 (1999): 50–7.

Linthicum, M. Channing. *Costume in the Drama of Shakespeare and His Contemporaries*. Oxford: Clarendon Press, 1936.

Loren, Diana DiPaolo. *Archaeology of Clothing and Bodily Adornment in Colonial America*. Gainesville: University Press of Florida, 2010.

– "Dress, Faith, and Medicine: Caring for the Body in Eighteenth-Century Spanish Texas." In *Archaeology of Culture Contact and Colonialism in Spanish and Portuguese America*, edited by Pedro Paulo, A. Funari, and Maria Ximena Senatore, 143–53. Cham: Springer International Publishing, 2014.

– "Social Skins: Orthodoxies and Practices of Dressing in the Early Colonial Lower Mississippi Valley." *Journal of Social Archaeology* 1, no. 2 (1 October 2001): 172–89.

Louis XIII (Roi de France; 1601–1643). *Déclaration, portant règlement général sur la réformation des habits. Vérifiée en Parlement le 9 may 1634*. Paris: A. Estiéne et P. Mettayer, 1634.

Macdonald, Alexander, and Roberta Clowater. "Natural Ecosystem Connectivity across the Chignecto Isthmus – Opportunities and Challenges. A Collaborative Project of CPAWS New Brunswick and CPAWS Nova Scotia." Canadian Parks and Wilderness Society, 1 January 2005.

MacMechan, Archibald, ed. "Nova Scotia Archives Commission Book, 1720–1741." In *A Calendar of Two Letter-Books and One Commission-Book in the Possession of the Government of Nova Scotia, 1713–1741*. Halifax, NS: Herald Printing House, 1900.

– *Original Minutes of His Majesty's Council at Annapolis Royal, 1720–1739*. CIHM/ICMH Digital Series = CIHM/ICMH Collection Numérisée; No. 83344. Halifax, NS: McAlpine, 1908.

Mahallati, Amineh. "Women in Traditional Sharīʾa: A List of Differences between Men and Women in Islamic Tradition." *Journal of Islamic Law and Culture* 12, no. 1 (1 April 2010): 1–9.

Maillard, Abbé. *An Account of the Customs and Manners of the Micmakis and Maricheets Savage Nations, Now Dependent on the Government of Cape-Breton: From an Original French Manuscript-Letter, Never Published, Written by a French Abbot, Who Resided Many Years, in Quality of Missionary, among Them*. London: Printed for S. Hooper and A. Morley, 1758.

Majewski, Teresita, and David Gaimster, eds. *International Handbook of Historical Archaeology*. 2009 ed. New York; London: Springer, 2011.

Mandel, Massimiliano. *Scissors*. Wingston: First Glance Books, 1990.

Martin, Calvin. "The European Impact on the Culture of a Northeastern Algonquian Tribe: An Ecological Interpretation." *William and Mary Quarterly* 31, no. 1 (1974): 4–26.

Mascarene, Paul. "A Narrative of Events at Annapolis From the Capture in Oct., 1710, till Sept., 1711." In *Collections of the Nova Scotia Historical Society*, vol. 4. Halifax: Nova Scotia Historical Society, 1885.

Mays, Dorothy A. *Women in Early America: Struggle, Survival, and Freedom in a New World*. Santa Barbara, CA: ABC-CLIO, 2004.

McCracken, Grant David. "The Fashion System." In *The Fashion Reader*, edited by Linda Welters and Abby Lillethun, 135–37. Oxford: Berg Publishers, 2011.

McKenney, Jenny. "That 'Bossy Shield': Money, Sex, Sentiment, and the Thimble." In *Lumen: Selected Proceedings from the Canadian Society for Eighteenth-Century Studies / Lumen: Travaux choisis de la Société canadienne d'étude du dix-huitième siècle*, 34: 1–23. London, 2015.

McKenzie, Matthew. "Reassembling the Greater Gulf: Northwest Atlantic Environmental History and the Gulf of St Lawrence System." In *The Greater Gulf: Essays in Environmental History on the Gulf of St. Lawrence*, edited by Bryan J. Payne, Edward George, and Claire Elizabeth Campbell, 13–31. Montreal and Kingston: McGill-Queen's University Press, 2020.

McNeil, Peter, and Giorgio Riello. "The Material Culture of Walking: Spaces of Methodologies in the Long Eighteenth Century." In *Everyday Objects: Medieval and Early Modern Material Culture and Its Meanings*, edited by Tara Hamling and Catherine Richardson, 41–56. Farnham, Surrey, UK: Ashgate, 2010.

Meulles, Jacques de. "Account of the Voyage of Monsieur de Meulles to Acadie, 1685–1686." In *Acadiensia Nova (1598–1779): New and Unpublished Documents and Other Data Relating to Acadia (Nova Scotia, New Brunswick, Maine, Etc.; the Actors, Sir William Alexander, Jacques De Meuelles Gargas, Vincent De Saccardy, Marquis De La Roche, Delabat and J.F.W. Des Barres*, vol. 1, edited by William Inglis Morse. London: Bernard Quaritch, 1935.

Miller, George L., Olive R. Jones, Lester A. Ross, and Teresita Majewski, eds. *Approaches to Material Culture Research for Historical Archaeologists*. 1st ed. Tucson: Society for Historical Archaeology, 1991.

Molière. *Le bourgeois gentilhomme, comédie ballet par M. Molière (1670)*. Chez Jean Mossy, imprimeur-libraire à la Canebiére, 1789.

Montfort, Louis-Marie Grignion de. *The Secret of the Rosary (c. 1700–1716)*. Translated by Mary Barbour. Bay Shore, NY: Montfort, 1954.

Montgomery, Florence M. *Textiles in America, 1650–1870*. New York: W.W. Norton, 1984.

Morgan, Gwenda, and Peter Rushton. "Visible Bodies: Power, Subordination and Identity in the Eighteenth-Century Atlantic World." *Journal of Social History* 39, no. 1 (2005): 39–64.

Morgan, Robert J. "Louisbourg – Block 16." In-house report. Researching the Fortress of Louisbourg National Historic Site of Canada / Recherche sur la Forteresse-de-Louisbourg Lieu Historique National Du Canada, June 1975.

Morin, J. *Manuel du bottier et du cordonnier ou Traité complet et simplifié de ces arts: contenant les meilleurs procédés à suivre pour confectionner les chaussures de toute espèce*. Librairie Encyclopédique de Roret, 1831.

Morris, Charles. "Breif Survey of Nova Scotia [*sic*]," 1748. Charles Morris Fonds, MG 18 vols. F.4–F.10. Library and Archives Canada.

– "Judge Morris' Account of the Acadians, Drawn Up in 1753, with Causes of the Failure of the British Settlement in Nova Scotia, 1749, 50, 53." Halifax, NS, 1881. Collections of the Nova Scotia Historical Society.

Morse, William Inglis. *Acadiensia Nova (1598–1779): New and Unpublished Documents and Other Data Relating to Acadia (Nova Scotia, New Brunswick, Maine, Etc.; the Actors, Sir William Alexander, Jacques de Meuelles Gargas, Vincent de Saccardy, Marquis de La Roche, Delabat and J.F.W. Des Barres*. 2 vols. London: B. Quaritch, 1935.

Muraca, David, John Coombs, Phil Levy, Laura Galke, Paul Nasca, and Amy Muraca. "Small Finds, Space, and Social Context: Exploring Agency in Historical Archaeology." *Northeast Historical Archaeology* 40, no. 1 (31 January 2014).

Nadon, Pierre. "Field Journals for Digs at Beaubassin, Fort Beausejours and Fort Cumberland." Nova Scotia, 1968.

– "The Isthmus of Chignecto: An Archaeological Site Survey of Acadian Settlements, 1670–1755." Ottawa: National Historic Parks and Sites Branch, Parks Canada, Dept. of Indian and Northern Affairs, 1968.

New England Historic Genealogical Society. *Vital Records of Duxbury, Massachusetts to the Year 1850*. Published by the New England Historic Genealogical Society, at the Charge of the Eddy Town-Record Fund, 1911.

Noël, Stéphane. "Archaeological Survey and Testing at the Melanson Settlement National Historic Site, Nova Scotia." *Society for Historical Archaeology Newsletter* 43, no. 4 (Winter 2010): 10–12.

– "Archaeology at the Melanson Settlement NHS." *Annual Report of Research and Monitoring in the Greater Kejimkujik Ecosystem*, 2012, 96–7.

– "Inventory of Archaeological Records of the Melanson Settlement National Historic Site, Nova Scotia." Parks Canada Mainland Nova Scotia Field Unit, March 2011.

Noël, Stéphane, and Anne-Marie Faucher. "Recent Excavations of Pre-Expulsion Acadian Middens (c. 1664–1755) at the Melanson Settlement National Historic Site." Conference Poster presented at the Council for Northeast Historical Archaeology Annual Conference, Utica, New York, 20 October 2011.

Noël Hume, Ivor. *A Guide to Artifacts of Colonial America*. 1st ed. New York: Knopf, 1970.

Oelsner, Gustaf Hermann. *A Handbook of Weaves*. New York: Macmillan, 1915.

Offen, Karen. *The Woman Question in France, 1400–1870*. Cambridge: Cambridge University Press, 2017.

Ordoñez, Margaret T., and Linda Welters. "Textiles from the Seventeenth-Century Privy at the Cross Street Back Lot Site." *Historical Archaeology* 32, no. 3 (1998): 81–90.

Parker, Rozsika. *The Subversive Stitch: Embroidery and the Making of the Feminine*. London; New York: I.B. Tauris, 2010.

Parthasarathi, Prasannan. *Why Europe Grew Rich and Asia Did Not: Global Economic Divergence, 1600–1850*. Cambridge: Cambridge University Press, 2011.

Patterson, Stephen. "Indian-White Relations in Nova Scotia, 1749–61: A Study in Political Interaction." *Acadiensis: Journal of the History of the Atlantic Region / Revue d'histoire de la région atlantique* 23, no. 1 (10 October 1993): 23–59.

Paul, Daniel N. *We Were Not the Savages: A Mi'kmaq Perspective on the Collision between European and Native American Civilizations*. Halifax, NS: Fernwood, 2000.

Payne, Brian J., George Edward MacDonald, and Claire Elizabeth Campbell. *The Greater Gulf: Essays on the Environmental History of the Gulf of St. Lawrence*. Edited by Brian J. Payne, George Edward MacDonald, and Claire Elizabeth Campbell. Montreal and Kingston: McGill-Queen's University Press, 2020.

Peace, Thomas G.M. "Two Conquests: Aboriginal Experiences of the Fall of New France and Acadia." PhD dissertation, York University, 2012.

Pellegrin, Nicole. "Le genre et l'habit. Figures du transvestisme féminin sous l'Ancien Régime." *Clio. Femmes, genre, histoire*, no. 10 (1 November 1999).

Pelletier, Gaby. "From Animal Skins to Polyester: Four Hundred Years of Micmac and Maliseet Clothing Styles and Ornamentation." In *Papers of the Tenth Algonquian Conference*, 10 (1979): 118–30.

Pennautier. "Enchantillon de drap du XVIIIme Siecle." Textile sample book, ca 1740. Accession Number: 156.415 EC4 F. Metropolitan Museum of Art.

"Polie des Habitans de la bans lieux du fort du Port Royal speciffie famile par famille du 25 October 1710." Great Britain. Colonial Office: Nova Scotia and Cape Breton, Original Correspondence reel c-9119 104282 MG 11 CO 217. Library and Archives Canada.

Preston, Brian. "An Archaeological Survey of Reported Acadian Habitation Sites in the Annapolis Valley and Minas Basin Areas." Curatorial Report 20. Halifax: Nova Scotia Museum Publications, 1971.

– "Excavations at Site BeDi-2 Belleisle Annapolis County, 1972." Curatorial Report 21. Halifax: Nova Scotia Museum Publications, 1975.

Preston, David L. *Texture of Contact: European and Indian Settler Communities on the Frontiers of Iroquoia, 1667–1783.* Lincoln: University of Nebraska Press, 2009.

"Procès verbal de levée de scelle et inventaire faits chez la d'Ile Péré." Louisbourg, 9 June 1735. Vol. 194, doss. 80. Louisbourg.

"Procès verbal de levée des scelles et inventaire des meubles et effets de la succession de deffunte Dame Jeanne Thibaudo, Veuve Degoutin," 11 April 1741. G2, vol. 197, dossier 151. Centre des Archives d'Outre-Mer.

"Procès verbal de vente des effets de feu François Gassot." Louisbourg, 19 August 1752. Section Outre-Mer, Série G2, Vol. 201, Dossier 251. Archives de la Marine.

Proulx, Gilles. *Between France and New France: Life aboard the Tall Sailing Ships.* Toronto: Dundurn Press, 1984.

Prown, Jules David. "The Truth of Material Culture: History or Fiction?" In *History from Things: Essays on Material Culture*, edited by Stephen Lubar and W. David Kingery, 14. Washington, DC: Smithsonian Institution, 1993.

Quinn, D.B. "The Voyage of Étienne Bellenger to the Maritimes in 1583: A New Document." *Canadian Historical Review* 43, no. 4 (1962): 328–43.

Racette, Sherry Farrell. "My Grandmothers Loved to Trade: The Indigenization of European Trade Goods in Historic and Contemporary Canada." *Journal of Museum Ethnography*, no. 20 (2008): 69–81.

Rahman, Fazlur. "Boots and Shoes from Fort Beausejour." Manuscript Report Series 13. Ottawa: National Historic Sites Service, Dept. of Indian Affairs and Northern Development, 1971.

Rameau de Saint-Père, François-Edme. *Une colonie féodale en Amérique: l'Acadie (1604–1881).* Paris/Montreal: E. Plon, Nourrit; Granger frères, 1889.

Raynal, Abbé (Guillaume-Thomas-François). *Histoire philosophique et politique des établissements et du commerce des européens dans les deux Indes.* Amsterdam, 1773.

"Recensement de l'Île Royale et de l'Île Saint-Jean Dressé par Le Sieur de La Roque en 1752." Census, 1752. Dépôt des papiers publics des colonies; état civil et recensements: Série G1: Recensements et documents divers: c-4582. Library and Archives Canada.

"Recensement de l'Isle Saint-Jean. Noms des chefs de familles et lieux d'origine." Census, 1728. Accession 2702/670. Smith-Alley Collection, Public Archives and Records Office of Prince Edward Island.

"Recensement des habitants de l'Isle Saint-Jean, 1730. Le présent est conforme aux nottes que m'en a donné Le Sieur Du Buisson." Census, 1730. Accession 2702/670. Smith-Alley Collection, Public Archives and Records Office of Prince Edward Island.

"Recensement fait par de Meulles, Intendant de La Nouvelle-France, de tous les peuples de Beaubassin, Rivière Saint-Jean, Port-Royal, Isle Percée et Autres Costes de l'Acadie, s'y étant

luy même transporté dans chacune des habitations au commencement de l'année 1686."
    Census, 1686. Dépôt des papiers publics des colonies; état civil et recensements: Série GI:
    Recensements et documents divers: c-2572. Library and Archives Canada.

"Record of the Sale after Death of the Possessions of Pierre Lambert." Louisbourg, 6 April 1756.
    Id. vol. 205, doss. 393. Fortress Louisbourg.

Rees, Jane. *A Directory of Sheffield: A Reproduction of the 1787 Directory of Sheffield Which Includes the
    Marks of the Cutlers, Scissor and Filesmiths, Edgetool and Sickle Makers.* Sheffield: Tool & Trades
    History Society, 2004.

"Registre de baptêmes mariages et sepultures pour la paroisse de St Jean Baptiste à Annapolis
    Royale ... 1727–1755." 1755. Diocese of Yarmouth; Nova Scotia Archives.

Reid, John G. "Acadia and the Acadians: In the Shadow of Quebec." *Beaver: Exploring Canada's
    History* 67 (November 1987): 26–31.

– "Pax Britannica or Pax Indigena? Planter Nova Scotia (1760–1782) and Competing Strategies of
    Pacification." *Canadian Historical Review* 85, no. 4 (2004): 669–92.

"Rescensement du Port Royal à l'Accadie de l'année 1707." Census, 1707. Dépôt des papiers publics
    des colonies; état civil et recensements: Série GI: Recensements et documents divers: c-2572.
    Library and Archives Canada.

"Research Notes on File, Archaeology Section, Nova Scotia Museum," n.d.

Richardson, Catherine. "Domestic Objects and the Construction of Family Identity." In *The Medieval
    Household in Christian Europe, c. 850–c. 1550 Managing Power, Wealth, and the Body*, edited by C.
    Beattie, A. Maslakovic, S. Rees Jones, 433–47. Turnhout, Belgium: Brepols Publisher, 2004.

– "'Havying Nothing upon Hym Saving Onely His Sherte': Event, Narrative and Material Culture
    in Early Modern England." In *Clothing Culture 1350–1650*, edited by Catherine Richardson,
    209–21. Aldershot: Ashgate, 2004.

Richelieu, Louis-François-Armand de Vignerot Du Plessis. "Echantillons d'etoffes et toiles des
    manufactures de France recueillis par le Marechal de Richelieu, tome III," 1735. Bibliothèque
    nationale de France.

– "Echantillons d'etoffes et toiles des manufactures de France Recueillis par le Marechal de
    Richelieu, tome IV," 1737. Recueil. Collection Richelieu. Echantillons de tissus. Bibliothèque
    nationale de France.

– "Manufactures à Rouen // 1737 // Siamoises: [échantillons de tissus]," 1737. Ark: / 12148 /
    btv1b6936131f. Bibliothèque nationale de France.

Ricker, Darlene A. *L'sitkuk: The Story of the Bear River Mi'kmaw Community.* Lockeport, NS:
    Roseway, 1997.

Riello, Giorgio. "Asian Knowledge and the Development of Calico Printing in Europe in the
    Seventeenth and Eighteenth Centuries." *Journal of Global History; Cambridge* 5, no. 1 (March
    2010): 1–28.

– *Cotton: The Fabric That Made the Modern World.* Cambridge: Cambridge University Press, 2013.

– *A Foot in the Past: Consumers, Producers, and Footwear in the Long Eighteenth Century.* Oxford;
    New York: Pasold Research Fund/Oxford University Press, 2006.

– "The Object of Fashion: Methodological Approaches to the History of Fashion." *Journal of
    Aesthetics & Culture* 3 (2011): 1–9.

Rivers-Cofield, Sara. "A Guide to Spurs of Maryland and Delaware ca. 1635–1820." *Northeast
    Historical Archaeology* 40, no. 1 (31 January 2014).

Roach-Higgins, Mary, and Joanne Eicher. "Dress and Identity." *Clothing and Textiles Research Journal* 10, no. 4 (1992): 1–8.

Roach-Higgins, Mary Ellen, Joanne Bubolz Eicher, and Kim K.P. Johnson. *Dress and Identity.* New York: Fairchild Publications, 1995.

Rocha Burguen, Francisco de la, and Pedro Patricio Mey. *Geometria y traça perteneciente al oficio de sastres: Donde se contiene el modo y orden de cortar todo genero de vestidos españoles y algunos franceses y turcos ... Por Francisco de La Rocha Burguen.* Valencia: En Valencia por Pedro Patricio Mey ... acosta del mismo autor, 1618.

Roche, Daniel. *La culture des apparences: une histoire du vêtement (XVIIᵉ–XVIIIᵉ siècle).* Paris: Fayard, 1989.

– *The Culture of Clothing: Dress and Fashion in the Ancien Régime.* Cambridge University Press, 1996.

Rogers, James E. Thorold (James Edwin Thorold), and Arthur G.L. Rogers. *A History of Agriculture and Prices in England: From the Year after the Oxford Parliament (1259) to the Commencement of the Continental War (1793).* Oxford: Clarendon Press, 1866.

"Rolle des habitans de l'Isle Saint-Jean, divisé par havres et rivières, pour l'année 1734." Census, 1734. Accession 2702/670. Smith-Alley Collection, Public Archives and Records Office of Prince Edward Island.

Rosenthal, Margaret F. "Cultures of Clothing in Later Medieval and Early Modern Europe." *Journal of Medieval and Early Modern Studies* 39, no. 3 (2009): 459–81.

Ross, Sally, and J. Alphonse Deveau. *The Acadians of Nova Scotia: Past and Present.* Halifax, NS: Nimbus, 1992.

Rothstein, Natalie. "Silk in European and American Trade before 1783: A Commodity of Commerce or a Frivolous Luxury?" In *Textiles in Trade: Proceedings of the Textile Society of America Biennial Symposium, September 14–16,* Washington, DC, 1990. 1-14.

Roy, Pierre-Georges, ed. "Lettre de Talon au Ministre Colbert (11 Novembre 1671)." In *Rapport de l'archiviste de La Province de Québec pour 1930–1931,* 163–7. Quebec: Rédempti Paradis, Imprimeur de sa Majesté, 1931.

Ruddel, David Thiery. "Domestic Textile Production in Colonial Quebec, 1608–1840." *Material Culture Review / Revue de la Culture Matérielle* 31, no. 1 (1 January 1990).

Ryder, M.L. "Medieval Sheep and Wool Types." *Agricultural History Review* 32, no. 1 (1984): 14–28.

Rygiel, Judith. "'The Homespun Economy': Persistence of Handweaving in New Brunswick in the Nineteenth Century." PhD dissertation, Carleton University, 2004.

– "Thread in Her Hands – Cash in Her Pockets: Women and Domestic Textile Production in 19th-Century New Brunswick." *Acadiensis: Journal of the History of the Atlantic Region / Revue d'histoire de la région atlantique* 30, no. 2 (3 March 2001): 56.

Sabatier, Antoine. *Sigillographie historique des administrations fiscales communautés ouvrières et institutions diverses ayant employé des sceaux de plomb 14ᵉ–18ᵉ siècles: plombs historiés de la Saône et de la Seine / Antoine Sabatier.* Paris: H. Champion, 1912.

Schmeisser, Barbara. "The Population of Louisbourg," Manuscript Report Number 303, Parks Canada, 1976.

Scholz, Susanne. *Body Narratives: Writing the Nation and Fashioning the Subject in Early Modern England.* Houndmills and New York: Palgrave Macmillan, 2000.

Schreiner, Olive. *From Man to Man, or Perhaps Only.* New York: Harper & Brothers, 1927.

Scott, Anne M., and Barbezat, Michael David, eds. *Fluid Bodies and Bodily Fluids in Premodern Europe: Bodies, Blood, and Tears in Literature, Theology, and Art.* Amsterdam: Arc Humanities Press, 2019.

Séguy, Jean. "Millénarisme et 'ordres adventistes': Grignion de Montfort et les 'Apôtres des Derniers Temps.'" *Archives de sciences sociales des religions* 53, no. 1 (1982): 23–48.

Severa, Joan, and Merrill Horswill. "Costume as Material Culture." *Dress: Journal of the Costume Society of America* 1, no. 1989 (March 2015): 22–51.

Sewell, William H. "The Empire of Fashion and the Rise of Capitalism in Eighteenth-Century France." *Past & Present* 206, no. 1 (1 February 2010): 81–120.

Shears, Robert H.J. "Examination of a Contested Landscape: Archaeological Prospection on the Eastern Shore of Nova Scotia." Master's thesis, Saint Mary's University, Halifax, NS, 2013.

Shovlin, John. "The Cultural Politics of Luxury in Eighteenth-Century France." *French Historical Studies* 23, no. 4 (Fall 2000): 577–606.

Shukla, Pravina. "The Study of Dress and Adornment as Social Positioning." *Material Culture Review / Revue de la culture matérielle* 61, no. 1 (1 January 2005).

Smith, David Kammerling. "Learning Politics: The Nîmes Hosiery Guild and the Statutes Controversy of 1706–1712." *French Historical Studies* 22, no. 4 (1999): 493–533.

Smith, Jared. "Acadia's Outpost: Beaubassin before the Deportation." Honours thesis, Acadia University, 2014.

Sonenscher, Michael. "The Hosiery Industry of Nimes and the Lower Languedoc in the Eighteenth Century." *Textile History* 10, no. 1 (1 October 1979): 142–60.

Sorge-English, Lynn. *Stays and Body Image in London: The Staymaking Trade, 1680–1810.* London: Routledge, 2011.

Spector, Janet D. "The Interpretive Potential of Glass Trade Beads in Historic Archæology." *Historical Archaeology* 10, no. 1 (1976): 17–27.

– *What This Awl Means: Feminist Archaeology at a Wahpeton Dakota Village.* 1st ed. St Paul: Minnesota Historical Society Press, 1993.

Spufford, Margaret. *The Great Reclothing of Rural England: Petty Chapman and Their Wares in the Seventeenth Century.* London: Bloomsbury Publishing, 1984.

Steele, Valerie. *The Corset: A Cultural History.* New Haven, CT: Yale University Press, 2003.

Stevens, S.K., Donald H. Kent, and Autumn L. Leonard. *The Papers of Henry Bouquet*, vol. 2: *The Forbes Expedition.* Harrisburg: Pennsylvania Historical and Museum Commission, 1951.

Stewart, Omer Call. *Forgotten Fires: Native Americans and the Transient Wilderness.* Norman: University of Oklahoma Press, 2002.

Stone, Lyle M. *Fort Michilimackinac, 1715–1781: An Archaeological Perspective on the Revolutionary Frontier.* East Lansing: Publications of the Museum, Michigan State University, 1974.

Surette, Paul. *Atlas of the Acadian Settlement of the Beaubassin, 1660 to 1755: The Great Marsh, Tintamarre and Le Lac.* Sackville, NB: Tantramar Heritage Trust, 2005.

– *Atlas of the Acadian Settlement of the Beaubassin 1660 to 1755*, vol. 2: *Mesagoueche and LaButte.* Tantramar Heritage Trust, 2015.

Taylor, Lou. *Establishing Dress History.* Manchester: Manchester University Press, 2004.

Têtu, Henri, and Charles-Octave Gagnon. *Mandements, lettres pastorales et circulaires des évêques de Québec.* Vol. 4. Quebec: Imprimerie Générale A. Coté et Cie, 1888.

Thelagathoti, Joseph Raja Rao. *The Mystical Experience and Doctrine of St. Louis-Marie Grignion de Montfort*. Rome, Italy: Gregorian University Press, 2005.

Thepaut-Cabasset, C. "Fashion Encounters: The 'Siamoise,' or the Impact of the Great Embassy on Textile Design in Paris in 1687." In *Global Textile Encounters*, edited by Marie-Louise Nosch, Feng Zhao, and Lotika Varadarajan, 165–70. Philadelphia: Oxbow Books, 2015.

Thomas, Nicholas. *Entangled Objects: Exchange, Material Culture, and Colonialism in the Pacific*. Cambridge, MA: Harvard University Press, 1991.

Thwaites, Reuben Gold, ed. *The Jesuit Relations and Allied Documents: Travels and Explorations of the Jesuit Missionaries in New France, 1610–1791; the Original French, Latin, and Italian Texts, with English Translations and Notes*. 73 vols. Cleveland: Burrows Bros. 1896.

Tilley, Christopher Y. *Handbook of Material Culture*. London; Thousand Oaks, CA: Sage, 2006.

Tingle, Elizabeth C. *Purgatory and Piety in Brittany, 1480–1720*. Ashgate, 2012.

Tiramani, Jenny. "Pins and Aglets." In *Everyday Objects: Medieval and Early Modern Material Culture and Its Meanings*, edited by Tara Hamling and Catherine Richardson, 113–22. London: Routledge, 2016.

Tomczyszyn, Pat. "Sifting through the Papers of the Past: Using Archival Documents for Costume Research in Seventeenth- and Eighteenth-Century Quebec." *Material Culture Review / Revue de la culture matérielle* 55, no. 1 (1 January 2002).

Tommaselli, Giovanni A., et al. "Using Complete Breastfeeding and Lactational Amenorrhoea as Birth Spacing Methods." *Contraception* 61, no. 4 (1 April 2000): 253–7.

Tortora, Phyllis G., and Ingrid Johnson. *The Fairchild Books Dictionary of Textiles*. New York: Fairchild Publications, 2013.

Tremblay, Eric. "Beaubassin 2: Sacré-Coeur de Vendée." Powerpoint, 2003.

– "A Typological Analysis of the Stone Pipes of the Isthmus of Chignecto, Eastern Canada." Conference paper presented at the Council for North-East Historical Archaeology Annual Conference, Halifax, NS, 20 October 2018.

Trueman, Howard. *The Chignecto Isthmus, and Its First Settlers*. Toronto: William Briggs, 1902.

Tubières, comte de Caylus, Anne Claude Philippe de. *Peddler of Knives, Scissors and Combs*. 1742. Etching with an engraving, 23.9 × 18.5 cm. 53.600.588(39). Metropolitan Museum of Art.

Turgeon, Laurier. "Material Culture and Cross-Cultural Consumption: French Beads in North America, 1500–1700." *Studies in the Decorative Arts* 9, no. 1 (1 October 2001): 85–107.

Ulrich, Laurel Thatcher. "Cloth, Clothing, and Early American Social History." *Dress* 18, no. 1 (1 January 1991): 39–48.

– *A Midwife's Tale: The Life of Martha Ballard*. New York: Knopf: Distributed by Random House, 1990.

– "Wheels, Looms, and the Gender Division of Labor in Eighteenth-Century New England." *William and Mary Quarterly* 55, no. 1 (1998): 3–38.

Varenne, Monsieur de la, and Ken Donovan. "A Letter from Louisbourg, 1756 (with an Introduction by Ken Donovan)." *Acadiensis: Journal of the History of the Atlantic Region / Revue d'histoire de la région atlantique* 10, no. 1 (9 September 1980): 113.

Vasile, Marian. "The Gender of Silk." *Journal of Research in Gender Studies* 3, no. 1 (2013): 102–7.

Vila, Anne. "Elite Masculinities in Eighteenth-Century France." In *French Masculinities*, edited by Christopher E. Forth and Bertrand Taithe, 15–30. Basingstoke: Palgrave Macmillan, 2007.

Voltaire. *The Age of Louis XIV. To Which Is Added, a Summary of The Age of Louis XV*. Translated by R. Griffith. London: Fielding and Walker, 1779.

Walder, Heather. "'... A Thousand Beads to Each Nation': Exchange, Interactions, and Technological Practices in the Upper Great Lakes c. 1630–1730." PhD dissertation, University of Wisconsin-Madison, 2015.

Wallace, Birgitta Linderoth. "The Nicolas Denys Site: Test Excavations, 1985." Manuscript on file. Nova Scotia: Nova Scotia Parks Canada, Atlantic Region, 1985.

Waller, T. *A General Description of All Trades, Digested in Alphabetical Order: By Which Parents, Guardians, and Trustees, May ... Make Choice of Trades Agreeable to the Capacity, Education, Inclination, Strength, and Fortune of the Youth under Their Care ... To Which Is Prefixed, An Essay on Divinity, Law, and Physic.* London: T. Waller, at the Crown and Mitre, 1747.

Walton, Perry. *The Story of Textiles: A Bird's-Eye View of the History of the Beginning and the Growth of the Industry by Which Mankind Is Clothed.* Boston: J.S. Lawrence, 1912.

Washburn, Wilcomb E. "Symbol, Utility, and Aesthetics in the Indian Fur Trade." *Minnesota History* 40, no. 4 (1966): 198–202.

Waugh, Norah. *The Cut of Men's Clothes: 1600–1900.* New York: Routledge, 2013.

– *The Cut of Women's Clothes: 1600–1930.* New York: Routledge, 1968.

Webber, Frederick Roth. *Church Symbolism; an Explanation of the More Important Symbols of the Old and New Testament, the Primitive, the Mediaeval and the Modern Church.* 2nd ed., rev. Cleveland, OH: J.H. Jansen, 1938.

Webster, John Clarence, and Joseph Robineau Villebon. *Acadia at the End of the Seventeenth Century; Letters, Journals and Memoirs of Joseph Robineau de Villebon, Commandant in Acadia, 1690–1700, and Other Contemporary Documents.* Saint John, NB: New Brunswick Museum, 1934.

Wellington, Donald C. *French East India Companies: A Historical Account and Record of Trade.* Lanham, MD; Oxford: Hamilton Books, 2006.

Welsteed, William. "Certificate by William Welsteed," 12 January 1696. Suffolk Court Files XXXVIII, 3007, 9th paper. Suffolk County Court.

White, Carolyn L. *American Artifacts of Personal Adornment, 1680–1820: A Guide to Identification and Interpretation.* Lanham, MD: Rowman Altamira, 2005.

– "Constructing Identities: Personal Adornment from Portsmouth, New Hampshire, 1680–1820." PhD dissertation, Boston University, 2002.

– "Knee, Garter, Girdle, Hat, Stock, and Spur Buckles from Seven Sites in Portsmouth, New Hampshire." *International Journal of Historical Archaeology* 13, no. 2 (1 June 2009): 239.

White, Carolyn L., and Mary C. Beaudry. "Artifacts and Personal Identity." In *International Handbook of Historical Archaeology*, edited by David Gaimster and Teresita Majewski, 209–25., New York: Springer, 2009.

White, Richard. *The Middle Ground: Indians, Empires, and Republics in the Great Lakes Region, 1650–1815.* 2nd ed. Cambridge: Cambridge University Press, 2010.

White, Sophie. "'To Ensure That He Not Give Himself Over to the Indians': Cleanliness, Frenchification, and Whiteness." *Journal of Early American History* 2, no. 2 (2012): 111–49.

White, Stephen A. *Dictionnaire généalogique des familles acadiennes.* 2 vols. Moncton, NB: Centre d'Études Acadiennes, Université de Moncton, 1999.

– "RE: [AFC] From Stephen A. White – Some Corrections to John Farragher's Book." E-mail. *ACADIAN-FRENCH-CANADIAN – L Archives*, 18 April 2010.

Whitehead, R.H. "Plant Fibre Textiles from the Hopps Site: BkCp-1." Curatorial Report 59. Halifax: Nova Scotia Museum Publications, 1987.

Whitehead, Ross. *Buckles 1250–1800*. Witham: Greenlight Publishing, 1996.

Whittle, J., and M. Hailwood. "The Gender Division of Labour in Early Modern England." *Economic History Review* 73 (2020): 3–32.

Whitmore, William Henry, and William Sumner Appleton. *A Report of the Record Commissioners of the City of Boston: Containing the Boston Town Records from 1742 to 1757*. Vol. 14. City Document 70. Boston: Rockwell and Churchill, 1885.

Whitmore, William Henry, William Sumner Appleton, Edward Webster McGlenen, and Walter Kendall Watkins. *Records Relating to the Early History of Boston: Selectmen's Minutes, 1764–1768*. Vol. 20. Boston: Rockwell and Churchill, City Printers, 1889.

Wicken, William C. "Encounters with Tall Sails and Tall Tales: Mi'kmaq Society, 1500–1760." PhD dissertation, McGill University, 1998.

– "Mi'kmaq Decisions: Antoine Tecouenemac, the Conquest, and the Treaty of Utrecht." In *The "Conquest" of Acadia, 1710: Imperial, Colonial, and Aboriginal Constructions*, edited by John G. Reid, 86–100. Toronto: University of Toronto Press, 2004.

– *Mi'kmaq Treaties on Trial: History, Land and Donald Marshall Junior*. Toronto: University of Toronto Press, 2002.

– "Re-Examining Mi'kmaq–Acadian Relations." In *Habitants et Marchands, Twenty Years Later: Reading the History of Seventeenth- and Eighteenth-Century Canada*, edited by Louise Dechêne and Sylvie Dépatie, 93–114. Montreal and Kingston: McGill-Queen's University Press, 1998.

Williams, Roger. *A Key into the Language of America*. Carlisle, MA: Applewood Books, 1997.

Winslow, John. "Journal of Colonel John Winslow, 1755." *Collections of the Nova Scotia Historical Society*, Vol. 4, 1884, 113–246.

Wood, William. *The Great Fortress: A Chronicle of Louisbourg, 1720–1760*. Toronto: Glasgow, Brook, 1915.

Index